ADMINISTRATION AND SUPERVISION OF SAFETY EDUCATION

ADMINISTRATION AND SUPERVISION OF SAFETY EDUCATION

DON CASH SEATON
PROFESSOR AND FORMER CHAIRMAN
DIVISION OF HEALTH, PHYSICAL
EDUCATION AND RECREATION
UNIVERSITY OF KENTUCKY

HERBERT J. STACK
FORMER PROFESSOR AND DIRECTOR
CENTER FOR SAFETY EDUCATION
NEW YORK UNIVERSITY

BERNARD I. LOFT
PROFESSOR OF HEALTH
AND SAFETY EDUCATION
DIRECTOR, CENTER FOR SAFETY
AND TRAFFIC EDUCATION
INDIANA UNIVERSITY

THE MACMILLAN COMPANY
NEW YORK

COLLIER-MACMILLAN LIMITED
LONDON

First Printing

Library of Congress catalog card number: 68-10249

THE MACMILLAN COMPANY, NEW YORK
COLLIER-MACMILLAN CANADA, LTD., TORONTO, ONTARIO

Printed in the United States of America

Dedicated to Three
Dedicated Wives
LOUISE
FRANCES
SADYE

HERBERT J. STACK 1893-1967

Dr. Herbert J. Stack, one of the authors, died unexpectedly during the final phases of the preparation of this textbook. Dr. Stack might well be called the father of safety education in America. He received his doctorate, with his dissertation in safety, from Columbia University in 1929 and since then served for nearly twenty years as Director of the Center for Safety Education at New York University.

Dr. Stack was pre-eminently a man of action, of great energy and un-flagging zest for his many interests in safety. He influenced hundreds of his students and thousands of leaders in the fields of traffic, industry, home, and recreation safety. Dr. Stack was a noted lecturer and a prolific writer. He authored numerous textbooks, contributed hundreds of articles, and created many courses of study.

In recognition of his eminent leadership in the field of safety education, Dr. Herbert J. Stack received many honors. These include an honorary Doctor of Education degree from the University of Massachusetts, the first Paul Gray Hoffman Award, the Arthur Williams Memorial Medal, and numerous certificates, plaques, and honorary life memberships.

Safety education will miss his dignified and dedicated leadership.

FOREWORD

by Lyman V. Ginger

DEAN, COLLEGE OF EDUCATION
UNIVERSITY OF KENTUCKY
FORMER PRESIDENT OF THE
NATIONAL EDUCATION ASSOCIATION

Safety is a desired way of life; but danger, not safety, is a normal condition of existence. Practically every activity in life contains some element of hazard, ranging in severity from a pinprick to a head-on collision of two automobiles. Technological advances have produced hazards so great, and the intellectual and emotional preparation required for living among them is so extensive, that safety has emerged as one of the major problems of our civilization. And natural instincts of self-protection can no longer be relied upon. Modern safety involves learning far beyond the scope of home training. It is principally to the school and community, then, that we must look for the development of skills, habits, and attitudes that are necessary if we are to live with reasonable safety in the modern world.

In many instances, because of the complications of modern life, individuals are powerless to protect themselves unless they function as a group. Hence, we have a large number of protective measures in the form of laws, regulations, governmental agencies, and other organizations whose functions are to provide guidance and leadership in meeting life's safety problems. Ben Miller says that the safety movement is based upon the instinct of self-preservation, modified by ideas of mercy and justice and transplanted by the imagination, so that self-preservation becomes a right recognized and extended to one's neighbor.

Safety education in schools was prescribed by law in some states as early as 1920. The recognition of the need for safety education spread rapidly but developed rather spasmodically, tending to be the concern of large school systems in large cities. During this period, until the early 1940's, emphasis was upon school safety patrols, posters, safety campaigns, slogans, contests, and negative instruction integrated with the school curriculum. Then in 1940 the American Association of School Administrators devoted their Eighteenth Yearbook to safety education, placing a stamp of approval upon its "stepchild." This decade witnessed the phenomenal growth of driver education, which had been introduced early in the 1930's by one of the authors of this text, Herbert J. Stack, in New Jersey, and by Amos E. Neyhart at Pennsylvania State College High School.

The rapid growth of this popular activity, especially behind-the-wheel training, was responsible in a large measure for the development of courses to train teachers in the colleges and universities of the United States. Many of these institutions have expanded their programs, especially at the graduate level, until they have become centers for safety education offering a wide range of programs, including teacher education, traffic engineering, police administration, and research.

The basic approach, however, has been focused largely upon the removal of hazards, safeguards against injury, and the enforcement of safety rules by public servants. The authors have recognized the need for a redefinition of goals and the seeking of effective methods of modifying attitudes through realistic administrative procedures and modern patterns of supervision. They stress the great need for creative and pertinent research.

School and college administrators and students of safety education should find the text a most helpful and welcome edition.

PREFACE

The authors have long felt the need for a text that would stress the organization plans, administrative functions, and supervisory procedures of safety education. Many safety educators have encouraged us to produce such a textbook and your authors have spent a good many months in its preparation. A number of fine texts have been published to be used in "catchall" classes of safety education, and an even larger number for driver education, but this one has been produced for two specific purposes: (1) to provide a textbook for the large number of graduate courses that stress administration and supervision in safety education, accident prevention, and injury control; (2) to make available to school and university administrators a guide or handbook for use in establishing, implementing, and conducting a modern program of safety and accident prevention.

The authors have purposely omitted the so-called content material of safe practices (i.e., home, traffic, industry, and so on) and have tried not to burden the book with teaching methodology. Rather, we have made an honest effort to prepare a text with a pragmatic approach to the science of administration and supervision based on experiences of the three authors in safety education.

The text is divided into five parts. Part I deals with the general organizational plans, overall administrative practices and suggested supervisory responsibilities, and measurement and evaluation. The next three parts offer practical guides and recommended procedures. Part II covers elementary and secondary schools; Part III is concerned with the college and university programs; and Part IV is devoted to safety in the area of athletics, physical education, and recreation. Since more than 50 per cent of all school and college accidents occur in these areas, the authors felt that the amount of material devoted to them was warranted. In fact, Part

IV would be a most welcome addition for use in many undergraduate courses in first aid and safety, safety and training, and a number of other advanced safety courses offered in schools and colleges. Part V outlines the future development and trends of safety education.

D. C. S.
H. J. S.
B. I. L.

ACKNOWLEDGMENTS

The authors wish to acknowledge their debt to all of those who co-operated in a study which resulted in the publication of this volume. They also wish to express their appreciation to the following persons and groups who so graciously permitted the use of materials from their studies and publications.

Dr. James E. Aaron, Southern Illinois University
The late Professor Homer Allen, Purdue University
Mr. Ralph W. Beechner, Lincoln Public Schools, Nebraska
Dr. Frank Bennett, Baltimore Public Schools
Dr. Charles A. Bucher, New York University
Dr. Donald M. Clark, Phillips Academy
Mr. James W. Crowe, Instructor, Department of Health and Safety Education, Indiana University
Miss Jean K. Dissinger, Santiago High School, Garden Grove, California
Dr. J. Duke Elkow, Brooklyn College and New York University
Dr. Hollis F. Fait, University of Connecticut
Mr. Charles C. Forsythe, Michigan State University
Mr. George S. Hjelte, Los Angeles, California
Dr. Otto Johansen, Royal Norwegian University of Church and Education, Oslo, Norway
Miss Ann Kibrick, Boston University
Dr. Giuseppe La Cava, National Institute of Physical Education, Rome, Italy
Professor Emeritus Emerson Langfitt, New York University
Dr. Lawrence Morehouse, University of California, Los Angeles
Mr. Emil Nyman, Lafayette School, Salt Lake City
Dr. Stanley Pechar, New York University

Dr. John Reichart, Northwestern University Medical School
School of Health, Physical Education, and Recreation, Indiana University,
    Graduate students in the course Problems of Driver Education and
    Highway Safety, Summer Session, 1962
Dr. William H. Solly, Western State University (Kentucky)
Dr. Arthur Steinhaus, Visiting Distinguished Professor at Michigan State
    University
Dr. Augustus Steinhilber, United States Office of Education
Mr. Richard Vollmer, Valley Stream High School, Long Island, New York
Dr. Vivian Weedon, National Safety Council, Chicago

The authors also wish to acknowledge the help of their secretaries for
their patient assistance in preparing the manuscript—our thanks to Mrs.
Mary K. Black, Miss Manila Lyman, Miss Joyce Arthur, and Miss Ellen
O'Dea.

CONTENTS

xiii

PART IV: SAFETY IN SPORTS

PART V: THE FUTURE OF SAFETY EDUCATION

PART I AN APPROACH TO SAFETY

Today safety education is an integral aspect of formal education. The development of safe behavior involves the same laws of learning as do all types of classroom activities. Furthermore, it is a basic tenet of our educational system that the primary responsibility for formal education resides with educators in our nation's schools. Therefore, the opportunity to develop safe behavior is a responsibility of all members of the profession regardless of their primary tasks.

WILLIAM G. CARR

INTRODUCTION

Accident prevention is an undeniable moral and legal obligation of all school and college personnel. In a sense, safety education is the obligation of all, but it is usually assumed to be the responsibility of the operational staff. A total school and college safety program will recognize the obligations of the administrative staff, teachers, and students in organizing, administering, and supervising such a program. The program must be designed to create safe conditions for school living, for study and research, for service and employment, as well as to promote safe practices by the student body, the faculty, and the staff. Above all, the safety program must not become the exclusive responsibility of the safety department, the supervisor or coordinator, the safety committees, or the school safety patrols. If the program is to be successful, all of these groups must become a part in planning the program.

All school or college safety programs must be approved by the school board or the college board of trustees which controls the budget, approves construction, authorizes maintenance, establishes policies, and designates authority. Most school administrators have found that the best safety programs result when a thoroughly qualified person is designated to administer it. Small colleges have had similar experiences, but large universities have found their safety problems to be so diverse and enormous that the authority has been vested in various departments and colleges.

If the safety program is to become educationally sound and effective it must be based on the following principles:

1. Safety is a sociological problem of great significance founded largely upon the psychological and philosophical aspects of accident and injury prevention.
2. Recognition that accident prevention is fundamentally based upon every individual's attitude toward and respect for the safety and well-being of others as well as for himself.
3. Sound principles of organization, administration, and supervision must be practiced.
4. The needs of the students, staff, and faculty as revealed by the accident experience of these groups must be the underlying foundation of the program.
5. The success of all programs depends upon constant, helpful, and understanding supervision.
6. Measurement and evaluation are prerequisites for determining the effectiveness of the safety education program.

FUNCTIONS OF THE SAFETY PROGRAM

As so simply stated in *Suggested School Safety Policies*,[1] the ultimate responsibility for accident prevention rests with the administrator. The objective of a healthful and safe environment will be attained through a comprehensive program that includes:

1. Maintenance of a safe school (or college) facility through the elimination of physical hazards.
2. Establishment of policies and procedures that are known, understood, and practiced.
3. Designation of an individual (or individuals) to organize the program and stimulate participation.
4. Assumption of safety responsibility by all school (and college) personnel and students.
5. Cooperation of related outside groups.
6. Education in safety skills and knowledge, and the development of attitudes of safe living.
7. Preparation for emergencies and training in first aid.

Obviously, the organizational structure and operational plans will depend upon the type, size, and location of the school or college and its educational objectives. Part I of this text sets the stage for all types and sizes of organizations and gives guidance in the realization of the objectives or goals of safety education.

[1] American Association for Health, Physical Education and Recreation, *Suggested School Safety Policies* (Washington, D.C.: The Association, 1964), p. 3.

CHAPTER 1 PHILOSOPHICAL AND PSYCHOLOGICAL ASPECTS OF SAFETY

Less depends on seeing something new than on thinking something new about what everyone sees.

SCHOPENHAUER

Safety educators and other personnel engaged in accident prevention and injury control need to recognize that there are axioms of safe behavior and safety programing. And they need to build on these axioms as the fundamental sciences have built on theirs. To some extent this has been done, and out of the accumulation of reasoning, experience, and evidence, certain facts and opinions have filtered down. They are of this order:

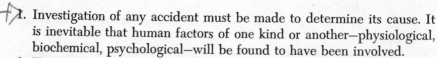

1. Investigation of any accident must be made to determine its cause. It is inevitable that human factors of one kind or another—physiological, biochemical, psychological—will be found to have been involved.
2. Human factors are nevertheless limited in significance without reference to specific physical and social environments—that is to say, the nature of the task being performed at the time of accident occurrence, the nature of interpersonal and societal factors then in effect, and sheer physical or chemical aspects of the environment.
3. Given the proper combination of human factors and environmental conditions, an accident may ensue.
4. Chance has much to do with the occurrence of the "effective" combination, and indeed with the consequence thereof.
5. Because of the role of chance, the consequence may not be fatal, or injurious, or even damaging to property. But accident *potential* is always present.
6. As long as there is such potential, the primary concern of safety personnel must lie with environmental conditions that are questionable, and with human conditions that are questionable, whether or not they evidence any statistical correlation with accident involvement. Study-

ing such conditions, therefore, is likely to be more profitable than studying accidents, or even near accidents, *per se.*

7. By the same token, there apparently is an irreducible minimum in accident rates—to the extent that there are irreducible, or unpredictable, chance factors. For example, automobile collisions must be regarded as a *random* mathematical result of poor driving practices by countless millions of drivers on four million miles of varying roadways in the United States, under an infinite number of conditions.

Assuming the validity of the foregoing approach to the problem of accidents, one may suggest certain principles for the guidance of teachers and other practitioners in the field. Thus, within the reducible range of accidents, traffic and otherwise, at least three categories of remedial effort are possible and necessary. They are commonly referred to as engineering, enforcement, and education, and optimally they have a variety of interrelationships.

Engineering, as applied, for example, to vehicle, roadway, and other aspects of the physical environment, makes possible a reduction in the range of human error (by driver or pedestrian) and in the severity of its consequences. (In a sense it imposes some *physical* restriction on human behavior.)

The enforcement of laws and regulations relating to motor-vehicle operation, if widely applied, offers the advantage of more or less immediate correction. In a sense this is tantamount to *social* control or limitation of human behavior. (But enlightened enforcement may have educational benefits as well.)

Education, with a primary objective of *self*-control, is particularly compatible with our culture. (At the same time it supports adaptation to changing cultures and environments.) Such education needs to take into account cognitive, attitudinal, and manipulative or skill factors.

Attitudinal factors, considered basic to the accident problem, require a long-range and multifaceted approach for development or modification through education in and out of the classroom. Such education can provide appropriate opportunities through preschool, in-school, and extension activities ranging from regular curricula to parent education and continuing education for all.

To accomplish this effectively, of course, an understanding of certain psychological knowledge and theory is essential. One cannot clearly separate the concept of attitudes from the concept of personality make-up. And in a society where, with the problems of present times, a high percentage of the population show symptoms of some degree of mental illness; where perhaps half of physicians' patients evidence functional disorder rather than organic disease *per se,* the crux of the accident phenomenon tends to suggest itself. Despite remarkable technological advances in our era, it will be many years, for practical and economic reasons, before further advances "minimize" (or optimize) the role of the human being's mind, hands, and feet. To illustrate these generalizations, the "psychology" that follows is largely in terms of the traffic accident problem. However, as is noted later, this same "psychology" has a high degree of relevance to safety in most areas of human activity.

CHARACTERISTICS OF ADOLESCENCE AND THEIR IMPLICATIONS

Adolescence is a period of life that requires special attention for two obvious reasons: (1) adolescents of course comprise the student body in the high schools where we teach safety and driver education; (2) it is a matter of fact that drivers under twenty-five years of age have the worst highway record and pay the highest liability rates. Ironically, from the viewpoint of physical qualifications, those under twenty-five are best able to drive. Moreover, they have the most to lose in an accident. Yet the under-twenty-five group, which holds about 15 per cent of all accidents— in spite of the fact that they do relatively little of the nation's driving, compared with heads of families and older occupational groups such as salesmen. On this basis the per-mile record of those under 25 is even worse than basic figures indicate.

To explain this phenomenon one could of course conduct a whole series of research studies seeking to determine relationships between the psychological make-up of adolescents and their traffic accident involvement. Undoubtedly many such studies would be valuable in efforts to understand and control the problem. One does not, however, need to wait for the completion of these studies, for there is already a wealth of clinical and other information regarding the personality profile of adolescence, and it requires no stretching of the imagination to apply this information to the area of immediate concern.

As Whitehorn [1] notes, no matter how vaguely it is defined, "personality" is a useful and necessary term. It connotes—and this may be construed as one of the "vague" definitions—the individuality of a particular human being in relation to the social and cultural context and the physical environment in which that individual is functioning. Whitehorn has presented a very succinct portrait of adolescent personality:

> In the usual course of events in our culture, one feels in adolescence an increased need to achieve and assert some sense of individual personal significance—sometimes very assertively against authority figures such as parents, sometimes in exhibitionistic physical exploits, and often, during

[1] J. C. Whitehorn, *The Human Personality and the Development of Mature Individuals.* Unpublished paper presented before the Adult Education Association, 1956.

later adolescence in a rather exaggerated radicalism or excessive reactive conservatism.

According to Hurlock,[2] moderation is hardly characteristic of the adolescent, who shows excesses in almost every activity. She notes, further, that adolescent emotions are intense, lack control of expression, show inconsistency, and frequently take the form of moods.

As a final example, Blos [3] reports that the adolescent is very difficult to teach by the traditional methods. His attention becomes distracted very easily, hence it is very difficult to have him engage in concentrated work. Much of his time is taken up by daydreaming, and many things serve to distract him.

Knowledge such as the preceding has been accumulated over the ages and carefully documented throughout the era of modern psychology. If one accepts the findings of current research (cf. Brody and Haddon et al.[4]) indicating the fundamental relationship between personality make-up and involvement in accidents and violations, statistical studies of adolescent drivers would probably serve only to reinforce the known and the obvious. It would seem, therefore, that one can proceed with appropriate recommendations on the basis of established psychological facts— facts which indicate that the characteristics of adolescence are likely to be incompatible with traffic safety.

The foregoing is not to be construed as a tirade at teenagers. The characteristics noted, difficult or undesirable as they may be from an adult point of view, are more or less typical of the adolescent process. Similarly every stage of growth, from childhood to senescence, has its own problems which are peculiar to it and may in a sense be regarded as "normal."

The fact remains that adolescent characteristics are uncomfortably of the same order as the characteristics of adult problem drivers and that intrinsically there is conflict with the requirements of safe driving. As a result, it seems reasonable to some to recommend that the driver's license be unavailable until at least the age of eighteen. At the present time, many states specify a minimum age of sixteen or less.

This may appear to be a drastic recommendation. Nevertheless, it seems warranted. And in no way does it weaken the need for driver education and general safety education in our schools. Such programs must continue and, as in the case of other courses of study, should be viewed as *preparation* for living.

[2] E. E. Hurlock, *Adolescent Development* (New York: McGraw-Hill, 1949).

[3] Blos, P. *The Adolescent Personality* (New York: Appleton-Century, 1941).

[4] L. Brody, *Basic Aspects and Applications of the Psychology of Safety* (New York: New York University, 1966); L. Brody, *Human Factors Research in Occupational Accident Prevention* (Chicago: American Society of Safety Engineers, 1962); W. Haddon, Jr., E. A. Suchman, and D. Klein, *Accident Research: Methods and Approaches* (New York: Harper & Row, 1964).

Needless to say, such a license requirement would deny the license to an unknown number of adolescents who might be ready for this responsibility, for maturity occurs at different ages among different individuals.

Of course if there were adequate screening tests of attitude and personality, age would not have to be a factor at all. But in this regard psychology is now approximately at the stage medicine was when the physician would taste the urine to see if it was sweet, or look at it with his naked eye to see what he could detect—the era before the laboratory test came to provide specific qualitative and quantitative estimates of the urine. But some day there will be valid psychological tests for application in driver licensing and driver re-examination. Indeed, there may be physiological and biochemical indexes of personality or personal adjustment.

In the meantime the educational process must recognize that, innately, youth wants to *know*, to *belong*, to feel *secure*. These are among his most basic needs. To the extent that our educators can guide him to a realistic appreciation of these needs, progress in safety will be accelerated and human conservation advanced.

THE ADULT DRIVER PROBLEM

As previously suggested, youth's disproportionate share of traffic accidents and violations still represents the smaller part of the problem. Some authorities say that it would be more sensible "to put off" the problem of influencing the behavior of about 100 million drivers and concentrate on automotive redesign, a matter that is presumed to be subject to control by a handful of manufacturers. This is an oversimplification of the problem.

For example, studies [5] involving autopsies now indicate that in 50 per cent or more of automobile fatalities, there is a significant presence of alcohol in the blood of victims. Will vehicle redesign prevent drivers from drinking? Severity of accidental injury might thereby be reduced, which is good, but collisions would continue. Moreover, it is conceivable that the knowledge of added protection afforded by vehicle redesign could engender even more risk-taking than is now in evidence. And, finally, how can one "package" the pedestrian, who is involved in one fifth or more of total traffic fatalities?

The big problem remains how to influence the behavior of drivers to achieve the objectives of safety. It is not appropriate here to consider the various types of "formal" educational programs that may be employed

[5] W. Haddon, Jr., E. A. Suchman, and D. Klein, *Accident Research: Methods and Approaches* (New York: Harper & Row, 1964); President's Committee for Traffic Safety. *Health, Medical Care and Transportation of the Injured* (Washington, D.C.: U.S. Government Printing Office, 1965).

for this purpose. However, some remarks need to be made about public safety campaigns through mass media. These apparently have fallen far short of set goals. One is challenged to attempt to explain this failure, and at least two considerations seem relevant. The first has to do with *feelings of immediacy of danger.* The other is concerned with the nature or degree of *ego involvement* in the consequences of an accident. It would seem that both factors have to be taken into account in safety campaigns—and it would appear that they have *not* been taken into account in any substantial degree.

With regard to the factor of immediacy, it may be said that we are largely a "gambling" people. Our culture seems conducive to such a characteristic. When an appeal is made to the public to drive safely on a holiday weekend, it is frequently based on a preholiday estimate of traffic fatalities. Thus, for a given holiday weekend, 400 deaths may be predicted. At the same time the message to the public is likely to indicate that during those days, 50 or 60 million cars may be on the road. Subconsciously or otherwise, our minds are likely to convert these figures to odds of several hundred thousand to one against *"me" being involved.*

With regard to the second factor, extent of ego involvement, campaigns have tended to emphasize fatalities. Death is something that people do not generally care to contemplate, but at the same time they realize that it is a terminal affair, with no ego involvement thereafter. On the other hand, if the danger is one that may result in personal disfigurement or permanent disability, the ego is much concerned.

Perhaps safety campaigns should change their previous emphases to the *lower* odds on injury and the *personal* significance of disfigurement or permanent disability. This may well have been the explanation for the phenomenal success of public officials in New York State in the late 1940's, when, through a massive media campaign, some five and one half million people were "persuaded" within a few weeks to seek preventive innoculations during a smallpox epidemic scare.

Fundamental psychological principles are also operative in point systems which provide for loss of a driver's license, highly valued by most people, upon accumulation of a specified number of demerits for traffic violations. Sound point systems should be established in every state. Although *prediction* of driving history on the basis of tests is still difficult, there can be little doubt that a record of repeated violations and/or accidents is indicative of something fundamentally wrong in the individual as a driver, at least temporarily.

When one refers to point systems, one is in effect dealing with a motivational approach to the traffic safety problem. The approach is essentially a negative one, because of the possible penalties involved.

Needless to say, there are positive motivations as well. Some of these are implicit in the content and methodology of high-quality programs of driver education. But other positive approaches are possible. For example: If traffic accidents do constitute a major *national* problem, *might not consideration be given to the provision of income tax credit for a year of accident-free (and possibly violation-free) driving?* With the advent of high-speed computers and the trend toward centralization of records, such action may be feasible and appropriate. Bonus measures of some insurance companies are also positively motivational, but they fall in a separate, private-enterprise category.

Related to the negative approach is the historical concept that a license is a privilege, rather than a Constitutional right. Thus, the privilege might be suspended or revoked under certain conditions—conditions that are still hard to define or justify.

But this concept is changing.[6] Courts increasingly tend to recognize that a license should not be withheld or denied unless it has been *established* that by reason of abuse of the privilege or other just cause it is necessary, in the interest of public safety, to do so. Such decisions are based on recognition of the growing social and economic necessity to drive. "There is seeming reluctance on the part of the courts to exclude summarily from licensure a person so unfortunate as to be ill or disabled, unless it is shown, and supported by factual data, that his impairment affects his driving ability under the usual conditions of use . . . a decision as to causality should be based upon a high level of proof."

THE GENERALITY OF ATTITUDES AND EMOTIONAL FACTORS IN SAFETY

With substantial indications of the importance of attitudes and emotional make-up in the occurrence of accidents in various areas of everyday living, it may be helpful to illustrate that there are common denominators. For purposes of demonstration in the classroom a relatively simple procedure may be employed. Administer the following three "tests" to a group of students, advising them to imagine they are adults in the situations specified. One set of items deals with traffic situations, another with home incidents, and the third concerns work conditions. Preferably, the three "tests" should not be administered consecutively. That is to say, some regular classroom activity should intervene, without discussion of the "tests," so that any "halo effect" may be reduced.

(a) Indicate the extent to which the following traffic situations are usually irritating or annoying to you by using a scale from 0 to 5. In this scale, the figure 0 means *"not the least bit irritating or annoying"*; the figure 5: *"extremely irritating or annoying—*to the point where you are just

[6] President's Committee, *op. cit.*

about ready to fly off the handle." On the line in front of each item write the figure from 0 to 5 that corresponds as closely as possible to the degree of your annoyance or irritation with the situation indicated.

___ Driver behind you blowing his horn
___ Driver behind you following your car closely
___ Driver "cutting in" ahead of you
___ Driver ahead of you "hugging" the middle of the road
___ Driver ahead of you going too slow for traffic
___ Pedestrian crossing the street and disregarding your car
___ Traffic light turning red just as you get to the intersection
___ Coming to a stop sign at an intersection with very little traffic
___ Driving on a road with too low a speed limit
___ Being criticized by a traffic officer

(b) Indicate the extent to which the following home situations are usually irritating or annoying to you by using a scale from 0 to 5. In this scale, the figure 0 means *"not the least bit irritating or annoying"*; the figure 5, *"extremely irritating or annoying*—to the point where you are just about ready to fly off the handle." On the line in front of each item write the figure from 0 to 5 that corresponds as closely as possible to the degree of your annoyance or irritation with the situation indicated.

___ Frequent borrowing by your neighbor
___ Wife (husband) nagging you to mail a letter when you are comfortably situated
___ Milkman shifting bottles outside your bedroom in early morning
___ Difficulty in reaching an object you want, while standing on a ladder
___ Garbage bag coming apart as you are carrying it downstairs
___ Light fuse blowing while you are watching favorite T.V. program
___ Being constantly told by wife (husband) how to do things around the home
___ Child marking up the living-room wall
___ Continual faulty operation of bathroom fixtures

(c) Indicate the extent to which the following work situations are usually irritating or annoying to you by using a scale from 0 to 5. In this scale, the figure 0 means *"not the least bit irritating or annoying"*; the figure 5, *"extremely irritating or annoying*—to the point where you are just about to fly off the handle." On the line in front of each item write the figure from 0 to 5 that corresponds as closely as possible to the degree of your annoyance or irritation with the situation indicated.

___ Being criticized by your supervisor
___ Constant talking by someone you work with
___ Not being praised for superior work
___ Someone else receiving an award for an idea that you also had

___ Careless work by other employees in your department

___ Being watched closely by your supervisor

___ Constant repetition of safety rules and regulations

___ Being required to report very minor injuries

___ Being required to attend employee training programs

___ Being asked to do work occasionally that is below the level of your training and experience

When the "tests" have been completed by everyone, the group should total their responses on each form. Then their totals should tallied in tables such as the following:

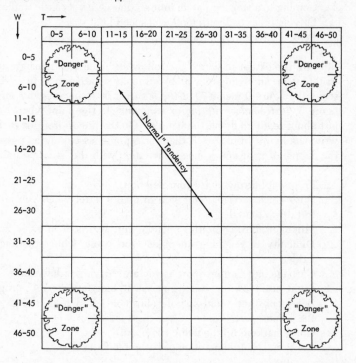

Figure 1–1. Table for illustrating the interrelationships of human responses in different areas of everyday activity. (W = work situations; T = traffic situations.)

In each table the horizontal boxes apply to tallies for one area of activity, the vertical boxes to another. Thus, there would be three tables, permitting comparison of tallies for driving situations versus those for home situations; driving situation responses versus work situation responses; and home situation responses versus work situation responses.

What distribution of responses may be expected in each table? Of course, these are not strictly scientific tests. Apart from questions of clarity of wording, a more scientific test might entail forty or fifty situations instead of ten in each set, and these would have been pretested and validated according to accepted procedures of test construction. Nevertheless, experience has shown that the devices as they are yield results that tend to serve the purposes of demonstration and discussion of some basic assumptions and principles relating to safe behavior. These are as follows:

1. In each chart there seems to be a central or "normal" tendency, with tallies clustering somewhat below the median, at least in the case of safety-oriented persons. This suggests that such individuals as a group are not inclined to over-react, and indeed tend to be somewhat on the placid side. There are likely to be few, if any tallies in the upper left-hand and lower right-hand quadrants.
2. Statistically, there is usually a high degree of correspondence between tallies for one set of situations and those for another set. This strongly suggests that the hypersensitive person in one area may also be hypersensitive in another area; and similarly with hypersensitive drivers, workers, or homemakers. This supports the cliché that "a man drives as he lives"; that a man's psychological makeup is not compartmentalized according to different areas of everyday activity. His is a consistent, unitary personality.
3. If the consistency evidences itself on the over-reactive side (lower right-hand quadrant), his behavior will tend to be incompatible with safety because of limited self-control. If the consistency evidences itself on the under-reactive side (upper left-hand quadrant), his behavior will also tend to be incompatible with safety because of limited awareness of environmental hazards or happenings.

Based on data obtained from the preceding demonstration "tests," the preceding generalizations would indeed seem theoretical. But the files of psychiatry and psychosomatic medicine abound in supporting case histories.

THE NATURE AND ROLE OF SCIENTIFIC INVESTIGATION

To pursue the previous issue and related problems through scientific investigation poses some basic questions.

To begin with, it is natural to undertake to define the term "research." Beveridge [7] has very realistically stated that scientific research is "simply the search for new knowledge." But one may find as many definitions of the term as there are researchers. This leads to all kinds of ramifications.

[7] W. I. B. Beveridge, *The Art of Scientific Investigation* (New York: Vintage Books, 1957).

In the sense of the Beveridge definition, one may say that we are concerned with questions that need to be answered before further progress can be made in accident prevention. This may well entail activity that does not fit traditional, if not mystical, connotations of the term.

Other interpretations, however, readily involve us in a veritable labyrinth. Thus, the concept of human factors research becomes "entangled" with factors anthropological to sociological, with epidemiological, experimental, and systems approaches among others. And phrases like human engineering, engineering psychology, and operations research are seemingly bandied about with perhaps as much interlocking and overlapping as one finds in the terms "perception," "attitude," and "motivation."

Such problems of concept and definition are compounded by the increasingly apparent need to interpret our principal character, "accident," along both philosophical and practical lines. No wonder, then, that progress in accident reduction has been relatively slow.

Thus, it can be said with confidence that no test yet devised can adequately measure two of the three ingredients of superior (safe) performance: character and motivation. For in attempting to measure such things as attitudes, we are dealing with the resultants of so many factors that empirical findings are seldom significant.

There is still another explanatory ogre—in the pitfalls of statistics. In our natural search for objectivity and quantification we seem to have undertaken to measure everything and to correlate everything. And so it is not surprising to note the report of a fantastic correlation, .87, between the membership size of an American labor union and the death rate of the state of Hyderabad. Incidentally, where there are genuine causal connections we should expect statistical correlation, but the converse is not necessarily true.

Even more important to teachers and administrators in the field of safety is this fact: the existence of a certain correlation or average at a given time must not be taken to mean that this correlation or average must prevail in the future. There is no law of nature that compels the normal family to have 2.7 children; or the normal man to have a seven-year itch, maritally speaking; or the average driver to incur 10,000 errors annually; *or* . . . the "unsafe" student ever to be earmarked for poor performance— or destruction. He is *educable*.

In view of the foregoing, it seems wise for safety educators to drop a few phrases from their vocabulary. The phrases are "most important" and "the best way." It is pointless at this time to ask, "What is *the* most important cause of traffic accidents?" And, "What is *the* best way of teaching driver and traffic safety education?" With regard to the former (*the* most important cause), there are so many variables involved, and these variables are so variable, that one can become enmeshed in an endless chain of *proof*. As for the second question, regarding *the* best way of teaching, there simply cannot be one best way. It was difficult enough to come up with the old formula of 30-and-6 for driver education. It could have been 32-and-4, or 26-and-10, if one insists on adding up to 36. But why not 30 and 16? Or 16 and 16? And so on *ad infinitum*.

Instead of pursuing the end of the rainbow *now*, the safety educators' concern should be: How *well* are we doing? How can we do things *better* (not "best")?

A CONCLUDING PHILOSOPHICAL VIEW

In these times it is impossible to separate the benefits of science and technology from concomitant risks. And because society seems unwilling to forego the benefits, it becomes saddled with the risks.

This is not to presume that risks must be accepted willy-nilly. Instead, the search for acceptable controls must be intensified. At the same time it must be recognized that we appear to be heading toward an era of push-button people; and technology without philosophy is like earth without water.

One must admit, of course, that technological advances have removed many rough edges from our environment with unquestionably salutary results. But to give a final dimension to the current challenge of human conservation and development, is it feasible or desirable to send a human being through life in a stress-free, shock-resistant package? An existence free of risk and stress may well be devoid of interest or purpose. Indeed it may be harmful. And so it appears appropriate, finally, to reaffirm a concept of perhaps critical significance in our times: the concept of *safety for essential adventures*.

REFERENCES

Beveridge, W. I. B., *The Art of Scientific Investigation* (New York: Vintage Books, 1957).

Blos, P., The *Adolescent Personality* (New York: Appleton-Century, 1941).

Brody, L., *Basic Aspects and Applications of the Psychology of Safety* (New York: New York University, 1966).

———, *Human Factors Research in Occupational Accident Prevention* (Chicago: American Society of Safety Engineers, 1962).

Bunge, M., *Causality: The Place of the Causal Principle in Modern Science* (Cleveland: World Publishing, 1963).

Dunbar, F. "Homeostasis During Puberty," *American Journal of Psychiatry*, 1958, 673–82.

Haddon, W., Jr., E. A. Suchman, and D. Klein, *Accident Research: Methods and Approaches* (New York: Harper & Row, 1964).

Hurlock, E. E., *Adolescent Development* (New York: McGraw-Hill, 1949).

President's Committee for Traffic Safety. *Health, Medical Care and Transportation of the Injured* (Washington, D.C.: U.S. Government Printing Office, 1965).

Whitehorn, J. C., *The Human Personality and the Development of Mature Individuals.* Unpublished paper presented before the Adult Education Association, 1956.

CHAPTER 2 ACCIDENT
· FACTS

An assessment of the various sources of statistical data regarding injuries and death makes it obvious that accidents are a most serious social and economic loss to the nation.

The National Safety Council estimates that for the first sixty years of this century there were at least 5.25 million accidental deaths and 500 million injuries resulting in a total economic loss of at least $100 billion. In 1966 there were 113,000 accidental deaths, 10.8 million nonfatal injuries (400,000 of which were permanent impairments) with an estimated economic loss of $20 billion (wage loss $5.9 billion, overhead cost of insurance $43 billion and medical expense, $2 billion), motor vehicle property damage of $3.3 billion, fire loss of $1.5 billions and indirect cost of work accidents of $3 billion.

The prevention of accidents has become the concern of practically every facet of our governmental agencies, public institutions, private industry and business, and particularly our educational system.

For the student and the administrator to understand the problems of safety education it is necessary to examine and analyze the national accident picture—which usually reflects the same picture he will find in his own state and community. Stratemeyer [1] cautions us, however, about the accuracy and exact meaning of the data presented.

> Even the accuracy of the data presented must, to a degree be regarded as open to question. Investigators in this area have not yet arrived at accepted methods of securing and reporting accident information. The criteria used for defining an accident vary greatly. And it is almost impossible to gather data on accidents not resulting in injury and so not requiring medical attention. Yet such events must be included in any investigation of accident causation.

Most of the following statistics have been furnished by *Accident Facts* [2] of the National Safety Council and by the Public Health Service, Accidental Death and Injury Statistics, U.S. Department of Health, Education, and Welfare.[3] (For sports injury statistics, see Chapter 15.)

[1] Clara G. Stratemeyer, *Accident Research for Better Safety Teaching* (Washington, D.C.: National Commission on Safety Education, N.E.A., 1964).
[2] National Safety Council, *Accident Facts* (Chicago: The Council, 1966). Published Annually.
[3] United States Department of Health, Education, and Welfare, *Accidental Death and Injury Statistics* (Washington, D.C.: 1963).

TABLE 2-1
PRINCIPAL CLASSES OF ACCIDENTAL DEATHS, 1949 TO 1965

YEAR	TOTAL*		MOTOR-VEHICLE		WORK		HOME		PUBLIC NONMOTOR-VEHICLE	
	DEATHS	RATE†	DEATHS	RATE†	DEATHS	RATE†	DEATHS	RATE†	DEATHS	RATE†
1949	90,106	60.6	31,701	21.3	15,000	10.1	31,000	20.9	15,000	10.1
1950	91,249	60.3	34,763	23.0	15,500	10.2	29,000	19.2	15,000	9.9
1951	95,871	62.5	36,996	24.1	16,000	10.4	30,000	19.6	16,000	10.4
1952	96,172	61.8	37,794	24.3	15,000	9.6	30,500	19.6	16,000	10.3
1953	95,032	60.1	37,955	24.0	15,000	9.5	29,000	18.3	16,500	10.4
1954	90,032	55.9	35,586	22.1	14,000	8.7	28,000	17.4	15,500	9.6
1955	93,443	56.9	38,426	23.4	14,200	8.6	28,500	17.3	15,500	9.4
1956	94,780	56.6	39,628	23.7	14,200	8.3	28,000	16.4	17,500	10.3
1957	95,307	55.9	38,702	22.7	14,300	8.5	28,000	16.7	16,000	9.6
1958	90,604	52.3	36,981	21.3	13,300	7.7	26,500	15.3	16,500	9.5
1959#	92,080	52.2	37,910	21.5	13,800	7.8	27,000	15.3	16,500	9.3
1960#	93,806	52.1	38,137	21.2	13,800	7.7	28,000	15.6	17,000	9.4
1961	92,249	50.4	38,091	20.8	13,500	7.4	27,000	14.7	16,500	9.0
1962	97,139	52.3	40,804	22.0	13,700	7.4	28,500	15.3	17,000	9.1
1963	100,669	53.4	43,564	23.1	14,200	7.5	29,000	15.4	17,000	9.0
1964	105,000	54.9	47,700	24.9	14,200	7.4	28,500	14.9	18,000	9.4
1965	107,000	55.2	49,000	25.3	14,100	7.3	28,000	14.4	19,000	9.8
Changes										
1955 to 1965	+15%	−3%	+28%	+8%	−1%	−15%	−2%	−17%	+23%	+4%
1964 to 1965	+2%	−1%	+3%	+2%	−1%	−1%	−2%	−3%	+6%	+4%

Source: Total deaths and motor-vehicle deaths from 1949 to 1963 are NCHS totals for the United States. All other figures are National Safety Council estimates based on data from NCHS, state and city health departments and other sources. [Courtesy National Safety Council.]

* Duplications between Motor-Vehicle, Work and Home are eliminated in the TOTAL column.

† Rates are deaths per 100,000 population.

1959 includes Alaska; 1960 and later years include Alaska and Hawaii.

18

Despite the fact that practically all citizens are aware of the ever-increasing toll of motor vehicle deaths, relatively few have a clear understanding of the total accident picture. Let us examine some of the facts.

1. *International Rate*

Death rates for 1964 among nations compiled by the World Health Organization of the United Nations disclose a low of 12.1 deaths per 100,000 population in the Philippines to a high in Chile of 74.9.

The United States, with a death rate of 55.7, stands eighth highest among the nations of the world. Other highly industrialized and mechanized nation exceeding this rate include France with 69.5, Switzerland with 62.3, and West Germany with 60.6. Italy and England have much lower rates—44.4 and 39.3, respectively.

2. *Where Accidents Occur*

Motor-vehicle accidents kill and maim more people in the United States than any other kind of accident. In 1966 53,000 persons were killed in traffic accidents; 14,500 at work; 29,500 in the home; and 19,500 in public. Accompanying this startling death toll were 10.8 million disabling injuries.

3. *How Fatalities Occur*

Next to motor-vehicle deaths, falls account for the next highest

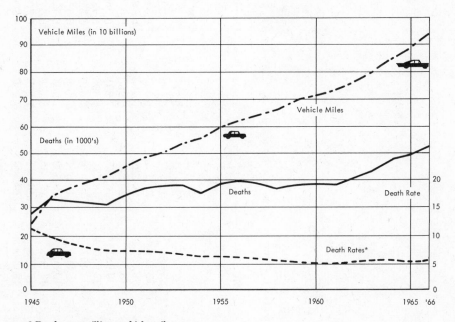

° Deaths per million vechicle miles.

Figure 2-1. The traffic situation since World War II. (Courtesy of the National Safety Council.)

TABLE 2-2
Principal Types of Accidental Deaths, 1953 to 1965

(Deaths)

Year	Motor-Vehicle	Falls	Fires, Burns *	Drown-ing †	Railroad	Fire-arms	Poison by Gas	Poison (solid, liquid)
1953	37,955	20,631	6,579	6,770	3,187	2,277	1,223	1,391
1954	35,586	19,771	6,083	6,334	2,616	2,281	1,223	1,339
1955	38,426	20,192	6,352	6,344	2,834	2,120	1,163	1,431
1956	39,628	20,282	6,405	6,263	2,696	2,202	1,213	1,422
1957	38,702	20,545	6,269	6,613	2,614	2,369	1,143	1,390
1958	36,981	18,248	7,291	6,582	2,480	2,172	1,187	1,429
1959	37,910	18,774	6,898	6,434	2,291	2,258	1,141	1,661
1960	38,137	19,023	7,645	6,529	2,391	2,334	1,253	1,679
1961	38,091	18,691	7,102	6,525	2,246	2,204	1,192	1,804
1962	40,804	19,589	7,534	6,439	2,209	2,092	1,376	1,833
1963	43,564	19,335	8,172	6,347	2,272	2,263	1,489	2,061
1964	47,700	18,941	7,379	6,709	2,516	2,275	1,360	2,100
1965	49,000	19,500	7,200	6,800	2,600	2,200	1,500	2,000

Death Rates Per 100,000 Population

Year								
1953	24.0	13.0	4.2	4.3	2.0	1.4	0.8	0.9
1954	22.1	12.3	3.8	3.9	1.6	1.4	0.8	0.8
1955	23.4	12.3	3.9	3.9	1.7	1.3	0.7	0.9
1956	23.7	12.1	3.8	3.7	1.6	1.3	0.7	0.9
1957	22.7	12.1	3.7	3.9	1.5	1.4	0.7	0.8
1958	21.3	10.5	4.2	3.8	1.4	1.3	0.7	0.8
1959	21.5	10.6	3.9	3.6	1.3	1.3	0.6	0.9
1960	21.2	10.6	4.2	3.6	1.3	1.3	0.7	0.9
1961	20.8	10.2	3.9	3.6	1.2	1.2	0.7	1.0
1962	22.0	10.5	4.1	3.5	1.2	1.1	0.7	1.0
1963	23.1	10.2	4.3	3.4	1.2	1.2	0.8	1.1
1964	24.9	9.9	3.9	3.5	1.3	1.2	0.8	1.1
1965	25.3	10.1	3.7	3.5	1.3	1.1	0.8	1.0

Changes in Rates

1955 to 1965	+8%	−18%	−5%	−10%	−24%	−15%	+14%	+11%
1964 to 1965	+2%	+2%	−5%	0%	0%	−8%	0%	−9%

Source: National Center for Health Statistics, Interstate Commerce Commission, and National Safety Council.
° Includes burns by fire, and deaths resulting from conflagration regardless of nature of injury. Totals for 1958 and later years are not comparable to earlier years—some deaths formerly classified to hot substances are now classified as fires, burns deaths.
† Includes drownings in water transport accidents.

toll 20,000. Following in order are fires and burns, 7,900; drowning, 7,000; machinery, 2,100; firearms, 2,600; poisoning (solids and liquids), 2,100; gases and vapors, 1,500; and, others 16,800.

4. *Accidents Leading Cause of School-Age Fatalities*

Accidents are the leading cause of death among all persons aged 1 to 37. The school-age accident rate is the highest of all. Those in the 17 to 28 age group experience the highest incidence rate with the peak year being 21 years of age. In 1966, 21,200 school-age (15 to 24) children lost their lives in accidents, 15,600 in motor vehicle accidents. There were 8,000 accidental deaths among school-age children from 5 to 14 years of age. Of these, 4,000 were motor vehicle (1,450 of which were pedestrian), 1,500 occurred in the home, 2,300 were public (nonmotor-vehicle), and 200 occurred at work. Accidental deaths among school-age groups for 1965 were as follows:

AGE IN YEARS	DEATHS	RATE (per 100,000 population in each group)
1 to 4	5,270	31.8
5 to 9	3,911	19.1
10 to 14	3,480	18.4
15 to 19	9,625	56.8
20 to 24	9,063	68

Each school day some 65,000 students 6 to 16 years of age are absent due to schooltime or playtime injuries.

5. *Males Experience More Accidental Deaths Than Females*

The male sex experiences more than two thirds (69 per cent) of the accidental deaths. Five out of six victims in the 15 to 24 age group were male, with approximately 16,900 killed in 1966.

6. *Work Accidents*

In 1966 there were 14,500 work deaths and 2.2 million disabling injuries in the United States. Government service (3,200) and agriculture (2,900) recorded the highest numbers, the construction industry was third with 2,800, followed by manufacturing with 1,900; transportation and public utilities with 1,700; trade with 1,300; and mining and quarrying with 700. The rates in all of these industries except transportation, agriculture, and mining decreased as did the total number of lives lost (down 100 from 1966). Disabling injuries, however, increased by 10,000.

7. *Public Accidents*

The term *public accidents* refers to deaths in public places that do not involve vehicles or industrial accidents. It includes sports and recreational deaths. A total of 19,500 persons lost their lives this way in 1966—5,300 by falls, 4,500 by drowning, 1,000 by firearms, 700 by fires

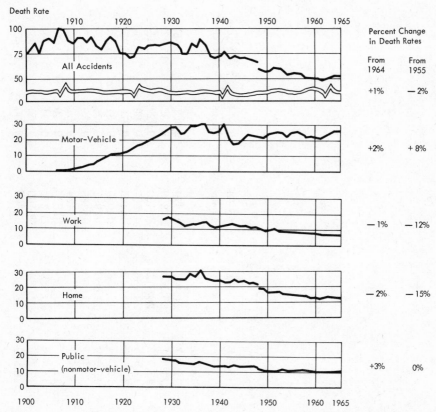

FIGURE 2–2. Trends in accidental death rate. (Courtesy of the National Safety Council.)

and burns, 1,200 in air transport (including military personnel) 1,100 in water transport, 800 in railroad transport, 200 in other transport (streetcars, bicycles, and animal-drawn vehicles). All other public deaths amounted to 4,700. These figures do not include automobile accidents.

8. *Home Accidents*

There were 29,500 persons killed and 4.4 million disabled in home accidents in 1966. The rate per 100,000 was 15.1, with urban homes accounting for 27,700 deaths and farm homes only 1,800. Oddly enough, more males are killed in home accidents despite the greater number of females in the population and the greater amount of time they spend at home. The excess of male deaths over female deaths is greatest for firearms, followed by poisoning by gases and vapors, fires and burns, and suffocation and poisoning by solids and liquids.

9. *Farm Accidents*

At least 8,200 farmers lost their lives in 1966 in accidents. Motor vehicles accounted for the largest number, 3,700 (approximately 1,000

TABLE 2-3
ACCIDENTAL DEATHS AND DEATH RATES, BY AGE, 1953 TO 1965

YEAR	ALL AGES	UNDER 5 YEARS	5–14 YEARS	15–24 YEARS	25–44 YEARS	45–64 YEARS	65–74 YEARS	75 YEARS AND OVER *
				DEATHS				
1953	95,032	8,678	6,136	12,837	21,422	19,479	9,927	16,553
1954	90,032	8,380	5,939	11,801	20,023	18,299	9,652	15,938
1955	93,443	8,099	6,099	12,742	20,911	19,199	9,929	16,464
1956	94,780	8,173	6,316	13,545	20,986	19,207	10,160	16,393
1957	95,307	8,423	6,454	12,973	20,949	19,495	10,076	16,937
1958	90,604	8,789	6,514	12,744	19,658	18,095	9,431	15,373
1959	92,080	8,748	6,511	13,269	19,666	18,937	9,475	15,474
1960	93,806	8,950	6,836	13,457	19,660	19,385	9,689	15,829
1961	92,249	8,622	6,717	13,431	19,273	19,134	9,452	15,620
1962	97,139	8,705	6,751	14,557	19,955	20,335	10,149	16,687
1963	100,669	8,688	6,962	15,889	20,529	21,262	10,194	17,145
1964	105,000	8,670	7,400	17,420	22,080	22,100	10,400	16,930
1965	107,000	8,600	7,400	18,500	22,200	22,600	10,300	17,400

Death Rates †

Index									
1953	60.1	64.0	49.5	22.1	61.4	46.3	60.5	106.7	383.6
1954	55.9	59.5	46.7	20.5	56.4	43.0	55.9	100.7	354.4
1955	56.9	60.8	43.9	20.3	60.1	44.7	57.7	100.8	350.2
1956	56.6	60.9	43.3	20.2	63.3	44.7	56.7	100.6	335.6
1957	55.9	59.8	43.5	19.9	59.5	44.7	56.6	97.5	333.3
1958	52.3	55.8	44.5	19.6	56.2	42.0	51.7	89.3	292.7
1959	52.2	55.8	43.6	18.9	56.6	42.1	53.2	87.7	284.7
1960	52.1	55.7	44.0	19.1	55.6	42.0	53.6	87.8	281.4
1961	50.4	54.1	41.7	18.1	54.0	41.2	52.1	84.6	267.3
1962	52.3	55.8	42.0	18.0	55.1	42.8	54.5	90.1	276.1
1963	53.4	57.2	41.9	18.3	57.2	44.0	56.2	90.0	275.0
1964	54.9	59.1	41.9	19.1	59.9	47.4	57.5	90.9	262.4
1965	55.2	59.5	42.1	18.7	61.1	47.8	58.0	89.7	260.9

Changes in Rates

1955 to 1965	−3%	−2%	−4%	−8%	+2%	+7%	+1%	−11%	−26%
1964 to 1965	+1%	+1%	0%	−2%	+2%	+1%	+1%	− 1%	− 1%

Source: 1953 to 1963 are NCHS national totals, 1964 and 1965 are NSC estimates. [Courtesy National Safety Council]

° Includes "age unknown." In 1964 these deaths numbered about 80.

† Death rates are deaths per 100,000 population in each age group. The *All Ages* crude rates are based on U.S. Census Bureau figures. The index numbers are based on rates which are standardized for age to remove the influence of changes in age distribution that occurred between 1903 and 1965.

in tractor accidents), whereas 2,200 occurred in farm work and 300 in nonfarm work; 1,800 happened in the home and 800 in public non-vehicular accidents. The death rate for farming is 66.3 which places it just below mining and construction in hazardousness.

TRENDS IN ACCIDENT PREVENTION

There can be little doubt about the effectiveness of the safety education movement. Spectacular progress has been made during the past century in the reduction of accidents in industry, rail and sea transportation, in public and in the home. It was estimated by the New York Center for Safety that the school safety programs saved nearly 30,000 lives from 1930 to 1945.

It is difficult to perceive the fact that between 1912 and 1966, accidental deaths per 100,000 population were reduced 29 per cent, from 82 to 58. They have been reduced 24 per cent in the past twenty-five years. This reduction in rate during a period when the nation's population has nearly doubled has resulted in 1.2 million fewer people being killed accidentally than would have been killed if the rate had not been reduced. (See Fig. 2-2.)

However, when limited to the population which is thirty-five years of age and under, the overall decline in the number of deaths resulting from accidents has been negligible in spite of the sharp reduction of deaths from other causes. This reduction has resulted in deaths from accidents becoming a larger and larger percentage. This trend, caused largely by motor-vehicle deaths, presents an ever-increasing challenge to the community and to school administrators. (See Table 2-3.)

Motor-Vehicle Deaths

During the past 25 years the public has been goaded into concern about the rising number of deaths and injuries as a result of motor-vehicle accidents. Despite the fact that the total number of fatalities mounts steadily each year, the rate per 100,000 population has been reduced by about 10 per cent since 1912. Motor-vehicle deaths still account for about 47 per cent of the loss of life caused by all types of accidents. The death rate of school-aged children continues to be high.

The total number of drivers and miles driven increases yearly. In 1966, 102 million drivers used 91.1 million registered vehicles to drive 935 billion miles with a death rate of 5.67 per 100 million miles of travel. Motor-vehicle deaths increased 8 per cent while the mileage increased 5 per cent, the number of vehicles increased 5 per cent and the population only 1 per cent.

Drivers who are drunk are twenty-five times more likely to cause accidents than they would if they were sober. An analysis of 1,134 fatally injured drivers in California showed that 65 per cent of those responsible for accidents had been drinking. Among the 353 pedestrians killed, 45 per cent had been drinking. School and college health and safety education programs have a most challenging obligation in coping with this drinking problem.

MOTORCYCLE-RIDER DEATHS

The use of motorcycles and scooters has increased rapidly and has become a major safety problem in many schools and colleges. They increased by 38.5 per cent in 1966 so that Americans owned 1,914,700 of them. During the past five years the deaths have increased faster than the number of motorcycles. Last year 2,160 died in motorcycle and scooter accidents. The year before, the death rate increased 43 per cent while the number of motorcycles increased only 9 per cent. The Safety Council estimates that the fatality rate for motorcycles is between 20 and 40 deaths per 100,000 vehicle miles of travel compared to 5.7 for all motor vehicles including pedestrian and other nonoccupant deaths as well as occupant deaths. If this rate continues, at least 3,260 deaths from motorcycles and scooters can be expected in 1971.

DEATH-RATE TRENDS AMONG YOUTH

Despite the fact that accidents are the principal cause of death among children, rates of fatalities have declined since 1922: 1 to 4 years, 58 per cent 5 to 9 years, 60 per cent: 10 to 14 years, 47 per cent. The rates for the next higher age groups have increased by +15 per cent for the group 15 to 19 years old and +27 per cent for the group 20 to 24 years old.

IMPLICATIONS

In the preceding pages we have tried to present the nature and scope of the accident problem as it confronts the American people. This material has presented the national situation which pertains, in general, to state and local communities but all school and college accident prevention programs should be based upon their own accident records. Accident report forms and methods of collection and reporting will be discussed in the following chapter. Such surveys are necessary to locate the most hazardous areas, to ascertain which students and faculty members are injured most often, and what the underlying as well as immediate causes of accidents are. At the same time such a survey, or surveys, determines which persons are *not* being reached by the safety education program.

Strasser *et al.*[4] say, *"Determination of needs should be established upon a priority basis,* giving first priority to those problems which are contributing most seriously to the accident problem of the organization. This procedure will assure the concentration of effort on the problems with the greatest need for improvement and with the greatest potential for making an effective reduction in the accident frequency and severity rates."

With the ever-increasing threat of mechanization and an almost unbelievable increment of leisure time, the school and college programs of safety and safety education must meet the unforeseeable challenge to improve the safety standards of the nation.

REFERENCES

Florio, A. E., and G. T. Stafford, *Safety Education* (New York: McGraw-Hill, 1962).

National Safety Council, *Accident Facts* (Chicago: The Council, 1966, published annually).

Stack, Herbert J., and J. Duke Elkow, *Education for Safe Living*, 4th ed. (Englewood Cliffs, N.J.: Prentice-Hall, 1966).

Strasser, Marland K., James E. Aaron, Ralph C. Bohn, and John R. Eales, *Fundamentals of Safety Education* (New York: Macmillan, 1964).

Stratemeyer, Clara G., *Accident Research for Better Safety Teaching* (Washington, D.C.: National Commission on Safety Education, National Education Association, 1964).

United States Coast Guard, *Recreation Boating Statistics* (Washington, D.C.: Treasury Department, C.G. 357, published annually).

United States Department of Health, Education, and Welfare, *Accidental Death and Injury Statistics* (Washington, D.C.: No. 1111, published annually).

———, *The Facts of Life and Death* (Washington, D.C.: Revised 1965, No. 600).

University of Kentucky, *Employee and Student Accident Experience* (Lexington: The Department of Safety, 1966).

[4] Marland K. Strasser, James E. Aaron, Ralph C. Bohn, and John R. Eales, *Fundamentals of Safety Education* (New York: Macmillan, 1964), p. 103.

CHAPTER 3 ORGANIZING FOR SAFETY EDUCATION

It has been nearly fifty years since Albert W. Whitney challenged the NEA Delegate Assembly to provide all students with the safety education that is their inalienable right. During this time safety education has become an important means of fostering effective living. Rapid progress toward total programs is occurring in numerous places and only needs continued enlightened leadership at the national, state, and local levels, and sufficient financial support to achieve its purposes.

However, safety education was a late-comer to the curriculum, and because it developed rather rapidly and haphazardly, the school program is seldom organized and administered in the most efficient and comprehensive manner. Teacher-education colleges and universities are beginning to accept leadership but often have vaguely defined programs as well as inadequate curricula. Many school administrators have not recognized the need for an organized plan of operation and instruction. This chapter is offered to provide guidance of those administrators who wish to check their present organization and to establish a type of plan which is recommended by leaders in safety education.

Before discussing the organizational and administrative plans let us examine the growth of the safety education movement.

GROWTH OF THE SAFETY EDUCATION MOVEMENT

The literature used in the first schools of our country refers to safety long before the days of Horace Mann. It was integrated into books like the McGuffey readers and texts on science and health education. Going still further back, there was some safety taught in the schools organized by the Pilgrims.

The safety education movement as we know it today began in the 1920's. Although there were some discussions of school safety at the meetings of the National Safety Council as early as 1914, interest in the subject was not fully aroused until 1919 when Albert W. Whitney addressed the annual convention of the National Education Association in Milwaukee.[1] In 1922 the National Bureau of Casualty and Surety Underwriters made a grant of funds to the National Safety Council which resulted in the organization of the Education Division,[2] which aided in the organization of demonstrations of safety programs in several cities and issued a series of publications for teachers and in 1926 published the magazine *Safety Education*. In the meantime, the first well-organized safety program was planned for Detroit under the direction of the first School Safety Supervisor, Harriet E. Beard. This program included (1) a study and analysis of traffic accidents to school children, (2) the construction of a course of study in safety education for the elementary schools, (3) the instruction of a class of students at Detroit Teachers College in the principles of safety education, and (4) the cooperation with all civil agencies concerned with public safety.

MILESTONES OF PROGRESS

There were several important milestones that occurred during this period. The first was the meeting of the National Education Association that was addressed by Albert W. Whitney. The second was the organization of the Education Division of the National Safety Council in 1922. The third milestone was passed in 1926 when the National Society for the Study of Education devoted its 25th Yearbook to safety education.[3] The White House Conference on Child Health and Protection was called by President Herbert Hoover in 1932 and included a section on safety education. Finally, the American Association of School Administrators devoted its 1940 Yearbook to safety education.[4] This Yearbook had a very important effect on school safety programs. It covered all phases of safety and included the organizations of programs in the elementary and secondary schools and in colleges and universities. It served for many years as a guide in the organization of programs of safety education. Because it covered the whole field of safety education, it was used for many years as a guide for organizing the planning of school programs. Even though it was approved by school administrators, many school districts and colleges were slow in organizing programs recommended in the Yearbook.

[1] National Commission on Safety Education, *The History of Driver Education in the United States* (Washington, D.C.: The Commission, 1936).

[2] Center for Safety Education, New York University, *Safety for Greater Adventures* (New York: The Center, 1953).

[3] National Society for the Study of Education, Twenty-fifth Yearbook, *The Present Status of Safety Education* (Bloomington, Illinois: Public Schools Publishing Company, 1926). (Out of Print.)

[4] American Association of School Administrators, Eighteenth Yearbook, *Safety Education* (Washington, D.C.: The Association, 1940).

Several nonschool agencies, including the American Automobile Association, the Casualty and Security Companies and the National Safety Council assigned members of their staffs to aid states in the organization of driver education programs. They assisted in preparing teachers, aided in developing courses of study, and distributed materials.

In 1943, the National Commission on Safety Education [5] was organized as a part of the National Education Association. It derived its main support from the Automotive Safety Foundation. In recent years additional support has come from the Insurance Institute of Highway Safety, the petroleum and tire companies, and automobile manufacturers.

The Commission has made a valuable contribution to the safety movement, especially in the areas of driver and traffic safety education, teacher education, fire prevention, and pupil transportation. It has aided in arranging four national conferences in high school driver education and has issued many valuable publications in various fields of safety.

Another department of the National Education Association—the American Association for Health, Physical Education and Recreation—has also aided in the development of the program. It has a Safety Division which holds meetings at the Association conferences and aids cities and states in planning safety activities. Its publications, *Annual Safety Education Review* and *Suggested School Safety Policies*, have been most helpful.

NATIONAL SAFETY CONFERENCES

We have already mentioned the White House Conference on Child Health and Protection held in 1932. In 1924, Herbert Hoover—at that time Secretary of Commerce—called the first national conference on street and highway safety. A second was held in 1934 and a third in 1946. Each of these conferences made recommendations for driver education. In 1954 the White House Conference on Highway Safety was held, and it completed the organization of the *Action Program*. It included a publication covering various phases of traffic safety education. National conferences were also held on fire prevention and protection and industrial safety, both of which recommended school and college safety programs.

GROWTH OF STATE PROGRAMS

Organizations, agencies, and national conferences have had a useful effect on the organization of state safety programs. For example, the number of high schools teaching driver education has grown from a few hundred in 1949 to well over 13,000 in 1967.[6] The number of colleges offering courses in various phases of safety has grown from 50 in 1940 to well over 600 by 1966.

[5] National Commission on Safety Education, *op. cit.*
[6] National Safety Council, *Accident Facts* (Chicago: The Council, 1966).

There has been one serious weakness in state departments of education. As late as 1957–1958, Key [7] reported that only 14 of 48 states had safety personnel with titles of supervisor or director of driver or safety education. At that time, fifteen states required only a single college-level course in driver or safety education for the supervisor. Supervisors with such backgrounds could not be very effective in organizing state programs.

If states are to assume the responsibility of developing programs, directing the preparation of publications, aiding in the preparation of teachers and advisory administrators, they must have supervisors who are well prepared and competent. The Elementary and Secondary Education Act of 1965 offers intriguing possibilities to state and local communities.

EFFECTS OF SAFETY PROGRAMS

The acid test of safety education is its effects on accidents. Fortunately, most programs have shown a reduction in accidents. In 1923, the number of deaths of children of ages 5 to 14 was 9,500, with a death rate of 39.4.[8] This was followed by a steady reduction in accidental deaths to 6,099 in 1956, and the rate dropped to 20.3. Since 1956, deaths have shown a steady increase while the death rate has dropped to 18.7. The increase in deaths was almost entirely attributable to the increase in motor-vehicle accidents.

If the death rate for the 5 to 14 age group had remained the same as it was in 1923 for the following 43 years, many thousands more children would have been killed. There is no satisfactory way to estimate the saving in nonfatal injuries. The safety education movement—including the work of the schools, police and fire departments, and dozens of other community agencies—has paid real dividends in the saving of lives of children.

From 1923 to 1967, accidental deaths for those in the 15 to 24 age group, have shown an increase of from 12,800 to 18,500, attributable almost entirely to motor-vehicle accidents and to falls. During the same period, deaths from drowning decreased from 9,200 to 7,200, although the use of the water for swimming, boating, and other activities has shown an outstanding growth. Deaths from firearms accidents also dropped from 3,000 to 2,200 during the same period in spite of the striking increase in the use of firearms for hunting and target practice. These two causes are mentioned because a large percentage of the deaths caused by both drowning and the use of firearms involves teen-agers. Education has played a part in reducing deaths from both these causes.

[7] Norman Key, *Status of Driver Education in the United States* (Washington, D.C.: National Commission on Safety Education, 1960).
[8] National Safety Council, *op. cit.*

ORGANIZATION AND ADMINISTRATION

Planning a school or college safety program begins with a determination of objectives sought and the needs to be met. It should be based upon sound basic principles of curriculum selection and organizational structure. If it is to function effectively the administrative responsibilities must be clearly defined and delegated to appropriate personnel.

It is obvious that the plan and structure will differ in various schools and colleges but all plans should include a sound instructional curriculum, a safe environment, a workable first-aid and accident-reporting system, and a teacher-training program.

The primary objective of every safety program is the prevention of accidents and injuries and the development of proper attitudes. Specific objectives should be formulated for all phases of the program. The next step would be to determine the needs.

DETERMINING THE NEEDS

The Illinois Curriculum Program Consensus Study formulated the following survey of needs, as quoted by Florio.[9]

A. Survey of present program
  1. Analysis of legal requirements
  2. Analysis of types and extent of previous training in safety
B. Determination of the safety problems of the age group
  1. Analysis of local, state, and national accident records of age group to discover educational shortage
    a. Frequency and types of accidents
    b. Time of accidents
    c. Accident trends
  2. Analysis of environmental hazards to discover exposure to accidents
    a. Analysis of school hazards
      (1) Buildings
      (2) Grounds
      (3) Equipment
      (4) Transportation
      (5) Organization
    b. Analysis of home hazards
      (1) Socioeconomic status
      (2) Nationality of parents
      (3) Occupation of parents
      (4) Types of homes
      (5) Location of homes
      (6) Safe places for play
    c. Analysis of community hazards
      (1) Population
      (2) Type—rural, urban, industrial, agricultural

[9] A. E. Florio and G. T. Stafford, *Safety Education*, 2nd ed. (New York: McGraw-Hill Book Company), p. 49.

(3) Playgrounds
(4) Recreational facilities
(5) Street hazards
(6) Industries
(7) Accident frequency at certain danger spots
3. Analysis of activities of children by season to determine probable exposure to accidents
   a. In school
     (1) Types of activities
     (2) Frequency of accidents
   b. Out of school
     (1) Types of recreational activities
     (2) Part-time employment
4. Analysis of safety responsibilities in the home, school, and community
5. Technics for determining safety problems
   a. Study of available accident records
     (1) School accident reports
     (2) Reports from local and state safety organizations
     (3) Police, motor-vehicle, and fire-department reports
     (4) Health-department reports
     (5) Reports of supervisors of recreational departments
     (6) Reports of insurance companies
   b. Systematic surveys
     (1) Check lists
     (2) Home-inspection blanks
     (3) Traffic counts
   c. Questionnaires
     (1) Children
     (2) Parents
   d. Inquiry, or personal interviews with
     (1) Recreation supervisors
     (2) Teachers
     (3) Police
     (4) Fire chief
     (5) Physician
     (6) Nurse
     (7) Parents
   e. Observations
   f. Diary records
C. Comparison of findings with experience of similar groups; analysis of courses of study and textbooks
D. Analysis of characteristics and interests of age groups
E. Survey of community agencies interested in promoting safety, their programs, and aids for schools

DUTIES OF THE ADMINISTRATORS

Organization and administration are closely related functions. The school superintendent and the principals organize and administer the school's program and also devote some time to supervision. Even though the board of education is legally responsible for the educational system, much of its work is carried on through the superintendent's office. He in turn delegates certain parts of the school safety responsibility to his assistants, the principals, or the safety supervisors.

Each board of education should see to it that the safety responsibilities of the superintendent and his assistants are clearly defined for the protection of schoolchildren, inspection of buildings and grounds, accident reporting, fire and civil defense drills, safe practices in school shops, gymnasiums, and playgrounds, duties of school custodians, and in some cases, the duties of street crossing guards. This chapter will consider several of these responsibilities; others will be discussed in later chapters.

Administration deals with the following aspects of the school program. According to Gulick,[10] these include:

1. *Planning* the program is the process of outlining the work to be done, and allocating responsibilities.
2. *Organization* refers to the relationship between the various activities, the structure, and assignment of responsibilities.
3. *Staffing* refers to the selection and assignment of personnel. In most instances this is the responsibility of the superintendent working with principals.
4. *Directing* is one of the most important functions of the superintendent. In school systems where there are well-organized programs, he has been active in initiating programs and establishing policies. Like the manager of an industry, he can make or break the safety program.
5. *Coordinating* refers to combining the various elements of the program to eliminate overlapping and duplication.
6. *Reporting* refers not only to accident report, but the reporting of all activities that are related to safety. Teachers and principals must be informed about all phases of the program which they should know about.
7. *Budgeting* refers to financial planning. A budget should be prepared especially for driver education, and the superintendent should be ready to defend it.

PRINCIPLES OF ORGANIZATION AND ADMINISTRATION

At the outset, the safety coordinator and other school administrators must recognize the fundamental truth that a successful safety education program is the result of a carefully planned structure in which all individuals clearly understand their responsibilities. Such a structure must be based upon proved principles of organization and administration which

[10] Luther Gulick, and L. Urwick, *Papers on the Science of Administration* (New York: Institute of Public Administration, Columbia University, 1937).

grow out of a sound educational philosophy. The principles of good administration are universal, inasmuch as success in every type of undertaking is dependent upon them. To be termed "good," administration must be *at once democratic*—offering to each individual and group the opportunity to cooperate—and the product of responsible leadership—leadership whose effectiveness may be judged by the extent to which it is able to delegate responsibility. This delegation of responsibility is not limited to the faculty alone; it is extended, under proper guidance, to the students as well, and provides them with an opportunity to learn by doing. Good administration makes use of *every resource at its command*, not only capitalizing upon the peculiar talents of the school faculty, but enlisting the cooperation of students, patrons, various levels of administrative personnel, and other groups. Another important duty of administration is to *provide a safe and adequate physical environment* for the student body. Last but not least, good administration is sound to the core, each of its parts being encouraged to *contribute to the whole, and each receiving recognition in the measure of its contribution.*

PITFALLS OF DEMOCRATIC ADMINISTRATION

Griffith [11] warns school administrators about the pitfalls of democratic administration. (Portions omitted.)

Democracy is the most misunderstood term in educational administration. Many schoolmen do not grasp its limitations. Their mental image of democracy as applied to education is fuzzy, like a view seen through an out-of-focus telescope. In the name of democracy, as they misunderstand it, they justify their blundering, indecisiveness, and buckpassing.

Six mistaken meanings of education democracy are prevalent. They need to be swept away so that the true meaning of democratic administration can be perceived.

ERROR 1: Democratic administration is a laissez-faire procedure.

A measure of freedom is desirable in teaching and administration, but it must be exercised in a framework of established policy and all school activities must be subject to inspection and evaluation. The administrator who allows his teachers to do as they please on the ground that he is being democratic is shirking his legal responsibility.

In a well-run school there must be statements of policy which all are bound to observe. There must be guidance, direction, and, when necessary, interference from above. A good school does not run by itself. Confusion is not an ingredient of freedom. Leadership and authority are essential.

ERROR 2: Democratic administration means guiding persons to accept an administrator's viewpoint.

Democratic administration is not an exercise in human engineering. It

[11] Frances Griffith, "Six Mistaken Meanings of Democratic Administration," *Phi Delta Kappen,* Vol. XLVIII, No. 2 (October 1966).

does not mean influencing subordinates to adopt a policy reached in advance of consultation. It does not mean adroitly manipulating persons to think and act as an administrator wants them to.

The gentle guidance of others into acceptance of a predetermined course of action is a perversion of democracy. *Democratic group discussion is a procedure for hammering out truth, for testing the merit of proposals by submtiting them to critical analysis, and for creative thinking.*

ERROR 3: Democratic administration avoids the firm exercise of authority and insistence on obedience.

Some administrators confuse firmness with authoritarianism. They are reluctant to issue orders and to demand compliance.

Indecisiveness is not an essential of democratic administration. There is a world of difference between the guarded and legitimate exercise of power and its arbitrary exercise without consideration of the interests, abilities, and welfare of those affected by its use. No organization can be effective without direction from above and compliance from below.

ERROR 4: Democratic administration means majority rule.

Educational problems cannot be solved by majority rule. An administrator's proposed solution may be sound even though his faculty considers it fallacious and unworkable. A majority's opposition may be based on ignorance, fear of change, or an incomplete knowledge of the elements in a situation.

Few educational matters are so urgent that they require immediate attention. For reasons of expediency an administrator may defer action when a poll shows widespread opposition to a proposal he favors. He may continue to try to convince his teachers and supervisors of the wisdom of a proposal, realizing that it will fail unless his subordinates are convinced of its validity.

ERROR 5: Democratic administration is a means of avoiding unpleasant decisions.

Every administrator faces at least one problem which requires an unpopular solution. A mature administrator will reflect on it thoroughly, discuss it with his associates and those affected, and after due consideration announce his ruling accompanied by a statement of his reasons therefor. He should not be concerned with the effect on his popularity. If he wishes to curry popularity, he should enter some field other than school administration.

When problems are important and complex, committees are indispensable instruments in school administration. But when committees are used to evade responsibility they negate rather than promote democratic administration.

ERROR 6: Democratic administration means the absence of formality.

A school in which every staff member is on a first-name basis with his fellow teachers and superiors is not necessarily democratic. A school in which the principal addresses everyone as "Mr.," "Mrs.," or "Miss" may be more truly democratic than one in which the principal backslaps his teachers, calls them by their first names, and discusses their personal affairs with them.

Every administrator needs to be aware of these six pitfalls. Democracy is a term which has been bandied about so much that it is assuming strange connotations. The beginning administrator, particularly, should realize that democracy does not mean abdicating authority, steering attitudes into a predetermined mold, or evading responsibility. He should also distinguish between democracy's trappings—voting, committee procedure, and informality—and democracy's essence, a respect for every individual.

SAFETY PLANS IN SELECTED SCHOOLS

The organizational and administrative plans of schools and colleges vary and the accident prevention and safety education programs will have to be planned to fit the given structure.

After a study of selected school systems known to have superior safety programs, Englehart made several important recommendations which have been abstracted as follows: [12]

1. Boards of education and superintendents should develop policies to help teachers and administrators provide adequate instruction to all students in all appropriate instructional areas.
2. One staff person should be designated to guide the safety education program for all schools in the system with a full-time supervisor in cities that can afford them, particularly in cities with a population of 50,000 or more.
3. The supervisor should have formal preparation in the field.
4. Each school system should have an advisory committee to plan the program.
5. Each school should have a teacher and/or committee to plan and guide safety activities.
6. All teachers should have preparation in safety education. An in-service program may be a substitute for a pre-service one.
7. All systems should appoint a committee at least once every three years to review and revise its safety education curriculum guide.
8. All systems should prepare and distribute materials describing policies and procedures in safety education.
9. Elementary schools should integrate safety education with all areas of instruction and seize every opportunity to teach safety.
10. High schools should offer a comprehensive safety education course which includes general safety education, driver education, and first aid. In addition, it should be integrated.
11. Schools should emphasize instruction in the following areas, depending on local conditions: traffic, fire, school, home, recreation, farm and rural, defense, occupational, and first aid.

[12] Melvin E. Englehardt, *The Administration of Safety Education in Selected School Systems.* Dissertation, Columbia University, 1961.

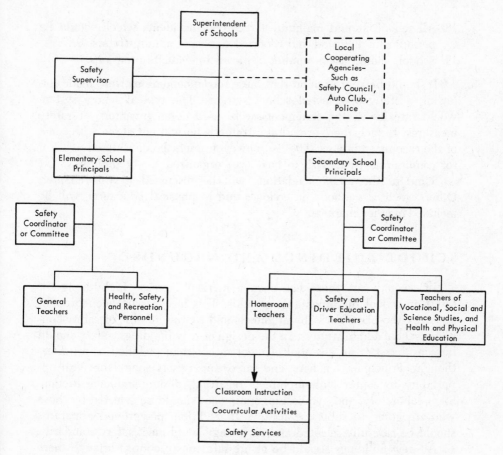

FIGURE 3-1. A school system's plan for student safety education.

12. In the high school, general safety education should be included in social studies, science, home economics, industrial arts, and physical education.
13. In the administration of the driver education program, schools should adopt the recommendations of the Third National Conference on Driver Education (1960).
14. School systems should adopt a definite procedure together with criteria for selecting textbooks and supplementary materials.
15. Schools should adopt student activity programs such as assemblies, safety projects, safety patrols, student organizations, and conferences to supplement classroom instruction in safety.
16. School systems should continue to seek the cooperation of all local agencies, civic groups, and national organizations.
17. State departments of education should provide more safety educational leadership and services to schools.

18. All schools should maintain a record of accidents which should be periodically analyzed and reported to school administrators.
19. Schools should use a number of means to evaluate programs.

It should be kept in mind that these recommendations were made following a study of *selected* school systems. The typical school system would rate low if the statements were used as an inventory of safety measures. In fact, there are administrators who will not agree with some of the recommendations. The list, however, might be considered as ideal for communities that wish to have well-organized safety programs.

Some of the recommendations will be discussed in this chapter. Others, such as methods on colleges and in physical education, will be included in other chapters.

SCHOOL BUILDINGS AND GROUNDS

In recent years there has been a marked increase in building for safety in school buildings and grounds. This has in part been brought about by the plans made by architects and by the interest of safety-conscious school administrators. In the design of new buildings, safety should be considered as an essential element rather than included as an afterthought. Principals, teachers, and safety supervisors should have an opportunity to confer with architects regarding design and construction. Shop, laboratory, and gymnasium equipment should be selected by those who are going to supervise its use. In addition, playground apparatus should be carefully selected and surfacing should meet safety standards.

All new buildings should be of fire-safe construction. Although there are far too many school fires, they are for the most part in old buildings, most of which are fire traps. Fortunately, most of the new buildings are of one or two story construction and built of brick, glass, concrete, or stone. In addition, much of the equipment in the building, such as desks, chairs, and tables are built of nonflammable materials.

SCHOOL SITES

Schools should be located as far as possible from other buildings and heavily traveled highways. This means that the Board of Education should plan for its schools well in advance and purchase property accordingly. All buildings should have adequate space for playgrounds and atheletic fields. Only too often the Board of Education acts too late and the acquisition of adequate area involves a great expense. Sufficient land should be available for parking and in high schools for a driver training range.[13]

[13] Florida now has 72 ranges at high schools.

There are certain accident prevention measures that are important in both new and old buildings. There should be a periodic inspection of buildings (see p. 70) to locate hazards and deficiencies and recommend remedial action. Sometimes this inspection will be carried on by members of the school board with the assistance of the principal, the custodian, and a safety engineer. All schools where school buses are used should have designated areas for loading and unloading. Moreover, separate, well-protected delivery entrances should be included for the full storage area, cafeterias, and shops. Rooms, hallways, and stairs should be adequately illuminated according to recommendations of the American Standards Association and the Society of Illuminating Engineers.

REGULATIONS

Special regulations should be published by the Board of Education and should cover the following areas:

Duties of Custodians
School Shops
First Aid Plans and Procedures
Fire and Civil Defense Drills
Responsibilities of Principals and Teachers
School Bus Regulations

It is important to have regulations of this type. In case of damage suits arising from accidents, the fact that the Board has published regulations covering various aspects is helpful in showing that it has not been negligent.

When schools or playgrounds are located close to streets the area should be protected by fences not less than 8 feet in height. They should not be located close to industries or railroads which could disturb the schools by offensive noise or odors. All exit doors should swing outward. They should be equipped with self-closing devices and bolts that operate easily.

Whether the ventilation system is of the open window or the mechanical pressure type, it should be sufficient to provide adequate fresh air in the rooms and halls.

It is further recommended that whenever possible the heating plant be located in a separate building. Even though buildings are fire resistant, adequate fire protection equipment should be provided, especially where fires are most likely to start or spread rapidly, such as in the boiler room, in corridors, in laboratories, and kitchens. When rebuilding or repairing an old building it is essential to check all wiring and enclose exposed wiring in conduits, rebuild wooden stairways with fire resistant materials, and install the furnace and fuel storage rooms outside the building—or if this is not possible, enclose them with fire resistant walls and ceilings. It is also desirable to install an automatic sprinkler system.

School Shops

It would appear that many accidents would be common in school shops, because there is so much machinery used that *could* be hazardous. However, only a part of the student body takes industrial arts or vocational courses. Moreover, shops generally follow the practices used in industry. Machines are guarded, personal protective equipment such as goggles are worn when using grinders, band saws, and other equipment. Helmets, aprons, and gloves are worn when welding. Instructors demonstrate the use of machines before individuals are allowed to use them. In addition, teachers insist on good housekeeping. As a result, school shops are comparatively safe.

Maintaining a Safe Environment

The mechanical and physical environment should be controlled in all shops. Factors such as illumination, disposal of waste materials, layout of machines, housekeeping and maintenance, and daily inspection should be stressed. It is of interest to note that even though school shops could be hazardous, the accident rate is about one fourth that in physical education activities. Blake's *Safety Subjects* [14] is a good manual to use in preparing an accident prevention program.

Regulations

It is essential that all shops have definite regulations especially with regard to power machinery and inspection of apparatus. There should be a daily inspection, which in some cases is conducted by a student safety inspector under the direction of the teacher. Regulations should be posted in a prominent place.

Student Safety Foreman

Many shops appoint student foremen or supervisors. They check tools from the crib, aid students in selecting tools and equipment, and, under the leadership of the instructor, act in the capacity of safety supervisors. In many shops, especially in junior high schools, students are not allowed to use certain machines, such as bandsaws or shearing machines.

[14] R. P. Blake, *Industrial Safety*, 3rd ed. (Englewood Cliffs, N.J.: Prentice-Hall, Inc., 1963).

Home Economics Laboratories

The same general principles of safety are used in home economics laboratories as in shops. Students are taught how to use stoves, irons, washers, and other equipment. There is good supervision and serious accidents are rare.

Chemistry Laboratories

There are many potentially dangerous chemicals used in laboratories. Among them are sodium, phosphorus, strong acids and caustics, and many others. Students are cautioned about the dangers in the use of the materials and are supervised at all times. As a result, most of the accidents that occur are minor, such as cuts from broken glass and burns from heating apparatus, acids, or caustics.

Public Relations

Good public relations are especially important in connection with the safety program. There are many local and state agencies that are directly concerned with accident prevention. The school system and the individual schools should take advantage of these agencies and cultivate good relationships. Some examples follow:

The police and bicycle dealers aid in conducting bicycle inspection programs.

Fire departments conduct inspection of buildings and put on demonstrations of fire prevention and fire-fighting methods.

The police arrange for setting aside certain streets for coasting and playing.

If a school has no pools, the Y.M.C.A. arranges to give swimming instruction in its pool.

The police arrange to equip the high school driving range with signs, signals, markings, and other traffic-control devices.

The local safety engineers arrange to inspect school shops.

The police department aids in supervising the work of safety patrols.

It can readily be seen that while these agencies aid in the work of the schools, the schools in turn provide help to the programs of the agencies. The police department wants to reduce accidents, the fire department wants to prevent fires. There are few subjects in the school curriculum that can get greater support from community agencies than safety education.

There are also several national organizations that aid in the work of the schools. Among these perhaps the best known are the National Safety Council, the American Automobile Association, the National Commission on Safety Education, the Insurance Institute for Highway Safety, individual insurance companies, the American National Red Cross, and others.

COCURRICULAR ACTIVITIES

In the junior high schools, cocurricular activities have unusual value. Many of these schools will devote five or more auditorium programs to phases of safety such as driving, fire prevention, water safety, home safety, and others. These programs include dramatizations, motion pictures, debates, demonstrations, and talks by experts, all of which may have unusual value in improving attitudes. Some cocurricular activities provide opportunities for actual practice, for example, clubs, such as the following: rifle, safety patrol, safety council, drivers, water safety, school parking, bus patrols, home economics, industrial arts, and others. Such programs can take on added life and strength if administrators, supervisors, and teachers take real interest in them. Mention should be made of other activities such as teen-age safety conferences, road-e-o's, publications, campaigns, physical education leaders corps, hunting, scouting, archery, and motor boating. Several of these can be carried on in cooperation with community organizations. For example, motor boating courses are conducted in many schools in cooperation with the Coast Guard Auxiliary or the United States Power Squadrons. Schools are fortunate if there is a local safety council in their community for there are many contributions that safety councils can make to aid a school's safety program.

USE OF VISUAL AIDS

If a school system is large enough, it will have a visual aids library and a full time director. This library should include a number of the best films on various safety subjects for both elementary and secondary schools. Each school should have at least one motion picture projector and a slide and film-strip projector.

The director of visual education should also arrange for the loan of visual aids from producers or distributors. Since there is a strong demand for the better films, schools should order them from the director so they will be available for long-term loans. Thus they can be used by many schools, without being shipped back and forth to distributors.

The usual plan is to stress one phase of safety each month, such as

September—Traffic
October—Fire and hunting
November—School

December—Home
January—Winter
February—Public
March—Street and Highway
April—Play and Recreation
May—June—Swimming and Vacation

There are many distributors of safety films, but unfortunately not too many good titles are available for the lower grades. Among the best known distributors are the following:

National Safety Council
Insurance Companies
State Department Depositories
Coronet Films
State University Libraries
Automobile Manufacturers
School Bus Manufacturers
Bureau of Mines
American Red Cross
National Fire Protection Association
American Automobile Association
National Rifle Association
Encyclopedia Britannica
Petroleum Companies
United State Department of Agriculture
United States Fire Service
United States Coast Guard
Public Utilities

Films should be previewed by a committee of teachers and the list of the most suitable ones sent to schools so that they can be ordered. When the school system is not large enough to have a director of visual education, the work should be done by a committee of teachers.

The standard 35-millimeter slides are also used extensively. One of the best methods of teaching safety is to prepare sets of slides featuring the various hazards in the community and use them as a basis for talks and discussions.

TELEVISION

Many school systems are making extensive use of television. Miami, for example, is using television programs in driver education in all high schools. A number of other cities have also had good results especially if programs are followed by discussion. Many cities have had televised programs covering other phases of safety education. Although little research has been conducted, it is generally believed that good television programs, followed by discussion, will be valuable. Good programs should include demonstrations, dramatizations, and in some subjects, laboratory experiments. A nationally televised quiz on safe driving practices for the general public was most successful.

THE SCHOOL AS A COMMUNITY SAFETY CENTER

In many cities there are local safety councils or committees. It has been found that over a period of years, these cities have developed the best programs. The councils are made up of representatives of the police and fire departments, health and recreation departments, the Red Cross, Boy and Girl Scouts, Parent-Teacher Associations, insurance agents, industries, chambers of commerce, and other organizations. Each of these agencies provides aid to the school program. They are interested in reducing accidents, and they know that one of the best ways to do so is through education. There are dozens of ways in which the police can cooperate—they act as school crossing guards, aid in conducting bicycle safety programs, give talks in the schools, assist in the driver education program, train crossing guards, and perform other useful services. Health and recreation departments are also active, as is the Red Cross.

Many high schools conduct driver education courses for adults and out-of-school youth. They also aid in "Hunter Safety" courses and in boating safety taught by U.S. Power Squadrons and the Coast Guard Auxiliary. In addition, evening schools include courses in first aid, cooking, vocational education, chemistry, physics, and other subjects in which safety can be emphasized. In some systems, each school has a safety or a health and safety coordinator who works with various organizations to strengthen the school program. Parent-Teacher organizations are usually active in safety programs, for safety is one of the major objectives of the national organization. The same is true of the American Red Cross and the Boy and Girl Scouts. Schools want the help of these agencies to strengthen their programs and the agencies want the aid of the schools to reduce accidents and fires.

REFERENCES

American Association of School Administrators, Eighteenth Yearbook, *Safety Education* (Washington, D.C.: The National Education Association, 1940).

Blair, G. M., R. S. Jones, and R. Simpson, *Educational Psychology*, 3rd Ed. (New York: Macmillan, 1968).

Center for Safety Education, New York University, *The Administrator and the School Safety Program* (New York: The Center, 1955).

Florio, A. E., and G. Stafford, *Safety Education* (New York: McGraw-Hill, 1962).

Higgins, T. J., "Check List for Safety in School Construction," *Safety Education* (January 1954).

Lane, W. R., R. G. Corwin, and W. G. Monahan, *Foundations of Educational Administration* (New York: Macmillan, 1967).

Miles, James B., "The School Principal and Accident Prevention," *Safety Education* (February 1957).

Morphet, E. L., *et al.*, *Educational Administration* (Englewood Cliffs, N.J.: Prentice-Hall, 1963).

National Commission on Safety Education, *The Elementary School Principal Plans for Safe Living* (Washington, D.C.: The Commission, National Education Association, 1961).

———, *Our Schools Plan for Safe Living* (Washington, D.C.: The Commission, 1956).

———, *Safety Guides for You—In the Intermediate Grades* (Washington, D.C.: The Commission, 1961).

———, *Safety Guides for You-In the Primary Grades* (Washington, D.C.: The Commission, 1961).

National Safety Council, *Foundations for Safe Living* (Chicago: The Council, 1948).

National Society for the Study of Education, *In-Service Education for Teachers, Supervisors, and Administrators*, The Fifty-sixth Yearbook (Chicago: University of Chicago Press, 1957).

Nihan, J., "State Laws and Regulations for Safety Education." Doctoral Thesis, New York University, 1961.

Office of the Superintendent of Public Instruction, *The Challenge of Safety Education* (Springfield, Ill.: Office of the Superintendent, 1959).

Silverwood, G. P., "Safety in the School Environment," *Journal of Health, Physical Education, and Recreation* (March 1960).

Stack, H. J., and J. D. Elkow, *Education for Safe Living* (Englewood Cliffs, N.J.: Prentice-Hall, 1965).

Strasser, M. K., J. E. Aaron, R. C. Bohn, and J. R. Eales, *Fundamentals of Safety Education* (New York: Macmillan, 1964).

Wasson, N. E., "Supervision in Safety Education," *Safety* (March–April, 1966.) (Washington, D.C.: National Commission on Safety Education, 1966.)

Wiles, K., *Supervision for Better Schools* (Englewood Cliffs, N.J.: Prentice-Hall, 1961).

Yost, C., *Teaching Safety in the Elementary School* (Washington, D.C.: American Association of Health, Physical Education, and Recreation, 1962).

CHAPTER 4 LIABILITY, FIRST AID, AND ACCIDENT REPORTING

LEGAL LIABILITY FOR SCHOOL ACCIDENTS

The system of law in the United States is such that every individual has the right to be free from bodily injury that is caused by other persons either intentionally or through an act of careless behavior. A universal principle of the law is that every person is individually liable in damages for his own contributory negligence. The application of this general rule similarly is designed for school personnel in their responsibilities to pupils. School administrators have a major role in the prevention of accidents to pupils on the school grounds, the corridors, and stairways of school buildings, the school playground, or the classroom. Exposure to injuries appears to be prevalent in gymnasiums, science laboratories, industrial arts classes, and on field trips. School bus transportation is likewise of concern to the school administrators and school bus drivers because of the possibility of injuries to pupils while they are being transported by school-owned buses. It is also of concern to private operators of school buses. The possibility of being sued by the parents of an injured pupil for an act of contributory negligence should be a concern of all school employees.[1]

Legal Definitions

Immunity from damage suits where school districts are involved has frequently been a target for criticism and challenge. In court procedures previous experience along with precedence may well be the determining factors in an ultimate court decision. For this reason there is a tendency for misunderstanding by educators concerning their personal legal status and the limits of their liability in cases of student injuries. Particularly important for the educator is an understanding of the fundamental con-

[1] Henry Campbell Black, *Black's Law Dictionary*, 3rd Ed. (St. Paul: West Publishing Company, 1933).

cepts that form a basis for court decisions in tort suits where school personnel are subjected to a trial.[2] An understanding of the following terminology is imperative.

Assumption of risk is a term defined by Leibee [3] as a person's voluntary involvement in a hazardous situation with full knowledge of the dangers attendant upon his action. A spectator at an athletic contest, for example, subjects himself to bodily injury where flying objects may come in contact with him.

Attractive nuisance can be an unguarded hazardous device, structure, apparatus, property, or environmental condition which a child may use or possibly engage in some form of play.

Contributory negligence is a charge imposed on a plaintiff who failed to exercise ordinary care in preventing an injury that he subsequently sustained through actions of negligence by another person.

Damages is a term used to indicate the compensation, recompense, or satisfaction assigned by the court to a person having received injuries through the wrongful act of another person.

Foreseeability is a designation that may be applied to an act that could have been anticipated and therefore prevented by prudent action. From all indications the court relies heavily upon the foreseeability of hazards in judging cases where accidents take place involving schools. School personnel should continually strive to eliminate whenever possible and compensate for any existing hazards in the school and surrounding environment.[4]

Liability is a legal responsibility involving indebtedness that is enforceable by court proceedings.

Last clear chance is the designation of a final opportunity to prevent injury to another who has placed himself in a dangerous situation through his own negligent acts.

Malfeasance is a term indicating evil doing, ill conduct, the commission of some act which is positively unlawful and which ought not to be committed at all.[5]

Misfeasance is the improper performance of some act which a man may lawfully do.[6]

Nonfeasance is the nonperformance of some act which ought to be performed, omission to perform a required duty, or total neglect of duty. *When* will the law impose a duty to act? There are numerous publica-

[2] *Ibid.*

[3] Howard C. Leibee, *Liability for Accidents in Physical Education, Athletics, and Recreation* (Ann Arbor: Ann Arbor Publishers, 1952).

[4] A. E. Florio and G. T. Stafford, *Safety Education,* 2nd Ed. (New York: McGraw-Hill, 1962).

[5] Howard C. Leibee, *Tort Liability for Injuries to Pupils* (Ann Arbor: Campus Publishers, 1965).

[6] *Ibid.*

tions containing possible answers to this question. This is referred to as the law of torts. Once a duty is imposed, it is always the same in negligence cases—that is to act as a "reasonable man in the consideration of circumstances." Limited emphasis should be placed on the distinction between misfeasance and nonfeasance in view of the fact that courts will always find a duty to act where, in general, reasonable men would recognize it and agree that it exists.[7]

Plaintiff is one who presents or initiates the court action, with a desire for enforcement or protection of a right, or the redress or prevention of a wrongful act; it represents one who invokes the assistance of the law.

Proprietary functions are those functions which could equally be performed by private individuals or corporations and do not have a relationship to sovereignty. For example, nongovernmental functions are classified as proprietary.

Save harmless statute is a law that exists in Connecticut, New York, New Jersey, and Wyoming stipulating that the school district reimburse a teacher who is judged liable for injury occurrences resulting from negligence. The enforcement of this law has on occasion stimulated the question of illegal use of school finances. In some states there is a specific authorization liability insurance to protect school personnel in transportation liability cases.

Tort, according to Black's definition, is a "wrong; injury; the opposite of right." Essentially it represents a civil wrong, where there is no involvement with a breach of contract, that infringes upon personal rights of another person and justifies the injured person to bring suit on the responsible person. A tort infraction refers to harm received by an individual rather than involvement with the public. It is conceivable this could be an infraction related to some form of public duty.

Vis major is a term applied to accidents that may have been inevitable such as those caused by lightning or a hurricane. Prevention would not have been possible by reasonable foresight, experience, or care.

A knowledge of the legal concepts will be of considerable assistance to school personnel in seeking legal counsel and possible interpretation in various types of liability cases.

LIABILITY FOR PUPIL INJURY

In the event that contributory negligence in the performance of duties with school pupils can be assessed, the school employee is legally re-

[7] *Ibid.*

sponsible for the outcome of existing injuries. Compensation from personal funds will be required unless he is employed in a state where there is a provision in the law whereby the school district as an employer is obligated to reimburse him for financial loss, or the district is liable for alleged employee negligence. A pupil can always make an effort to claim redress from the individual charged with contributing negligence that could have caused him some type of injury. This employee may be a teacher, an administrator, school bus driver, another pupil, or any employee of the school district. If the case is settled in favor of the student he may get a money judgment, but actual payment may not be possible if the individual sued lacks the necessary financial resources. A pupil sustaining injuries has a better possibility of satisfying his judgment if the state in which he resides is one where the law permits or requires school districts to provide protection of school employees from having to make a payment out of personal funds.

The purpose of this chapter is to assist school personnel in understanding the problem of legal liability and the importance of school employees in accepting responsibility for the prevention of pupil injuries. In establishing negligence as a contributory factor there must be sufficient evidence to substantiate a failure in complying with this duty. A direct relationship exists between "negligence" and teacher liability.

LEGAL DEFINITION OF NEGLIGENCE[8]

"*Negligence* is the failure to act as a reasonably prudent person would act under the particular circumstances." All school personnel must have a complete understanding of this definition and each constituent part of this principle of law:

Failure to act. Negligence can consist of inaction as well as of action. If one fails to do something expected of him by the law, he can be negligent. Likewise, actively doing something contrary to what the law expects can also be negligence.

A reasonably prudent person. This is a mythical person established by law; "foresight" is his major characteristic. If a reasonable man of ordinary prudence could have, or should have, foreseen the harmful consequences of his behavior, it is negligent to disregard them by failing to take the necessary precautionary steps to obviate or prevent such harmful consequences. Thus, negligence consists of the failure to avoid trouble that reasonably could or should have been foreseen or anticipated. Need one have been able to anticipate the particular accident that actually occurred? No, it is enough if reasonable prudence could or should have foreseen that some such accident might or could happen in the absence of precautionary safeguards.

[8] *Legal Liability for School Accidents*—Remarks by Harry N. Rosenfield, Attorney, at the National Conference on Accident Prevention in Physical Education, Athletics, and Recreation, Washington, D.C., December 7, 1963.

A liability law suit presents this critical question: Could or should the teacher, in the exercise of reasonable prudence and foresight, have anticipated danger or hurt to another under the particular circumstances? If the answer is yes, the teacher is negligent if he failed to act so as to avoid such foreseeable danger or harm. In other words, if in the reasonable exercise of care one could or should anticipate trouble under the circumstances before him, his failure to take precautionary measures is imprudent and therefore negligent.

Under the particular circumstances. The specific facts in a case are all important in the determination of negligence. What would be prudent with high school students may be highly imprudent with kindergarteners. What may be prudent for a teacher assigned to a playground may be no test of the prudence of a principal who fails to assign enough teachers to supervise that playground. Even partially different facts may change the situation, as for example whether the players sent by the football coach into scrimmage are trained or untrained. In other words, in legal terminology, "negligence" is a question of fact for the jury to decide.

ACTS OF NEGLIGENCE

Before an accident can be classified as unavoidable, the principle of the law of negligence must be applied to the situation. After all the facts have been established, if no negligence is revealed, the accident may be of such a nature that it was unavoidable, and thus no liability is involved. Court decisions involving cases of negligence are predicated on such factors as the kind of behavior or conduct, the legal aspects of the injury cause, and the foreseeability in relationship to a harmful outcome. Negligent conduct may be placed in two categories: (a) an act in which a reasonable man would have been cognizant of an unreasonable risk involving injury to others, and (b) failure in the performance of an act which is apparent in the protection or assistance to another and one for which a person dutifully has a responsibility.

The act of negligence is usually identified as an unreasonable risk of injury to others, even though there is evidence of reasonable care, preparatory considerations, skill, and previous warning. The fact is that some aspect of negligence has been inherently related to the act. In certain types of conduct, the harmful act may become an act of negligence through improper care, skill, warning, or preparation, even though the act in itself may not have been related to negligent conduct if adequate care, skill, warning, or preparation had been exercised.

A school employee is negligent as stipulated by the law when there is a display of conduct that does not conform to the established standard set forth by law with regard to the protection of others against risk or harm considered to be an unreasonable act. A standard of conduct is evaluated on the comparative basis of what a reasonable man displaying ordinary prudence would have done in similar circumstances or the same situation. In the profession of teaching, this standard would be in relationship to that of a prudent teacher, and not that of the so-called prudent layman. In situations where negligent action on the part of a teacher contributes to a pupil injury, the liability involvement may have similar extensive consequences as a private negligent individual being a party to the act of negligence. In this instance the teacher would not only be liable in damages where there was physical harm he caused, the same individual may also be liable for

1. Physical harm resulting from fright or shock or other similar or immediate emotional disturbances caused by the injury or the negligent conduct causing it.
2. Additional bodily harm resulting from acts done by third persons in rendering aid irrespective of whether such acts are done in a proper or negligent manner.
3. Any disease which is contracted because of lowered vitality resulting from the injury caused by his negligent conduct.
4. Harm sustained in a subsequent accident which would not have occurred had the pupil's bodily efficiency not been impaired by the original negligence.[9]

Further implications for teacher liability when there is pupil injury may result where a pupil's previous physical condition was not known. All teachers should possess a thorough familiarity with the legal implications of personal liability and the proper procedures and precautions for personal protection. Liability laws are established with the purpose of protection rather than persecution of the innocent. These laws have a function to serve such purposes as

1. Protection for the innocent by organizing and developing safety standards that may have been eliminated without the existence of liability laws. This represents a contribution to accident reduction resulting from such laws.
2. Designation of fault and the basic contributory factors related to accident causation. With corrective action being applied a similar occurrence contributing to an accident may have been eliminated.
3. Provisions for a financial reimbursement to innocent victims to relieve the monetary burden resulting from accident involvement.[10]

RESPONSIBILITY OF SCHOOL ADMINISTRATORS

The school administrator is not legally liable for pupil injuries unless it can be established that he is personally guilty of acts of negligence. Obviously, the school administrator has a primary responsibility to the pupils and staff for safe and efficient management of the total school

[9] National Commission on Safety Education, *Who Is Liable for Pupil Injuries* (Washington, D.C.: The Commission, 1963).

[10] Marland K. Strasser, James E. Aaron, Ralph C. Bohn, and John R. Eales, *Fundamentals of Safety Education* (New York: Macmillan, 1964).

complex. In establishing policies and procedures much can be accomplished by the administrator in minimizing hazards throughout the school environment and the promotion of accident and injury prevention to all school personnel. This would include an effective program of supervision in all aspects of the school program.

The safety of pupils can be strengthened when the school administrator establishes procedures that would include

1. Procedures for school personnel to report the existence of dangerous practices and unsafe conditions as they are observed.
2. A plan for a regularly scheduled inspection program to include all buildings, grounds, facilities, and equipment. A search for hazardous and dangerous conditions would be a part of the periodic inspection program.
3. Elimination and repair of any defects or unsatisfactory items used by school personnel.
4. Scheduling of periodic faculty and staff meetings, including maintenance and service personnel, to appraise the school accident experience and devise means to eliminate accidents.[11]
5. Regulations for student traffic to include stairs, corridors, and other areas of the school's premises.
6. Provisions for competent supervision of students on field trips and other excursions away from the school building.
7. Provisions for adequate supervision where pupils congregate for recreational and play periods.
8. Adherence to rules and regulations for an efficient system of school bus transportation.
9. Investigation of all accidents occurring throughout the school complex.
10. An accident-reporting and analysis procedure to be followed by all faculty and staff.

School administrators have a highly significant role in the prevention of school accidents. Their responsibility includes an understanding of the contributory causes of accidents and how they can best be eliminated or minimized. All faculty and staff must have the administrator's full cooperation in this essential phase of the school program if the school is to be managed efficiently.

PUPIL AND SCHOOL PERSONNEL INSURANCE

In consideration of a satisfactory plan whereby school liability cases can be expedited, a large number of states are utilizing insurance programs that will provide medical attention for injuries suffered by pupils and

[11] National Committee on Safety Education, *op. cit.*

protect school personnel from judgments and legal claims. This procedure is highly recommended when considering the slow judicial procedure to settle by court proceedings the variety of legal liability cases that may be presented to a jury. In particular, teachers should be aware of their personal liability and seek professional guidance concerning the availability of insurance protection. Failure by either the school district or individual to purchase adequate insurance coverage could be an expensive form of economy.

TEACHER INSURANCE PROTECTION

The teacher having a responsibility for a phase of the instructional program and possibly cocurricular activities should adhere to the recommended procedures for obtaining proper insurance protection. He should consider the following points.[12]

1. Obtain an insurance liability policy that would provide for payment of damages assessed against the teacher for accidents related to his teaching responsibility. A variety of professional teacher organizations subscribe to an insurance program that makes such protection available to their membership on a group basis. Individual members' names are added to an original contract that is written by the insurance carrier for the sponsoring organization. The cost for this protection is minimal, with a fee for a $10,000 liability policy being one or two dollars annually.
2. Apply for liability protection through a "Homeowner Insurance Policy." This form of insurance usually provides liability coverage for accidents occurring on the policy holder's personal property. With the exception of automobile liability, this policy is considered as blanket protection against personal liability cases in the community, on the job, or at home.
3. Purchase personal liability insurance from a reputable insurance company that would provide for complete liability protection, with the exception of automobile liability. Automobile liability protection customarily must be purchased in a separate policy.

In view of the fact that many safety educators have a teaching assignment in Driver Education they should be aware of the need for insurance protection in the practice-driving phase of this discipline. A special clause can be written into the regular policy that will cover the driver education instructor while he is engaged in his teaching responsibility.

Legal liability of teachers is reduced considerably when the state has a legal provision to rescind immunity. Teachers should be certain to have adequate insurance protection against all conceivable aspects of legal liability.

[12] *Ibid*, pp. 242–43.

School District

A school district will have a concern for insurance coverage in those states where there has been legislative action to either completely remove or alter the district immunity provision. The legislatures in some states have granted permission to school districts for the purchase of various types of insurance policies with approval of a court suit in keeping with the stipulation of the policy. In certain instances this may be partial coverage as is the case with driver education instructors in the practice-driving phase of the instructional program. Conversely, there are certain aspects of the school program where all phases will be covered by the insurance policy.

There are indications that some school districts have entered into a self-insured program whereby payment of claims will be made to meet the existing situation. Obviously a school district for the most part is not in a position to establish an individual budget for the settlement of claims. The majority of school districts where there is authorization by legislative action to purchase insurance have obtained adequate coverage for the student body, staff, and teaching personnel.

Student Insurance Protection

A representative number of insurance companies have developed an insurance protection program for students who receive injuries while participating in school activities. School districts participating in this plan provide an opportunity for parents to purchase insurance protection for their children that have various benefits including medical payments for school accidents. Payments can be made for optical service where glasses are necessary as the result of an eye injury and for dental attention for injuries to the teeth. The coverage can also include clauses similar to workmen's compensation. This would make available financial settlements for losses to sight, hearing, and limbs. Purchase of orthopedic devices can also be stipulated as a part of the policy.

School districts can avoid court cases, by seeing that an injured pupil receives payment for all justifiable medical expenses. Significantly important is the protection made available in the policy for pupil protection and payment of medical fees resulting from school jurisdictional accidents.

FIRST AID AND ACCIDENT CASES

GENERAL ADMINISTRATION. Every school, regardless of size or level of education, should have a definite policy for handling student, staff, and faculty accidents. All administrators, supervisors, teachers, and members of the health and physical education staff should be thoroughly informed of this procedure. Many should also be properly qualified to render first aid. It is advisable, especially below college level, to have the names, addresses, and telephone numbers of the parents and the family physician, of each student in accessible files. First aid is defined by the American Red Cross as "the immediate, temporary treatment given in case of accident or sudden illness, before the services of a physician can be secured."

The National Safety Council recommends that the school administration make definite arrangements with a nearby hospital or clinic to handle emergency cases when the family or school physician is not available. If, after notification, the parents want their child to have medical attention at some place other than the designated hospital, the parents should assume responsibility for this procedure. In the case of a moderate injury, if the parent is reached before the student is sent to a doctor, the student should be taken wherever the parent directs. The college situation presents different administrative procedures which are usually well established.

A first-aid room should be provided with adequate equipment, including a stretcher, and made available to all activity areas. Making such equipment available to all areas of activity may present quite a problem, but every effort should be made to do so. Often a laboratory or the playing field is some distance from the first-aid room, and if a telephone call is necessary, valuable time can be lost before aid can be secured. Specific mention is made of a stretcher, because this valuable piece of equipment is usually not included in school first-aid rooms and it should be by all means. The stigma that once accompanied its use is rapidly disappearing, especially at football games, where one should always be available. Dr. George G. Deaver,[13] New York University orthopedist, sees its use as an educational device as well as the only sensible means of transporting the injured. He says,

> When one observes the methods used by many schools and colleges in transporting injured players to the sidelines, there can be no doubt that many simple injuries are aggravated by the rough treatment. If schools and colleges used proper methods of transporting injured football players, instead of pulling them off the field with head, arms, and legs dragging, it would be an excellent method of educating the spectators on the proper treatment of injury.

Administering treatment at the scene of the accident, especially to serious injuries, may upset class morale and should not be done unless it is absolutely necessary. Also, the injured person ordinarily prefers privacy and the person administering first aid should have a suitable place to work.

[13] George G. Deaver, "First Aid Emergencies," *Journal of Health, Physical Education, and Recreation* (April 1941), p. 233.

AVAILABLE FIRST AID. It is apparent that much of the severity of injuries is caused by a lack of adequate and immediate treatment. College statistics indicate that first aid is best offered by a medical doctor, and second a teacher of physical education. In high schools where the teacher of physical education renders first aid there is a lower average severity incidence than in schools where first aid is offered by other teachers or the principal. It is desirable to have medical service available for all types of periods, class instruction, laboratories, intramurals, and interschool competition.

RECOMMENDED PROCEDURE IN ADMINISTERING FIRST AID. School organization and the conditions under which accidents occur vary so much that it is difficult to establish first-aid procedures that will cover all cases. The following steps, therefore, are given to serve as guiding principles.

1. *The nearest qualified first aider should act in case of injury.* If the first aider happens to be one of the students, the coach or teacher should take over as soon as he or she arrives.

   He should determine the location, nature, and seriousness of the injury. The first aider will have to call upon his knowledge and experience to make this preliminary decision.

2. He should then determine the proper course of action.

   If the injury is minor, he should give first-aid treatment and then refer the decision with regard to further treatment to parents, school nurse, or health service.

   If the injured person can walk or be carried safely to the first-aid room, he should be taken there. This applies particularly if the injured person is in such condition as to alarm others. The first-aid room is a more suitable place for treatment.

   If a back or neck injury is suspected he *must not be moved.*

3. If the injury is serious, the following steps should be carried out: *Telephone or send a dependable messenger to notify the school physician, nurse, or trainer as well as the principal.*

   Instruct him to tell the location of the injured person and the nature, cause, and probable extent of injuries.

   Instruct him to tell what first aid has been given and ask what to do until one of the above-mentioned persons arrives.

4. *Continue first-aid treatment in accordance with Red Cross recommendations and school policy* until the physician, nurse, trainer, or principal takes over. In most serious cases experienced in the shop, laboratory, or physical education program, it is advisable to make the patient as comfortable as possible and await the arrival of a physician. It often becomes the first aider's role to protect the injured player from the excited and foolish actions of would-be helpers.

5. The physician, nurse, trainer, teacher, or administrator should determine the seriousness of the case, decide whether an ambulance should be called and/or the parents notified and their disposition of the case requested, and act accordingly. Some administrators feel that only a physician should make this decision, which is probably true in metropolitan areas, but in rural areas it might be necessary for one of the others to make this vital decision. The utmost tact must be used in contacting the parents, and the principal should probably handle this task.

6. *Transportation to the home or hospital should be provided by the parent* or by the administrator at the parent's request if an ambulance is not available. A doctor, nurse, or a person designated for the purpose should accompany the injured party, if necessary. Some schools may find this procedure unsatisfactory, but practice has shown it to be most desirable. A former director of health and safety of the Boy Scouts of America, had this to say:

> Of all things related to care of the injured by lay persons, this matter of transportation is perhaps the most serious. I doubt that if the injury is serious the person should be transported without specific instructions from a physician, unless weather conditions make movement absolutely necessary to prevent further harm being done. The question of whether the patient will be transported by parents or otherwise is also a matter to be decided by a physician.

THE FOLLOW-UP. *Investigation of the cause of the accident should be made immediately.* It should include the injured person's version and witnesses' testimony. The teacher in charge should have taken the precaution to insure that the apparatus or facility involved in the accident is maintained in *status quo* until an inspection has been made. It is understandable, of course, that often no facilities are involved, or that it is not possible to retain them in *status quo* or to investigate immediately, but every effort should be made to do so. In such an investigation the instructor should seek the true cause of the accident, which lies deeper than the unsafe act or the physical hazard. Then, by examining the health record of the student, it may be possible to determine the true cause and prescribe intelligent corrective measures. "This task of knowing each pupil's needs will, under any system, be greatly simplified by a strong system of diagnosis and cumulative records (including accident reports and items from anecdotal behavior journals). Faculty cooperation on the problems of particular students will be helpful." [14]

As soon as possible, *a written report*, on a standard form, of all injuries which force the student to miss one or more classes, should be made. (See pages 64, 65.) The accompanying forms are recommended. An effort has

[14] National Safety Council, *Safety in Physical Education and Recreation* (Chicago: The Council, 1941), p. 21. (Out of Print.)

been made in these reports not only to record the facts of the accident, but also to stimulate the recorder to delve into the background of the causes and prescribe intelligent methods of correction or compensation. Such elaborate investigation and study would not be necessary in all accident cases, but would be most useful in helping accident repeaters. Many school systems have their own form that is used for reporting accidents. Others use the standard National Safety Council form (see page 66) but these blanks do not usually include sufficient information for all departments. Many such forms are designed only to protect the school from law suits. The use of a special form for certain departments might be in addition to the regular school report and could be treated confidentially. As an educational device, it is desirable to have the injured person assist in filling out the accident report. Not only should this form be filled out, but a follow-up should be made and the factors involved in the accident corrected. Sometimes this may entail no more than the repairing of a board or reemphasizing some safety practice. However, a number of serious accidents may require a major reconstruction job or the improving of teaching techniques.

HOSPITALIZATION OF THE INJURED. For many years it has been customary for colleges to offer health service plans, usually covering limited periods of hospitalization, to all students upon payment of a relatively small insurance fee. Members of athletic teams are usually covered in case of accident by special health service plans. On the other hand, high schools have been slow to recognize their responsibilities in regard to insuring all students. In many communities local physicians have provided free service for injured players of athletic teams, or the school has arranged to pay nominal fees for the service.

Probably a stronger case could be made for the provision of such services for *all* students. Some persons reason that their children are compelled to attend school and to engage in dangerous shop or physical education activities; therefore, when children are injured in those activities, it is the school's responsibility to pay for the resulting medical care. Therefore, the present trend seems to be to make the benefits of an accident benefit plan available to *all* students who wish to subscribe. Wisconsin has been a leader in this movement.

ACCIDENT INVESTIGATION AND REPORTING

The following material is adapted from the *Safety Manual* [15] of the University of Kentucky.

[15] University of Kentucky, *Safety Manual, Safety Program, and Standards for Safety* (Lexington: University of Kentucky, 1966).

General

An essential element of any safety program is the immediate investigation, reporting, and analysis of all accidents resulting in injury to persons or damage to equipment or property. Prompt, precise investigating and reporting is extremely important in order that essential information may be properly recorded and evaluated to indicate trends, identify causes, and provide the basis for formulating plans and actions to prevent recurrence. Accident reporting is the keystone of a viable accident prevention program.

Reportable Accidents

For the purpose of this program, an accident may be defined as any act, to include occupational disease, which causes an interruption to an intended course of action resulting in a reportable injury to a person or damage to equipment or property. A reportable injury is one which requires the injured to desist from the activity, absent himself for a period of time and require either first aid or medical attention. Any injury to the head, neck, or spine must be reported, regardless of how slight it appears to be. It can therefore be assumed that any accident, including traffic accidents involving school-owned vehicles, which comes within the purview of this definition, must be investigated and reported. The magnitude of the accident will determine the depth of the investigation.

Accident Investigation

Accurate, precise accident investigation will fulfill the requirement for full information as to causes—all the correctable causes that led to the accident. It should be clear to those conducting an investigation that their purpose is not to determine who is to be held responsible for the accident. If those providing information mistakenly believe this is the intent, vital information may be withheld or facts may be distorted.

The investigation of accidents has other purposes and advantages. Efficient investigation procedures indicate to the employee, student, or visitor that the school or university is displaying an interest in determining the cause of accidents. Carrying procedure further, arriving at a good sound explanation of the accident and then correcting the situation that caused it, is proof that the school or university is sincere in its efforts.

In many instances the individual making an investigation is quick to analyze the contribution to the accident made only by the individual involved. He should look further to determine what contribution the supervisor and the conditions made, if any. The individual has but one responsibility, the other two require equal investigation to determine the underlying causes of an accident.

The supervisor is expected to know the job of which he is in charge, whether he is a teacher, janitor, professor, laboratory manager, office manager, or dormitory supervisor. The supervisor is the representative assigned to get the job completed in the most efficient manner.

In view of this responsibility, it is expected that the supervisors be the key persons in investigating accident occurrences within their operation. Accidents should be met with and dealt with as their problem first. If underlying causes are outside the supervisors' responsibility, they should be brought to the attention of the superior as would be done in the case of an operational problem.

An investigation should not be looked upon as a necessary evil, or extra paper work, but rather as an opportunity to bring about more effective control of hazardous conditions—whether they be in the process itself, the machinery used in the process, or in the individuals themselves. Nothing should be assumed or taken for granted. Every alleged fact must be examined until the investigator knows exactly what happened.

Investigations should not be considered complete until all actions that will prevent recurrences have been taken. Investigators will find in many cases that some action should have been taken previously; in others, the accident will point out measures that could not have been foreseen. They should understand such actions that might be indicated by any of the causes assigned to the accident, whether unsafe conditions, unsafe acts, or unsafe personal factors.

For example, unsafe conditions should be studied to determine the reason for their existence, for anything the supervisor or higher management levels might have done or might do to prevent those conditions from arising. In a similar manner, unsafe acts should also be studied to learn why the employees acted as they did—to discover the causes underlying the acts. These causes will often be found in unsafe personal factors which should clearly direct attention to the needed corrective measures. The supervisor is helped when he knows that the individual lifted improperly, held work unsafely in the hand, or hurried unnecessarily, but he can take corrective actions that promise to be effective only when he recognizes that the individual's act stemmed from such unsafe personal factors as inadequate training, a willful disregard of instructions, bodily defects, or other causes. The underlying causes are therefore extremely important to the investigation and should always be reflected in the corrective measures taken or recommended.

The following corrective measures should be considered by supervisors. Some corrective actions should be taken immediately. Others will be outside their authority and will need to be recommended to their superiors or the local safety committee.

1. Correct unsafe conditions or take steps to have corrections made.
2. Improve housekeeping.

3. Provide proper tools, equipment, etc.
4. Restudy equipment, tools, processes, etc.
5. Restudy arrangement of work space or department.
6. Request sufficient equipment to do work safely.
7. Inspect tools, equipment and work area more frequently.
8. Supply proper protective equipment.
9. Give more adequate and/or complete instructions to the injured or other individuals.
10. Instruct individuals properly and make certain they understand.
11. Be particularly observant of individuals for evidences of inexperience.
12. Observe work practices more closely and stop those found to be unsafe.
13. Assign or secure sufficient help to do work safely.
14. Enforce regulations regarding protective equipment.

INVESTIGATION STEPS

The following steps should be followed in the conduct of an investigation. The sequence is not intended to be followed in the order enumerated; however, all areas should be considered by the investigator.

1. See the injured person immediately, if possible.
2. Get the complete story of the accident. Ask the injured party or witnesses to demonstrate, within the limits of safety, how it happened. (In cases of accidents involving machinery, never permit demonstrations with the power on.)
3. Review the physical causes that may have been involved:
   a. Poor housekeeping.
   b. Lack of proper guards.
   c. Improper apparel.
   d. Defective equipment, floors, and so on.
   e. Poor working conditions.
4. Review the personal causes:
   a. Dangerous practices.
   b. Inability to perform job properly (inexperience, poor judgment).
   c. Disobedience of rules.
5. Find all the contributory causes that are present. Trace each item to its cause.
6. Describe a good preventive remedy. Report defective equipment to the proper authority.
7. Tell others about the accident and show them how to avoid it.

ACCIDENT REPORTING

In order to assure that the administration is cognizant of all accidents and serious illnesses, one or two of the standard reporting forms listed should be used. A number of school systems and colleges have programmed the reports for IBM data processing which provides fast and effortless summarizations.

Record of Injury/Illness

These forms are intended to be used to record all injuries of students and employees or sudden serious illnesses of students. It is the record and the initial notification on which the supervisor may base an investigation. Part I may be prepared by the patient's immediate supervisor or other responsible individual and forwarded with the patient, when possible, to the medical facility rendering aid. Part II of the form should be completed by the physician or medical attendant. The form should then be torn apart and copies for the supervisor, safety department, and personnel division dispatched to the respective offices. The medical copy may be used as a record for the medical facility.

UNIVERSITY OF KENTUCKY
Record of Injury / Illness

PART I
(To Be Completed By Supervisor, and Delivered By Patient, If Possible, To Health Service Or Hospital Emergency Room)

1. LAST NAME FIRST NAME MIDDLE INITIAL | 2. SOCIAL SECURITY NO. | 3. AGE | 4. ACCIDENT REPORT NUMBER (Safety Department Use)

5. OCCUPATION OR STATUS __Employee __Student __Other | 6. INJURY/ILLNESS hour date | 7. RELEASED hour date | 8. EXACT LOCATION WHERE INJURY/ILLNESS OCCURRED:

9. HOW INJURY OCCURRED | 10. FIRST AID TREATMENT RENDERED

11. PATIENT INTENDS TO FILE CLAIM UNDER WORKMEN'S COMPENSATION ACT: ____Yes ____No

12. COLLEGE OR ADMINISTRATIVE OFFICE | 13. NAME OF SUPERVISOR TELEPHONE NUMBER

PART II
(To Be Completed By Medical Facility And Copies Returned To The Supervisor (White), Personnel Department (Pink), And The Safety Department (Buff). Green Copy May Be Retained By Medical Facility).

1. DIAGNOSIS

2. TREATMENT

3. DISPOSITION: __Return To Class/Work __Hospital __Sent Home/Residence __Other, specify: ____

4. ESTIMATED ABSENCE IN DAYS BEYOND DAY OF INJURY OR ILLNESS | 5. NAME OF PHYSICIAN/ATTENDANT | 6. TELEPHONE NUMBER

SAFETY FORM 5

FIGURE 4–1.

Standard Accidental Injury Report

The Standard Accidental Injury Report is intended to be used to report the facts derived from the investigation of all accidental injuries and contracted occupational diseases. The form is a single sheet, designed to provide ease of reporting (in most instances by checking blanks) and is compatible with automatic data processing systems.

This form should be prepared by the injured person's immediate supervisor, or other person assigned to conduct the investigation, within 24 hours of an injury. The report should be prepared in duplicate; the

UNIVERSITY OF KENTUCKY
Standard Accidental Injury Report

TO: UNIVERSITY SAFETY OFFICER, ROOM 102, KINKEAD HALL, UNIVERSITY OF KENTUCKY, LEXINGTON, KENTUCKY

| 1. NAME   (Last, First, Middle Initial) | 2. LOCAL ADDRESS | ___ On Campus |
| | | ___ Off Campus |

| 3. AGE ___ Years | 4. SEX ___ Female ___ Male | 5. CLASSIFICATION: ___ Faculty ___ Staff ___ Visitor ___ Freshman | ___ Sophomore ___ Junior ___ Senior ___ Graduate ___ Special | 6. POSITION & SSN (Employees Only) | 7. EMPLOYED ___ Months Years |

8. YEAR, MONTH & DAY OF ACCIDENT   9. HOUR ___ AM ___ PM   10. ESTIMATE OF SEVERITY: ___ Non-disabling (loss of less than a full day from normal activity)   ___ Disabling (loss of one or more full days from normal activity) Estimate number of lost days   ___ Fatal

11. COLLEGE/ADMINISTRATIVE DIVISION   12. NAME OF IMMEDIATE SUPERVISOR   13. WAS STUDENT AN EMPLOYEE AT TIME OF INJURY ___ Yes ___ No   WAS EMPLOYEE A STUDENT AT TIME OF INJURY ___ Yes ___ No

14. JURISDICTION   ___ On or in UK property, or in University conducted or supervised activity   ___ Off campus in non-University conducted activity   15. ACTIVITY AT TIME OF ACCIDENT (e.g. driving vehicle, diving from low board, lifting crate)

16. EXACT LOCATION OF ACCIDENT   17. ACTION TO PREVENT SIMILAR ACCIDENTS (Indicate if taken or recommended)

18. TYPE OF FACILITY (Use more than one block for clarity if necessary)
___ Administrative Office   ___ Physical Education
___ Auditorium or library   ___ Playing field or track
___ Athletic competition   ___ Private activity
___ Bath, shower or locker room ___ Public activity
___ Building exterior or grounds ___ Recreation or entertainment
___ Classroom or lecture hall ___ Retail shop or professional office
___ Eating place   ___ Service or maintenance area
___ Exterior walk or sidewalk ___ Shop
___ Farm, field or woods   ___ Sports area
___ Food preparation or service ___ Storeroom
___ Gymnasium   ___ Street or highway
___ Home Economics   ___ Swimming pool
___ Housing or domicile   ___ Transportation
___ Interior corridor or hall ___ Undeveloped area
___ Interior stair or ramp   ___ Water area
___ Intramurals   ___ Other, specify:_____
___ Laboratory

19. PROPERTY DAMAGE: (Include cost estimate)

20. NATURE OF INJURY
___ Amputation   ___ Fracture   ___ Puncture
___ Bruise, contusion   ___ Foreign body   ___ Shock, electrical
___ Burn, scald   ___ Heat exhaustion, sunstroke ___ Shock, fainting
___ Concussion   ___ Inhalation - dust   ___ Sprains, strains,
___ Cuts, open wounds   ___ Inhalation - fumes - gases   dislocation
___ Dermatitis, infection ___ Internal injury   ___ Suffocation, drowning, strangulation
___ Exposure, frostbite ___ Poisoning, internal   ___ Rupture, hernia
___ Other, specify:_____

21. PART OF BODY INJURED
___ Generalized   ___ Neck   ___ Shoulder   ___ Thigh
___ Skull or scalp ___ Spine   ___ Upper arm ___ Ankle
___ Eye   ___ Chest   ___ Elbow   ___ Knee
___ Nose   ___ Abdomen   ___ Wrist   ___ Foot
___ Mouth   ___ Back   ___ Hand   ___ Hip
___ Jaw   ___ Pelvis   ___ Finger   ___ Lower leg
___ Other, head   ___ Other, trunk   ___ Toe
___ Other, specify:_____

22. AGENT CAUSING ACCIDENT
___ Animal bites   ___ Hand tools   ___ Radiation
___ Athletics   ___ Hot liquid/object   ___ Sharp edged object
___ Broken glass   ___ Icy conditions   ___ Sharp pointed object
___ Broken pavement   ___ Lifting/carrying object ___ Slipping
___ Chemicals   ___ Miscellaneous kitchen ___ Striking with body
___ Falling/moving object equipment   ___ Tripping
___ Foreign object in eye ___ Off balance   ___ Welding light
___ Gases   ___ Office equipment   ___ Miscellaneous
                       ___ Power tools and machinery ___ Unknown

23. WITNESSES

24. DETAILS OF ACCIDENT (Describe full events, conditions including environmental, physical and emotional personal factors, which contributed to the injury. Indicate specific human failure, unsafe equipment or conditions, unsafe acts, as applicable. Use additional sheets if necessary).

25. EMERGENCY CARE & PATIENT STATUS:
___ First aid only, not at hospital or by doctor
___ Treatment at University Health Service or hospital or by medical personnel
___ Confinement at University Health Service, hospital, or in residence
___ Other, specify:_____

26. PREPARED BY (Signature)
_____
Title_____ Date_____
Address_____
_____
Signature of Injured

Safety Form 6   (Cooperating with the National Safety Council)

FIGURE 4–2.

original forwarded directly to the safety department and the duplicate submitted to the appropriate academic department or administrative division.

SUMMARIES OF EXPOSURE

The safety department will prepare and periodically distribute summaries and analyses of the accident exposure experience. The reports

STANDARD ACCIDENTAL INJURY REPORT	FORM COLLEGE 1	COLLEGE OR UNIVERSITY STUDENT

INJURED PERSON

1. NAME (Last, First, Middle Initial)

2. ADDRESS AT COLLEGE Address and name of dorm or house ☐ On campus ☐ Off campus

THE PURPOSE OF THIS REPORT is to provide information which can be used in preventing similar accidents in the future, hence every accidental injury severe enough to require first aid or medical treatment should be reported. See reverse side for instructions and additional space for explanations. Record file number; cut at dotted line for confidential study purposes.

FILE NO.

FILE NO.

3. AGE _____ years
4. SEX ☐ Female ☐ Male
5. STUDENT CLASSIFICATION ☐ Freshman ☐ Junior ☐ Graduate ☐ Sophomore ☐ Senior ☐ Special
6. ENROLLMENT AT this college _____ years

7. Date, day, and hour of accident

8. Estimate of Severity ☐ Non-disabling (loss of less than a full day from normal activity) ☐ Disabling (loss of one or more full days from normal) ☐ Fatal

9. College (or school) in which enrolled

ACCIDENT

10. School or department supervising activity at time of accident

15. Activity at time of accident (e.g. driving auto, diving from low board, lifting crate)

11. Was student an employee at time of injury? ☐ Yes ☐ No

16. Details of accident (Describe fully events, conditions including environmental, physical and emotional personal factors, which contributed to the injury. Use reverse side or additional sheets if needed)

12. JURISDICTION
☐ On or in college property, or in college conducted or supervised activity
☐ Off campus in non-college conducted activity

13. TYPE OF FACILITY
☐ Athletic or physical education
☐ Recreation or entertainment
☐ Instruction
☐ Housing
☐ Exterior walk or sidewalk
☐ Street or highway
☐ Commerce or industry
☐ Service or maintenance
☐ Undeveloped area

14. SPECIFIC LOCATION
☐ Gymnasium
☐ Sports arena or play field
☐ Swimming pool
☐ Pub. recreation or entertain
☐ Pvt. recreation or entertain
☐ Bath, shower or locker room
☐ Interior stair or ramp
☐ Interior corridor or hall
☐ Classroom or lecture hall
☐ Auditorium or library
☐ Laboratory
☐ Other, specify
☐ Shop (mechanical)
☐ Home economics
☐ Storeroom
☐ Food preparation or service
☐ Eating place
☐ Public transportation
☐ Private transportation
☐ Bldg. exterior or grounds
☐ Water area
☐ Farm, field or woods
☐ Retail shop or professional office

17. Action to prevent similar accidents (Indicate if taken or recommended)

INJURY

18. NATURE OF INJURY
☐ Amputation
☐ Bruise, contusion
☐ Burn, scald
☐ Concussion
☐ Cuts, open wounds
☐ Dermatitis, infection

☐ Exposure, frostbite
☐ Fracture
☐ Foreign body
☐ Heat exhaustion sunstroke
☐ Inhalation - dust, fumes, gases
☐ Internal injury

☐ Poisoning, internal
☐ Shock, electrical
☐ Shock, fainting
☐ Sprains, strains, dislocation
☐ Suffocation, drowning, strangulation
☐ Rupture, hernia

☐ Other, specify

19. PART OF BODY INJURED
☐ Generalized
☐ Skull or scalp
☐ Eye
☐ Nose
☐ Mouth
☐ Jaw
☐ Other head
☐ Other, specify
☐ Neck
☐ Spine
☐ Chest
☐ Abdomen
☐ Back
☐ Pelvis
☐ Other trunk
☐ Shoulder
☐ Upper arm
☐ Elbow
☐ Forearm
☐ Wrist
☐ Hand
☐ Finger
☐ Hip
☐ Thigh
☐ Knee
☐ Lower leg
☐ Ankle
☐ Foot
☐ Toe

20. WITNESSES AND THEIR ADDRESSES

TREATMENT

21. EMERGENCY CARE & PATIENT STATUS
☐ First Aid only, not at hospital or by doctor
☐ Treatment at College Health Service or hospital or by medical personnel
☐ Confinement at College Health Service, hospital, or in residence
☐ Other specify

22. This report prepared by (Signature) _____ Date _____
Title or Status _____
Address _____

NATIONAL SAFETY COUNCIL
SMS6199
PRINTED IN U.S.A.
425 N. Michigan Ave., Chicago 11, Ill.
Stock No. 429.26

FIGURE 4–3. Standard student accident report form. (Courtesy of the National Safety Council.)

will present in summary form a picture of the accident experience of all elements of the school or university. Summaries will be in terms of kinds of accidents, circumstances associated with the occurrence of those accidents, and the results of the accidents. The summaries can be used for safety committee study in indicating trends, hazardous areas or operations, unsafe acts, and the nature and extent of injuries.

GUIDE FOR ACCIDENT INVESTIGATION

The systematic investigation of accidents generally requires surveying them for unsafe acts, unsafe mechanical or physical conditions, and unsafe personal factors.

The following factors are those most frequently encountered, but are not to be considered as all-inclusive. Answering each item with a Y (yes) or N (no) will greatly assist the investigator in arriving at his conclusions as to the primary and proximate causes of the accident.

UNSAFE ACTS

—Calling/talking/unnecessary noise
—Carrying or pushing with obstructed vision or restricted clearance
—Cleaning/adjusting moving equipment
—Failure to clean up area
—Failure to check before using
—Failure to place caution signs
—Failure to report injury promptly
—Failure to report unsafe tools or equipment
—Failure to secure against unexpected movement
—Failure to shut off equipment not in use
—Failure to use guard, pusher, etc.
—Failure to use handrail
—Failure to wear protective equipment
—Horseplay
—Improper discarding of materials
—Improper storage of material
—Jumping on/over object
—Jumping on/off moving equipment
—Lifting/carrying/pushing too heavy a load
—Lifting objects too bulky
—Lifting while in awkward position

—Lifting with bent back
—Lifting while twisting back
—Not using proper equipment
—Operating without due caution
—Overloading
—Quarreling
—Removing without due caution
—Running, hurrying
—Self-treatment of injury without authorization
—Standing under suspended loads
—Starting/stopping/moving without giving proper signal
—Throwing material rather than passing it
—Throwing object
—Unsafe use of equipment
—Using defective equipment
—Using hands instead of tools
—Using tool improperly
—Using wrong tool
—Walking into fixed object
—Wearing jewelry
—Wearing loose hair
—Wearing unsuitable clothing
—Working on equipment with electric power on

UNSAFE MECHANICAL OR PHYSICAL CONDITIONS

—Congestion in work area
—Defective guard
—Exposure to fumes
—Glare
—Inadequately guarded
—Insufficient/improper lights
—Insufficient ventilation

—Poorly constructed
—Poorly designed
—Protective equipment defective/inadequate
—Protective equipment not supplied
—Protective equipment not worn
—Sharp/rough edges

UNSAFE MECHANICAL OR PHYSICAL CONDITIONS

___Misalignment
___Overloading
___Poor housekeeping

___Slippery floors
___Unguarded
___Worn condition

UNSAFE PERSONAL FACTORS

___Allergies/sensitivity
___Body defects
___Disregard of instructions
___Disturbed, excited, nervous
___Existing hernia
___Fatigue
___Haste
___Heedless to warnings
___Inadequate training
___Inattention
___Intoxication (drugs or alcohol)
___Lack of acclimation
___Lack of concentration

___Lack of cooperation
___Lack of coordination
___Lack of practice or skill
___Lack of safety consciousness
___Muscular weakness
___Overconfidence
___Oversight/forgetfulness
___Recklessness
___Startled
___Unfitness/incompetence for job
___Unawareness of safe practice
___Violent temper
___Worried

SAFETY INSPECTIONS

GENERAL

Preventing accidental injuries and losses of property is the basic objective of the safety program. Accident prevention inspections, although not as glamorous as after-the-accident corrections, has proven economical, both in reduction of property loss and enhancing life safety. Safety inspections are not the exclusive responsibility of certain agencies or departments; instead, each member of the school or university family in pursuing normal daily routines should form the habit of observing and correcting or reporting safety hazards.

Several agencies conduct formal inspections of school and university property. Some agency inspections are required by state law; others are conducted to determine hazards and potential losses that have direct bearing on insurance rates. The safety department inspections are conducted in an attempt to preclude loss of life or property and to eliminate unsafe conditions. It is axiomatic that internal inspections and the correction of deficiencies will make the school or university a safer place to live, work, and learn.

Inspections conducted by the safety department will be made utilizing the Building Safety Checklist, page 70. Safety committees and individuals making safety inspections will find the checklist helpful in their efforts.

Inspection Agencies

State and state contractual agencies conduct periodic life-safety inspections of school or university property. The following is a brief description of the major inspection agencies and their primary areas of interest.

The Department of Insurance (State Fire and Tornado Fund) is the designated agency which assumes insurance liability, usually up to $300,000, for all state properties. Life-safety inspections will be made by that agency under authority of KRS 56.170 which states: "The Division of Insurance shall annually have an inspection made of each building and its contents owned by the state or any agency having control or custody of the building relative to the removal or correction of the hazard. Reasonable differences in the premium chargeable against the agency on account of the building and its contents may be made contingent upon compliance with such recommendations."

The State Inspection Bureau conducts annual inspections of all school and university property for the purpose of establishing premium rates to be charged by the Division of Insurance and private insurance companies which carry liability insurance above the $300,000 limit of the Division of Insurance.

Inspections by the Underwriters' Insurance and Claims Company are conducted to assist in helping to eliminate unsafe working conditions or practices which may be in existence. This service is rendered as a means of assisting the school or university in making every effort to reduce the total costs involved in conducting the Workmen's Compensation Program.

The safety department inspections encompass all facets of safety. The department conducts, or causes to be conducted, an annual general life-safety inspection of all property including community colleges and facilities exterior to the main campus. Safety department inspections will be made approximately six months after the annual state insurance inspection. The checklist (page 70) will be used to ensure complete coverage and uniformity of inspections.

In addition to the annual general safety inspection, the safety department will conduct, or cause to be conducted, the following inspections:

1. Fire alarm and automatic sprinkler systems.
2. Fire hydrants and standpipe systems.
3. Fire inspection.
4. First-aid fire equipment. (Extinguishers and hoses.)
5. Fires.
6. Fallout shelter areas and supplies.
7. Accidents of a serious nature.

REPORTS OF INSPECTIONS

The deans and other proper university officials will be furnished with complete copies of all blank inspection reports. All appropriate officials will be furnished copies of all completed inspection reports concerning areas under their operational control. In addition, the physical plant division will be furnished copies of reports that contain recommendations as to physical structure modifications.

Upon the receipt of inspection reports the individual exercising operational control should review the report and initiate corrective measures where applicable.

FOLLOW-UP ACTION

Subsequent to completion of corrective actions required by the inspection report, the deans and administrative heads should furnish the designated vice president a summary of action taken and recommendations for further action, if any is required. For areas requiring long-range action, interim summaries at thirty-day intervals will be submitted. After review in the administrative head or vice president's office the summaries should be forwarded to the safety department for follow-up action.

BUILDING SAFETY CHECKLIST

Building_____   Number of Occupants_____

General Building Factors

A. Stairs & Ramps
    Repair   S   U
    Risers   S   U
    Treads   S   U
    Handrails   S   U
    Adequacy of access and numbers in relation to occupancy
        of the floor and stories above ground   S   U
    Dangerous slopes   S   U
    Headroom   S   U

B. Floors
    Repair   S   U
    Surface slickness   S   U
    Resistance to fire or other stresses to be inspected within
        the building   S   U
    Proper warning and protection when waxing or repairing
        is underway   S   U

C. Walls
    Repair   S   U

Building Safety Checklist

    Surfacing   S   U
    Adequacy of windows and ventilation   S   U

D. Ceilings
    Repair   S   U
    Freedom from leaks   S   U
    Adequate protection if pipes and conduits traverse them   S   U

E. Windows
    Repair   S   U
    Adequacy of ventilation   S   U
    Screening   S   U
    Storm windows where necessary   S   U

F. Doors
    Repair   S   U
    Outward openings   S   U
    Panic hardwear and absence of dead bolts   S   U
    Screen doors   S   U

G. Fire Escapes
    Adequate   S   U
    Working condition   S   U
    Obstructions   S   U

H. Security
    Locks   S   U
    Screens   S   U
    Window guards   S   U
    Latches   S   U

I. Fire Aid Fire Fighting Equipment
    Adequate number   S   U
    Location   S   U
    Charged   S   U
    Checked within 1 year   S   U

Utilities

A. Electricity
    Grounding   S   U
    Fusing   S   U
    Unsafe wiring and extension cords   S   U
    Proper location of switches   S   U
    Unauthorized appliances   S   U

B. Gas
    Adequacy of supply   S   U
    Routine checking for leaks or equipment which has been
       left on   S   U

C. Water and Plumbing
    Equipment in compliance with appropriate codes   S   U
    Absence of crossing of lines   S   U
    Absence of possibility of back siphonage   S   U

Building Safety Checklist

Proper use of vacuum breakers	S	U
Use of an approved source	S	U
Use of approved disposal techniques	S	U
Electric cords on pipes	S	U

D. Heat

Method of heating	S	U
Preventive maintenance and repair of equipment	S	U
Automatic controls and warning devices	S	U
Flues and vents (include location)	S	U
Periodic inspection for excessive concentration of carbon monoxide or other noxious vapors	S	U
Ventilation and air supply	S	U

E. Telephone

Proper installation	S	U
Adequacy of phone lines and relation to notifying others in the event of need for help	S	U

Special Requirements

A. Chemicals

Use	S	U
Storage (include amounts)	S	U
Special hazards	S	U
Dangers from solvents (such as carbon tetrachloride xylene, benzol, etc.)	S	U
Proper location of deluge valves	S	U

B. Wiring

Special requirements for equipment	S	U
Adequacy of grounding	S	U
Adequacy of fusing	S	U
Adequacy of instructions and safety programs	S	U

C. Machinery

Type	S	U
Usage	S	U
Proper type and guarded	S	U
Proper instruction of operators	S	U
Proper protection when not in use	S	U
Condition of bearings	S	U

D. Routine Laboratory

Adequacy of ventilation	S	U
Adequacy of functioning of fume hoods	S	U
Familiarity with common hazards such as mercury vapor concentration above allowable limits	S	U
Such special considerations as are appropriate	S	U
Radioactivity	S	U

E. Housekeeping

Storerooms, basements	S	U
Waste and rubbish	S	U

BUILDING SAFETY CHECKLIST

Custodian closets	S	U
Periodic disposal of waste	S	U

F. Special Topics

Care of animals	S	U
Radiation hazards	S	U
Nuclear research programming	S	U
Proper handling of compressed gases, etc.	S	U
Fire Alarms	S	U
Sprinkler system (Use Safety Form)	S	U
Standpipes	S	U

Inspector:_____   Date:_____

Safety Form 1

REFERENCES

American Law Reports, Vol. 86, "Tort Liability in Public Schools and Institutions of Higher Learning," pp. 489–601, 1962.

American Medical Association, "First Aid for Athletic Injuries," *Today's Health,* Vol. 42, No. 10 (October 1964), p. 49.

Badgley, Carl E., "Sports Injuries of the Shoulder Girdle," *Journal of the American Medical Association* (January 20, 1960), pp. 444–48.

Bolen, J., "Hand Trouble, the Gymnastic Bugaboo," *Scholastic Coach.* (December 1952), p. 16.

Center for Safety Education, New York University, *The Administrator and the School Safety Program* (New York: The Center, 1952).

Cerney, J. V., *Athletic Injuries* (Springfield, Ill.: Charles C. Thomas, 1963).

Clarke, K. S., "The Trainer's Greatest Contribution," *Fourth Annual Safety Education Review,* American Association for Health, Physical Education, and Recreation (Washington, D.C.: 1965), pp. 22–37.

Conway, F. J., "Who's Liable?" *Safety Education* (October 1960), p. 3.

Dollar, J., "Reducing Knee Injuries," *Scholastic Coach.* (May 1956), pp. 40–41.

Drury, R. L., ed., *Law and the School Superintendent* (Cincinnati: W. H. Anderson, 1958), Chapter 15.

Dzenowagis, J. G., "An Accident Reporting System, Why Bother," *Journal of Health, Physical Education, and Recreation* (February 1962), p. 24.

Edwards, N., *The Courts and the Public Schools* (Chicago: University of Chicago Press, 1955), Chapter 15.

Ferguson, A. B., and J. Bender, *The ABC's of Athletic Injuries and Conditioning* (Baltimore: Williams and Wilkins, 1964).

Florio, A. E., and G. T. Stafford, *Safety Education*, 2nd ed. (New York: McGraw-Hill, 1962), pp. 112–34.

Friedman, S. L., "Can Driver Education Teachers Be Held Liable?" *National Safety Congress Transactions* (Chicago: National Safety Council, 1960), pp. 117–18.

Kigin, D. J., "Tort Liability Affecting Shop Teachers with Provisions for Avoiding Accidents and Litigation," Dissertation, University of Missouri, 1959, pp. 1–209.

Matthews, D. O., and R. A. Thompson, *Athletic Injuries* (Dubuque, Iowa: William C. Brown, 1963).

Muscle Injuries, Their Prevention and Care (New York: National Distribution Center of Associated Films, Inc.).

National Safety Council, *Accident Facts* (Chicago: The Council, 1968).

Raywood, R., "Care and Prevention of Cauliflower Ear," *Scholastic Coach* (October 1956), p. 42.

Research Division for the National Commission on Safety Education, *Who Is Liable for Pupil Injuries?* (Washington, D.C.: National Educational Association, 1963).

Rosenfield, Harry N., "Legal Liability and the Cost of Accidents," *Safety Education* (April 1957), p. 4.

Stack, H. J., and J. D. Elkow, *Education for Safe Living*, 4th ed. (Englewood Cliffs, N.J.: Prentice-Hall, 1966), pp. 317–30.

Strasser, M. K., J. E. Aaron, R. C. Bohn, and J. R. Eales, *Fundamentals of Safety Education* (New York: Macmillan, 1964).

Stromgren, G., "A Practical Technique for an Injury Prevention Check-up Program," *Journal of Health, Physical Education, and Recreation* (May 1964), pp. 24–25.

Thorndike, A., *Athletic Injuries* (Philadelphia: Lea and Febiger, 1961).

Wall, Norman M., Physical Educators Need to Know About Heart Disease," *Journal of Health, Physical Education, and Recreation* (March 1960), pp. 26–27.

CHAPTER 5   SUPERVISION IN SAFETY EDUCATION

Increasing importance is placed on the need for designating a qualified safety educator to be responsible for the implementation of administrative policies as established by the school board and superintendent of public instruction. A variety of titles have been used in designating this individual's job classification such as supervisor, consultant, coordinator, or chairman. The selection of an appropriate title must be determined by administrative policy in the local school system.

The supervisor's role is fundamentally related to the achievement of excellence in teaching and learning in the nation's public schools. McKean and Mills [1] indicate that supervision is not a single unilateral function, nor will it be entirely accomplished by a person with the title of *supervisor*. Supervision, more realistically, is a multiple, complex, and frequently intangible assignment. In essence, supervision is a product and responsibility of many educators working together in a harmonious relationship. McKean and Mills offer the following principles of modern supervision as a guide to action and a technique in evaluating the instructional process.

1. Supervision is directed toward the improvement of learning and teaching. This has remained the overall objective, and it provides the ultimate criterion in appraisal of successful supervision.
2. The total program of supervision is directed to accepted purposes. Effective supervision seeks to help teachers recognize and accept general aims and then works consciously toward these purposes. For example, teachers may come to accept the proper role of supervision as a specialized service which attempts (a) to help them see beyond their present performance and seek improvement; (b) to identify and coordinate efforts and resources for more efficiency and greater impact on important educational problems: (c) to increase the amount and quality of learning by students; and (d) to promote continuous appraisal of performance of all who are engaged in the educational process.
3. Supervision seeks the cooperative participation of all concerned. Intelli-

[1] Robert C. McKean and H. H. Mills, *The Supervisor* (Washington, D.C.: Center for Applied Research in Education, 1964).

gent and effective supervision is genuine cooperative endeavor, not skillful manipulation of others. This principle results from the strong belief that school personnel affected by certain decisions should have a part in making these decisions.

4. Modern supervision strives to utilize the talents and strengths of all. The emerging concept of democratic leadership recognizes the necessity of releasing and using the potential which resides within various members of the group. The most effective group problem-solving results from the joint efforts of individuals, each making contributions in line with his own special abilities and skills.

5. The existing situation provides the setting for supervision. The nature and characteristics of the staff, the student group, the community, and the past and present school program are the basic elements with which the supervisor must deal. Thus he must know well the present situation and its antecedents before proceeding to make improvements.

6. Supervision offers assistance to all. The astute supervisor knows that the most likely places to begin are with those teachers who recognize needs and who are willing to work for improvement. He knows that often the teachers who seem to be doing the best job are those with greatest potential for sustained progress. He works with all, not merely the inexperienced or ineffective.

7. Supervision is flexible. The supervisor tends to be eclectic in approach. A concern about the means as well as the end requires a flexible adaptive approach rather than adherence to a single approved procedure.

8. Supervision seeks evidence regarding the results and value of change. The supervisor uses his skills in evaluation to this end. Judgments should be based upon the weight of evidence and logic rather than upon hunch or sheer opinion.

9. Supervision strives to enhance the satisfaction in their work of the educational staff. The procedures of supervision should result in improved staff morale and job satisfaction. As a consequence of the work of the supervisor, teachers should develop more confidence in themselves, feel more adequate to handle their own problems, and experience the fuller realization of their capabilities.

SUPERVISION APPLIED

Barr, Burton, and Bruckner [2] make the following recommendations which are closely affiliated with the supervisory process in safety education.

1. Supervision should be theoretically sound to provide for technical accuracy in the presentation of factual and established authentic information.

2. Supervision should use the scientific approach in the systematic improvement and evaluation of techniques.

[2] A. S. Barr, William H. Burton, and Leo J. Bruckner, *Supervision, Principles and Practices in the Improvement of Instruction* (New York: Appleton-Century-Crofts, 1938).

3. Supervision should be democratic with a respect for personality and individual differences that may exist between personalities and should endeavor to develop these traits to the fullest capacity of each.
4. Supervision should be creative in locating inherent capabilities that will reflect originality, and imagination that will render unique contributions in the instructional process.

In the administration and supervision of a school safety education program the previously mentioned recommendations when effectively applied will have significant value in producing desirable results.

SAFETY SUPERVISOR JOB ANALYSIS

To provide assistance for a school system in selecting a safety educator to administer and supervise the safety education program, the National Safety Council Safety Supervisor's Section has prepared a job analysis for this school position. The analysis presents in outline form a detailed set of job specifications and responsibilities for the supervisor. The Job Analysis was approved by the Council's School and College Conference in December of 1958. A digest of significant aspects from the adminstrative guide and analysis is herein included as model for administrators and supervisors of school safety education.[3]

1. Determination and coordination of administrative policy in safety.

Someone must be assigned the responsibility to develop this function thus preventing an oversight of important educational elements. Safety education is unique in that it cuts horizontally and vertically through all areas of the school curriculum and is related to many facets of administrative concern. The supervisor frequently has administrative responsibility that would include such duties as:

a. The collection, analysis, and use of data from the accident reporting system.

The supervisor devises a method whereby the accident reports are collected at specific intervals using the Standard Student Accident Reporting System that will include all school personnel. A monthly summary of the accident experience is submitted to the National Safety Council as required. This summation should also be routed to teachers and various administrative units throughout the school system as prescribed by the administration. An annual analysis of all reports should be made available to all personnel and community groups having a mutual interest in safety and accident prevention. These reports can serve as a basis for curriculum adjustment and development.

[3] National Safety Council, A *Job Analysis for Safety Education Supervisors* (Chicago: The Council, 1959).

b. The safety program will also be related to functions outside the school building. To this extent desirable public and community relations will be of importance.

All activities and procedures established by the supervisor should be in conformity with policies set forth by the local administration. Interpretation of the school safety program to the public will assist in gaining resources and support for the program. Leadership both from the faculty and community groups will aid in program development. In the selection of safety education materials prepared by outside agencies, the supervisor should establish criteria to aid classroom teachers in making a wise choice of all available information. Publicizing the safety program through the use of all mass medias of communication is a primary function of the supervisor.

c. Instructional procedures and accident prevention controls for beginners in school represent a significant supervisory responsibility.

The supervisor communicates to teachers, parents, and others the importance of safety and accident prevention for schoolchildren recognizing their individual differences. Child growth and development patterns must be recognized as a means of providing for specific needs and interests. Cooperation with local civic organizations and community groups in organizing protective programs for children should be initiated by the supervisor.

d. Fire and emergency drills taking into consideration all legal, instructional, and supervisory controls.

The supervisor exerts leadership in formulating evacuation drills for all school buildings. Exit drills procedures designated for fires, explosions, and other emergencies requiring rapid removal from buildings or school buses should be checked and revised periodically. In the preparation of such plans special consideration will be directed to children having physical disabilities and handicaps. The principal in each building should understand his responsibility for exit drills in providing the maximum of protection for children and all personnel in the school building.

e. Safety and accident prevention procedures must be designed for all areas in the school with emphasis on shops, home economics, science laboratories, physical education complex and other locations where accident possibilities exist.

The supervisor should participate in conferences with teachers for removal or compensation of hazards. Safety education resource materials that can assist teachers will be of importance in implementing various programs. Teachers will need to be provided with orientation for proper use of the accident reports and how the data can be used in curriculum development.

f. School building construction.

The supervisor can assist in the blueprint stage of new construction by meeting with administrators, architect, or building director to eliminate hazards in the building.

g. Community responsibility for the development of attitudes and safety practices.

The supervisor assumes responsibility for advising the community wth local, state, and national data relative to desirable school safety procedures. In this function he provides assistance for persons and community agencies in their understanding, enforcing fire prevention, sanitary, building, zoning, traffic control, nuisance abatement, and additional codes and laws enacted to prevent accidents and improvement of living standards.

2. Safety education curriculum.

Safety education to be presented at all levels of instruction either through integration or direct instruction is an integral part of the total school program. The supervisor has a significant responsibility for implementing all aspects of safety education instruction.

As the accident prevention consultant on the central curriculum committee the supervisor suggests and assists the committee with the development of instructional materials. Coordinating with principals and teachers, he works continuously to achieve the objectives identified with the safety education curriculum.

3. Improving the quality of safety instruction.

Safety education involves numerous technical elements related to efficiency in safety instruction. Techniques associated with school safety organizations, adoption of instructional methods, organization of driver education courses, and efficient use of all medias of instruction are all of importance in supervisory practices. The supervisor has a responsibility for being informed of the most recent developments in research and modern techniques in program development.

With this background of information he should periodically conduct in-service training programs for teachers and administrators. Teachers should be encouraged to utilize sound methods of teaching that will include a variety of audio-visual aids and to participate at their level in research studies.

4. Evaluating the effectiveness of school safety programs.

Evaluation is a highly skilled process requiring supervisory assistance with a comprehension for all aspects of the total school program and its relationship to safety instruction. This requires a precise plan for evaluating the quality of instruction and effectiveness of the program. The supervisor's responsibility in evaluation will consist of such duties as those outlined below.

a. Understand the goals and objectives of safety instruction.

b. Accumulate data of success or weaknesses in producing attitudinal and behavior changes.

c. Participate annually in the National School Safety Honor Roll.

d. Review and analyze all forms of accident statistical data.

e. Study recommendations from the *Annual Inventory of Traffic Safety Activities* and make a comparison with the results evident in this program.

f. Coordinate with principals and teachers in preparing evaluation instruments to determine program effectiveness.

MONTHLY WORK SHEET FOR SAFETY EDUCATION SUPERVISORS

To assist safety education supervisors in establishing a monthly schedule of responsibilities and duties, the following pattern developed at the Center for Safety Education, New York University [4] can serve as a guide in charting a program for the school year.

September

1. Discuss safety program with other safety supervisors.
2. A detailed explanation of safety objectives in regard to the community, to the school patrons and other citizens. This would involve press, radio, and TV.
3. Provide time for safety education supervisors to analyze, catalog, distribute, and place on ready reference the flow of safety materials printed each month by various organizations.
4. Get fire prevention materials ready to be sent out to schools.
5. Arrange for first meeting of city safety education committee.
6. Attend first meeting of school principals and/or teachers and speak for 15 minutes.
7. Send out material on National Safety Council Honor Roll awards.
8. Arrange with the police department for assistance in training patrols.
9. See that each patrol is supervised by safety coordinator.
10. Receive a report on patrols.
11. Send out to principals suggestions for a fire prevention week.
12. Working with principals and custodians, inspect five of the school buildings.
13. Aid in getting cars for high school driver education.
14. Establish sound techniques of evaluating student progress in safety objectives.

[4] Center for Safety Education, *Supervisors Set Up Schedule* (New York: New York University, 1960).

15. Speak at two PTA meetings called for September.
16. Arrange with principals for fire department demonstrations in October.
17. Meet with department chairmen of high schools to discuss integration of safety in program.
18. Discuss school parking arrangements with school principals and safety committee.

October

1. Check to see how the patrols are functioning.
2. Speak on fire prevention at two school assemblies.
3. Send out home safety materials for use in November.
4. Inspect several school buildings.
5. Speak at a local service club meeting.
6. Arrange for the monthly meeting of the safety education committee.
7. Confer with supervisors of other subjects regarding safe practices.
8. Find out why certain schools do not have patrols and try to organize, working with principal.
9. Meet with new teachers in the school system.
10. Speak on safety at a conference of teachers of industrial arts.
11. Speak at a meeting of scout officials regarding follow-up of Safety Good Turn.
12. Send out booklet on hunting safety secured from state department.

November

1. Attend State Teachers Convention; speak at Driver Education Conference.
2. Check with principals for proper exit methods for emergency drills.
3. Speak to physical education teachers at their monthly meeting.
4. Check the safety features of high school football.
5. Attend the monthly meeting of civic clubs to solicit help in obtaining safe play areas for winter sports.
6. Confer with superintendent of recreation to arrange for safety instruction to his instructional crew.
7. Send out a bulletin on Thanksgiving safety. Distribute it to all teachers and administrators.

December

1. Send suggestions to principals for a Christmas safety program.
2. Distribute information on home safety.
3. Discuss accident reports in order to incorporate safety in the program.
4. Arrange movies for distribution on winter sports, such as ice skating, coasting, and skiing.
5. Check to see whether or not schools are having fire drills.

January

1. Review first half of school year program. Check on safety practices and any weaknesses of the program.
2. Discuss the need for emphasis on safe driving during the winter months with high school teachers.
3. Send out materials on winter sports.
4. Be prepared to talk to PTA meetings about winter home safety.
5. Secure cooperation of news media stressing city ordinances concerning winter safety.
6. Make sure that all play areas are well supervised.
7. Consult with police in getting their cooperation to set aside certain areas for coasting.
8. Continue to check several school buildings.

February

1. Secure material, to be distributed in March, on safety in spring clean-up, playground, bicycle, roller skating, kite flying.
2. Prepare and send out summary of first term accident reports.
3. Continue inspection of schools with principals and custodians.
4. Check practices in civil defense drills.
5. Send memos to school principals and custodians to prepare for playground safety next month.
6. Arrange for in-service safety course for teachers in school system.

March

1. Spring clean-up campaign.
2. Continue inspection of school buildings.
3. Speak at two assembly programs.
4. Make preparation for bicycle programs in elementary schools and make plans for bike rodeo in April.
5. Establish class visits to observe safety education projects and activities in action.
6. Receive forms and start to evaluate program for National School Safety Honor Roll Awards.
7. Attend state Driver Education Association meeting.
8. Distribute information (data sheets) on first aid instruction.
9. Distribute seasonal material and posters on the hazards of kite flying.
10. Distribute material on playground safety.

April

1. Secure and distribute materials on fishing and boating from the state department.
2. Have building safety coordinator check playgrounds and playground equipment.

3. Talk at monthly physical education teachers' meeting emphasizing spring sports.
4. Send out materials on bicycle safety.
5. Check to make sure National School Safety Honor Roll program has been submitted.

May

1. Prepare safety awards for schools with the best records.
2. Be prepared to give outdoor safety talks to any interested group.
3. Consolidate school year reports for accident evaluation.
4. Present recent safety films to committee for its approval for the coming year.
5. Send out materials on summer vacation hazards and pedestrian warnings.

June

1. Emphasize water safety (secure and send out films and literature on fishing, boating, water skiing, swimming, and sunburns). Check with owners of public and private swimming pools.
2. Emphasize camping safety (knives and hatchets, fires, poison ivy, wood ticks, and snakes). Utilize boy scouts to present assembly programs.
3. Prepare accident summary of the past year and distribute with recommendations for the coming year.
4. Send out materials emphasizing farm safety, recreational safety and water safety for the coming summer vacation.
5. Meet with visual aids committee about placing order for films, safety literature, posters, and magazines for the coming year.
6. Arrange for the collection, washing, and storing of school safety patrol belts.
7. Evaluate the past year and revise the plans for the coming year to have ready for the teacher's workshop before school opens in the fall.
8. Order a supply of accident report blanks for the coming year.
9. Meet with a committee to arrange for the purchase of safety readers and textbooks. (In some schools, this should be done earlier.)
10. Arrange for tests to be given in elementary grades.
11. Reporting and summarizing accident data with special distribution and emphasis to all faculty and nonteaching personnel.
12. Prepare a report of the year's program to be submitted to the superintendent.

July and August

1. Spend at least two of the eight free weeks preparing plans for next school year.

Although there has been limited research concerning the relative values of different methods that can be employed to provide special assistance for teachers, the necessity for expert guidance in special areas is generally recognized.[5] In certain school systems the special supervisors will devote considerable time as special teachers. In other school systems they perform duties primarily as consultants and resource persons, being guided by leadership principles that are applicable to other educational leadership personnel. Supervision in safety education is adaptable to each of these methods with various adjustments to meet the local needs.

The supervisory program in schools and school systems will be observed to have considerable variability depending upon the number of students, size of faculty, characteristics of the community and school environment. Supervisory responsibilities, however, will contain numerous common functions in serving the interests and needs in the school safety education program. Periodically the supervisor should present a total plan for the safety program to his immediate superior or designated administrator. Fundamentally, the superintendent is responsible for all school safety programs as stipulated in policy by the Board of Education. Through delegation by the superintendent, the safety supervisor receives a complete job description of his duties.

REFERENCES

Aaron, James E., A Study of Supervisory Practices in Safety Education in Selected Cities in the United States, Dissertation, New York University, 1960.

Center for Safety Education, New York University, The Administrator and the School Safety Program (New York: The Center, 1951).

Kaywood, Richard, "Supervision—Key Factor in Driver Education," Safety Education (February 1962), pp. 8–10.

Miles, James B., "The School Principal and Accident Prevention," Safety Education (February 1957), p. 6.

Miller, Van, The Public Administration of American School System (New York: Macmillan, 1965).

National Commission on Safety Education, Checklist on Safety and Safety Education in Your School (Washington, D.C.: National Education Association, 1953).

——, Our Schools Plan Safe Living (Washington, D.C.: National Education Association, 1956).

——, The Elementary School Principal Plans for Safe Living (Washington, D.C.: National Education Association, 1945).

Nihan, James F., State Laws and Regulations for Safety Education, Safety

[5] Jane Franseth, Supervision As Leadership (New York: Harper & Row, 1961).

Monographs for Colleges and Universities No. 15 (Chicago: National Safety Council, 1962).

Ovard, Glen F., *Administration of the Changing Secondary School* (New York: Macmillan, 1966).

Wiles, Kimball, *Supervision for Better Schools* (Englewood Cliffs, N.J.: Prentice-Hall, 1961).

CHAPTER 6   MEASUREMENT
AND EVALUATION

Teachers and school administrators both in public schools and colleges need to know how to measure and evaluate their safety programs. This is especially true because it is important to find out whether or not safety education, which is a relatively new subject and often not too well defined, is achieving its objectives.

Obviously, the most important objective is to reduce accidents. This is the ultimate test of the program, and there have been many illustrations of how a well-organized activity has resulted in a marked reduction of accidents over a period of years. This is true both for public school systems and colleges. There are other methods of measuring the success of safety activities which will be discussed in this chapter.

WHAT TO MEASURE AND EVALUATE

How successful is our safety program? How does it compare with that of other schools and colleges? What are the weaknesses in our activities? Where are we strong? What do the citizens in our community think of our program? How are we cooperating with the local safety council or committee? What use are we making of local and state non-school agencies such as the police and fire departments, the Red Cross, and the many other agencies that are concerned with accident prevention?

These are some of the questions that school and college administrators and supervisors should be asking. Accident prevention is an important objective of both the schools and the colleges. The school and college administrators and their boards should be vitally concerned with the protection of their students, faculty, and staff. As has been said many times before, "What good does teaching the command of the fundamental processes—reading, writing, and arithmetic—do, if a child as a result of lack of instruction is accidently killed or seriously injured?" Health and safety are basic in the school program.

This chapter will not go into the details of the techniques of measurement and evaluation. It is chiefly concerned with informing administrators about methods—where aids can be secured, how programs can be organized. The descriptions of the various methods will be necessarily brief, only enough to inform the administrator of their significance.[1]

A SCHOOL EVALUATION PROGRAM

The following are some of the essential elements in a well-rounded program:

What are the kinds of accidents, their frequency, and severity?

What are we doing to promote safety in pupil transportation?

Where are the hazardous areas in our community? Where are students being hurt?

What are the hazards in our school buildings and grounds? Are they being corrected?

Can we measure safety instruction in our schools? How does it compare with that of other schools? Are our schools provided with textbooks, readers, and other helpful materials?

What about the safety activities in our system?[2] Are we teaching swimming and water safety? How well are the patrols functioning? What about bicycle safety? Are schools devoting time to assembly programs? How many of our high schools teach driver education, and what percentage of the eligible students are we reaching each year? What about safety on our school playgrounds?

What does the public think about our program? Do we have cooperative arrangements with other community agencies such as the police and fire departments?

What are our high schools doing? These are usually the weak spots in the school program. Yet the secondary school period in life has the highest accident frequency for many kinds of accidents. We cannot accept driver education as the high school safety program; it is just a part of it.

ACCIDENT REPORTS AND TRENDS

One test of a safety program will be found in the accident trends. Every school system should have an accident reporting system. The most widely used system is that published by the National Safety Council.

[1] Ralph H. Ojemann, *Tests and Evaluation Methods Used in Driver and Safety Education* (Washington, D.C.: The National Commission on Safety Education, 1959. (Out of Print.)

[2] The National Safety Council Honor Roll is awarded to schools following an evaluation of safety activities.

This has been discussed in Chapter 4. Copies of report blanks can be secured from the Council.

There are several important uses of accident reports:

1. Adjusting the safety curriculum to immediate student needs.
2. Individual student guidance.
3. Modifying the structure and use of the building and grounds.
4. Protecting the school from unfortunate publicity and liability suits growing out of accident cases.
5. Enabling the schools to compare their records with those of previous years and with those of other cities.

In addition to the reports, summary sheets are provided. Many school systems analyze the reports once a month and send the results to principals, supervisors, and to the safety council. In addition, in a number of cities accident reports of the police department are furnished to the schools.

Accident reporting is especially valuable in states in which legislation provides for legal liability for suits following accidents. State Workmen's Compensation in all states cover the custodial services and, in some cases, the teachers.

It is a curious fact that while all motor vehicle accidents must be reported, as well as all industrial accidents and all fires, only a small percentage of the public schools in the country have installed an accident reporting system. Yet such a system is the foundation for a good safety program. Schools are required by law to report accidents involving the janitor and the school bus. In most states, accidents in athletics must be reported to the governing body of the state athletic benefit association. Student accidents should also be reported by a regulation of the state board of education.

Mention should be made of one weakness that exists in some school systems that report accidents. The reports are often filed in the administrator's office and remain there; teachers are not informed about them. Yet these reports provide excellent case studies around which to organize safety instruction and provide special emphasis in the curriculum. Monthly reports should be sent out to schools.

SAFETY CHECKLISTS

The most extensive safety checklist for schools has been published by the National Commission on Safety Education.[3] It includes over 300 items covering such areas as (1) general administration; (2) structures,

[3] National Commission on Safety Education, *Checklist on Safety and Safety Education in Your School* (Washington, D.C.: The Commission, 1953).

equipment, and grounds; (3) daily school routine and maintenance; (4) exit drills and fire fighting equipment; (5) civil defense preparedness; (6) personnel; (7) street and highway safety; (8) school transportation; (9) industrial and home arts rooms, laboratories, and cafeterias; (10) stage and auditorium; (11) playground, gymnasium, pool and shower rooms; (12) supervision and guidance; (13) classroom instruction; (14) instructional materials; and (15) community relations.

It involves a thorough survey of all activities. A school that can check a majority of these items in a positive way surely has an all-round program. A checklist of this type would be valuable for making a *thorough* survey of the safety activities of individual schools.

OTHER SAFETY CHECKLISTS

1. Fire safety lists are provided by the local fire department, the National Safety Council, and the National Fire Protection Association. These are widely used and the home inspection carried on with the aid of parents.
2. The National Fire Protection Association also has a number of lists of standards for safety in building construction and maintenance.
3. Civil Defense also has checklists.
4. The state boards of health often have standards for first aid, for swimming pools, and camps.
5. The American Red Cross has tests and standards for first aid and water safety.
6. Other standards exist in most states for pupil transportation, building maintenance, and the construction of playing services and playgrounds.
7. Inventories are provided by the National Safety Council for evaluating the traffic safety education activities of the community. These are valuable for appraising the total educational program in traffic safety. Hundreds of cities are now cooperating in utilizing these inventories. Although the schools are chiefly interested in the education phases, other phases cover enforcement, engineering, public support, and other activities.
8. The *National Pedestrian Protection Contest* of the American Automobile Association has an inventory for these activities. This is usually filled out by police officials.
9. The *National High School Driver Education Achievement Program* [4] has an inventory to be filled out by the schools teaching driver education. They are sent out by the State Department of Education, and the results forwarded to the Insurance Institute for Highway Safety. This has been useful for appraising the quality and quantity of driver

[4] Insurance Institute for Highway Safety, *National High School Driver Education Achievement Program* (Washington, D.C.: The Institute, published annually).

education in individual schools and the state program in comparison with other states.

There are a variety of other checklists and inventories. Lest the school administrator feel that he is overburdened with lists, most of the forms can be filled out by teachers, the school nurse, the principal and supervisors, and the results forwarded to his office. Through such reports he will know how safety is measuring up in his schools.

TESTS AND SCALES

Althogether too little has been done in the public schools in the use of tests and scales. There are few standardized tests available for either the elementary or secondary schools. Without standardized tests it is difficult for the teacher or school administrator to know how his program is going and how it compares with programs in other cities. Much more should be done in the construction of tests of knowledge, skills, and attitudes among schoolchildren. Several of the basic safety readers include achievement tests, but they are not standardized. In addition, many of the workbooks include tests and scales.

Teachers are generally familiar with the various types of knowledge tests such as *true-false, multiple-choice, matching, completion,* and several others, one of which is known as the *judgment type.* The latter, which is not enough, sets up situations in which the pupil makes a decision on how he would act or respond.[5]

In the absence of standardized tests, schools will have to depend on those prepared by teachers and those taken from textbooks and state courses of study. However, it would be most beneficial if a series of standardized tests could be prepared for use in the schools.

HIGH SCHOOL DRIVER EDUCATION TESTING

Driver education is a field in which there has been extensive testing—in fact, more than in all of the other fields of safety combined. The tests used can be generally divided into four types, (1) knowedge and information, (2) attitude scales, (3) performance or road tests, and (4) judgment in traffic situations or emergencies.

Practically all of the high school driver education textbooks and workbooks include two types of tests, those administered at the end of a chapter or unit, and final tests. They are for the most part achievement tests, with items based on textbooks. The New York University Center for Safety Education has published a standardized test, *National Test in*

---

[5] The most striking response to testing was the Columbia Broadcasting System's tests for drivers, a program in which millions of drivers participated in radio and television tests.

Driver Education [6] which has age and grade norms and a reliability of .86. The test is based on several books and publications on driving practices. Many schools administer tests at the beginning and at the end of a course to measure growth. Neyhart also has prepared a series of tests[7]

The *Siebrecht Attitude Scale* [8] is the most widely used scale for measuring safety attitudes. It is essential that the manual of directions be followed carefully to get valid and reliable results. The same could be said for the Conover *Driving Attitude Inventory*.[9]

The state driver's license tests have improved during recent years. The American Automobile Association also publishes road and knowledge tests. One road test was developed by McGlade [10] as a part of a doctoral thesis. It has high validity and reliability and is especially useful for accurate measurement of road performance.

Psychophysical tests are also widely used for measuring characteristics of drivers. These tests are of value in acquainting students with their characteristics, and especially in locating individuals with extremely poor scores on vision tests.

Tests of this type can be purchased from [11] The American Automobile Association, Washington, D.C., and The Porto-Clinic Instruments, 298 Broadway, New York.

EVALUATION BY A COMPARISON OF THE RECORDS OF TRAINED AND UNTRAINED DRIVERS

It is desirable for a school to keep records of drivers who have completed courses, but it is difficult to make reliable comparisons between trained and untrained drivers. Some 30 such research studies have been carried out in the last decade. Most of these lack validity and reliability. The difficulties in carrying through such studies are discussed in the National Commission on Safety Education publication, *A Critical Analysis of Driver Education Research*.[12] This publication concludes with this statement: "The evidence of this report shows clearly the extreme difficulty of scientifically measuring so complex and complicated a phenome-

[6] Center for Safety Education, *National Test in Driver Education* (New York: The Center, New York University, 1958).

[7] Amos Neyhart, *Tests for Drivers* (Washington, D.C.: American Automobile Association, n.d.).

[8] Elmer Siebrecht, *The Siebrecht Attitude Scale* (New York: Center for Safety Education, New York University, 1941).

[9] Donald Conover, *Driving Attitude Inventory* (Ames, Iowa: Iowa State University of Arts and Sciences, n.d.).

[10] Francis McGlade, *A New Road Test* (New York: Center for Safety Education, New York University, 1958).

[11] More elaborate tests can be purchased from the American Optical Company, Southbridge, Massachusetts; the Keystone View Co., Meadville, Pennsylvania; and Bausch and Lomb, Rochester, New York. These are all tests of vision and are used in industries and by some motor vehicle departments.

[12] National Commission on Safety Education, *A Critical Analysis of Driver Education Research* (Washington, D.C.: The Commission, 1963).

non as driving behavior. At the same time, the contention that a traffic safety program reduces accidents is a plausible one."

STANDARDS

There are many published standards for both safety and driver education. For illustration, most state departments of education have standards for pupil transportation, school buildings and play areas, industrial arts shops and laboratories, school patrols, and a number of others. In addition, there are standards for high school driver education, especially in those 35 states that have some form of state financial support. The National Commission on Safety Education also has standards for driver education in its publication *Policies and Practices for Driver Education*.[13] As a matter of fact, the administrator can find standards for practically any type of school building and activity from civil defense to school building construction and maintenance.

The reliability and validity of test and scales is highly important. As an illustration of this, seven different research studies have been reported, five of which were doctoral theses. They tried to determine the value of simulators or ranges, and although the research designs of the studies was quite different from each other, the principle purpose of each study was to compare the learning of prospective groups of drivers. One group received instruction largely on simulators; the other received the traditional classroom and practice lessons. Improvement was measured by the use of tests and scales, most of which were standardized, but their value is questionable.

One very surprising result appeared in the conclusion of each study. In general there were no *significant differences* between the gains in the groups that used the simulator and the traditional groups. Research specialists have suggested several explanations for this curious result. Perhaps the instruments used (tests and scales) are not valid or reliable enough to distinguish differences. Students interested in these studies will find abstracts in *Driver Education and Driving Simulators*.[14]

PROOF OF THE VALUE OF DRIVER EDUCATION

As has been mentioned above, well over 30 studies have been carried on of the value of driver education.[15] It is the opinion of many of the leaders in the field that too many poorly planned studies have been undertaken.

[13] National Commission on Safety Education, *Policies and Practices for Driver and Traffic Safety Education* (Washington, D.C.: The Commission, 1964).

[14] James H. Fox, *Driver Education and Driving Simulators* (Washington, D.C.: National Commission on Safety Education, 1960).

[15] National Commission on Safety Education, *Results of Studies Evaluating Driver Education* (Washington, D.C.: The Commission, 1961).

In research conducted in Illinois, which included several hundred thousand drivers in both the trained and untrained groups, the trained group emerged with better accident records.

Brody, in the December, 1957, issue of *Safety Education,* suggests that "further studies of this kind are unnecessary. Proof is not required that social studies make better citizens, that health education produces better health or that mathematics pays off in everyday living. We do not have to prove the value of every course in the curriculum statistically. Is education for safe living justifiable? What educator would argue that it is not?" Mahony in *Teaching Driver and Traffic Safety Education* [16] re-emphasizes this point.

OTHER FORMS OF EVALUATION

There are subjective forms of evaluation that may at times be more valuable than elaborate surveys and testing programs. Often public opinion, the consensus of faculty judgment, the recommendations of the State Department of Education, or the evaluations of national authorities and organizations can be even more effective than statistical measurement.

SAFETY IN COLLEGES AND UNIVERSITIES

Although the measurement and evaluation of safety are not too far advanced in the public schools, they are considerably ahead of safety evaluation and measurement in higher education. There are various explanations for this situation.

Although state legislation and regulations regarding safety exercise considerable influence over the public schools, no such control is maintained over colleges and universities.

Although health and safety have been considered major objectives in the public schools, such objectives seem to be remote in higher education.

Although most elementary and secondary schools will have some form of safety instruction, it will be difficult to find much safety instruction in the colleges.

National and state agencies exert influence over public schools, but few such influences affect the colleges.

As will be noted in other chapters in this text, only a few hundred colleges have a campus safety program—a small percentage of the total number of colleges.

Institutions of higher learning feel that safety and accident prevention should have been taken care of in the public schools. College admin-

[16] American Automobile Association, *Teaching Driver and Traffic Safety Education* (New York: McGraw-Hill, 1965).

istrators might also insist that safety has been woven into the fabric of their regular courses.

Other reasons could be given for these differences, some undoubtedly more significant than those above, but the fact remains that in many colleges in the United States and in those in foreign countries, safety education has been given but little attention.

Some college administrators would say that safety education is not too important, that it is not college level material, or that it is taken care of by insistence on safe practices in college courses where there are elements of danger. Others would say that we just do not have accidents, our students are responsible enough to take care of themselves. This may all be quite true, but in institutions that have taken the trouble to investigate accidents, it has been found that one student out of ten is involved in an accident each year—a rate considerably higher than that in most industries. So few colleges have reporting systems that they do not know how many accidents they have.

It should not be construed from this discussion that all colleges are doing little to measure and evaluate safety. Many have good programs, especially the state-supported institutions and the technical and teachers colleges. The following are some of these activities:

1. Standards of safety for school buildings, laboratories, gymnasia and athletic fields, and other parts of the school plant have been fairly well followed.
2. Most private institutions are covered by fire and liability insurance and their buildings must pass inspections by insurance carriers.
3. Workmen's Compensation Insurance must be carried by all institutions. Losses from claims can become costly. This is especially true of private institutions.
4. Most colleges take care of injured students in infirmaries. This is better than what the public schools are doing.
5. Many of the coaches have shown a definite interest in accident prevention. They know that injured players do not make a winning team.
6. Many colleges are strengthening their health services. Some of these efforts are in advance of the work being done in the public schools. Physical examinations are generally better.
7. Many of the shops and laboratories are being constructed and maintained according to the standards set by the American Standards Association and other agencies.

OTHER METHODS OF EVALUATION

There are other methods which colleges can use to evaluate their safety programs. The following are illustrations.

Teachers colleges and university schools of education can compare their safety offerings with those of other institutions.

Engineers of the insurance carrier can inspect and evaluate operations in shops, farm buildings, heating plants, and laboratories. Inspection can be provided by safety engineers, industrial hygienists, and other specialists.

Civil defense officials can make inspections of all facilities, or this can be done by members of the faculty.

The accident record of school transportation facilities can be studiesd and compared.

There should be a complete accident reporting system for students, faculty, and other employees. The results can be compared to others and national standards.

Residence halls and laboratories can be studied, especially for fire hazards.

All colleges should have someone responsible for campus safety and report on conditions.

Standards of one kind or another are to be available for chemistry laboratories, school shops, residence halls, parking areas, athletic areas and facilities—in fact, for almost every area in the school.

If administrators really want to know how they stand on safety, there are dozens of evaluating tools available.

The fact remains that altogether too many college administrators and teachers appear to be little concerned with problems of safety. Only a few have accident reporting systems. Yet there are institutions where several students are killed in accidents in a single year—usually motor vehicle accidents or drowning, and generally off-campus. In accidents of this kind there is rarely legal responsibility or negligence on the part of the college. But there is a moral responsibility to make some effort to protect students off-campus as well as on. The armed forces are making determined efforts to reduce off-post accidents; colleges can certainly do more than they are at present.

REFERENCES

Gronlund, N. E., *Measurement and Evaluation in Teaching* (New York: Macmillan, 1965).

Insurance Institute for Highway Safety, *National High School Driver Education Achievement Program* (Washington, D.C.: The Institute, published annually).

McFarland, R. A., *et al.*, *Human Variables in Motor Vehicle Accidents* (Boston: Harvard School of Public Health, 1955).

Michels, W. J., and M. R. Karne, *Measuring Educational Achievement* (New York: McGraw-Hill, 1950).

Myers, F. H., "A Safety Attitude Scale for the Seventh Grade," *Research Quarterly* (October 1958), AAHPER, 29:320–21.

Remmers, H. H., *et al.*, *A Practical Introduction to Measurement and Evaluation* (New York: Harper & Row, 1960).

National Commission on Safety Education, "Tests and Evaluation Methods Used in Driver and Safety Education (Washington, D.C.: The Commission, National Education Association, 1959).

Stanley, Julian C., *Measurement in Today's Schools* (Englewood Cliffs, N.J.: Prentice-Hall, 1947).

Stack, H. J., and J. D. Elkow, *Education for Safe Living*, 4th ed. (Englewood Cliffs, N.J.: Prentice-Hall, 1966).

Strasser, M. K., J. E. Aaron, R. C. Bohn, and J. R. Eales, *Fundamentals of Safety Education* (New York: Macmillan, 1964).

PART II THE SCHOOL
SAFETY
PROGRAM

No cause, not even the highest and purest, can prosper in our day without education as its ally.

HORACE MANN

INTRODUCTION

In a recent publication [1] it was emphasized that the health and safety of children as participants in the school program continues to be a primary concern of educators. This regard for the health, welfare, and protection of the school-age population came into existence with the beginning of public education in this nation. The relationship of safety education to the school program is basic in assisting youth to make an effective adaptation in their environment.

The application of this concept is evident by many educators as they present an educational program that utilizes the school and community as a laboratory for living and learning. Efficient living in an ordered world includes intelligent standards of behavior, precautionary measures, and skills in the home, school, traffic, playground, and recreational activities. The accomplishment of this goal will be largely dependent upon all teachers accepting the responsibility for a school program that presents learning experiences contributing to the development of desirable habits, attitudes, knowledge, and skill.

There is general agreement among educational authorities that a successful school safety education program is a major responsibility

---

[1] Bernard I. Loft, "Emphasis and Sequence in Safety Education," *Current Administrative Problems* (Washington, D.C.: American Association for Health, Physical Education, and Recreation, 1960), pp. 170–71.

of the school administrator. Through his dedicated leadership an effective safety program should contribute to decreased absenteeism, increased morale, and sound principles in administering the total school program. The administrator's belief in the significance of safety education and accident prevention will be a source of motivation for everyone affiliated in the school. Initially, the administrator should establish the fact that safety is not to be considered as an adjunct in the school curriculum.

All members of the faculty and staff have an important role in teaching students how to live efficiently. Every area of the school program, either by correlation or integration techniques, can provide teachable moments for instruction in safe living.

In student acceptance of the safety program, there should be a realization of the positive concept whereby greater adventure can be enjoyed without harmful results. Hence, safety has contributed to an increase of adventure through intelligent behavior. Numerous examples of this concept exist in a variety of school activities, particularly where action is involved.

The community must also be convinced by the administrator and faculty that an investment in safety education is directly related to productive citizenship for the future. In many communities there will be apparent evidence that to eliminate this area of education would be false economy. Sustained economic losses resulting from accidents and human suffering can soon prove that a safety-minded individual is a distinct community asset. The administrator, faculty, students, and community all have a mutual responsibility in the human conservation problem.

CHAPTER 7 THE ELEMENTARY SCHOOL PROGRAM

The elementary school by virtue of its organizational structure provides numerous opportunities for experiences in safety education. A comprehensive elementary school safety program should contribute to the desirable formation of knowledge, attitudes, skills, and habits that will be a basis for applying safety procedures in daily practices. Success of the program will depend on cooperative effort by all persons and organizations affiliated with the school and community in developing the safety and accident prevention program.

A significant goal of education at the elementary school level includes emphasis upon the prevention of school accidents and on instructional programs in preparing the child to make an efficient adaptation to his environment. If the aim of education functions in preparing children for participation in lifelike situations and effective citizenship, the school has an obligation for presenting instruction in safe living. Thus safety education must be recognized as an integral phase of the total school process.

The preschool child should receive his first introduction to safe living through the teaching and experiences provided by parents in the home environment. This will be a continued process by the parents in cooperation along with safety instruction presented throughout the elementary school. In school the child will experience a variety of situations that may not occur in the home. During this period a foundation is established for future learning experiences and behavioral patterns for the children in their role as worthy citizens in a democratic society.

The administrator, classroom teacher, and supervisor of safety education have a challenging responsibility in making safety instruction meaningful, interesting, and dynamic. Everyone in the school should recognize that accident prevention and instruction for safe living is not a supplement to the school program but a vital part of the total curriculum. The administrator must provide an opportunity for teachers to include safety instruction with an appropriate amount of time assigned to each topical area. A similar arrangement is also necessary for practical experiences that should be included in the school environment. When effectively presented, safety education not only prepares the child for proper living but also permits him to participate in related skills that will have considerable value. Safety education offers numerous opportunities for sound judgment to be developed so that the child can carry over his learning experiences and apply them to everyday needs. Self-direction and self-guidance must necessarily be an outcome of safety education at the elementary school level.

SAFETY EDUCATION EXPERIENCES

The Elementary School Section of the National Safety Council in 1952 prepared a significant statement which was revised in 1959 with reference to desirable experiences in safety education for elementary school pupils. In consideration of the significant contribution made by a committee of this section, the official statement is included in the same manner as produced for the Safety Education Magazine, March, 1959.[1]

Meaningful experiences in elementary school safety are extremely important since they form the foundation for future behavioral patterns.

An elementary school that is providing desirable experiences in safety education should be able to point to definite accomplishments in seven specific areas according to the Elementary School Section, School and College Conference, National Safety Council.

1. Schools with desirable programs provide safety instruction to meet the needs of the pupils. The needs may be determined by:
   a. An analysis of the temporary and permanent hazards of the pupils' environment.
   b. An analysis of the hazards associated with the pupils' activities.
   c. An analysis of the records collected through the standard student-accident reporting system.
   d. An analysis of the hazards associated with the seasons and with such special days as Christmas, Halloween, the Fourth of July.
   e. A consideration of individual pupil's abilities, limitations, and problems.
2. Schools with desirable programs provide for the active participation of pupils in caring for their own safety. For example,
   a. Provision for pupil safety organizations, such as junior safety councils, school safety patrols, student safety committees, school building patrols, monitors, and bicycle clubs.
   b. Provision for pupil information and evaluation of rules for action.
   c. Provision for inspections by pupils.
3. Schools with desirable programs utilize instructional aids for a well-rounded program of school, recreation, traffic, fire, seasonal, civil defense and home safety. Such aids could include:
   a. Text materials: books, lesson units, work sheets.

[1] National Safety Council, "Desirable Experiences in Elementary Safety Education," *Safety Education* (Chicago: The Council, 1959).

b. Audio-visual aids: motion pictures, film strips, glass slides, posters, models.

c. Pupil-made materials.

4. Schools with desirable programs provide realistic opportunities for supervised practice in meeting hazards. For example:

   a. In crossing streets and railroad tracks.

   b. In using school equipment, such as pencils, scissors, saws, stoves, slides, swings.

   c. In using transportation systems.

   d. In emergency drills.

   e. In performing science experiments.

   f. In physical education and recreation activities.

5. Schools with desirable programs keep safety in the forefront of the consciousness of pupils, parents and teachers. Among the tools to accomplish this are:

   a. Exhibits and bulletin boards.

   b. Slides or drawings of accident statistics.

   c. Posters and other art work.

   d. Assemblies, radio broadcasts, and television shows.

   e. School and community newspapers.

   f. Maps showing prevalent accident locations and safe routes for walking.

   g. Home and community inspections.

6. Schools with desirable programs cooperate with other community agencies. Opportunities for such cooperation are:

   a. Conducting an active safety program among patrons.

   b. Aiding in the preparation of the community's report for the Annual Inventory of Traffic Safety Activities, the American Automobile Association Pedestrian Program, the Inter-Chamber Fire Waste Contest of the Chamber of Commerce.

   c. Cooperating in communities' safety activities, such as Fire Prevention Week, Clean-up Week.

   d. Supplying a safety speaker for a community enterprise.

7. Schools with desirable programs take the steps necessary to:

   a. Establish and maintain school plant, equipment, transportation facilities in safe condition.

   b. Provide in-service education for the school faculty and other personnel, including opportunities for serving on safety committees, helping to write teachers' guides or courses of study and attending safety conferences.

ADMINISTRATIVE RESPONSIBILITY

Responsibility for the organization, administration, and supervision of safety education at the elementary-school level is a function of boards of education and superintendents of public instruction. Through cooperative effort they should establish policies and procedures for the development of a safety program that will be structured according to sound educational practices. Essentially this will include safety education for all elementary students in the appropriate areas of instruction. Implementation of the established policies and procedures then become the responsibility of school personnel such as administrators, supervisors, teachers, bus operators, custodians and other related staff, and faculty members. In the initial planning by school administrators there should be thoroughness and precision in order to establish a solid foundation for relating safety education to the total school program.[2]

PRINCIPLES CONTRIBUTING TO EFFECTIVE ORGANIZATION AND ADMINISTRATION

In developing a complete safety program in the elementary school the areas of safety instruction, safety services, and a safe school environment are to be considered. Each individual aspect in the planning stage requires the application of sound basic principles of organization and administration. The following educational principles can be applied in keeping with their relationship to the elementary safety program:

1. Success in commercial, industrial, governmental, and educational enterprises is conditioned by the degree to which sound principles of administration operate in the organizational structure.
2. Good administration seeks the active cooperation and participation of all individuals and groups concerned.
3. It is centered in a responsible and effective executive head.
4. Good administration recognizes the principle of delegated authority and responsibility. It is physically impossible for the chief executive to retain active supervision of all functions of his school, therefore he delegates to responsible persons the power to act in given functions.
5. The school administrator places a premium upon the abilities, special interests and training of staff members by assigning them to positions where they can do the most good.
6. In establishing policies, good administration invites the participation of all persons and groups concerned: students, teachers, the staff, school employees, the board of education, school patrons, and community groups.
7. Good administration makes possible the systematic collection and use of facts as a basis for policies and procedures.
8. It also provides opportunities for pupils to bear responsibilities under the guidance of the school staff, thus recognizing the principle of "learning by doing."

[2] E. J. Brown, *Secondary School Administration: Its Practices and Theory* (Boston: Houghton Mifflin Company, 1938).

9. Good administration provides safe buildings, grounds, equipment, and supplies, and seeks in every manner to advance the health and well-being of the child.
10. It recognizes as well that an administrative machine is no stronger than its weakest part. It makes possible a maximum contribution to the program from all members by giving appropriate recognition to each individual and groups.

CURRICULUM PLANNING

An effective approach as recommended by educational authorities is to design a custom-built curriculum planned cooperatively by teachers and students. Primary consideration should be related to the needs existing in the community and individual student requirements for safe living. A complete study should be made of all hazards that can be identified in the community and environment surrounding the school building. The safety curriculum must take into consideration all of the safety aids and services that are available in the community. Proper use of all the available resources will enhance the effectiveness of a safety and accident prevention program in the school and community. Recognition of community hazards and safety resources with proper direction can be a project for groups of students. This technique can provide a central core around which many additional learning experiences can be planned for students. In some locations the schools have solicited the assistance of parents in the making of school and community surveys. Parents and students should be made aware that their contribution in conducting safety surveys will benefit the total school and all students presently enrolled and who will be enrolled in future years. To be effective, surveys should be completed on a yearly basis with different groups assuming responsibility for collecting and assimilating the desired information. In a dynamic society new hazards will be constantly developing in all communities. Hopefully many of these hazards will be eliminated or compensations made where the hazard cannot be eliminated. Particularly important is to contain the accident problem so that accident frequencies and accident severities will be at a minimum. As survey teams become aware of new safety-resource materials, their prepared lists will be maintained with all of the recent aids and developments to prevent accidents.

BASIC ELEMENTS IN THE SAFETY CURRICULUM

1. Safety education should be concerned with a positive approach rather than the negative aspects so as to add greater adventure to life rather than detract from wholesome living.
2. The movement and exposure of people to hazards necessitates that

every aspect of human endeavor be approached quantatively and qualitatively.

3. Community needs should be given thorough consideration in planning the safety curriculum. Both present and new developments in the community environment must be recognized.

4. Emphasis should be placed upon child growth and development in assuming safety and accident prevention responsibilities.

5. Wherever feasible practical experiences should be included in the safety curriculum through use of techniques as simulation, role playing, and mimetic drills.

6. The safety curriculum should be structured upon the best known practices in school health education and mental hygiene as a means of enhancing personal security.

7. Periodically the safety curriculum should be evaluated in conformity with the established objectives including the direct and indirect outcomes. The National Safety Council's Standard Student Accident Reporting Form can be used to evaluate the direct results. (See p. 66.)

8. The total school curriculum is conducive to the integration of safety education. In some areas of instruction the effectiveness can be increased by an independent unit of instruction or a special course.

9. Modern curricular trends are compatible with the fundamental concepts of safety education.

ORGANIZING THE CURRICULUM FOR SAFETY INSTRUCTION

A fundamental question centers on how the elementary school curriculum should be organized to provide proper direction in the process of instructing students. Decisions related to organizing the curriculum should be determined by needs of the learner, subject matter, and the accomplishment of educational achievement. The teacher will gain direction by decisions that are made at the institutional level, the school, or school system. These decisions are of considerable importance since they establish a working procedure for teachers to have a basis for individual instructional responsibilities. Should there be an absence of curriculum planning at the school level, teachers then find themselves in situations requiring decisions and the use of whatever instructional resources may be available.

At the school level there is no substitute for effective planning. A framework is necessary if safety instruction is to be included as an essential phase of the elementary school program. This framework provides for a systematized approach to including instructional programs in keeping with sound educational practices.

In a study [3] of selected practices in elementary and secondary schools, included as a phase of the Project on Instruction, school administrators were requested to rank, in accordance with their use, ten resource areas for development of the school program. The findings from this study indicated that textbooks outrank all other resources as materials utilized in developing the school program. Curriculum materials prepared by state departments of education, school systems, or faculty personnel followed next in order. Ranking considerably lower on this list of resources were reports by outstanding educators and laymen.

WHAT SHOULD BE TAUGHT AND WHEN

Decisions by administrators and teachers concerning what to teach and when to teach it should be determined by the student's capability to understand and the values placed on a variety of methods to use the learner's time throughout the various aspects in his school experience.

Parents and educators should consider the current trends to place subject-matter areas further down in the curriculum. From all indications this trend has implications for the teaching of safety education at the elementary school level. The pressures related to this trend should be examined and understood from the validity and justifiable explanations that have been presented by educational authorities. Essentially the reasons behind placing subject matter lower in the curriculum are

Underestimation of the child's ability to comprehend difficult subject matter and learning experiences at a young age. There is evidence that young children can absorb aspects of subject matter that was initially designated for advanced study.

With the rapid increase of knowledge in many areas of learning there is a need for more teaching at an earlier period in the child's school experience.

In preparing the child for his place in a rapidly progressive society of adults he will need high-level skills to qualify him for effective citizenship.

Children who receive early educational experiences in subjects such as mathematics, science, and safety education will probably be prepared to rapidly advance academically and in areas of their particular interest.

If freedom from accidents is to become a way of life there is a need to begin safety education for children at the earliest possible opportunity. In the early stages of the child's development, parents and elementary teachers need to coordinate their efforts in providing a fundamental foun-

[3] *The Principals Look at the Schools: A Status Study of Selected Instructional Practices* (Washington, D.C.: National Education Association, April, 1962).

dation that will aid the child in preparing for adulthood with freedom from accident and injury.

School Organizations for Pupils

The elementary school provides many opportunities for pupils to participate in learning experiences that will contribute in the development of cooperation and leadership abilities. Routine activities in the school environment present a wide range of situations for pupils to learn safety practices and procedures. Interest and enthusiasm should be increased as a result of experiences where students have responsibilities to share in the management of school activities. In giving pupils a share in this phase of the school program they will learn that safety is a process of cooperation that becomes everybody's responsibility. The formation of desirable habits and attitudes should be important outcomes obtained by pupils from their experiences in pupil organizations.

Junior Safety Council

Junior safety councils have proved to be a worthy organization in the elementary school program. The entire school is closely affiliated with the council by selecting a representative from each homeroom. Council representatives have the responsibility of communicating information from the council meetings to the respective homerooms. In organizing a council the school administrator should carefully establish a plan to include provisions for general organization, sponsor, constitution, qualifications for memberships, officers and their duties, committee functions, program content for meetings, special events, and interschool activities.

Regulations for the safety and protection of schoolchildren are designated by the board of education in cooperation with the superintendent of schools. The administrators, teachers, custodians, supervisors, and all others concerned [4] are then responsible for implementing the various aspects of the program. In organizing a Junior Safety Council the administrator should study school safety programs that continue to produce favorable results.

The following constitution for developing a school safety council as prepared by the School Safety Committee for the Pittsburgh public schools presents the necessary steps to be included in organizing the council.

Article I.   Name

The name of this organization shall be the Junior Safety Council of_____ School.

[4] Pittsburgh Public Schools, *Constitution of the Junior Safety Councils of the Pittsburgh Public Schools*, Pittsburgh, Pennsylvania, Schools Safety Committee.

(Note: In those schools in which other pupil organizations promote safety thru a standing committee, these organizations may be considered as units of the Junior Safety Council.)

Article II.   Affiliation

This organization is affiliated with the Western Pennsylvania Safety Council, a branch of the National Safety Council.

Article III.   Supervision

This organization shall operate under the general supervision of the Schools Safety Committee, a group of principals appointed by the superintendent of schools.

Directly, this organization shall operate under the supervision of the principal of this school, or of a teacher appointed by the principal.

Article IV.   Purpose

The purpose of this organization shall be to promote individual, school, and community safety.

Article V.   Membership

Active membership in this organization shall include a representative or representatives from each room (Grades IV to XII, inclusive), elected by the pupils in the room represented, unless otherwise provided for under Article I.

Associate Membership shall include all other pupils in the school. All members shall memorize the Junior Safety Council pledge.

Article VI.   Officers

The officers of this organization shall include a president, vice-president, secretary, and treasurer.

Officers shall be elected by the majority vote of the active members.

Article VII.   Meetings

Meetings shall be held at least once a month.

Article VIII.   Committees

This organization shall function thru standing and special committees. Standing committees should include committees on Program, Publicity, Accident Reporting, and Inspection. The School Safety Patrol may operate as a Standing Committee.

Special committeees may be appointed as the need arises.

Article IX.   Star Membership

Any pupil who performs an outstanding act in the interest of safety, such as saving a life or preventing a serious accident, shall be eligible to receive a Gold Button award from the Western Pennsylvania Safety Council upon the following conditions:

1. The written application for such award containing the signature of

at least one witness to the act, approved by the Junior Safety Council and principal, shall be submitted to the School's Safety Committee.

2. The application shall be submitted not later than ten days after occurrence of the act if during the school term, or if during a vacation period, within ten days after resumption of school.

3. The School's Safety Committee shall have final jurisdiction in making the award.

4. To be favorably considered, acts performed by patrol members in the course of duty must represent an exceptionally high standard of safety accomplishment. This is in line with the policy followed by the Carnegie Hero Fund Commission.

Article X.   Safety Pledge

The Junior Safety Council Safety Pledge shall be:

1. I will work for the safety of others, as I would want them to work for my safety.

2. I will not take unnecessary chances, for in doing so, I may lead into danger a younger child who is not so well able to take care of himself as I am.

3. I will do my part to reduce the number of accidents in this city this year.

4. I will try to take care of my health and to be clean in thought, words, and deed.

5. I will try to do right at all times, telling the truth, and respecting the rights of others.

6. All this I will do for the sake of humanity and the honor of my school.

Article XI.   Amendments

This Constitution may be amended at any regular meeting of this organization, subject to the approval of the School's Safety Committee.

PROTECTION OF PUPILS TO AND FROM SCHOOL

SCHOOL SAFETY PATROLS

The purpose of a school safety patrol is to provide assistance in directing and controlling student pedestrian traffic while crossing streets and highways in the school's vicinity. Patrol members can also contribute to the safety instruction program by teaching pupils how to cross streets and highways properly. Under no circumstances should members be considered as a substitute for police enforcement or be assigned responsibilities for the direction of vehicular traffic.[5]

[5] American Automobile Association, *School Bus Patrols* (Washington, D.C.: The Association, 1960).

Primary responsibility for determining the school safety patrol overall policy is a function of the superintendent. The principal assists faculty personnel in establishing an understanding relationship between the patrol and all pupils in the school. Additional administrative responsibility by the principal is directed to selection, training, supervision, procurement of materials, necessary for the efficient development of the patrol.

The faculty member selected as supervisor or sponsor of the patrol represents a key factor in determining the success of this pupil organization. His direct contact with individual patrol members affords numerous opportunities for counseling and guidance. As the faculty representative he is responsible for the patrol in all of its efforts and activities. The individual selected for this important responsibility needs to be exceedingly interested in the safety service potentiality of the patrol. Further, he should be continuously aware of the importance in providing safety education for all members of the patrol.

Police departments can be of assistance by designating a qualified police officer to cooperate with the faculty representative and patrol members in making an analysis of existing street hazards where individual patrol members are to be assigned. Instructional programs for the patrol units can also be arranged by utilizing the police personnel for this purpose.

A recommended organizational chart for the school safety patrol is shown in Table 7-1.

A complete guide for the organization and development of a school safety patrol can be found in the American Automobile Association, *Safety Patrol Handbook*.[6]

BICYCLE SAFETY

The elementary school principal should make provisions for a continuous bicycle safety program. Many pupils use bicycles as a means of transportation to and from the school. Learning desirable bicycle safety practices can form a basis for habits, attitudes, and skills that are impor-

TABLE 7-1

SCHOOL SAFETY PATROL ORGANIZATION

	Superintendent
	Principal
Auxiliary	Faculty Representative
Lieutenants	Captain (Student)
	Sidewalk Lieutenants
	Sidewalk Patrol
	Members

[6] American Automobile Association, *Safety Patrol Handbook* (Washington, D.C.: The Association, 1961).

tant during this period of the pupils' growth and development. One method for organizing a bicycle safety program is by forming a bicycle club under the direction of an interested member of the school faculty. Membership in the club can be made available to all pupils riding bicycles to and from school and other interested members of the school. In a cooperative manner the faculty representative and club members can establish a set of objectives and program for the school year. Of considerable importance is the accomplishment of the stated objectives. A majority of states and cities have rules and regulations governing the proper use of bicycles. All members of the club and student body in general should know and understand the application of these rules and regulations. Special club programs can be organized to familiarize pupils with such matters as the proper selection and maintenance requirements for various kinds of bicycles. Bicycle safety clinics involving events such as steering, balancing, stopping, and turning can be sponsored by the club for their own participation and as a service to other pupils in the school. The clinic is a means of periodically presenting a bicycle safety education program for everyone in the school with the club membership assuming a major leadership role.

CONCLUSION

A comprehensive program of safety education should be a phase of all elementary schools. The program should be of such a nature to include learning experiences that will assist the pupils in freedom from accidents in daily activities and provide for a carry over to the community and home. Routine activities in the elementary school provide numerous opportunities for pupil participation in safety and accident prevention procedures. This is in addition to the safety instruction presented by the classroom teachers. Special programs in connection with national holidays and safety campaigns can be used as a theme for assembly activities, school newspaper articles and projects sponsored by clubs within the school.

The principal has a major role in providing the necessary leadership to keep the school environment safe and free from accidents. His enthusiasm, attitude, and understanding of all aspects that contribute to a complete safety program will be of utmost importance in achieveing desirable results.

REFERENCES

American Association of School Administrators, Eighteenth Yearbook, *Safety Education* (Washington, D.C.: National Education Association, 1940).

California State Department of Education, *Education for Safety* (Sacramento: Education Department, 1963).

Education in a Changing Society (Washington, D.C.: National Education Association, 1963).

Florio, A. E., and G. T. Stafford, *Safety Education,* 2nd ed. (New York: McGraw-Hill, 1962).

How Children and Teacher Work Together (Washington, D.C.: U.S. Government Printing Office, 1952).

Kilander, H. F., *School Health Education,* 2nd ed. (New York: Macmillan, 1968).

Loft, B. I., "Positive Approach to Safety," *Journal of Health, Physical Education, and Recreation* (May 1961), pp. 34–35.

National Commission on Safety Education, National Education Association, Washington, D.C.:

> *The Elementary School Principal Plans for Safe Living,* Part 2, 1945.
>
> *They Found a Way,* Report of National Conference on Safety Education in Elementary Schools, 1953.
>
> *Our School Plans Safe Living,* 1956, p. 32.
>
> *Unit Guides for You, Safety in the Primary Grades,* 1959, p. 100.

National Safety Council, *Curriculum Planning for Safety—A Report of the Committee on Curriculum Planning for Safety, Safety Education* (Chicago: The Council, 1941 and 1956).

National Safety Council, *Foundation for Safe Living* (Chicago: The Council, 1948).

National Safety Council, *Safety Education* (Series of Articles on Correlating Safety Teaching into the Curriculum) (Chicago: The Council):

> No. 1. Zahn, W. D., "Time to Impress" (September 1959), Vol. XXXIX, pp. 2, 3, 39.
>
> No. 2. Fea, J. L., "Science and Safety Education Are Inseparable" (October 1959), Vol. XXXIX, pp. 2, 3, 4, 21.
>
> No. 4. Manley, H., "It's All in the Game" (December 1959), Vol. XXXIX, pp. 4, 6.
>
> No. 5. Thurston, L. B., "Sociograms to Safety" (January 1960), Vol. XXXIX, pp. 20, 23.
>
> No. 6. Rappaport, M. G., "An Apple a Day" (February 1960), Vol. XXXIX, pp. 4–6.
>
> No. 7. Anthony, F., and C. Mertz, "Art for Safety Sake" (March 1960), Vol. XXXIX, pp. 2–3.

Planning and Organizing for Teaching (Washington, D.C.: National Education Association, 1963).

Russell, E., "What to Teach When," *Safety Education* (October 1960), p. 6.

Schools for the Sixties: A Report of the N.E.A. Project on Instruction (New York: McGraw-Hill, 1963).

Yost, C. P., *Teaching Safety in the Elementary School* (Washington, D.C.: N.E.A. American Association for Health, Physical Education, and Recreation, 1962).

CHAPTER **8** THE SECONDARY
SCHOOL
PROGRAM

The importance of a high school safety-and-accident-prevention program is evident in the excessively high rate of accidents involving adolescent youth in the secondary schools. Many of these accidents could have been avoided or minimized by providing an adequate program of safety education. The high school principal has an important responsibility to provide a program that will enable students to develop desirable attitudes, acquire skills, habits, and knowledge to enhance safe living in our rapidly moving society. In administering the high school safety-education program, the principal must recognize several prevalent characteristics of adolescence. The desire for adventure and distaste for restrictions is constantly a force in the growth and development of youth. Unless the safety education program is presented in a positive manner, the high school pupil may develop a severe distaste for the negative aspects of safety. His need for understanding proper standards of performance and behavior continues to increase throughout this period of adolescence. The experience of meeting new hazards is encountered as youth begins to stray away from influences in the sheltered environment of the home and school. A concern for the protection and welfare of others becomes significant as high school pupils approach driver-licensing age. In consideration of a variety of problems to be overcome, the necessity for an effectively organized program of safety education in the secondary school is of significant importance.

The various safety education programs established in secondary school usually follow one or a combination of the following patterns:

1. Organizing safety education as a separate course on a required or elective basis.
2. Presenting safety as an individual unit of instruction included in existing school subjects.
3. Relating safety to and integrating it with related aspects of the curriculum and cocurricular activities.
4. Developing the safety education program through pupil organiza-

tions and projects conducive to safety and accident prevention experiences.

Frequently several types of the aforementioned programs will be organized within the secondary school. There are various possibilities for providing variations of the four programs designed to meet specific needs and interests.

SECONDARY SCHOOL ACCIDENT PROBLEM

As adolescent youth seek the challenge for greater adventure many of the activities in which they participate have an element of danger. Participation is constantly on the increase in the use of small craft, power boats, and in such activities as water skiing, swimming, fishing, hunting, hiking, camping, skin diving and scuba diving, competitive sports, and school physical education programs. Large numbers of secondary school students are involved in agricultural responsibilities where heavy-duty farm implements are used in farming. At this stage of the adolescent's development there appears to be a desire for adventurous living. The negative aspects of safety impose restrictions and limitations that reduce the freedom youth is seeking. Experiences in safety education should be convincing so that the opportunity for increased adventure is clearly understood. The positive application of safety and accident-prevention principles should be presented by the educator with an approach that will capture the interest and enthusiasm of secondary school students.

Accident statistics reveal that secondary school accidents are on the increase while a steady decrease has been taking place in the accident experience in elementary schools. Accidents in motor vehicles, swimming, hunting, fishing, physical education, athletics, and recreation are on the increase for secondary school students. An understanding of the problem is related to the increased exposure in the previously mentioned activities. Obviously the motor vehicle compounds the problem since many teen-agers begin their driving experience as they approach the minimum driver-licensing requirement at age sixteen in a large number of states. During this period there is also a strong desire for participation in competitive sports. This desire provides a partial explanation for the increase in accidents involving secondary school students. "The fatality rate for accidents among those in the 15 to 19 age group is 2.6 times that of the 10 to 14 age group. This is chiefly due to the incidence of motor vehicle accidents."[1]

The high school student has an increasing need for an understanding of human conservation as it applies to every aspect of his environment.

[1] National Safety Council, *Accident Facts* (Chicago: The Council, published annually).

His need for safety education must be efficiently administered as an integral phase of the total school program. There is increasing evidence that with the growth of driver education many schools are simultaneously developing comprehensive school safety education programs.

SPECIFIC OBJECTIVES FOR SAFETY EDUCATION ON THE SECONDARY SCHOOL LEVEL [2]

1. To teach pupils to take an active interest in the protection of the life, health, and property of the community in which they live.
2. To bring about an appreciation of the responsibility of the individual for the safety of the group and the effect of individual conduct on the safety of others.
3. To develop cooperation in the solution of such safety problems as traffic hazards, safe driving, and fire prevention.
4. To create a respect for—and an understanding of—safety rules, regulations, laws, and practices.
5. To understand the common causes of accidents and ways by which accidents may be prevented.
6. To develop knowledges and skills applicable to all traffic situations involving pedestrian responsibilities, bicycle riding, and automobile riding and driving.
7. To develop appreciations of occupational hazards and skills in minimizing these hazards.
8. To develop knowledges and skills that may be applied to such emergency health problems as wounds, suffocation, poisoning, fractures, dislocations, and burns.

PROGRAM PLANNING

The initiative for the organization and administration of a quality safety program is a responsibility of the high school principal. Recognizing that all aspects of the total school program are of importance, teaching pupils how to make an effective adaptation to their environment is of primary concern.

In some situations, the principal will seek counsel from the superintendent and board of public instruction prior to establishing policy and procedure for the program. In schools with a small enrollment, the principal may desire to assume a major responsibility for the organization and implementation of all program aspects. In larger schools the need for a delegation of responsibility becomes an administrative procedure. Initially, the principal should actively participate in establishing

[2] American Association of School Administrators, National Education Association, Eighteenth Yearbook, *Safety Education* (Washington, D.C.: The Association, 1948).

plans that will be compatible with existing school policy. Precise planning will eliminate the occurrence of problems that may require considerable attention by the principal at a future time. In assigning responsibility, there should be a complete job analysis outlining duties and lines of authority with respect to the assignment. The administrator must recognize that every faculty member has a significant role in the total school safety program. A lack of cooperation in any one phase of the prorgam could cause a severe limitation in the desired results.

Familiarization with related safety-education and accident-prevention literature will be of value to the principal in understanding the scope, organization, and administrative needs in formulating a sound program. This knowledge will also be helpful in providing guidance for the faculty in their assigned responsibilities.

The principal may adhere to the following plan in organizing a school safety and accident-prevention program. Depending on the established organizational school structure there will be a need for modifying the plan in keeping with local administrative policy.

Organizing the Safety Committee

The purpose of a safety committee is to serve in an advisory capacity to the principal during the organizational period and actively participate in a functional capacity in implementing the program. Committee membership should be determined by selecting personnel possessing outstanding qualifications to serve the school safety interests. Representatives of the student body, faculty, custodial staff, and school bus operators constitute a logical choice for this committee.

During an initial committee meeting the following suggestions should be presented by the principal:

1. The need for a complete program of safety throughout the school.
2. The need for a cooperative effort by all members of the committee as a fundamental prerequisite for a successful program.
3. The need for a process whereby the safety program can be established within the existing school program.
4. The need for the assignment of subcommittees and chairmen directly responsible to the principal.

In cooperation with the designated committees, the principal establishes plans to make a survey of the existing conditions through a fact-finding process. Accumulated data concerning local accidents and hazards will provide information to assist in developing the program. A definite period of time should be established for collecting the data with the faculty, students and committees being informed as to their respective duties.

Fact Finding

Fundamental to organizing an effective school safety program is an investigation of the accidents that have occurred throughout the school. Particularly significant is a determination of the contributory factors revealed during the period of fact finding. A school accident-reporting system is imperative to providing information concerning persons, unsafe acts and conditions that contribute to accidents. Complete accident investigation and analysis with a high degree of validity should be adopted by the total school system. The National Safety Council's Standard Student Accident Reporting System, is widely used and endorsed by administrators and safety educators as a desirable school instrument. An analysis of the school accident reports may reveal deficiencies and weaknesses in the safety education aspects of the school curriculum. Revisions in school plant facilities, materials, and equipment can also be detected by an analysis of the accident reports.

Accident reports should provide all the necessary data as indicated in the following items: [3]

Names, address, age, sex, grade, and school of injured student.
Date, time, place, and activity in which injury occurred.
Cause and nature of injury.
Treatment of injury—first aid or medical care.
Person who administered treatment.
Person in charge when accident occurred.
Witnesses to accident.
Structural or equipment defects contributing to accident.
Notification of proper persons for correction of such defects.
Notification of parents of injured student.
Number of school days lost due to accident.
Name of person filling out form.

The principal should have available in the school office the names, addresses, and telephone numbers of pupils' parents so that they can be contacted rapidly in the event of an emergency. Arrangements for emergency student medical care is an administrative matter to be provided by the principal with a nearby physician.

As a means of determining student accident experience after school hours, the safety committee should endeavor by means of questionnaires, surveys, and investigations to accumulate data concerning hazards and unsafe student practices in the community. A complete program of

[3] American Association for Health, Physical Education, and Recreation, National Association of Secondary School Principals, and National Commission on Safety Education, National Education Association, *The High School Principal and Safety* (Washington, D.C.: The Association, 1948).

safety education includes all aspects of the students' environment in and out of school. Valuable information relative to the community can be obtained from the health agencies, police and fire departments, local safety council, chamber of commerce, American Red Cross, civic organizations, farm agencies, and traffic organizations.

ANALYSIS OF THE SCHOOL ACCIDENT PROBLEM

Having completed the survey, the committee should schedule a series of meetings to analyze all aspects of the findings. An understanding of the who, when, why, where, and how, of student accident experience can be classified for additional study and remedial action. Similarly, the early detection of hazards can be placed in categories with relation to student exposure.

The analysis procedure including an investigation of accident experience and existence of hazards may prove to be significant in revealing a desirable comprehensive school safety program that would include the following areas:

Scope of program [4]

A. Administrative phase.
  1. Construction and maintenance of safe school buildings.
  2. Maintenance of safe and adequate school grounds and equipment.
  3. Operation and maintenance of safe school buses, driven by carefully selected drivers trained in first aid and basic driving techniques.
  4. Provision in curriculum for safety teaching in all grades, driving instruction and first aid in secondary schools.
  5. Selection of teachers prepared to teach safety education, provision for in-service teacher education.
  6. Establishment of a complete student accident reporting system.
  7. Provision for adequate instructional materials such as books and visual aids.
  8. Provision for fire drills, inspection, removal of snow and ice.
  9. Provision of trained first-aider in each building to care for minor injuries.
  10. A well-established policy and plan of procedure in case of serious accidents and sudden illness.
  11. Adequate supervision of school activities by properly qualified and trained personnel.

[4] American Association of Teachers Colleges and National Commission on Safety Education of the National Education Association, *Safety Education for Teachers, Part II—A Guide for College Instructors of Safety Education* (Washington, D.C.: The Association, 1947).

12. Annual medical examinations of all children.
13. Provision of special safeguards for physically handicapped children.
14. Interpretation of existing school safety laws to the school personnel.
15. Consistent application of the principles of safety in the organization and operation of the school.
16. Assumption of responsibility for initiation, direction, development, and evaluation of the program.
17. A program of training for the custodial staff.

B. Instructional phase.
  1. Safety taught through general school routine.
     a. Conduct at recess period.
     b. Corridor traffic.
     c. Safety on the school bus.
     d. Conduct on the playground.
     e. Safety in the classroom.
  2. Incidental teaching, as in safe use of equipment.
  3. Direct instruction in safety.
  4. Integration or correlation with other subjects.
  5. Cocurricular activties.
     a. Fire drills.
     b. Accident reporting system.
     c. Junior Safety Council.
     d. School safety patrols.
     e. Safety clubs, such as a bicycle club.
     f. Excursions.
     g. School assemblies.
     h. Cooperation with outside agencies in safety activities
        (1) Fire Prevention Week.
        (2) Clean-up Week.

The curriculum in secondary schools provides for the teaching of safety education in various subject matter areas. Related to the fields of business and industry, industrial arts teachers have constantly directed emphasis in the prevention of accidents in school shops. For apparent reasons safety is continually emphasized in hazardous areas such as gymnasiums, athletic fields, swimming pools, science laboratories, lunch rooms, and home economics rooms. In various sections of the nation there is an indication that safety education programs in secondary schools are experiencing a wholesome period of growth. The increasing interest in driver and traffic safety education has been a contributory factor in this development.

APPOINTMENT OF COORDINATOR

In analyzing the school accident-prevention problem and safety-education considerations, the administrator should obtain assistance in determining the administrative policies. There will be a need to select one faculty member who will be given the responsibility for coordinating all phases of the safety and accident prevention program. This can be accomplished by designating a full-time supervisor or a part-time safety coordinator. In the developmental stages of the program provisions should be made to have active participation by all faculty members and students.

ACTIVATING THE PROGRAM

The completed survey and analysis of the school accident problem now provides an opportunity for the principal and the safety committee to begin planning procedures in a direct attempt to obtain effective accident reduction. During the early stages of program development, emphasis should be placed upon a relatively small number of significant activities that will be planned to achieve an early satisfactory result.

A successful outcome will be established by initially alerting the student body, faculty, and community of existing hazards and accident problems to be remedied at the earliest possible opportunity. Public relations at this point becomes an important consideration by the principal. An understanding community can provide many resources that will be of value to the school safety program. Many organizations and agencies in the community will welcome the occasion to assist in various aspects of the program. In addition to the professional societies and civic organizations, there will be individuals having an interest in safety that will desire to give their assistance.

The mass communication media—television, radio, newspapers, and local magazines—can aid by communicating information to the general public. The success of the school and community safety and accident prevention program is largely dependent upon public support.

In appointing committees for specific projects, the principal should advise all members of the faculty and student body of the objectives established and procedures for each activity. A complete understanding throughout the school is essential in obtaining successful results.

In appointing the necessary subcommittees to perform specific functions, the principal should communicate information to all school personnel concerning membership and responsibility for the various assignments. There will be occasions when subcommittees should make inspections of the school plant, classrooms, laboratories, lunch room, swimming pool, gymnasium, playroom, playground, and athletic facilities. The collected data should be analyzed with a follow-up to either eliminate, correct, or compensate for existing hazards.

CORRELATING AND INTEGRATING SAFETY INSTRUCTION WITH SUBJECT MATTER

The integration and correlation of safety instruction with subject matter in the secondary school requires precise planning by a competent teacher. With little exception, every aspect of the school curriculum offers opportunities for a resourceful teacher to utilize teachable moments for safety instruction. If this method is not properly utilized a danger exists of underemphasis of essential safety topics and complete omission by the subject-matter-oriented teacher. The recognized weakness can be eliminated by careful administrative planning and assignment of instructional responsibility to all teachers in the secondary school. The Texas Education Agency Office of Instructional Services developed the following procedure for integrating safety instruction with existing school subjects: [5]

Agriculture: use of gas and electricity; home lighting and heating; safety in garage, yard, and garden; safety practices in agricultural employment; using hand tools on farm and ranch; maintaining personal safety in agricultural pursuits.

Aeronautics: rail, water, and air travel; the pilot and his plane; safe practices in commercial employment; safe practices in industrial employment.

Band: classrooms and auditoriums, school bus safety.

Biology: wounds, control of bleeding, asphyxia, fractures, poisoning, snakes, lunchrooms.

Chemistry: causes of fire, fire extinguishers, gas and electricity, cleaning materials, lighting and heating, use of science laboratories, handling fireworks, industrial employment.

Commercial subjects: safety on the job, handling electrical equipment, cost of accidents in terms of insurance.

English and journalism: identifying poisonous snakes and plants; seashore recreation and enjoyment; fishing, hunting and hiking as year-round sports; courtesy in the classroom or auditorium; community responsibility in fire prevention.

General mathematics: use of accident figures from local hospitals or officials; cost of accidents to individuals; comparison of the cost of accidents to amount spent for their prevention.

General science: fire prevention; sanitation; electricity; gas; bicycling;

[5] Texas Education Agency, Office of Instructional Services, *Safety Education in Secondary Schools,* Bulletin 533 (Austin: The Agency, September, 1952).

transportation by rail, water, and air; school bus safety; the pilot and his plane.

Health education: first aid for wounds, common emergencies, participation in public recreation.

Homemaking: use and care of household equipment; electrical appliances; first aid; handling gas, poisons, use of the family car.

Home room: halls and stairs, classrooms and auditoriums; cafeteria and lunchroom; restrooms; fire prevention; fishing, hunting and hiking; public recreation.

Physical education: physical education activities, swimming and life saving, public recreation in parks and playgrounds, first aid.

Physics: electricity, explosives, small crafts.

Social studies: handling fireworks, public transportation, industrial safety, safe practices in commercial employment, safe practices in agricultural employment.

Support by Community Organizations

A successful secondary school safety program will require active participation and support from community organizations. The following list of community groups should be encouraged to have an active role in the school safety program:

American Red Cross

Police Department

Fire Department

Board of Health

Recreation Department

Common Council

Traffic Commission

Urban and Rural Planning Commission

Parent-Teacher Association

Girl Scouts

Boy Scouts

Civic groups

YM and YWCA

YMHA

Fraternal organizations

Service Clubs

Chamber of Commerce

Community Chest

Schoolboard

Safety Council

Automobile Club

Newspapers

Radio stations

Television

Industrial Safety departments

Labor organizations

Transportation lines

Theaters

Zoning commission

Farm organizations

Evaluating the Safety Education Program

Evaluation of the school safety education program should be a continuous process in which the students, faculty, and community will participate. Effectiveness of the evaluation process will be primarily influenced by the leadership qualities of the school safety committee and principal. Proceeding cooperatively to ascertain the effectiveness derived from the program and determining areas in need of improvement provides a major purpose of evaluation. Information to be used in the counseling and guidance of individual students will also be obtained through program evaluation. Observation of pupil behavior, statistical data relative to accident elimination and reduction, skill tests, written tests, and opinion of teachers constitute means whereby the safety program can be measured in terms of results. The principal should be concerned with students who have graduated to determine the carry-over values of the school safety program. Such evaluation by the principal can be determined through parent-teacher cooperation and contact with local business and industrial organizations. This will further indicate aspects of the school safety and accident prevention program in need of improvement.

REFERENCES

Aaron, J. E., and M. K. Strasser, *Driver and Traffic Safety Education* (New York: Macmillan, 1966).

American Association for Health, Physical Education, and Recreation, *Current Administrative Problems* (Washington, D.C.: The Association, 1960).

Brody, L., and H. J. Stack, *Highway Safety and Driver Education* (Englewood Cliffs, N.J.: Prentice-Hall, 1954).

Florio, A. E., and G. T. Stafford, *Safety Education*, 2nd ed. (New York: McGraw-Hill, 1962).

Halsley, M. N., *Let's Drive Right* (Chicago: Scott, Foresman, 1964).

Kilander, H. F., *School Health Education*, 2nd ed. (New York: Macmillan, 1958).

National Academy of Sciences, *Driving Simulators and Application of Electronics to Highways* (Washington, D.C.: The Academy, 1960).

National Commission on Safety Education, *High School Driver Education—Policies and Practices* (Washington, D.C.: National Education Association, 1950).

——, *Policies and Guidelines for Teacher Preparation and Certification in Driver and Traffic Safety Education* (Washington, D.C.: National Education Association, 1965).

——, *Policies and Practices for Driver Education* (Washington, D.C.: National Education Association, 1954).

——, *Policies and Practices for Driver Education* (Washington, D.C.: National Education Association, 1960).

————, *Policies and Practices for Driver and Traffic Safety Education* (Washington, D.C.: National Education Association, 1964).

————, *Special State Financial Support for Driver Education* (Washington, D.C.: National Education Association, 1963).

————, *A Critical Analysis of Driver Education Research* (Washington, D.C.: National Education Association, 1957).

National Safety Council, *Accident Facts* (Chicago: The Council, published annually).

Sawers, K. T., *Group Discussion Techniques for Driver Education* (New York: New York University, Center for Safety Education, 1961), pp. 23–24.

Smith, L. K., "How You Can Build Public Support for Driver Education," *Safety Education* (April 1964), pp. 25–29.

Stack, H. J., and J. D. Elkow, *Education for Safe Living*, 4th ed. (Englewood Cliffs, N.J.: Prentice-Hall, 1966).

Strasser, M. K., J. E. Aaron, R. C. Bohn, and J. R. Eales, *When You Take the Wheel* (River Forest, Ill.: Laidlaw Brothers, Inc., 1963).

CHAPTER 9   DRIVER AND
TRAFFIC SAFETY
EDUCATION

A review of the motor vehicle's influence on the nation's social and economic development clearly establishes the fact that traffic accidents present a serious national problem. The necessity for developing desirable habits, attitudes, and skills continues to be of paramount importance in consideration of the annual occurrence of traffic accidents. Although traffic-enforcement programs, legislation, and automotive and highway engineering have made recognizable progress, the human element in traffic-accident prevention is of primary concern. Traffic authorities agree that an analysis of traffic-accident causation is attributed to the human factors of undesirable attitudes, insufficient skill, improper attitudes, and insufficient knowledge. The nature of these causes well establishes education as a potent force in approaching a solution to the traffic-accident problem. There is an abundance of evidence that teen-age drivers are in need of an organized instructional program in driver and traffic education.

Since the introduction of the automobile some sixty years ago, more than one million persons have lost their lives in automotive traffic accidents. In this same period, 40 million persons received injuries in vehicular mishaps and 12 million experienced disabling injuries. Further statistical information reveals that one traffic fatality occurs every fourteen minutes as a result of motor vehicle accidents.

The record for motor-vehicle fatalities for any one-year period was 52,300 persons in 1966 as reported by the National Safety Council. The Council also revealed that disabling injuries occurred to 1.9 million others and cost the nation $9.8 billion. Traffic fatalities in 1966 were approximately 7 per cent above 1965, when there were 49,000 fatalities.

In 1966 there were 96.1 million vehicles operated by more than 102 million motor vehicle drivers. During this period a total of 935 billion miles were logged on the nation's highways. Recent statistical data reveals that one half of the nation's population is licensed to drive. Drivers under the age of 25 represented 20.2 per cent of the total, 9.8 per cent were under 20 (teen-agers), and 10.4 per cent were between 20 and 24.[1]

[1] Automotive Safety Foundation, *Teen-Age Driving Facts* (Washington, D.C.: The Foundation, 1966).

Instructors of driver and traffic safety education should be constantly aware of their fundamental responsibilities by adherence to the following principles: [2]

1. The control of traffic accidents represents a problem in this nation of great magnitude related to social, economic, and human factors. Public officials and the general public have a moral and civic responsibility in striving toward a solution of the problem.
2. The physical, mental, and emotional behavioral characteristics of individual drivers are major determining factors in a reduction of traffic accidents.
3. The presence of public apathy resulting from a lack of knowledge related to traffic-accident prevention continues to hinder progress in accident reduction.
4. The need for increased enforcement of motor vehicle laws, driver improvement programs for traffic violators, upgrading of driving licensing procedures, periodic reexamination of all persons having an operator's license, a mandatory periodic vehicle inspection of all registered motor vehicles, and required chemical tests for intoxication.
5. The development of effective school traffic-safety-education programs to be available at the school and community levels.
6. The responsibility for the determination, administration, supervision, and evaluation of school driver- and traffic-safety-education instructional programs be delegated to a School Traffic Safety Education Division in the State Department of Education.
7. The need for a public relations program that will create statewide and national support for traffic accident prevention.

OBJECTIVES

A qualitative course of instruction in driver and traffic safety education should provide the high school student with educational experience that will contribute to the development of habits, attitudes, knowledge, and skill in the safe and efficient control of motor vehicles.

The specific objectives of driver and traffic safety education are herein presented as a foundation upon which to establish a course of instruction that will conform to sound educational procedure.[3]

1. To develop in the student self-confidence and a sense of pride in his ability to drive efficiently and safely.
2. To bring about a reduction in motor vehicle accidents throughout the nation.

[2] State Department of Public Instruction, Indiana, *Driver and Traffic Safety Education—A Guide for Administrators and Teachers,* Bulletin 240, 1960.
[3] *Ibid.*

3. To develop a knowledge and appreciation of motor vehicle traffic laws.
4. To develop efficient drivers that will constantly maintain a sense of civic and social responsibility in the sharing of streets and highways.
5. To stimulate a desire for both interest and participation by operators of motor vehicles in stimulating an improvement of traffic conditions.
6. To recognize the physical limitations which have an effect on driving ability.
7. To be aware that other drivers may have physical limitations of which they have no knowledge.
8. To develop a sensitivity to the potential mistakes and errors that can be anticipated in the behavior of other drivers.
9. To practice defensive driving constantly.

Relationship of Driver and Traffic Safety Education to the Total School Program

In many locations the growth of high school driver and traffic safety education has been motivated by the general public. The relationship between general education and driver and traffic safety education is illustrated in "the seven cardinal principles" of education set forth by the National Education Association. These principles and their relationships to driver and traffic safety education are [4]

1. *Citizenship.* Driver and traffic safety education is directly related to good citizenship, since one of the chief aims of the program is to teach people to express their good citizenship in the proper use of streets and highways.
2. *Health.* Physical, mental, and emotional health are essential to the safe operation of the motor vehicle. Driver and traffic safety education stresses these points in the teaching of approved driver attitudes and the importance to driving of good physical condition and emotional stability.
3. *Ethical Character.* Closely correlated with good citizenship at the wheel is the practice of ethical and courteous manners while driving.
4. *Command of Fundamental Processes.* Educators should place great importance on teaching those things well which will be used throughout a person's lifetime. We can safely assume that a great majority of our students will operate a motor vehicle for many years.
5. *Vocation.* Many people are employed in the motor-transportation industry as a livelihood. Driver and traffic safety education has significant implications for vocational guidance and training programs.
6. *Worthy Home Membership.* Since American families have learned to

[4] *Ibid.*

depend on the automobile for numerous occupational and recreational purposes, the person who can safely and efficiently operate an automobile is usually a more worthy home member. A person who displays desirable attitudes, practices, and habits while driving will tend to display desirable personal qualities in the home.

7. *Worthy Use of Leisure.* Many recreational and social activities are accessible only by automobile. Consequently, the automobile has become almost a necessity in traveling to and from such events. The total educational program strives to teach the worthy, as opposed to the unworthy, use of leisure time. The driver and traffic safety education program can support such learning.

Program Planning Characteristics

All regularly enrolled students in secondary schools should have an opportunity to complete a course of instruction in driver and traffic safety education as a phase of the school's safety education program. This should be scheduled as an integral part of the curriculum with preference to a full semester course.

The total program should include both classroom and laboratory instruction. Students having completed or currently enrolled in the classroom phase will be eligible for practice driving instruction and related laboratory experiences. Only those students having satisfactorily completed the total course of instruction should be encouraged to meet the examination requirements for the driver's license. Students having previously obtained a driver's license should also be required to complete both phases of the course. The driver and traffic safety education course should be made available to students who have vocational opportunities for positions requiring driving experience.[5]

Single-Car Plan

A dual-control car is used for laboratory instruction with one, two three, or four students being assigned to one instructor. The vehicle in this plan serves the purpose of a rolling classroom with all students having an equal opportunity for observation and instruction. With a maximum of four students participating the instructor utilizes teaching techniques that will involve participation in a simultaneous learning process. The in-car instruction should serve as a continuation of the classroom phase where in a small-group process, driver education continues in an effective manner.

[5] National Commission on Safety Education, *Policies and Practices for Driver and Traffic Safety Education* (Washington, D.C.: National Education Association, 1964).

MULTIPLE-CAR DRIVING-RANGE PLAN

This plan has the distinct advantage of providing for a number of cars to follow a prearranged pattern on an off-street location with one or more instructors serving the purposes of supervision and instruction.

The use of multiple-car, off-street ranges for driver education goes back to the early work at Lane Technical School in Chicago and later on in the high schools of Detroit. In recent years there has been a rapid development of the range program—Florida has 72; Michigan 44; and Illinois 35. According to the *19th Annual Report of the Driver Education Achievement Program,* most of the ten states that are leading in the percentage of eligibles trained are making use of ranges, simulators, or both. These leading states are reaching from 70 to 100 per cent of the eligibles while the average for all states is 50 per cent.

According to Williamson of Florida, the Florida plan is unique in several ways:

> Our ranges are quite different from those found in the Detroit area, since we have no permanent curbings, no permanent roadways, but only a paved area, roughly 200 by 400 feet. The size varies in different localities to meet local needs. We feel that our plan is more flexible than one that makes use of permanent curbings. If we wish to change the design, we only have to paint new lines. We make use of portable curbings when these become important. The fact that we have 72 ranges is an indication of our belief in them. We feel that there is no finer way to teach manipulative skills than in an isolated area constructed to simulate the traffic environment. We know that when a range is properly used that the pupil cost is drastically reduced by at least 40 percent and the quality of the program improved.
>
> Ordinarily, under the traditional approach in practice driving, one teacher can reach about 125 students per year. Using the range plan, this number can be increased to several hundred, depending upon the number of cars used.
>
> The cost varies widely. In some cases a parking area is already paved and the cost will be a minimum. In other cases, the city or county assumes some of the cost for grading and labor. We generally follow range instruction with two hours of practice driving in traffic. According to the most recent report of the 19th Annual Driver Education Achievement Program, in the school year 1965–1966, Florida used ranges in instructing 31,000 students, and simulators, 12,349.

Michigan now has sixty-five ranges used in instructing 52,000 students. In its complete program it is able to reach 150,000 students, or 100 per cent of the eligibles. The cost of off-street ranges varies widely. In some cases, they serve as parking areas or for school games and the cost will run under $1,000. In some cases garages are included which increases the costs. Michigan State University has had a model range for many years.

DRIVING SIMULATORS

Electromechanical driving simulators and special films are placed in a laboratory setting to enhance carry-over experiences for the follow-up, in-car instructional program.

Los Angeles is using mobile driving simulators in its high schools. These simulators are heated, air-conditioned, twelve-place units which can be moved from school to school. Mobile units (twelve-place) can be rented at $7,600 a year on a four-year lease-purchase; permanent classroom installations are $5,600 for a four-year lease-purchase. Like the range, simulators greatly increase the number of students that can be trained and are especially useful in large schools.

ADULT AND OUT-OF-SCHOOL-YOUTH PROGRAMS

The high school driver and traffic safety education program may also be extended to include additional instructional offerings for adults and out-of-school youth. Instruction at the beginner's level and specialized advanced classes may be established to meet the existing needs. A program for beginners would be comparable to that of the regular high school students. Specialized programs can be designed for such purposes as driver improvement, senior citizens, retraining for chronic violators, and rehabilitation to assist drivers having various types of disabilities. Advanced programs can be organized for individual desiring to qualify as commercial vehicle drivers and for in-service training for on-the-job employees having driving responsibilities.

COLLEGE PROGRAMS

Driver and traffic safety education courses at the higher education level have been organized by following a variety of procedures that best serve the institution and students. A variety of departments and divisions should be involved in providing enriched programs along with community agencies having the necessary resources. At this level there should be consideration for the possible integration of the program as a phase of general education, as a part of teacher education inclusive of student-teaching experience, or of offering it through the adult or continuing education service programs.

THE ROLE OF THE STATE DEPARTMENT OF EDUCATION

The state Department of Education has the responsibility for providing professional assistance in the general development and progress of driver and traffic safety education in the public schools throughout the state. In a leadership role the state Department of Education is structured to make available program assistance and supervision in the various aspects of the total program.[6]

The state Department of Education encourages local schools by

1. Stimulating thoughtful public interest in driver and traffic safety education at state and local levels.
2. Developing means for utilizing interested individuals and groups in an advisory capacity.
3. Maintaining proper relationships, on the state level, with public and private agencies interested in general highway safety, and in the development of driver education in the school system of the state.
4. Establishing and supporting high standards for driver education at the secondary school level.
5. Stimulating, encouraging, and supervising the establishment of teacher-preparation courses for driver and traffic safety instructors.
6. Developing procedures and standards for certification of high school teachers of driver education and providing leadership in the upgrading of these standards.
7. Developing record and reporting forms for driver education comparable to those for other curriculum subjects in the public schools.
8. Collecting, analyzing, summarizing, and interpreting these reports of driver education activities at the secondary school level.
9. Cooperating with the state driver licensing agency to upgrade driver licensing examinations.
10. Promoting driver education as a prerequisite for licensing.
11. Cooperating with existing agencies' efforts in behalf of the Uniform Vehicle Code.
12. Encouraging and assisting in improving the quality of instruction through such means as
    a. New teaching methods and techniques.
    b. New course organization.
    c. Classroom teaching devices.
    d. Supervision of the efficient and ethical use of dual-control cars.
    e. Placement of driver education on the same status as other subjects in the high school curriculum.
13. Suggesting program modifications as indicated by research findings.
14. Providing every possible financial aid for supporting the driver and traffic safety education programs in the public schools.

The state Department of Public Instruction assists local schools by

1. Helping to develop driver education and traffic safety courses.

[6] State Department of Public Instruction, Indiana, *op. cit.*

2. Supporting the local systems in adoption of such courses.
3. Publishing a course outline or syllabus for driver and traffic safety education.
4. Making available information concerning available text and reference materials.
5. Assisting schools with public relations programs in the interest of driver and traffic safety education.
6. Providing advisory and consulting services to local schools as to
   a. Organization and administration of driver education courses for high school students and for adults.
   b. Teaching methods, techniques, and materials.
   c. Proper methods of obtaining practice cars.
   d. Economical purchase and replacement of school-owned practice cars.
   e. Evaluation of the total driver education program in the school system.
7. Helping with local in-service training programs for driver education instructors.
8. Assisting in establishing a comprehensive library of teaching aids in the field of driver and traffic education.

ORGANIZATION AND ADMINISTRATIVE CONSIDERATIONS

As in all areas of education there are numerous decisions to be made for the inclusion of specific areas of instruction to be placed in the curriculum. The administrator of a secondary school in establishing a driver and traffic safety education course will be concerned with such matters as scheduling, finance, car procurement, teacher selection, and criteria for determining student enrollment. The fact that more than 12,000 high schools now offer driver and traffic safety education courses is an indication that practical solutions can be established in compliance with administrative policy and procedure.

TEACHER QUALIFICATIONS

A successful instructional program in driver and traffic safety education is primarily dependent upon the personality, character, capability, and professional qualifications of the teacher. Outstanding teaching ability should be designated as a number-one priority in selecting teacher personnel for this area. In conformity with the minimum standards as established by the National Commission on Safety Education, of the National Education Association, all teachers employed in either one or both phases (classroom instruction, practice driving instruction) should possess the following listed certification requirements for the teaching of driver and traffic safety education.[7]

1. Possess a bachelor's degree from an accredited institution of higher education.
2. Have a valid teaching certificate for employment in the secondary schools and authorizing the teaching of driver and traffic safety education [based on a total of 12 semester hours in (a) safety education; and (b) driver and traffic safety education].
3. Have physical qualities necessary for teaching in this field as validated by a health certificate.
4. Possess a valid driver's license from the state where employed.
5. Display an outstanding example for others evidenced by a satisfactory driving record.

State departments of education should establish requirements concerning the prospective teacher's driving record as a prerequisite consideration for teaching in this field. An established procedure should be organized to determine the nature of violations, recency and frequency. A definite standard is needed relative to possible suspension of teaching responsibility for an established period of time. Recommended guidelines that can be followed are:[8]

1. For a two-year period immediately prior to employment the beginning teacher should possess a valid driver's license without having any chargeable accidents or a conviction for a moving violation.
2. An automatic suspension of authorization to teach resulting from a conviction for a moving violation causing a revocation or suspension of the driver's license.
3. Where an authorization to teach has been suspended the instructor should be required to give evidence of a driving record with no moving violation convictions or chargeable accidents for two years before reinstatement will be considered.

SPECIAL QUALIFICATIONS FOR SUPERVISORS OF DRIVER AND SAFETY EDUCATION

The responsibility for supervision of school driver and safety education programs should be assigned to a qualified educator. Research studies have revealed that if this phase of the school program is to be effectively organized and administered, the responsibility must be delegated to a supervisor of driver and safety education.[9]

[7] National Commission on Safety Education (1964), op. cit.
[8] Ibid.
[9] James E. Aaron, A Study of Supervisory Practices in Safety Education in Selected Cities in the United States (Dissertation, New York University, 1960).

A supervisor of driver and safety education should qualify by meeting such requirements as

1. Completion of a master's degree with a major in driver and safety education.
2. Previous teaching experience of at least five years in driver and traffic safety education.
3. Possession of a supervisory certificate, if required in the state where employed.
4. Professional affiliation in the American Driver and Traffic Safety Association and the state driver and traffic safety education association.
5. The capability to administer the program efficiently with a constant interest in program development.
6. A personality that is conducive to gaining community and faculty cooperation.

Several alternatives may be considered in delegating supervisory responsibilities with consideration being directed to the size of the school district and then deciding on the best approach, such as (1) a full-time supervisor of driver and safety education; (2) a half-time supervisor of driver and safety education, half-time supervisor of pupil transportation; (3) half-time supervisor, half-time driver and traffic education instructor; or (4) one-third-time supervisor, two-thirds-time teacher of driver and traffic safety education.

TEACHER PREPARATION

The state of Indiana in a guide developed for administrators and teachers (Bulletin 240) indicates that teacher qualification plans should include preparation in the three following major areas of safety education: [10]

1. Driver Education.
   a. Basic driver education.
   b. Advanced driver education.
   c. Problem-solving in driver education.
   d. Seminar in driver education.
   e. Research in driver education.
   f. Tests and measurements in driver education.
2. Traffic Safety Education.
   a. Traffic regulation and control.
   b. Fleet safety supervision.
   c. Highway transportation problems.
   d. General traffic engineering.

[10] State Department of Public Instruction, Indiana, *op. cit.*

  e. Highway safety and traffic control.
  f. Thesis problems and research.
3. General Safety Education.
  a. Psychology of the accident prevention problem.
  b. Methods and materials course in safety.
  c. Organization and administration of safety education.
  d. Supervision problems of safety in the elementary schools.
  e. Industrial accident prevention.
  f. School shop safety.
  g. First aid.
  h. Fire prevention.
  i. Safety and human conservation.
  j. Safety engineering.
  k. Recreation and safety.
  l. Accident investigation.
  m. Intersection traffic control.
  n. Traffic administration and enforcement.
  o. Supervision and safety education.
  p. Safety education and safety equipment and practices on the playground.

SELECTION OF STUDENTS

All high school students having reached the qualifying age for obtaining a legal driver education or beginner's permit should be given the opportunity to enroll in the driver and traffic safety education class. Students who have previously received an operator's license should also be considered for selection. Frequently the licensed, nontrained teen-age driver is desperately in need of an organized course of instruction with a competent driver education instructor. Classroom instruction should be required of all students prior to graduation. The administrator may have to limit the number of students desiring to receive practice driving instruction because of limited facilities and the number of students that an instructor can effectively accommodate in a one-semester course. Criteria for selection of students may be established by considering those students having a special need such as vocational placement, immediacy of graduation, a means of transportation to and from school, availability of an automobile, and similar reasons as substantiated by the parents.

The instructor should arrange groupings for practice driving instruction with due consideration being given to factors of sex, comprehension ability, chronological age, previous training, experience, and physical, mental, and emotional stability. Proper student grouping for the practice driving phase is imperative to assure that each student will receive a significant learning experience, including time in the car as an observer.

Minimum Recommended Time Standards

A complete high school course of instruction in driver education should consist of forty-five to sixty clock hours. Within this period of time there should be a provision for each student to have no less than thirty hours of classroom instruction and at least six hours of practice driving instruction, exclusive of time in the car as an observer. Class hours should be interpreted on the basis of sixty minutes each or a composite equivalent total. Variations in time standards will be necessary so that individual student differences and special problems can be considered.

Class periods in individual secondary schools may vary in length from forty to sixty minutes. The following illustration is a guide to display the minimum recommended time standards when there is variation in class periods.[11]

To provide a minimum of thirty clock hours for each student in the classroom phase, check Table 9-1.

TABLE 9-1

Minutes Per Class Period	Minimum Number of Sessions for 30 Classroom Hours
40	45
45	40
50	36
55	33
60	30

To provide a minimum of six clock hours for each student in the practice driving phase, check Table 9-2.

TABLE 9-2

Minutes Per Class Period	Minimum Number of Sessions for Six Clock Hours		
	2 Pupils	3 Pupils	4 Pupils
40	18	27	36
45	16	24	32
50	15	22	29
55	14	20	27
60	12	18	24

The total driver education program is in most locations scheduled over one full semester consisting of eighteen weeks. If the program is to be offered during the summer months the same standards should be met

[11] *Ibid.*

in a concentrated period as indicated above. A summer program should be scheduled to last no less than six weeks.

SCHEDULING

Several different systems are used in scheduling classes for driver and traffic safety education in high schools. Each administrator must apply sound judgment in fitting driver education into the school curriculum. In attempting to place the course into the school program the following consideration should be taken into account.[12]

1. The number of students and how they are to be accommodated.
2. The number of weeks needed to complete the course.
3. The amount of time to be alloted to classroom instruction and practice driving.
4. The number of qualified teachers available.
5. The availability of dual-control cars.

Students will be selected as the principal indicates, from

1. Free periods.
2. Study halls.
3. Library periods.
4. Regularly assigned driver education classes.

TABLE 9-3
SAMPLE SCHEDULE FOR THIRTY-SIX STUDENT CLASS

PERIOD OF SCHOOL DAY	M	T	W	Th	F	M	T	W	Th	F	M	T	W	Th	F
I Classroom	C		C		C	C		C		C	C		C		C
II Driving	1	2	3	1	2	3	1	2	3	1	2	3	1	2	3
III Driving	4	5	6	4	5	6	4	5	6	4	5	6	4	5	6
IV Driving	7	8	9	7	8	9	7	8	9	7	8	9	7	8	9

TABLE 9-4
SINGLE-PERIOD SAMPLE SCHEDULE
(9 Student Class)

	WEEKS OF SEMESTER																	
	1	2	3	4	5	6	7	8	9	10	11	12	13	14	15	16	17	18
Mon.	C	C	1	2	3	1	2	3	1	2	3	1	2	3	1	2	3	C
Tues.	C	C	C	C	C	C	C	C	C	C	C	C	C	C	C	C	C	C
Wed.	C	C	2	3	1	2	3	1	2	3	1	2	3	1	2	3	1	C
Thurs.	C	C	3	1	2	3	1	2	3	1	2	3	1	2	3	1	2	C
Fri.	C	C	1	2	3	1	2	3	1	2	3	1	2	3	1	2	3	C

[12] *Ibid.*

In this schedule, the class consists of thirty-six students who meet collectively for classroom instruction but are divided into nine groups of four students each for practice driving. Refer to Table 9-1 and Table 9-2 for requirements to complete an eighteen-week semester.

In this schedule, the class consists of nine students, three driving groups of three students each. Each student will receive 30 classroom hours in instruction, six and two-third hours behind-the-wheel instruction, and thirteen and one-third hours of observation time.

TABLE 9-5
SINGLE PERIOD SAMPLE SCHEDULE
(12 Students)

WEEKS OF SEMESTER

	1	2	3	4	5	6	7	8	9	10	11	12	13	14	15	16	17	18
Mon.	C	C	1	1	1	1	1	1	1	1	1	1	1	1	1	1	1	C
Tues.	C	C	C	C	C	C	C	C	C	C	C	C	C	C	C	C	C	C
Wed.	C	C	2	2	2	2	2	2	2	2	2	2	2	2	2	2	2	C
Thurs.	C	C	3	3	3	3	3	3	3	3	3	3	3	3	3	3	3	3
Fri.	C	C	4	4	4	4	4	4	4	4	4	4	4	4	4	4	4	C

In this schedule, the class consists of 12 students, four driving groups of three students each. Each student will receive 30 classroom hours of instruction, five hours of behind-the-wheel instruction to be supplemented by one additional driving instruction hour. This extra hour, or more, may be obtained by the utilization of study periods and outside school hours.

SUGGESTED SUMMER SCHEDULE FOR DRIVER EDUCATION

In the following eight-week schedule, "C" indicates classroom instruction for twenty-one pupils. Each number (1-2-3-4-5-6-7) indicates a driving group of three pupils. Seven driving groups of three pupils each provide for a total enrollment of twenty-one pupils.

Week		M	T	W	T	F	M	T	W	T	F	M	T	W	T	F
1-2-3	8:00– 9:00	C	4	C	4	C	C	7	C	7	C	C	3	C	3	C
	9:00–10:00	1	5	1	5	1	4	1	4	1	4	7	4	7	4	7
	10:00–11:00	2	6	2	6	2	5	2	5	2	5	1	5	1	5	1
	11:00–12:00	3	7	3	7	3	6	3	6	3	6	2	6	2	6	2
Week																
4-5-6	8:00– 9:00	C	6	C	6	C	C	2	C	2	C	C	5	C	5	C
	9:00–10:00	3	7	3	7	3	6	4	6	4	6	2	6	2	6	2
	10:00–11:00	4	1	4	1	4	7	4	7	4	7	3	7	3	7	3
	11:00–12:00	5	2	5	2	5	1	5	1	5	1	4	1	4	1	4

Week
7–8	8:00– 9:00	C	1	C	1	C		C	4	C	4	C
	9:00–10:00	5	C	5	C	5		1	5	1	5	C
	10:00–11:00	6	C	6	C	6		C	6	C	6	C
	11:00–12:00	7	4	7	4	7		C	7	C	7	C

When credit is given, driver education should be scheduled as a one-credit course. The minimum summer term is forty days at two hours per day, or eighty hours. Minimum time for earning one credit hour is seventy-three clock hours of instruction, with the understanding that each student must spend adequate time in preparation.

If the teacher is scheduled for a four-hour day and the course extends over an eight-week (forty-day) period, up to twenty-one pupils may be scheduled for the course.

All pupils attend class every Monday, Wednesday, and Friday at eight o'clock and from 8 to 12 on the last Friday. Each driving group, by rotation, drives in the automobile as indicated by the numbers. To understand the schedule, let us follow Group 1 for the first two weeks. The members of Group 1 go to class Monday, Wednesday, and Friday of the first week at eight o'clock and drive at nine o'clock on the same days. The second week, Group 1 goes to class Monday, Wednesday, Thursday only. Now, in the first week, these pupils must report for supervised study on Monday, Wednesday, and Friday at nine o'clock and on Tuesday and Thursday at eight o'clock.

Every group follows a similar schedule according to pattern. During the periods a pupil is having supervised study, he will be in the library or study hall working on assignments. The class will use a textbook, teaching aids, workbooks, and other materials just as in a full semester course. Pupils will report to the teacher at the next class session following the completion of the assignment.

The suggested schedule provides the following fifty-five-minute periods for all pupils: class periods, 27; supervised study, 36; in-the-car, 19; total, 82.

The practice driving provides six and one-third hours behind the wheel and twelve and two-thirds hours of observation.

Credit should be one-half unit or one credit. The administrator will need to provide supervision for the hours that students are not attending class or driving, so that they will have two hours daily attendance for the eight-week (40-day) period.

CREDIT. Credit for driver and traffic safety education should be given only upon satisfactory completion of a course which meets the standards prescribed by the state Department of Education. The National Commission on Safety Education of the National Education Association recommends that driver and traffic safety education should be assigned credit contributing toward high school graduation. The state Department of Education recognizes this credit standard also when it meets the regular standards of credit courses. State-recommended standards include a minimum of thirty hours of classroom instruction and six hours of supervised practice driving instruction for each pupil.

CAR PROCUREMENT. The car used for student practice driving must be equipped with dual controls. Four methods by which an administrator may obtain a practice driving automobile are

1. Loan.
2. Rental.
3. Direct purchase.
4. Procurement of a war surplus car.

The most inexpensive method is the loan method. When this method is used, the car should be used only for instructional purposes in the driver education program. All the forms needed to complete such a loan transaction with the sponsoring car dealer are provided by the area motor clubs and the Division of School Traffic Safety Education of the State Department of Education.

The direct purchase method may have an advantage over other methods in that it provides for school ownership of the car. If the car should be used for other purposes, the driver education decal should not be displayed. It should be understood that the requirements of the driver and traffic safety education course take priority over any activity in the use of the automobile and scheduling for other activities should be done with the realization of the car's primary purpose. Under this system, a complete record of the use of the car should be maintained.

A war surplus car can sometimes be obtained through the state Agency for Surplus Property. Low initial cost for the automobile is the main advantage of procuring a car by this method. The disadvantage of this method is high renovation and maintenance costs since the car undoubtedly will have had prior use.

The rental plan gives the same advantage as the direct purchase plan, but the cost of obtaining the car must be met every year. On a long-term basis, therefore, the rental plan may prove to be more expensive than the direct purchase plan.

The type of dual-control mechanism purchased and installed will be determined by the type of car used. Usually dual controls for both standard-shift cars and automatic-transmission cars must be purchased every year to model specifications. The new hydraulic-cylinder brake for use in automatic-transmission cars, however, can be transferred to any model of car that has an automatic transmission. This type of dual control also has a cut-off switch which helps car control. Normally the high school auto shop can install this type of dual control in a few hours.

The usual cost of mechanical dual controls is about $25, plus installation charge. The cost of the hydraulic-cylinder controls is $40, plus installation cost.

Today, the two-car family is rapidly becoming the rule rather than the exception. In all probability one of the two cars will be an economy model equipped with a standard transmission. The ever-increasing number of foreign cars has further increased the number of standard-transmission cars in use today. In light of these facts, the school administrator and instructor should plan the training program to include practice driving in both standard and automatic-transmission automobiles.

INSURANCE AND LIABILITY. Because of the hazards of using an automobile on streets and highways, adequate public liability and property damage liability insurance coverage for the driver-education car is necessary for the school, the instructor, and the student. The purpose of such insurance is to protect such persons from claims for property damages, personal injury, or death arising out of the negligent or reckless use of a motor vehicle. Claims for negligence in court actions could be brought by any member of the general public, or by a passenger in the car, against the driver-education instructor, student operator, or such other persons who are legally responsible for the proper care, maintenance, and use of the vehicle, including the school administrator and the Board of Education. The Board of Education is responsible for making such insurance protection available to protect such persons against whom suits might be brought. It is suggested that such public liability and property damage coverage be extended to cover and protect the Board of Education, the school administrator, and the driver education instructor.

Generally speaking, negligence or recklessness is the exercise of a lack of due care in the operation of a motor vehicle. It might well be, in a particular case, that an error on the part of a student driver could be designated as a lack of due care on the part of the instructor or on the part of those under whose authority he acts.

Suggested coverage for the driver education car would include—but should not be less than—public liability of $100,000 to $300,000, and property damage of $10,000 to $20,000 with a $2,000 medical payment rider. Comprehensive coverage and collision protection would be an optional part of the total coverage.

The policy should specifically provide that the Board of Education, the administrator, the driver education instructor, and the students while they are behind the wheel of a dual-control car under the supervision of the driver education instructor are covered. It is not necessary to designate such persons by their individual names in such policies, but it is necessary to designate them by their class, type, or position held.[13]

[13] National Commission on Safety Education (1964), *op. cit.*

COMMUNITY RELATIONS

The role of community relations in driver and traffic safety education in the secondary schools is threefold. The purpose is to convince the school personnel, the student, and the community of the practical value of the course. One of the objectives of driver and traffic safety education is to promote good social adjustment by assisting people to learn how to stay alive in traffic and to keep others alive also.

Three groups must be considered in the development of the community relations program. They are the school personnel, the student, and the community. There is a different objective to be reached in each of these groups and many methods can be used to reach these objectives.

1. The School Personnel
   a. Objective: To improve the status of the program.
   b. Methods of reaching objective
      (1) Explain the program at teachers' meetings, before the school boards and school administrators.
      (2) Encourage all school personnel to observe films, practice-driving demonstrations, and classroom activities.
      (3) Invite staff members to take part in the overall planning.
      (4) Inform faculty, school administrator, and board members of progress being made.

2. The Student
   a. Objective: To develop interest.
   b. Methods of reaching objective
      (1) Documentary brochures, pamphlets, and displays.
      (2) Films about driver education shown in school assemblies.
      (3) Resource visitors.
      (4) Surveys.
      (5) Program publicity published through various school media.
      (6) Field trips.
      (7) Cocurricular activities.
      (8) Informative checklists and letters to parents.

3. The Community
   a. Objective: To obtain public acceptance of the program.
   b. Methods of reaching objective
      (1) School publications.
      (2) Local news media.
      (3) Parent-teacher meetings.
      (4) Photographic exhibits.
      (5) Parent-pupil gatherings.
      (6) Speakers' bureau.
      (7) Merchants' Association window displays.

(8) Community calendars.
(9) Civic meetings and luncheons.
(10) Local theaters.
(11) By having parents and key persons in the community ride in the car with student.

FINANCIAL SUPPORT FOR DRIVER AND TRAFFIC SAFETY EDUCATION

In 1966 the National Commission on Safety Education of the National Education Association made available a publication presenting a current status report devoted to financial assistance by the states, methods whereby funds are appropriated and disseminated, and suggestions for the preparation of legislative considerations at the state level. Significant legislative questions were raised such as [14]

1. In the initial planning for state financial assistance are all of the related groups included? This would give recognition to the state driver and traffic safety associations, state school boards associations, state departments of education, associations of school administrators, and state education associations.
2. Are nonschool groups having an interest in driver education and the prevention of traffic accidents included? The support for legislative proposals will be of concern to automobile clubs, youth organizations, safety councils, civic and service clubs, parents, business, rural, labor, professional, and religious groups. Interpretation to the public and legislative authorities will be necessary for a successful outcome.
3. Will the "legislative appeal" be consistent with how a new law can be understood and enforced?
4. Will legal counsel be procured to make certain that legislative proposals contain accurate terminology?
5. Do the legislative proposals conform with the state's procedure for consideration of funds to support new programs?
6. Are the long-range goals related to public education considered so as to eliminate undesirable effects of rapidly prepared legislation to expedite obtaining funds?
7. Are the legislative requests designed with due consideration to the circumstances and special needs of the state?
8. Is there a legislative information service that can assist so that all mutual interests in the proposed bill can be aware of progress through the legislative procedures, compromise desired, and can rapidly modify the text where necessary?

[14] National Commission on Safety Education, *State Financial Support for Driver and Traffic Safety Education* (Washington, D.C.: National Education Association, 1966).

9. Is there a practical plan established to enhance implementing the new program at an appropriate time?

Essentially there are two methods used by the various states for defraying the costs in administering a secondary school driver and traffic-safety education program. In some states the subject is considered as an integral phase of the curriculum in the secondary school comparable to all other subjects being offered with the instructional costs being included in the total budget. Where this method is predominant it may be concluded that all people in the local school district and state provide the finances for payment of the course.

An additional technique provides for driver and traffic safety education to be classified as a special curricular subject requiring a specific method of finance through state aid. Thirty states and the District of Columbia adhere to this procedure with variations in the procurement of special funds.[15] In these states there is a division into four subgroups utilizing one or more of the following techniques to obtain special funds that will be allocated to the various local school districts:

1. General state funds allocating an appropriation.
2. Driver license fees and funds made available from vehicle registrations.
3. Fees from learner permits.
4. Fines payed by traffic violators.

In comparison with the first method for obtaining funds to support the driver and traffic-safety education program, ultimately in the second method all people contribute financially either as vehicle owners, licensed operators, learners, or as traffic violators. Recently federal funds have been made available to states and school systems complying with approved standards and having noteworthy programs of instruction.

EXPANDING HORIZONS OF A NEW PROFESSION

The historical development of secondary school driver and traffic safety education has progressed with phenomenal growth. From the inception of this program in the nation's schools there was an obvious need that motivated numerous organizations and agencies to provide ingredients and cooperative assistance. Throughout this development, problems have arisen related to teacher-preparation, certification, facilities, academic recognition, finance, and status in the instructional program.

In the preparation of leadership particularly related to the "three E's" of traffic safety, the Traffic Institute at Northwestern University,

[15] *Ibid.*

The Bureau of Highway Traffic at Yale University, and The Center for Safety Education at New York University provided a major impetus to the movement. At New York University and Pennsylvania State University some of the pioneer teacher-preparatory courses in driver and traffic safety education were initially offered. The Association of Casualty and Surety Companies, the National Education Association, the American Automobile Association, and various state education agencies and bureaus of motor vehicles contributed extensively in the teacher preparatory programs to prepare qualified instructional personnel for the new profession.[16] In recent years the American Driver and Traffic Safety Education and the American Association for Health, Physical Education, and Recreation have provided sources of significant assistance and leadership.

The expanding horizon continues with the addition each year of colleges and universities throughout the nation including this discipline in their programs of academic studies. Similarly, secondary schools continue to add and expand the driver and safety education programs periodically. Numerous accomplishments both quantitatively and qualitatively must be achieved in a concentrated effort to eliminate, wherever possible, and to minimize and control the traffic accident and injury problem.

REFERENCES

Aaron, J. E., and M. K. Strasser, *Driver and Traffic Safety Education* (New York: Macmillan, 1966).

Dunbar, Flanders, and Leon Brody, *The Psychology of Safety* (New York: Center for Safety Education, New York University, 1959).

Florio, A. E., and G. T. Stafford, *Safety Education*, 2nd ed. (New York: McGraw-Hill, 1962).

Hilgard, Ernest R., *Theories of Learning* (New York: Appleton-Century-Crofts, 1956).

Leonard, J. Paul, *Developing the Secondary School Curriculum* (New York: Holt, Rinehart & Winston, 1953).

Loft, Bernard I., "Positive Approach to Safety," *Journal of Health, Physical Education, and Recreation* (May 1961), pp. 34–35.

Russell, Emerson, "What to Teach When," *Safety Education* (October 1960), p. 6.

Sawers, Kenneth, *Group Discussion Techniques for Driver Education* (New York: Center for Safety Education, New York University, 1961).

[16] Leon Brody and Herbert J. Stack, *Highway Safety and Driver Education* (Englewood Cliffs, N.J.: Prentice-Hall, 1954).

Stack, Herbert J., ed., *Safety for Greater Adventures* (New York: Center for Safety Education, New York University, 1953).

Strasser, M. K., James E. Aaron, Ralph C. Bohn, and John R. Eales, *Fundamentals of Safety Education* (New York: Macmillan, 1964).

Wiles, Kimball, *Supervision for Better Schools* (Englewood Cliffs, N.J.: Prentice-Hall, 1961).

Wood, Donald, "Co-Curricular Safety Activities in Secondary Schools," *Safety Education* (December 1958), pp. 8–10.

CHAPTER 10 SCHOOL BUS TRANSPORTATION

School bus transportation in the United States is "big business" and more than likely will continue to expand because of school consolidation and the tremendously increasing school population. The large number of vehicles and congestion found on roads and highways presents a safety problem in the administration of school bus transportation. More than 12 million students depend on this type of transportation in the United States. In most states one out of every four students is transported to school by bus. An approximate cost of $410 million is spent annually for the 190,000 buses that travel on the nation's roads 1.3 billon miles each year.[1] Even though the safety record in school bus transportation is commendable there is a need for constant improvement to increase efficiency and decrease the potentiality of accidents.

Transportation of students when properly administered represents a highly significant phase in providing a thorough educational program for youth attending the nation's schools. The increasing number of vehicles and the resulting congestion on roadways present a problem in school bus transportation from the standpoint of safety and accident prevention.

ORGANIZATION OF THE SCHOOL BUS PROGRAM

School buses are a safe and efficient method of transportation when parents, school administrators, teachers, city and state officials, the pupils, the public, and law enforcement agencies have a complete understanding of all aspects in organizing a school bus program and offer their cooperation in the conduct of a successful program.

The following procedures represent basic considerations for the organization and implementation of the school bus transportation program.

1. Use of efficient business methods in maintaining high standards in the selection of buses to comply with state and national specifications. This would apply regardless of whether the buses were purchased outright or contracted. Efficient business methods also include keeping

[1] Herbert J. Stack and J. Duke Elkow, *Education for Safe Living*, 4th ed. (Englewood Cliffs, N.J.: Prentice-Hall, 1966).

accurate records on drivers, equipment, routes, violations, accidents, commendations, and complaints.
2. Selection, inspection, and maintenance of equipment.
3. Establishment and supervision of transportation areas, routes, and stops.
4. Selection, education, and placement of the drivers.
5. Education of the pupil in safe transportation practices.

In organizing a school bus transportation program there is no place for laxity on the part of the responsible, designated school officials as "a pupil transportation operation that runs itself soon will develop into a costly and dangerous adventure."[2]

DRIVER SCREENING — SELECTION AND PLACEMENT

The man who drives a bus load of children to school every day, in all kinds of hazardous highway and weather conditions, is charged with grave responsibility. Together with a ship's captain, or an airline pilot, precious human lives depend upon his experience, skill, and judgment. Yet, despite the increasing dangers of highway travel, many communities pay minimum attention to the dependability of their school bus drivers.[3]

It is a vital responsibility, however, and the operators of school buses are discharging their duties capably. This is in part because of improvements in construction, development of supplementary materials and equipment, and the maintenance of school buses. However, the most significant factor has been the improvement in the selection and education of operators.[4] Established criteria for the selection instruction and supervision of school bus drivers are of paramount importance.

The primary steps in obtaining qualified drivers is the establishment of rigid standards which should include the following items.

1. *Age.* Every state has laws regarding the minimum age in qualifying for a motor-vehicle operator's license. In some instances, a higher age is required in chauffeuring a school bus. Also, a maximum age should be considered.
2. *Character.* This should include elements of reliability, dependability, honesty, initiative, desire to cooperate.
3. *Emotional Stability.* Factors of patience, temperament, calmness, and understanding.

[2] Herbert J. Stack and J. Duke Elkow, *Education for Safe Living*, 3d ed. (Englewood Cliffs, N.J.: Prentice-Hall, 1957).
[3] Paul W. Kearney, "Who Drives Your School Bus?" *Safety Education* (March, 1954).
[4] Leon Brody and Herbert J. Stack, *Highway Safety and Driver Education* (Englewood Cliffs, N.J.: Prentice-Hall, 1954).

4. *Physical Fitness.* Strength, normal use of limbs, freedom from disease, mental illness, adequate and proper visual acuity, field of vision, depth perception, and hearing. The driver should be able to pass a rigid physical examination by a medical doctor.
5. *Knowledge and Skill Requirements.* Should know all local and state vehicle regulations and be able to perform satisfactorily behind the wheel in all situations which would arise in carrying out his duties.
6. *Experience and Certificates.* Should possess at least three years' experience and be free of violations and chargeable accidents. Should also meet any certificated standards set up for school bus drivers by the state or other accrediting agencies.[5]

In addition to the previously mentioned standards, competency in first aid must be considered as a prerequisite for a driver in school bus transportation. All motor vehicles, especially a school bus, should be equipped with an emergency first-aid kit and a driver possessing both skill and knowledge in administering first aid. The school bus driver should assume responsibility for keeping the first-aid kit adequately supplied with all necessary emergency equipment and fresh materials.

INSTRUCTION FOR SCHOOL BUS DRIVERS

Every new driver should be required to satisfactorily complete a basic course of instruction before being assigned to the duties involved in transporting students. In this job classification the driver must possess desirable habits, attitudes, knowledge, and skill to assure safe and efficient transportation for students. The program of instruction will depend upon the capability and previous experience of personnel being considered for employment. Recommendations for a complete instructional program are contained in the National Commission on Safety Education publication, "Selection, Instruction, and Supervision of School Bus Drivers, 1965." In essence the basic course should follow a pattern that includes classroom instruction with emphasis on such topics as

1. Policies and procedures.
2. Traffic accident problems.
3. Human considerations in driving.
4. Natural laws and their relationship to driving.
5. Traffic rules and regulations.
6. A job analysis for the school bus driver.
7. Responding to emergency driving situations and providing first aid to injured passengers.

[5] National Commission on Safety Education, *Selection, Instruction, and Supervision of School Bus Drivers* (Washington, D.C.: The Commission, 1961).

8. Proper care and maintenance of the school bus.
9. Record keeping and required reports.

Practice driving instruction in the bus should emphasize

1. Basic driving skills that would include experiences in starting the engine, shifting to gear ratios, stopping, starting, turning, backing, and parking the bus.
2. Road training in traffic that will include a variety of situations requiring the application of defensive driving techniques. Length of the training program will depend upon individual needs of the driver.

Continuing education programs for school bus drivers should be planned and scheduled in advance as a phase of the total instructional program. This arrangement would provide for

1. Regular monthly meetings.
2. Meetings designated to consider special problems.
3. Literature and pertinent instructional information.
4. Liaison between the transportation supervisor and individual sessions with bus drivers.
5. Periodic recognition meetings to present awards for outstanding accident-free driving records.
6. Keeping the public informed concerning the efforts to increase the efficiency in school bus transportation by sponsoring driver education.

School Transportation Supervisors

To administer an effective school bus transportation program there is a need for employing a qualified supervisor. Providing leadership and guidance at the local level will be a primary determining factor in the success to be achieved in transporting the students. The supervisor should have competencies and knowledge that would include

1. Selection, screening, and driver instruction.
2. Routing and scheduling methods.
3. Standards and specifications for school buses.
4. Maintenance and vehicle function.
5. Accident investigation and analysis.
6. Procedures for purchasing school buses.
7. Problems encountered in traffic and transportation.
8. Coordinating with all school personnel to obtain cooperation for the school bus transportation program.

In some states the institutions of higher learning are offering workshops and short courses for school transportation supervisors in cooperation with the state Department of Education. These programs have assisted considerably in improving the school bus program. In the performance of his responsibilities the supervisor is in need of special preparation to equip him with the knowledge and skill to function efficiently. There is a need for additional colleges to include in-service training, workshops, and institutes for school bus transportation supervisors.

LEGAL CONSIDERATIONS AND SCHOOL BUS SPECIFICATIONS

LEGAL LIABILITY

The legal aspect of school bus transportation is an important factor not only to the bus driver, but to all persons involved in the administration of the school. In certain instances the driver will be directly involved, but the school board can also be responsible for specific legal liabilities.

Contributory negligence appears to be the most common charge brought against both bus drivers and students. The matter of contributory negligence may be related to the student either on or off the school bus. In some cases, negligence may include a third party and not involve the student in any manner. Negligence cases are handled with precision in considering all details involved in the case.

In a case, *Taylor* v. *Cobble* (Court of Appeals, 1945), the bus driver overran his usual stop. At the time he stopped, the door of the bus was open and a girl was thrown out of the bus, which led to injuries of the abdomen. The court ruled that the driver was negligent. It ruled that if the door of the bus had been shut, there would have been no occurrence of injury.

The following are specific cases where injuries occurred while a bus was moving. In the case of *Eason* v. *Crews* (Court of Appeals, 1953) a girl lost the sight of one eye when she was struck by a tree limb through an open window of a bus. The court ruled that the driver was negligent because it was his duty to either close the windows or to instruct the students of the hazards involved while windows are open. In another case, *Maley* v. *Children Bus Service* (Supreme Court, 1953), a girl lost the sight of one eye as a result of harmful play with sharp objects while the bus was in motion. The court ruled that the driver was negligent because this behavior could have been stopped before any problem was created. Also, the driver made no effort to take action or to exercise ordinary care.[6]

Another case which involved a third party—*Tilton* v. *Hansley*—concerned a situation where negligence resulted in a collision with another vehicle. This case involved Tilton, a bus driver, and Hansley, a motorist.

---

[6] H. H. Prinke, "Care, Injury, and Tort Liability in Pupil Transportation," *American School Board Journal* (October, 1955).

Tilton was driving along the highway at night with an empty school bus. Simultaneously, Hansley was approaching Tilton while passing over a bridge. Tilton did not have proper lights on the bus, which was 95 inches wide. Hansley, not anticipating the width of the bus, collided head on and was killed. The court ruled that Tilton was negligent because he did not check the electrical system of the bus prior to the trip. The court also made the point that the school board was responsible because it had not had the equipment checked properly.

In most cases dealing with the question of contributory negligence, it appears that the bus driver will usually be in a vulnerable position. The courts decide whether the responsibility is related to the nature of the driver's job or the circumstances prevailing on a given occasion.

SCHOOL BUS STANDARDS AND SPECIFICATIONS

Beginning in 1939, an initial National Conference charged with the responsibility to establish school bus standards, a series of objectives and guiding principles have served as a basis for the formulation of minimum standards applied to school buses.[7]

The objectives are essentially directed to safety and economy considerations. Safety includes those aspects providing for school bus construction which may have a direct or indirect bearing on transporting students in a safe and efficient manner. Economy is primarily concerned with the construction, procurement, mechanical efficiency, and maintenance at the minimum cost in keeping with the safety and welfare of students.

In the selection and purchase of efficient transportation equipment the national conferences on school bus standards have made available guiding principles to assist school administrators with technically accurate information.[8] The following eight principles should serve as guideposts for making decisions in keeping with the minimum standards.

1. Uniform state school bus standards should be applied in
    a. Conforming with the established objectives for safety and economy in the transportation of students.
    b. Eliminating the production of school buses considered to be unsafe.
    c. Minimizing the preparation of conflicting standards wherever possible among states in view of efficient production and economy of costs.
    d. Establishing exact dimensions as a means of increasing efficiency in mass production.

[7] National Commission on Safety Education, *Minimum Standards for School Buses* (Washington, D.C.: The Commission, 1964).
[8] *Ibid.*

e. Eliminating unnecessary luxury equipment to a degree consistent with safety and efficiency in the transportation of students.

2. Any modification of the nationally recommended minimum standards that is made at the state level in conformity with local interests may be considered only when the adjustments do not

    a. Enter into conflict with the fundamental recommended national minimum standards.

    b. Contribute to an undue increase in production costs.

3. Uniform state school bus standards should clearly indicate the desired safety and economy results, and specifications for efficient performance be stated when necessary in the enforcement of regulations.

4. Through cooperation among the states there should be a periodic evaluation and when necessary a revision of uniform state standards.

5. The use of new inventions and improvements should be made possible through the uniform state standards for school buses when the innovations are in conformity with safety and economy measures.

6. Construction of school buses as stipulated in the uniform state standards should provide for flexibility taking into consideration safety and economy within the limits of efficient construction to coordinate with the school bus manufacturing industry.

7. The uniform state standards for school bus construction should recognize that the engineering design for school buses is the manufacturers' responsibility.

8. The current revised minimum standards for school buses are considered presently in effect as recommendations and guidelines to serve the states. Future revisions of the current standards will be considered only when evidence is apparent that there is a need for modification.

FINANCE

COSTS OF THE SCHOOL BUS PROGRAM

In the past ten years school bus transportation has considerably increased as a result of an expanding population, and the trend in school consolidation. In many school districts students are confronted with greater distances to be traveled on school buses. The program of school bus transportation is of primary concern in the budgetary requirements for school systems throughout the nation.

Efficiency in school bus transportation requires numerous costs relative to equipment, maintenance, and personnel. Frequently job classifications are established as:

Director of Transportation

Area Supervisor
Mechanic
Body Repair Technician
Stock Clerk
Secretary

The maintenance program includes a complete preventive and repair department that will function in keeping the equipment in efficient condition for daily use.

School buses are usually purchased after receiving a prescribed number of bids as established by the school board or a designated administrative unit. This purchase frequently represents the largest single expenditure of funds to be considered by a school system. Members of the school board should be familiar with recommended procedures before making such purchases.[9]

1. School buses should be purchased on cooperative bids filed on detail specifications.
2. Old buses can sometimes be sold outright to better advantage rather than traded in on the purchase of new equipment.
3. A long-term purchasing plan should be adopted so the school board will not be called upon to purchase several buses in one year.
4. School boards believe there is little difference in the quality of approved bus bodies if they are bought to some clear-cut specifications.
5. If the bus is to be used for other activities, such as transportation of athletic teams or musical groups, extra room should be considered between seats.
6. Many times, boards buy a school bus chassis that is too small. This will cause more labor for the motor and therefore raise the expense of operating the bus.
7. Cost per pupil is less for transportation with seating capacities of 48, 54, and 60 than it is for smaller vehicles.

RELATED ASPECTS OF THE SCHOOL BUS PROGRAM

ROUTING AND SCHEDULING

Planning bus routes for enlarged school districts requires a comprehensive study with regard to each item contributing to safety and efficiency. This school-community responsibility represents a large expen-

[9] R. H. Paradise, "Hints in Better School Purchasing," *American School Board Journal* (June, 1959).

diture of funds. Sound business procedures and the application of fundamental principles tend to prevent the waste of funds that could be used
to finance other phases of the school program.

The first step in routing and scheduling is the preparation of maps.[10]
Base maps in black and white can frequently be procured from state
public works or highway departments or from county highway departments. Maps designating the locations of homes are preferable but are
not entirely essential. The second step is to establish boundary lines defining the school district, the location of schools, and limits of the service
areas for the schools involved. The map is now ready for duplication by
a commercial photographer to prepare a scale map. Several copies should
be obtained and placed in the school administrator's office where they will
be available to those who need them.

Various items of transportation policy must now be established. The
line between transported and nontransported pupils must be established
to facilitate which pupils are to be represented on the map by the use of
push pins. The heads of the push pins should be obtained in a variety of
contrasting colors to indicate the grade level of pupils and respective locations.

The maximum of efficient service using the least number of buses will
contribute to economy. The period of time for students to be enroute
should be carefully considered. Thirty to forty-five minutes is desirable,
with a maximum limit being set at one hour.

In establishing bus and routing schedules through a study of the spot
map and the use of the map measure, the bus mechanic and one or two
of the senior drivers longest in service, will be of assistance in determining
the best procedures for routing and schedules. All locations to be serviced
by the school buses should then be traveled in unloaded buses by all
school officials having an interest in the school transportation program.

> The largest buses operating within load and time schedules are the most
> economical. The best schedules are those that are best supervised with
> drivers, an all important factor in any successful transportation venture.[11]

School Bus Patrols

It is estimated that in the next ten years an additional 5 million students will be transported by school buses. The number of vehicles that
will be required to accommodate this increase has been estimated at 218,-
000, of which 193,000 will be school buses. In consideration of this increase
there is a need for organizing an effective bus patrol organization.

[10] Ted Sorenson, *Pupil Transportation,* published by AAA, Safety Patrol Handbook (Washington, D.C.: 1960).
[11] B. H. Belknap, "Preparing Bus Routes," *American School Board Journal* (May,
1957).

Bus Patrol Organization [12]

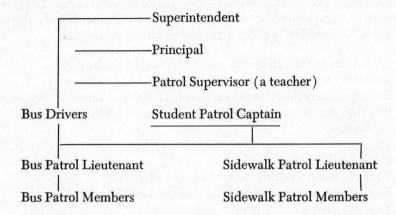

The growth of school bus transportation represents sizable hazards for the nation's school-age population. It also suggests that a highly organized program is needed by school officials in providing for accident prevention and improved safety-education experiences for children.

The most important responsibility in the safe transportation of students traveling to and from school by school bus is borne by the school bus driver. All school personnel have an obligation to help children develop desirable attitudes and practices to be followed as passengers on the school bus.

Efficiently organized bus safety patrols have proven to be helpful in maintaining order and preventing accidents to school bus riders—both when they are on buses and when they are crossing roadways. Bus drivers should welcome bus patrols as aides in safeguarding the children being transported.

Early in the school year the bus patrol can be organized by giving the students to be transported an opportunity to select their own patrol. When students are given an opportunity for this selection they will be inclined to comply with the requests and decisions of their elected patrol members. The duties and responsibilities of the patrol should be stipulated before their election. Requirements for selection of bus patrol members should include [13]

1. The command and respect of both older and younger students.
2. Living at or near the terminal point of the bus route so that supervision is available throughout the bus itinerary.
3. A good school attendance record.

[12] American Automobile Association, "School Bus Patrols," *Traffic Engineering Safety* (Washington, D.C.: 1960).
[13] Sorenson, *op. cit.*

The patrol members' primary function is to assist the driver in a safety and accident prevention program. Two patrol members assist the school bus driver, one positioned toward the front and the other toward the rear of the bus. Several of the important duties of bus patrols are

1. To determine that all riders are seated before the bus starts.
2. To check on proper behavior among riders.
3. To check such items as books, lunch boxes, and other objects to see that they are properly stored on the bus and carried safely when leaving the bus.
4. To observe and enforce the rule that students keep their heads and hands inside the bus.
5. To assist young children in getting on and getting off the buses.
6. To assist the bus driver in making an attendance check.
7. To assist the driver in emergency situations.

In assisting students in boarding the bus, the forward patrol member should step to the ground after the bus has completely stopped and stand in a safe and convenient position for carrying out his responsibility. Where students must cross the roadway, he gives the signal to children when the thoroughfare is clear and it is permissible to cross—but only after the driver has signaled to him that the students can proceed across the road.

The patrol member stationed in the rear of the bus should know how to open the emergency door so that, if necessary, he can aid the driver.

One phase of bus patrol procedures that the patrols must be prepared for is that of emergency stopping. The following is the recommended procedure for the emergency unloading of school buses by patrol members: [14]

1. Forward Bus Patrols
    a. Position flags or flares the legal distance both front and rear.
    b. Render assistance in unloading.
    c. Direct students to a safe location.
    d. Assist small children.
2. Rear Bus Patrols
    a. Open emergency door when instructed by the driver.
    b. Use sound judgment if the driver is injured, as to when to open the emergency exit.
    c. Be on the alert for any traffic hazards.
    d. Direct students to a safe location.

In the event of fire the bus patrol should adhere to the following recommended procedures.

[14] Sorenson, *op. cit.*

1. Assist where they can be of help to the driver.
2. Know how to use the fire extinguishers properly.
3. Direct the students to a safe location away from the bus.
4. Look for traffic hazards.

In the case of an accident the following suggestions are offered.

1. Driver not injured
   a. Assist driver in locating injured students.
   b. Assist the driver in administering first aid under his direction.
   c. Take telephone number card and go to the nearest residence for assistance.
   d. Remain with the bus and students until assistance arrives.
2. Driver injured
   a. Move into driver's seat and stop the bus if it is still moving.
   b. Turn off the engine.
   c. Set the hand brake.
   d. Supervise unloading students to a safe location.
   e. Take telephone number card and go to nearest residence for assistance.

Success of the bus patrol depends on the teacher-supervisor, who must understand its value and bring to this assignment an enthusiasm and attitude that will provide for an efficient program. He should conduct an educational program for patrol members on rules of procedure concerning emergency exit, fire extinguishers, and emergency care when first aid is necessary. During the last week of the school term, the teacher-supervisor should provide for the training of newly elected patrol members who will serve during the following school year.

Bus safety will be considered important by the students when teacher-leaders continuously display enthusiasm in and give proper support to this essential phase of school administration.

PREVENTIVE MEASURES

The following preventive measures are important concepts in the efficient administration of a school bus program and will contribute to safety and accident prevention.

1. When starting from home, use the safest route to the highway.
2. Along the highway walk to the left, and in single file.
3. Follow the established rules for getting on and getting off the bus as directed by the bus driver.
4. Cooperate with the bus driver and the front and rear bus patrols.

5. Never cross to the opposite side of the street or road in front of the bus without receiving a signal from the bus driver.

After boarding the bus, the following measures should be standard procedures.

1. The rider should remain in his seat unless otherwise instructed.
2. All portions of the rider's body should be inside the bus.
3. The rider should not disturb or distract the driver.
4. All large and heavy objects should be secured properly.
5. Practice safety manners while the bus is in transit.
6. Cooperation with the bus driver and the bus patrol is of primary importance.

The previously mentioned are directed measures basically for the students. Additional preventive measures include

1. Providing school bus safety education for the public at large stressing the significance of our most valuable resource, the school child.
2. Enforcing the recommended minimum standards and specifications for school buses.
3. Using only capable, select, and reliable bus drivers.
4. Obtaining the best equipment and specifying the most efficient routes and schedules.

The goal should be safe transportation by school bus for every student.

References

Belknap, Burton H., *The School Bus* (Minneapolis: Educational Publishers, 1950).

Featherstone, Glenn E., *State Laws on Stopping for and Passing School Buses* (Washington, D.C.: U.S. Government Printing Office, rev. 1958).

Harris, Richard, "Uncover School Bus Problems," *Safety Education* (March, 1959), p. 22.

Hyde, Wallace N., "Use of Student Drivers for School Buses," *National Safety Council Transactions*, Vol. 24, p. 169, School and College Division, 1959.

Kearney, Paul W., "Who Drives Your School Bus?" *Safety Education* (March, 1954), pp. 5–8.

National Commission on Safety Education, *The Expanding Role of School Patrols* (Washington: National Education Association, 1953).

———, *Minimum Standards for School Buses* (rev. ed.), 1964 (100 pages).

————, *Selection, Instruction, and Supervision of School Bus Drivers,* 1964 (36 pages).

National Safety Council, *Accident Facts* (Chicago: The Council, published annually).

————, *School Buses—Administrative Problems* (rev. ed.), *Safety Education Data Sheet No. 11* (Chicago: The Council).

————, *School Bus Safety: Education Pupil Passengers, Safety Education Data Sheet No. 63* (Chicago: The Council).

————, *Safety in Pupil Excursions, Safety Education Data Sheet No. 51* (Chicago: The Council).

————, *School Bus Safety: Operating Practices, Safety Education Data Sheet No. 73* (Chicago: The Council).

Noble, Marcus C. S., *Pupil Transportation in the United States* (Scranton, International Textbook Company, 1940).

Preece, Thomas William, *The Selection, Training and Evaluation of School Bus Drivers in California,* Dissertation, University of Southern California, 1961.

PART III THE COLLEGE
SAFETY
PROGRAM

It cannot be given to all of us to fight for freedom, but the fight for safety, the fight for adventure, the fight for a life that shall be the measure of a purpose instead of the marred result of purposeless chance is within the right of all of us.

ALBERT W. WHITNEY

INTRODUCTION

Twentieth-century society is changing with increasing rapidity; at the same time many new approaches to human understanding and the learning process are evolving. In the field of safety education there is a segment from inside the profession, at the higher-education level, that advocates stressing scholarship, publication, and research. This group believes that teachers of this caliber thereby enhance their effectiveness. As the safety movement continues to search for ways and means of improving status and effectiveness, colleges preparing teachers of safety education must recognize this trend.

Leaders of safety education must convey the idea that campus safety activities contribute to the abilities of colleges and universities to perform their stated missions, whether they be in the training of technical or professional workers, or in the preparation of teachers of future generations. College administrators and staff members must realize that campus safety is a means of conserving human and material resources.

SIGNIFICANCE OF SAFETY

In recent years there has been a significant number of new centers for safety and a gradual development of established safety programs in colleges and universities. Administrators are realizing that the health and safety of their students, faculty, and other employees is an inherent responsibility. This realization is especially important because the college-age population has the highest incidence of certain types of accidents of any period in the life span. Deaths occurring from automobile accidents, drowning, firearms, and recreational activities are especially numerous. It is distressing to hear of the large number of students killed each year in automobile and motorcycle accidents. In most instances students are on their way to and from college or on vacation.

In addition, there are many areas of the college curriculum in which safety is highly important. This is especially true in state universities. Safety in all forms of engineering, especially highway engineering is becoming more and more important. The use of a variety of dangerous chemicals and nuclear products has been increasing rapidly. It has been necessary to prepare new manuals covering safety in chemical engineering and in the use of nuclear energy. Transportation problems are growing year by year in every field except railroads. Air and water pollution has become a serious menace in our cities. The automobile industry has been told that from now on safety must be given more attention. All of the companies are moving ahead to meet the standards that have been set by Congress. More and more attention is being paid to safety practices in recreation, such as water skiing, skin diving, scuba diving, motor boating, swimming and dozens of other activities.

All of this attention has resulted in a new interest in safety in institutions of higher learning. Fire-resistant buildings are being constructed, students are being moved from off-campus frame residences to fire-resistant dormitories, employees are being trained in safety procedures, the use of automobiles and parking is being restricted, and campus safety programs are being organized.

Two decades ago, there were but few college courses in any phase of safety. Today all state colleges and universities and hundreds of private colleges have courses in the subject. Many of these colleges have made accident studies as the basis for establishing a safety program. Let us look at some.

DISTRIBUTION OF COLLEGE ACCIDENTS

Several years ago a joint study of accidents in eleven colleges was made by the American College Health Association and the National Safety Council.[1] It was found that during one year there

---

[1] American College Health Association and National Safety Council, *Survey of Accidents to College Students* (Chicago: The Council, 1955).

were 8,500 injuries reported, 9 per cent of which required hospitalization. A recent report of the University of Minnesota Health Service [2] showed that in one year there were 2,608 injuries to students, 1,259 of which occurred on the campus, 1,359 off-campus. One out of every eleven students was involved in an accident. A greater number of students are injured on and off the campus than had been realized.

In addition, one large university system employing 5,100 persons found that 385 persons, or one out of every thirteen, were injured during the year. Minnesota, in the report mentioned above, found 791 injuries among the 9,600 employees (one out of every twelve employees) including faculty, clerical staff, and all others employed by the institution. This ratio of one out of twelve is higher than one would find in some industries. Some of these accidents result in disabling injuries. They also cause a loss of time, and the costs of Workmen's Compensation Insurance, as well as hospitalization. It can readily be seen why the development of an accident prevention program for students, faculty, and other employees is important.

STUDENT ACCIDENTS

There is a great variation in the types of accidents. Minnesota,[3] for example, found that 51 per cent took place off the campus, 48 per cent on the campus. Those on campus were equally divided between athletic and nonathletic activities. The following table shows the distribution:

DISTRIBUTION OF STUDENT ACCIDENTS,
UNIVERSITY OF MINNESOTA

by Per Cent

ON CAMPUS				OFF CAMPUS	
ATHLETIC		NONATHLETIC			
Intramural	40.4	Laboratory	27.8	Recreation	32.5
Varsity	23.5	Other Buildings	24.7	Residence	27.9
Unorganized	22.6	Pedestrian	23.0	Automobile	20.6
Physical Ed.	13.5	Dormitory	13.5	Pedestrian	10.6
		Automobiles	6.4	Work	5.0
		Other	4.6	Other	3.4
Total	100		100		100

[2] University of Minnesota, *Employee and Student Accident Experience—1960–61* (Minneapolis: The University, 1961).
[3] *Ibid.*

The University of Minnesota is a metropolitan university and the greater percentage of students (over 85 per cent) live off campus. Off-campus accidents exceed those on the campus. This would be entirely different in institutions that house the majority of students in dormitories. It will be noted that a large percentage of all accidents take place in recreational activities and sports. (See Chapter 15.) It is also evident that pedestrian safety is always a problem, both on and off the campus.

CHAPTER 11 ORGANIZATION OF ACCIDENT PREVENTION PROGRAMS

Even though there are many kinds of institutions of higher education in the country, there is some similarity in the organization of accident prevention programs at the college level. These programs will be discussed in this chapter. According to Trabue, in *Safety Education by Colleges and Universities*,[1] "A great many changes which have taken place in our standard of living are due to the knowledge, inspiration, and skills instilled by colleges and the university. . . . A democratic state depends chiefly upon its educational institutions to prepare its citizens to live intelligently and safely in this increasingly dangerous environment. . . . The mere listing in a college catalog of a course in safety does not discharge the institution's obligation for building habits of safety."

This is a fine statement of one of the functions of a college. When one reads that several hundred college students are killed in automobile accidents each year, several hundred more drowned, and that the accident rate in some universities is as high or higher as that in some industries, one wonders whether the average college has an adequate safety program. Are the colleges educating their students for safe living?

There are no historical records that show when safety instruction was first integrated into college courses. It would naturally appear first in chemistry, physics, engineering, physical education, and in psychology, to which it has a direct relationship. As early as 1926, courses in safety education were included in the Normal Schools at La Crosse, Wisconsin, at Oswego, New York and at New York University. By 1940, at least 50 colleges offered courses in some phase of safety or driver education.[2] At that time, a number of universities also included instruction in industrial

---

[1] National Commission on Safety Education, *Safety Education by Colleges and Universities* (Washington, D.C.: The Commission, 1950).

[2] National Society for the Study of Education, *Twenty-fifth Yearbook, Safety Education* (Bloomington, Ill.: The Society, 1926).

FUNCTIONS OF A COLLEGE PROGRAM

safety and related subjects. Now, it is estimated that more than 400 colleges and universities are involved.

A college safety program would naturally be organized in the light of the needs of the nation and the immediate geographic area to be served. The three general accident prevention areas to be served are (1) the degree or academic program, (2) the service program for various areas and governmental agencies, and (3) a program of research. A college may choose to develop in one or more of these areas.

BASIC ELEMENTS OF THE SAFETY PROGRAM

The Campus Safety Association has generally agreed on ten basic elements of a complete program: (1) a college safety policy; (2) safety leadership; (3) safety organization; (4) maintenance of a safe environment; (5) fire prevention; (6) reporting and follow-up of accidents; (7) training; (8) promotion of interest in safety; (9) education for safe living; (10) off-campus activities. The degree to which each of these elements will develop will vary widely from the small liberal arts college to the large state university. The safety program must be tailored to fit the needs of the institution employing it.

Several developments have contributed to the growth of interest in campus safety. The first of these was the mounting costs of State Workmen's Compensation insurance. In some institutions there was also the increasing costs for public liability, property damage, as well as fire insurance. Something had to be done to reduce these costs. Another involved the increase in accidents among the student body, faculty, and other employees. College presidents were surprised to find the number of accidents that occurred both on and off the campus. There is a moral, if not a legal responsibility, for the administration to provide protection and safeguards for the college community. A fourth reason was the increase in problems related to the control of motor vehicles on and off campus, as well as the obligation to protect pedestrians and bicycle traffic. This was especially true in institutions in which a large percentage of the students were commuters. In addition, many colleges have large industrial, engineering, agricultural, and research laboratories as well as other operations that tend to be hazardous. Finally, as college presidents heard of the successful programs being carried on by other institutions and were informed as to the effect these had on accidents, they decided, with the support of their trustees, to inaugurate a campus safety program. In the last few years the number of colleges that have organized safety programs has shown a rapid increase.

THE COLLEGE SAFETY POLICY

One of the most important steps in organizing a college safety program is a general statement of policy from the president. This should be approved by a committee and sent out to all deans, directors, and other administrative heads. Ideally it should be printed and posted so that it can be read by the entire college family. The success of the program will be in direct proportion to the support it receives from the administration.

This policy statement should answer the following questions.

1. What is the Safety Program?
2. Why is it necessary?
3. What are its desired ends?
4. Who is responsible for its direction?
5. What are the roles of students, faculty, and staff in promoting the success of the program?

SAFETY LEADERSHIP

Leadership starts with the president. In some cases he may designate a vice-president or other administrative offcer to exercise the direct leadership of the program, but he is kept informed of developments. Much of the daily operation is carried on by the safety supervisor or coordinator, devoting full time or part time to the work. The next echelon of administrators—department heads and deans—are very important in leadership for they can influence members of their departments and students. A certain amount of leadership should come from chairmen of certain departments such as engineering, physical education, and agriculture. All successful programs utilize the help they can get from leaders in student government, editors of school newspapers, and college organizations.

ORGANIZATION

The committee type of organization has been adopted in some colleges to plan the programs. The central committee consists of from six to ten members with a chairman, usually an administrative officer. The latter may be the vice-president, the superintendent of buildings and grounds, or one of the deans. In smaller colleges the president often serves as chairman. The central committee is made up of deans or directors of the various departments. In the university, this would include the heads of the engineering, agriculture, medical college, arts and sciences, graduate school, the medical officers, the laboratory schools, buildings and grounds, and other departments. Some colleges also include representatives of the student body; in others, there is a separate student committee or council. In the larger universities there may be other committees to meet special needs. In the smaller institutions there is usually only the central committee or council. (See Fig. 12-1.)

No one department or division within the college or university could possibly assume all the instructional program responsibilities. In keeping with sound administrative and organizational policies this does not eliminate the need for specific courses or integrating and correlating safety units throughout the various divisions and departments.

ORGANIZATION IN DEPARTMENTS

Safety education in state universities is found in several departments. Among these are agriculture, teacher education, engineering, university extension and services, and safety in the college community. Some colleges also have separate departments of home economics and health, physical education, and recreation, which include safety instruction.

AGRICULTURE

Accident Facts, a publication of the National Safety Council,[3] shows that in recent years agriculture is one of the most dangerous industries. There are not only the hazards of the farm, ranch, and home, but also those of the highway. However, few colleges offer specific courses in farm safety. For the most part it is integrated into agricultural courses.

According to *Safety Education by Colleges and Universities* [4] "the land grant and other colleges in agriculture and home economics have the responsibility for incorporating safety education in nearly all of its courses. . . . It is also recommended that at least one general farm safety course be offered to prepare, not only the professional farm workers, but also teachers and leaders in the fields of agriculture and home economics."

Other useful activities are covered by the field services offered in connection with 4-H Clubs, F.F.A., the Grange, and other farm organizations. This service, often carried on by county agents, is valuable and should be extended.

ENGINEERING

Accident prevention has been integrated into many of the engineering courses. In addition, many colleges offer separate courses in industrial

[3] National Safety Council, *Accident Facts* (Washington, D.C.: The Council, published annually).

[4] National Commission on Safety Education, *Promotional and Procedural Guide for Traffic Short Courses and Conferences* (Washington, D.C.: The Commission, 1958).

safety and related subjects. Still others include a series of units in existing courses, taught by safety supervisors from state departments, from industries, or insurance companies. Over 200 colleges now offer one or more engineering or industrial safety courses. As a rule, these are in three major areas: (1) Industrial Safety; (2) Fire Prevention and Protection; and (3) Engineering Control of Health Hazards. Some of these courses are offered for credit but more often they are in the nondegree extension program.

The American Society of Safety Engineers lists ten courses for safety engineers:

Basic Industrial Safety
Industrial Safety Engineering
Industrial Fire Prevention
Design of Industrial Safety Program
Engineering Control of Health Hazards
Design of Machine Safeguards
Industrial Safety Standards
Safety Administration
Casualty and Liability Insurance for Industry
Research Problems in Industrial Safety

However, most colleges offer only a few courses, primarily for industrial safety supervisors and foremen. A number offer at least one course in traffic engineering, usually in the nondegree program.[5] There is an acute need for several thousand more traffic engineers, but a qualified traffic engineer should have at least a full semester's training in several courses in traffic engineering. Yale University, in its Bureau for Highway Traffic, requires a full year. It was surprising to find, according to *Courses in Highway Safety and Highway Traffic*,[6] that in the United States, 975 courses were offered dealing with traffic safety and driver education, traffic and highway engineering, enforcement, motor vehicle fleet operation, and specialized operations. The number is increasing year by year.

LIBERAL ARTS

Over 75 per cent of our institutions of higher education offer a curriculum in the liberal arts. As a rule no specific courses in safety education are offered in this curriculum except on an elective basis. Nevertheless, safety can be stressed in many liberal arts subjects such as the sciences, social studies, health and physical education, psychology, and sociology. In addition, all liberal arts colleges have a responsibility for the protection of students and employees.

[5] *Ibid.*
[6] National Commission on Safety Education, *Courses in Highway Safety and Highway Traffic* (Washington, D.C.: The Commission, 1958).

TEACHER EDUCATION

Twenty-three states have laws requiring the teaching of safety in elementary and secondary schools but only two state departments of education require certification to teach. It is essential that all elementary and safety teachers be prepared in this field.

As stated previously, well over 400 colleges offer one or more courses in safety education, driver and traffic safety education, or related subjects. In addition, state certificate requirements for driver education are increasing, with many states requiring at least nine semester hours of credit. According to *Policies and Guidelines for Teacher Preparation and Certification in Driver and Traffic Safety Education*,[7] "teacher preparation for driver and traffic safety education should be, for the most part, an undergraduate, pre-service program." However, in actual practice, since certificate requirements are increasing, many courses provide graduate credit.

TABLE 11-2

INADEQUACIES OF PREPARATION OF COLLEGE TEACHERS OF SAFETY EDUCATION

HIGHEST LEVEL OF SPECIAL PREPARATION	INSTRUCTORS		
	FULL-TIME	PART-TIME	TOTAL
None	3	0	3
A noncredit workshop, short course, institute, or seminar	44	2	46
A credit course	46	4	50
More than one credit course, but not a minor (16 s.h.)	64	20	84
A minor (16 s.h.) or major field on the undergraduate or graduate level	34	8	42
Total	191	34	225

Report by Charles H. Hartman and Lillian C. Schwenk in 1963.

Major emphasis in the preparation of these teachers should be selected in the areas of

1. Driver and traffic safety education
2. Safety education and accident prevention
3. Behavioral sciences

[7] National Commission on Safety Education, *Policies and Guidelines for Teacher Preparation and Certification for Driver and Traffic Safety Education* (Washington, D.C.: The Commission, 1965).

4. Physical sciences
5. Biological sciences

In addition, the prospective teacher should include student teaching in both classroom and laboratory instruction.

Various patterns have been established to indicate the courses in a minor in safety and driver education. One pattern lists four basic courses: [8]

	CREDITS
Introduction to Safety Education	3
Basic driver and Traffic Safety Education	3
Advanced Driver and Traffic Safety Education	3
Methods and Materials of Traffic Safety	2

In addition, students would elect several of the following courses to make up 20 credits, with five additional credits for student teaching:

	CREDITS
Traffic Law Enforcement	2
Problems of Research in Driver and Traffic Safety Education	3
Traffic Engineering	2
Auto Mechanics	3
First Aid	2
Mental Health	3
Municipal Government	3

This is a recommended program for colleges preparing minors in safety education. The great majority of the colleges are not equipped to offer a complete program of this kind because they do not have qualified college instructors. It is probable that the legislation on highway safety passed by Congress in 1966 will result in an upgrading of college programs and that within a short time all states will have some form of state financial support for driver education. This development will necessitate many more teachers. The colleges have a real responsibility in meeting this challenge. In addition, the national conferences on Fire Prevention and Protection, Highway Safety, and Industrial Safety have pointed up the need for better preparation of teachers and other educational workers in safety education.

SAFETY EXTENSION SERVICES

Safety is one of the most critical social problems needing public education. Extension and service activities of our colleges and universities are designed to meet the needs of many groups. Courses, institutes, conferences, and workshops devoted to safety have developed extensively in

[8] *Ibid.*

the last decade. In some cases they are offered for credit, but by far the larger number are noncredit. Among these are courses or conferences for police, firemen, industrial safety supervisors and foremen, civil defense workers, supervisors and drivers of commercial fleets, school bus drivers, traffic court judges and prosecutors, fire prevention engineers, public health workers, traffic engineers, coaches of various sports, adult drivers, traffic violators, ambulance drivers, motorboat operators,[9] lifeguards, farm youth and adults. A complete list would include almost every segment of our population engaged in activities in which there are elements of danger. Some colleges include safety programs in their radio and television series. Many also have visual-aid depositories which include films on various phases of safety. Others send out pertinent newspaper releases.

SAFETY CENTERS

There are a number of institutions that have bureaus or departments that could be called Safety Centers. The first of these was organized at Harvard University in 1926, called the Eskine Bureau for Street Traffic Research. In 1937, it was moved to Yale University and the name changed to the Bureau for Highway Traffic. According to *University Transportation and Accident Prevention Centers* [10] the Bureau's work consists of three basic elements—the graduate training program, research, and co-operation with other agencies seeking solutions to the many problems related to the movement of persons and goods by highway. The basic program requires a year of graduate work, but in 1959 a two-year graduate program was offered combining traffic engineering with city planning. Graduates of the Bureau hold key positions in traffic engineering in the country.

The Northwestern University Traffic Institute was organized in 1936, primarily to prepare enforcement officers. The Institute is now a divsion of the Transportation Center. The primary function of the Institute is the professional training of police, traffic court judges and prosecutors, and driver's license examiners. It offers a one-year course, but in addition conducts short seminars, courses, and conferences both on and off the campus. It also conducts a number of research studies.

The Center for Safety Education was organized at New York University in 1938, primarily for training teachers and supervisors, conducting research, and issuing publications. Since its organization its work has

[9] Usually offered in cooperation with the Coast Guard Auxiliary on the United States Power Squadrons.

[10] Association of State Universities and Land Grant Colleges and the National Commission on Safety Education, *University Transportation and Accident Prevention Centers* (Washington, D.C.: The Association and Commission, 1962).

expanded greatly, and it now offers over 30 different courses for teachers, supervisors, representatives of the armed forces, industrial safety supervisors, fire prevention engineers, state traffic coordinators, enforcement officers, traffic court magistrates, and many other groups. Its credit courses make it possible for a student to prepare a doctoral thesis in safety and over 45 graduates have completed the work for this degree.

These three centers have been described because they were the first major academic organizations in the field of safety. Later, the Institute for Transportation and Traffic Engineering was organized at the University of California; the Highway Traffic Safety Center at Michigan State University; the Highway Traffic Safety Center at the University of Illinois; the Institute of Public Safety at Pennsylvania State University; the Public Safety Institute at Purdue University; the Texas Transportation Institute at the University of Texas; the Safety Education Program at Iowa State University of Science and Technology; and, the Safety Center at Southern Illinois University. In 1965 the Board of Directors of Indiana University authorized the establishment of a Center for Safety and Traffic Education. There are other small centers—in fact, if a liberal interpretation was given for the term *center* there might be more than 50.

FINANCIAL SUPPORT

There is an important difference between the financial support of the first three centers that were described and those that have developed subsequently. For the most part the first centers were financed by private organizations: The Bureau for Highway Traffic received its basic grant from the Automotive Safety Foundation, as did the Traffic Institute at Northwestern University. On the other hand, for 25 years the Center for Safety Education received its main support from the Association of Casualty and Surety Companies, and in recent years from the Insurance Institute for Highway Safety. The latter now provides grants to both the Yale Bureau and Northwestern's Traffic Institute. Today each of these centers receives aid from many different organizations. Mention should be made of the Allstate Insurance Company, which gives scholarship grants to many colleges, the Esso Safety Foundation, the Aetna Casualty and Surety Company, the American Trucking Association, the Chrysler Corporation, and dozens of other companies. Nearly all of the centers that have been organized since 1950 are financed by state funds; this undoubtedly will continue to be the practice.

The following guidelines were prepared for the publication *University Transportation and Accident Prevention Centers*.[11] Although the publication is chiefly concerned with traffic safety and transportation, these guidelines are applicable to the whole field of safety.

[11] *Ibid.*

1. In its proper role the center in effect functions as an instrument of all of the schools, departments, colleges, and divisions within the institution.
2. Within the administrative structure of the institute the center functions in such a way as to utilize the institution's total resources on an interdisciplinary basis.
3. In helping to carry out the institution's basic purpose of instruction, research, and extension services, the center does not duplicate efforts elsewhere in the institution.
4. Those associated with the center program are employed and recognized on the same basis as their counterparts elsewhere in the institution.
5. The dimensions of the center program develop in the direction and to the extent that the institution believes will help it to fulfill its role in highway traffic and safety.
6. The institution provides the basic financial support for establishing and operating the center, with supplemental support coming from legislative appropriations, foundations, government grants, and other sources.
7. The president appoints an institution—wide *ad hoc* committee to explore the institution's role in improving transportation, traffic, and accident prevention in order to determine how its resources can best be utilized in this field.
8. The president appoints a temporary external committee to advise him as to how the institution can be of help to government agencies, business and industry, and the general public, and as to its off-campus relationships and activities, and its financial support.
9. Policy decisions on center organization, procedures, program and budget are vested in the president.
10. Administration of the center's program is the responsibility of its administrative head, under the supervision of an official designated by the president, whose rank and function are such as to provide authority for management of the program.
11. The president appoints a continuing institution-wide advisory committee with whom the center's administrative head consults on policy matters and program development.
12. The president appoints a continuing external advisory committee to serve after the center is organized.

These guidelines are very good, especially for universities, but since they were published few centers have been organized. Centers in teachers colleges might not require all of these guidelines. Although only a few centers exist today, it is probable that the action of Congress in 1966 in passing legislation "to provide aid to states and municipalities for traffic safety" may influence some states to organize centers.

The schools of higher education have an important responsibility to educate young people for safe living. Many colleges in the country are doing excellent work, but there are others that have not yet recognized the importance of safety education.

References

Aaron, J. E., and M. K. Strasser, *Driver and Traffic Safety Education* (New York: Macmillan, 1966).

American Association of Teachers Colleges and National Commission on Safety Education, *Safety Education for Teachers* (Washington, D.C.: National Education Association, 1947).

Brody, Leon, and Herbert J. Stack, *Highway Safety and Driver Education* (Englewood Cliffs, N.J.: Prentice-Hall, 1959).

Florio, A. E., and G. T. Stafford, *Safety Education* (New York: McGraw-Hill, 1962).

Hartman, Charles H., and Lillian C. Schwenk, *Teacher Preparation and Certification in Driver Education* (Abstracts of research studies), (Chicago: National Safety Council, 1963).

National Commission on Safety Education, *Policies and Practices for Driver Education* (Washington, D.C.: The Commission, 1964).

    Policies and Guidelines for Teacher Preparation and Certification in Driver and Traffic Safety Education (Washington, D.C.: The Commission, 1950).

    Safety Education by Colleges and Universities (Washington, D.C.: The Commission, 1950).

National Education Association and U.S. Department of Health, Education, and Welfare, *Courses in Highway Safety and Highway Traffic* (Washington, D.C.: National Education Association, 1958).

National Safety Council, *Standard Student Accident Report Form* (Chicago: The Council, 425 N. Michigan Avenue, 60611).

President's Committee for Traffic Safety, *Education* (Washington, D.C.: U.S. Government Printing Office, 1960).

Strasser, M. K., J. E. Aaron, R. C. Bohn, and J. R. Eales, *Fundamentals of Safety Education* (New York: Macmillan, 1964).

CHAPTER 12 SAFETY AND SECURITY IN THE COLLEGE ENVIRONMENT

The college and university today is often a self-sustaining community and a business enterprise of considerable magnitude. In many instances it is the largest enterprise in the city. It may have many thousands of students and faculty members. There has been a rapid increase in the size of institutions. Of 1,200 senior colleges and universities more than 40 have at least 10,000 students. Several have more than 30,000, while more than 70 have enrollments between 5,000 and 10,000. In addition, there may well be several hundred workers on the clerical payroll and even more other employees, chiefly assigned to buildings and grounds. Many institutions have large numbers of buildings—dormitories, laboratories, gymnasiums, and those assigned to special fields such as engineering, agriculture, the sciences, and the like. Some campuses cover many acres of land with several miles of driveways, walks, and paths. In addition, the college may own hundreds of acres of off-campus land devoted to recreation, farming, aviation, forestry, or other activities. In transportation it may operate many vehicles—trucks, buses, and passenger cars. In fact some institutions have over a hundred vehicles in their fleets. Many also have the safety problems of off-campus student housing. In most, there is a large percentage of commuters in both the student body and faculty. Since most of these use the automobile, the problem of traffic congestion and parking often becomes a serious one. The Highway Safety Law of 1966 [1] will undoubtedly stimulate action by the colleges.

As noted in Chapter 11, there has been a rapid development of interest in campus safety. As colleges have increased in size and activities there has been a corresponding growth in the various types of campus activities which require added safety measures. Moreover, there has always been the ever-present danger of fire, especially in off-campus housing. Several hundred institutions have developed campus safety programs with com-

[1] American Automobile Association, *Highway Safety Law of 1966*, Digest of provisions (Washington, D.C.: The Association, 1966).

mittees appointed to supervise safety activities. A National Campus Safety Association has been organized in cooperation with the National Safety Council and meets regularly to discuss problems and new developments. Campus safety should not be relegated to a minor role in the operation of the colleges. To implement the wishes of the trustees, the accident-prevention efforts of all of the colleges should be coordinated by the central administration. The diversified activities inherent in operating such a variety of colleges preclude the adoption of any one campus safety formula. The best accident prevention program is developed locally and adapted to the situation and requirements of each campus.

MAINTAINING A SAFE ENVIRONMENT

To maintain a safe environment is one of the most important goals of the campus safety program. Safe environment is an all-inclusive term and covers all the conditions and possible hazards in all college buildings, both on and off the campus. It also includes the physical features of the grounds—roadways, sidewalks, parking facilities, and recreational areas such as lakes, parks, playing fields, and playgrounds.

One of the important ways of maintaining a safe environment is to conduct periodic safety inspections. (See Chapter 4.) They can be conducted by members of the various committees. However, it is common practice in many colleges to invite community specialists in various fields—safety engineers, fire prevention specialists, health officers, laboratory safety experts, state labor department inspectors and the like—to make the inspections. These people are more experienced in the techniques of good inspection. Some colleges have students aid in these inspections, usually as recorders. They should always be present when fraternity or sorority houses and dormitories are being inspected. These inspections can be made on a regular monthly basis; some colleges prefer the semi-annual inspection. Remedial action is highly important. When hazards are located, steps should be taken to correct them. At its next regular meeting the commitee receives reports of progress made toward completing remedial assignments.

What are some of the conditions that inspections can reveal? They of course vary widely but the following are illustrations:

Unguarded or poorly guarded machinery in shops.
Noxious fumes in laboratories.
Poorly lighted stairways in dormitories or other buildings.
Lack of fire escapes in student housing.
Poor sanitation in cafeterias.
Exit doors not opening outward.
Accumulation of rubbish in buildings.

Inadequate parking facilities.
Unsafe conditions of temporary bleachers.
Slippery condition of floors.
Conflict of vehicle and pedestrian traffic.
Lack of fire extinguishers (or not serviceable).
Repairs needed in buildings.

All motor vehicles operated by the college should be inspected regularly. Some colleges also require the inspection of vehicles owned by students. This is especially true in states that require the periodic inspection of all vehicles.

Since accidents tend to be common in physical education and recreation activities, inspections should include the gymnasium and locker rooms, the swimming pool, and outdoor recreational facilities. Many institutions operate recreational, forestry, and other types of camps. These and all other off-campus facilities should be included in the inspection program.

Reporting and Follow-Up of Accidents

Accident reporting and follow-up are, in one sense, the keystone of the safety program for it is the only way in which the college can get the facts and take steps to prevent a recurrence. Moreover it is highly important in

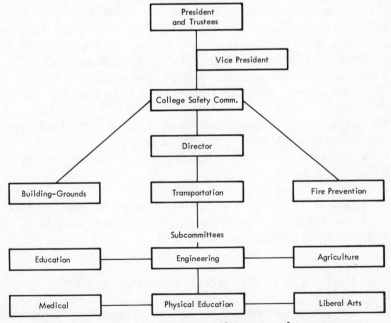

Figure 12–1.   Organization of campus safety program.

many universities to get all the facts and a complete report of the accident because of the possibility of public liability suits. However, laws in many states make it difficult to bring liability suits against state-owned institutions. This does not apply to Workmen's Compensation insurance, which covers all college employees in each state.

Some colleges make use of the Accident Report Form shown as Figures 4-2, 4-3. In some cases these are filled out by the immediate supervisor; in others, by the campus safety director.

The next step is corrective action. It will be noted on the accident report form that an attempt is made to get at the underlying causes of the accident and how it might have been prevented. Was it a poorly guarded machine, a slippery floor, obstructions in the way, poor lighting, unsafe procedure, or any other of hundreds of other conditions that might have contributed? If so, many of these conditions can be corrected, some by engineering changes, others by enforcement, and still others by training. When such conditions exist it becomes the responsibility of the safety director, working with the supervisor, to recommend changes. If many changes are to be made they may have to be approved by the department chairman, dean, or director. The following are illustrations of corrective action.

CORRECTIVE ACTION FOLLOWING INVESTIGATON

1. Visitor tripped going downstairs on steps leading from main entrance of University Heights Library. Handrail was installed.
2. Porter received severe cuts while emptying a trash can filled with glass and acid containers. Trash receptacles were color-coded in laboratories, red for glass refuse and silver for paper and related trash.
3. Several instances of students, visitors, and employees walking into glass doors. Large decals of University emblem placed at eye level on doors.
4. All classrooms with raised blackboards, desks, or chair platforms had edges painted yellow to contrast with the floor.
5. Entire sidewalk of Commerce Building torn up and repaired in order to level off all portions.
6. Loose coping on dormitory roof repaired.
7. Restraining bars placed at all landing windows at each stairway.
8. All low-wheeled stools in library removed as they were being used as step stools by students and staff.

FIRE PREVENTION AND PROTECTION

Fire prevention and protection, police activities, civil defense, and other emergencies usually reflect the protective features of city government. But inasmuch as many of our institutions are communities in themselves, they should have their own security and protection controls, especially large universities that have several hundred buildings either owned or leased.

In recent years a number of serious fires have ocurred in colleges that have resulted in a loss of lives and valuable property. Several years ago 46 students died in a residence-hall fire. The 1,800 colleges and universities have an average of 100 fires in residence halls during a school year; the probabilities, therefore, are one in eighteen that a residence building at each college will be visited by fire this year.

Many colleges and universities are still using wooden "temporary" barracks left over from World War II for housing students. There are also many fraternity and sorority houses without adequate fire escapes or other means of egress. In addition, many colleges have extensive laboratories, store houses, farm buildings, power plants, and other structures such as one would find in a typical community. Some of these buildings may be fire resistant, but they are not always fireproof.

STANDARDS FOR STUDENT RESIDENCES

The Campus Safety Association, in cooperation with the National Board of Underwriters [2] and the National Fire Protection Association, has prepared a National Standard Student Residence Fire Safety Check List.[3] The following is a brief summary of this list:

1. Stairway enclosures or smoke barriers of noncombustible materials. Wired glass in metal frames provide an acceptable enclosure for this purpose in most buildings.
2. Two or more ways out of each floor used in whole or in part for public rooms, study rooms, or sleeping quarters.
3. Automatic sprinklers provide the best fire protection for life and property and should be installed wherever possible.
4. Interior finish of safe types on walls and ceilings.
5. A working emergency plan published for residences and exercised through frequent exit drills.
6. Noncombustible decorations.
7. A program of effective maintenance and inspection based on knowledge of the causes of residence fires.

In connection with fire drills it is of interest to note the results of a survey conducted by the Campus Safety Association covering 341 returns of a questionnaire sent out to colleges:

[2] The National Board of Underwriters is now part of the American Insurance Association.

[3] Francis Quinlan, *Student Residence Fire Check List* (Chicago: The National Safety Council, 1959).

1. Thirty-five per cent of the institutions conducted no fire drills.
2. Eighty-four per cent of the junior colleges conducted drills.
3. Drills were seldom held in chapter houses except in women's sororities.
4. Less than 42 per cent reported drills in laboratory or shop areas.
5. Drills were conducted in women's dormitories but rarely in men's.

Many college buildings, constructed seventy to eighty years ago, have few provisions for fire protection. They have open stairwells, wooden floors, roofs, and joists, and will burn like tinder if a fire gets under way. These should be renovated or replaced.

Some colleges have limited fire fighting apparatus and in some instances volunteer fire departments. In a number of institutions the engineering staff works closely with the building and maintenance departments to see to it that buildings are inspected regularly and extinguishers and other apparatus are kept in good condition.

TRAFFIC CONTROL

Nearly all colleges have some type of police protection, night watchmen, and security officers. In other cases there may be a larger force, primarily assigned to traffic control. Still others utilize officers from the city department, especially at football games when traffic is likely to be heavy. Bennett Wells in an article, "University Campus Parking," in *Traffic Quarterly* [4] illustrates some of the traffic problems of the larger universities. "Like cities, the campus has parking lots, a road network, traffic signals, and traffic and parking problems that may often be complex. . . . Universities, like cities, are increasingly recognizing the need to pay for transportation and parking, and the values of technical, objective approaches."

In a study conducted at Cornell University it was found that 20,000 vehicles entered and left the campus on a single day; 3,000 had to be parked at one time. Other institutions have an even larger number. According to recommendations of the Wilbur Smith Associates, Traffic Consultants, reported in the Seventh National Conference on Campus Safety [5] "a campus parking program should pay its own way or, at least, most of it. . . . To obtain needed monies, conventional fee schedules should be established for the various parking facilities." The fee paid varies widely in the various universities from $3.00 a year to as high as $70.00. The problem of traffic congestion and parking is one that must be met by careful planning, usually in cooperation with the community

---

[4] Bennett Wells, "University Campus Parking," *Traffic Quarterly* (January 1956). (Saugatuck, Conn.: The Eno Foundation, 1956.)
[5] Wilbur Smith, and Associates, *Safety Monographs for Colleges and Universities*, No. 10 (Chicago: The National Safety Council, 1960).

planning agency. Restriction of student driving will help, but there is always the problem of vehicles driven by members of the faculty, other employees, and commuters. This is especially true where mass transportation facilities are limited. Many have a system of permits for student drivers in addition to parking permits.[6] Some require that automobiles be inspected periodically and carry inspection certificates. Others have traffic courts for trying violators, but in most colleges violators report to the city court.

Serious accidents on the campus are comparatively rare. The real trouble arises in off-campus driving, commuting from home, trips on holidays and vacations, and driving to athletic events. Some colleges have taken steps to encourage the use of public transportation—buses, railroads, and air transport. Railroads have arranged for special trains to athletic events, various groups have chartered buses. College buses are sometimes used for field trips. In addition, some have arranged for educational programs stressing safe driving and held just before holidays or vacations. Every effort should be made to reduce the serious menace of motor vehicle accidents.

PEDESTRIANS AND BICYCLISTS

It is essential that all institutions take steps to protect pedestrian and bicycle traffic at crossings. Officers should be assigned to major intersections during the hours of peak traffic. Lights should be installed where the volume of traffic is heavy, and stop signs at other intersections. Crosswalks should be painted. This tends to keep pedestrians from crossing in the middle of the block. As the use of the automobile by students is restricted, bicycles are coming into general use. The bicycle provides a relatively safe and economical method of getting around. To keep cyclists from using sidewalks, some colleges have built paths for the use of bicycles only. This plan has resulted in a reduction of accidents.

The problem of motor-vehicle safety among college students is a serious one. With the law passed by Congress in 1966 (Highway Safety Law for 1966), more attention will be paid to the training of youthful drivers, both in high school and college. One of the best steps is to *restrict* the use of cars and motorcycles to those who actually need them through the use of a special licensing system.

REFERENCES

American Association of School Administrators, Eighteenth Yearbook, *Safety Education*, 1940.

[6] Motorcycles and motor scooters have created a problem in many colleges. Some institutions require that they be licensed by the college.

Association of State Universities and Land Grant Colleges and the National Commission on Safety Education, *University Transportation and Accident Prevention Centers* (Washington, D.C.: The Association and Commission, 1962).

Florio, A. E., and G. Stafford, *Safety Education* (New York: McGraw-Hill, 1962).

National Commission on Safety Education, "Conferences on Teacher Preparation and Certification," *History of Driver Education in the United States* (Washington, D.C.: The Commission, 1966).

National Association of Deans of Women and National Commission on Safety Education of the National Education Association, *Fire Safety for College Residence Buildings* (Washington, D.C.: The Association, 1952).

National Safety Council, "Definitions of a Safety Center," *Transaction of the School and College Conference* (Chicago: The Council, 1961).

Nihan, James, "A Practical Approach to College Safety Programs," *Seventh National Conference on Campus Safety* (Chicago: National Safety Council, 1960).

Policies and Practices for Driver Education (Washington, D.C.: The Commission, 1964).

Safety Education by Colleges and Universities (Washington, D.C.: The Commission, 1950).

Sheehe, Gordon H., "The Growth and Role of Centers in the Decade Ahead," *Transactions,* National Safety Council, Vol. 23, 1960, p. 59.

Stack, Herbert J., and J. Duke Elkow, *Education for Safe Living* (Englewood Cliffs, N.J.: Prentice-Hall, 1965).

Strasser, Marland, *et al., Fundamentals of Safety Education* (New York: Macmillan, 1965).

United States Department of Health, Education and Welfare and National Education Association, *Courses in Highway Safety and Highway Traffic* (Washington, D.C.: The Association, 1958).

CHAPTER 13 PREPARATION FOR DISASTER

No community, school, or college is immune from disaster. In the last decade we have seen evidences of this in the Alaska earthquake, the California floods, hundreds of tornadoes in many states, hurricanes, forest fires, and other conflagrations. Although there are no facts available as to the yearly loss of life and property from natural disasters, it is probable that each year the number of deaths would be over 1,000 and the cost of the property destroyed would total well over a billion dollars. Disasters seem to strike in almost every state. For example, in successive years forest fires destroyed many homes in New England, New Jersey, California, Oregon, and Michigan, in addition to bringing about a heavy loss of valuable timber in these and many other states. Floods also cause great losses, especially in coastal areas.

Because the schools and colleges are important community centers they can often do much to aid the community through education and protection. Even though we are not able to stop tornadoes, hurricanes, or floods, we can predict violent storms and prepare people to meet emergencies. In recent years, for example, 110 districts were declared disaster areas by the Presidents. Almost every state had at least one of these areas.

TORNADOES. Several hundred torandoes occur each year, mostly in midwestern and southern states. They are violent, localized storms with a wind velocity that may reach over a hundred miles an hour—strong enough to carry everything in their paths, even heavy automobiles. Although they last but a short time, they can demolish buildings and cause severe damage.

The loss of life from tornadoes may not be great because people are warned. It is possible to predict them fairly accurately. Tornado warning services have been established in many states and their reports are sent by radio and television to areas where storms are likely to hit. College radio stations usually aid in this service. There are a few precautions that should be taken that will help reduce injuries from tornadoes.

1. Whenever possible seek shelter in a concerete or other reenforced building and keep away from windows.

2. In schools, pupils should go to the lower floors or basement and keep away from windows and doors.
3. At home, the corner of the basement in the direction the storm is approaching from is the safest.
4. If caught in the open in a rural section, lie down in a depression or behind a heavy wall or rock. Do not get behind trees or wooden buildings.
5. When a tornado approaches, electric power lines are likely to be blown down. Every home should have a battery radio, fire extinguishers, flashlights, and first aid equipment.

FLOODS. Destructive floods can occur wherever there are rivers or lakes. In addition, hurricanes and tidal waves sometimes cause heavy flooding along the coastal areas. The greatest danger occurs after a heavy rain when a dam breaks and a raging torrent rushes down on a community. Sometimes the rainfall may be as much as 15 inches within a few hours. One of the best illustrations of flood disaster is the Johnstown flood of 1889, in which over 1,200 lives were lost. Johnstown, Pennsylvania, is located at the confluence of two rivers, both of which are so shallow that one could wade across them during summer months. The great flood followed a heavy rain, which caused a poorly constructed earthen dam to give way, allowing the river to become a raging torrent which swept away everything in its path. A stone bridge across the river just below the point where the two rivers came together dammed up the waterway. Debris piled up behind the bridge and backed up the water which flooded the city up to 15 feet above street level. Many other flood disasters have occurred in the same way.

Although the normal average rainfall in the United States varies considerably from one part of the country to another, whenever 10 to 15 inches of rain fall within a short period of time, any city or town where such heavy rain occurs will be in trouble. Flash floods are one of the possible results. They are occasionally caused by a cloudburst over the headwaters of a stream. Hurricanes, too, are usually accompanied by heavy rainfall which often causes flooding.[1]

There are a few precautions that can be taken in cases of flood.

1. If your home is near a river, move to higher ground. In the case of flash floods where there is little time to escape, go to the upper floor of a sturdily constructed building.
2. Listen to the weather reports on radio or television. They give warnings to move to a safe place in time of flood danger.
3. If you live in a home near a river where there are annual spring floods,

[1] The disastrous floods in Italy in 1966 caused damage estimated at more than $1 billion.

do not use your cellar as a storehouse. Homes and stores have lost millions of dollars worth of merchandise stored in basements.

4. Use special precautions if it is necessary to drive during or after a heavy rainfall. Visibility may be poor, highways and bridges washed out, and trees blown down on the roadway.

Fortunately, on rivers like the Ohio and Mississippi where there are destructive floods every spring, reservoirs have been built on the headwaters to hold back the excess water, lessening the danger of floods.

HURRICANES. Hurricanes are violent tropical storms. Those which strike the United States originate near the equator, often in the Carribean. They cover a much larger area than tornadoes, and sometimes have a diameter of 500 miles. The wind velocity often exceeds 125 miles an hour and the storm is usually accompanied by heavy rainfall.

In the last two decades hurricanes have caused a great loss of life and property. Storms that have caused the greatest damage have first hit the Florida coast and then swept northward to strike the Middle Atlantic and the New England states, as in the cases of Hurricanes Carol and Hazel in 1954. The loss of life and property resulting from both of these storms was extremely high.

However, in recent years the Hurricane Forecasting Services tracks the paths of the storms, and the public is alerted by the Weather Bureau and the Coast Guard by radio and television. This service not only serves to protect shipping, but also provides a warning to communities in the path of the storm. Hurricane winds are extremely high, but the storm center often moves in peculiar fashion, sometimes only ten miles an hour and shifting from one direction to another. For example, a storm will hit the South Carolina coast, move northward toward Virginia, and then choose one of two paths, striking directly north toward the Middle Atlantic states or moving in a northeasterly direction out to sea.

There are a few steps that can be taken if you know that the storm is going to hit your community:

1. Move to higher ground or away from the coast. In the storm that hit Texas and Louisiana in 1965, many persons were saved by moving away from the coast.
2. Stone and brick buildings are much safer than those constructed of wood. If you cannot move inland, go to an upper floor of one of a well-constructed building.
3. If your home is not in the direct path of the storm, lay in a supply of foodstuffs, water, first aid equipment, and flashlights. The electric power is apt to be disrupted.
4. Avoid using the car. Trees are apt to be blown down and highways and bridges washed out.

5. If there is sufficient time, board up windows and doors and move valuable materials to an upper floor.

EARTHQUAKES. Fortunately, strong, destructive earthquakes are comparatively rare in the United States and, for the most part, are confined to the western area. The Alaskan earthquake of 1964 not only caused tremendous damage to cities and villages in Alaska, but the subsequent tidal waves caused by the quake destroyed valuable property 1,800 miles away in California. A large number of the world's earthquakes originate at the bottom of the ocean and therefore cause but little damage except from tidal or seismic waves. The greatest loss of life caused by a tidal wave happened in Galveston, Texas, in 1900, when more than 6,000 persons were killed.

Although many colleges have seismographs that record earth tremors, they cannot predict when or where earthquakes will occur.

FOREST FIRES. There is hardly a state that has not been struck by forest fires. Anyone who has seen communities like Bar Harbor, Maine, where well over 100 fine homes were destroyed can realize the terrible destruction that can be wrought by forest fires. The same is true for the communities in California, New Jersey, Michigan, and other states. Moreover, fires not only burn homes, but destroy millions of acres of valuable timber each year.

In the summer and fall months forest areas, which are often as dry as tinder, should be closed to campers, fishermen, and hunters. Moreover, since many highways run through forests, special care needs to be used by motorists not to throw lighted matches or cigarettes along the right-of-way. The Forest Services maintain lookouts in national and state forests which spot fires and sends out squads to fight them.

Forest fire prevention should be stressed in all of the schools as well as in the colleges. Most fires are caused by careless campers and motorists and prevention methods should be stressed on radio and television and through other media. In addition, in some communities, colleges and high school students are sometimes called upon to join fire-fighting squads. Too often fires get out of control, fanned by high winds, and are very difficult to extinguish.

BLIZZARDS. Blizzards are characterized by cold weather, strong winds, and blowing snows. The greatest danger is to motorists marooned on highways in rural districts. Following heavy storms cars are sometimes stalled for several days before snowplows and rescue squads can reach them. Of course, the best advice is to listen to weather reports and keep off the highways when a blizzard is predicted. Chains and snow tires will help but only too often a car is stalled because other vehicles do not have this equipment. If it is necessary to drive in a blizzard, the gasoline tank should be filled, oil and anti-freeze should be checked, and

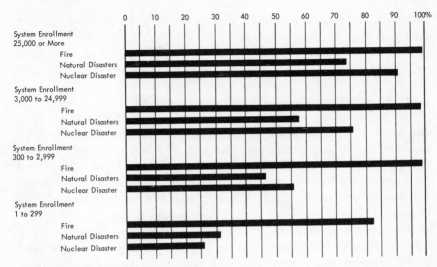

F I G U R E 13–1. Plans for meeting emergencies—per cent of school systems having definite plans.

a shovel should be carried in the car. The heating system should also be checked to see that it is functioning and the exhaust lines examined to see that there is no leakage of dangerous fumes containing carbon monoxide. Being marooned in a blizzard miles from a house in subzero weather can be a most unhappy experience.

CIVIL DEFENSE

In recent years many communities have been active in developing programs for civil defense, but little is being done by the colleges. Much has been said and written about the terrific loss that would occur if a nuclear bomb were detonated over a city. The tremendous explosion produces terrific heat, blast, and radiation that would not only result in many deaths and injuries but also destroy valuable property. Anyone who has seen the films of the destruction of Nagasaki and Hiroshima can get some idea of the terrible result of atomic bombing.

The reasons for the lack of interest in civil defense in schools and colleges is the feeling that most people have that (1) nations having the atomic bomb will not use it because of the fear of retaliation, and (2) in case of an atomic attack nothing much can be done to protect a community. Although the first statement may be true, the second is not. There are many things that can be done to reduce casualties.

It has been emphasized that fallout shelters will greatly reduce the casualties from fallout. It is said that shelters 10 to 12 miles from an atomic blast would have great value in reducing the dangers. Fallout shelters in the basements of college buildings will also aid.

WHAT COLLEGES CAN DO

There are many activities which can be carried on by colleges that will be helpful. Each institution should have an organization that will go into action in event of any type of disaster. In some instances it will be the campus safety organization. The United States Congress has prepared a *National Plan for Emergency Preparedness.*[2] Two other useful publications are the *Disaster Manual*[3] of the American Red Cross and *A Realistic Approach to Civil Defense*[4] published by the Office of Civil Defense.

The college can include discussions of preparation for disasters in many of its courses. Fire prevention and fire fighting can be included in the sciences and engineering. The dangers of poisonous chemicals and gases can be included in chemistry and chemical engineering. Preparation of nursing aids can be included in public health and nursing courses. The construction of the various types of shelters can be introduced in engineering and industrial courses. Home economics and household arts can devote time to emergency foods and mass feeding. First aid can be included in health and physical education courses. Civil defense is related to many fields of education.

In addition to the integration of materials into existing subjects, there is much that can be done in special courses. Some institutions offer training courses for local leaders. Others run extension courses and special institutes to assist communities in training personnel in case of disaster. Still others use members of their faculties who possess technical knowledge that can help in planning programs and training in the local community. They can assist in such problems as health education, traffic control, fire prevention, general safety, and first aid. It is difficult to recommend a general pattern to be followed. Much depends on the location and the size of the community in which the college is located.

COLLEGE PLANS AND OPERATIONS

It is most important in case of disasters that colleges not be found negligent. In fact, they should be the real leaders in preparing for the protection of their personnel and property. The president of the college

[2] Office of Emergency Planning, *National Plan for Emergency Preparedness* (Washington, D.C.: U.S. Government Printing Office, 1964).

[3] American National Red Cross, *Disaster Manual* (Washington, D.C.: The Red Cross, 1955).

[4] Office of Civil Defense, *A Realistic Approach to Civil Defense* (Washington, D.C.: Office of Civil Defense, 1966).

should take the official initiative with the trustees for the development of a program. This activity should be tied to that of the community, not only for assistance and training but also because some of the college facilities might well be used for temporary evacuation centers. In some states one or more members of the college faculty have civil defense responsibility and all or a part of their salaries is taken care of in the state budget. Yet according to *Disaster Readiness,* a report prepared by George Peabody College for Teachers in 1960.[5]

> Most college administrators *profess* to believe that their own institution should have plans for coping with potential disasters. But colleges and universities appear *not to have* such plans. Inasmuch as institutional management is primarily a trustee and presidential responsibility, it may be that governng bodies either disagree with or have not been guided by their administrators. None would dispute the fact, however, that patrons have a right to expect institutions of higher learning to safeguard the physical safety of their students.

INTERNAL OPERATIONS

The president should make certain that conditions and needs of his institution be studied and that plans for possible disaster are prepared. The plan suggested in *Civil Defense and Higher Education* [6] is one of the best that has been prepared. The following is a digest of this plan:

1. Planning Committee Membership
   The president should appoint a planning committee which should consist of:
   a. Chairman, who by experience and interest is capable of giving leadership to the committee and the college community in matters related to disaster protection.
   b. Committee members. The members will depend partially upon the size and type of institution, but consideration should be given in the selection to the regular responsibilities of the individuals. Civil defense should be a part of their regular duties and official activities. Student representation should be included.
2. Planning Committee: Duties
   Should be responsible for the master disaster plans and their revision.
   a. Making an inventory of the campus, considering:
      (1) Nature and extent

[5] George Peabody College for Teachers, *Disaster Readiness in Undergraduate Education* (Washington, D.C., and Nashville, Tenn.: George Peabody College, 1960).

[6] American Council on Education, *Civil Defense and Higher Education* (Washington, D.C.: The Council, 1954). Even though the plan is a very good one, few colleges use it.

    (2) Number and type of habitants

    (3) Location with respect to large centers of population, and industrial and military establishments

    (4) Types and conditions of structures

    (5) Routes of access and egress

    (6) Existing organization, facilities and equipment.

  b. Anticipating types and possible extent of disaster

    (1) Recognizing that all institutions would not be subject to the same kind of disaster

    (2) Being careful not to underestimate possible damage

    (3) Considering effects on personnel, buildings, water and gas pipes, sewage, power and telephone wires, equipment.

  c. Preparing plans for institutions

      In session or out of session, day or night, during and immediately following disaster.

  d. Merging plans with other agencies—Red Cross, local and state civil defense.

  e. Integrating plans with the normal operating schedule of the institution.

Instructional Operation

1. Basic Principles
Smaller institutions might have a single committee; larger will have several subcommittees.

  a. Overorganization can be as bad as underorganization

  b. The institution's organization should maintain its identity but should cooperate with local and state agencies.

  c. Existing agencies in the college, i.e., transportation facilities, health, fire control, and the like should be used.

  d. Organization should show the proper chain of command to prevent confusion.

  e. Reduction of disaster vulnerability is just as much a part of disaster preparation as organization for medical care and rehabilitation after disaster strikes.

  f. Special equipment should be secured.

2. Recruitment and Assignment

  a. Personnel should be drawn from their own regular staff and student body.

  b. Services which may be needed include:
Air raid warnings
Communications
Engineering
Evacuation

      Fire
      Law Enforcement
      Medical and Health
      Police
      Public Information
      Radiological
      Staff
      Supply
      Traffic Control
      Transportation
      Training
      Utilities
      Welfare (housing and feeding)

3. Training

   a. Key committee members should attend national, state or other defense schools.

   b. Courses should be conducted for employees and students.

   c. The faculty should include civil defense materials in existing courses.

A study conducted in 1965 showed that very few colleges had well-organized programs for civil defense. A publication of the National Commission on Safety Education [7] makes a statement on the responsibility of the schools in this area.

References

American Association of School Administrators, *Disaster Protection Handbook for School Administrators* (Washington, D.C.: The Association, 1959).

American National Red Cross, *Disaster Manual* (The Red Cross, 1955).

Bennett, Wells, "University Campus Parking," *Traffic Quarterly* (Saugatuck, Conn.: The Eno Foundation for Traffic Control, 1956).

Campus Safety Association, *National Standard Student Fire Check List* (Chicago: National Safety Council, n.d.).

Department of Health, Education and Welfare, Office of Education, *Education for National Survival* (Washington, D.C.: The Department, 1961).

Douglas, Marjorie S., *Hurricanes* (New York: Holt, Rinehart, 1958).

National Safety Council, *Preparing for Disaster* (Chicago: The Council, 1962).

Public Works (New York: *Civil Defense and Natural Disasters*, April, 1954).

[7] National Commission on Safety Education, *Civil Defense and You* (Washington, D.C.: The Commission, 1966).

Quinlan, Frances Jo, *Safety Monographs for Colleges and Universities,* (Chicago: The National Safety Council, 1959).

Sloan, Eric, *The Book of Storms* (New York: Duel, Sloan and Pearce, 1956).

Smith, Wilbur and Associates, *Safety Monographs for Colleges and Universities,* No. 10 (Chicago: National Safety Council, 1960).

State University of New York, State Educational Department, *Nuclear Survival: A Resource Handbook* (Albany, N.Y.: The Department, 1960).

Strasser, Marland, *et al., Fundamentals of Safety Education* (New York: Macmillan, 1964).

United States Congress Committee on Government Operations, *Federal Disaster Relief Manual* (Washington, D.C.: U.S. Government Printing Office, 1959).

CHAPTER 14 RESEARCH IN SAFETY EDUCATION

Each time the School and College Conference of the National Safety Council questions its membership on the most important needs of safety education, the one item that is most frequently checked is the need for research. Studies conducted by other organizations also reveal a similar need. Safety education is relatively new in the school and college curriculum—hardly a generation old. Other subjects, such as the sciences, social sciences, and mathematics are much older and far more research has been conducted in these areas. For example, between 1930 and 1946 over 420 doctoral dissertations were produced in the fields of health, physical education, and recreation, whereas not more than 40 were completed in the safety field. However, it is fortunate that in addition to research listed under safety education and accident prevention, many other studies have been completed in the related fields of psychology, sociology, engineering, and other subjects that have a direct or indirect application to safety and driver education. A recent publication of the Center for Safety Education at New York University, *The Human Element in Industrial Accident Prevention*,[1] listed over 100 studies related to industrial safety. Similarly, McFarland in *Human Variables in Motor Vehicle Accidents*[2] reviewed several hundred studies that have been completed in the traffic safety field alone. In addition, a recent publication of the National Commission on Safety Education, *Research in Safety Education: A Source Book on Research Studies*,[3] summarizes well over 100 studies, and another, *Accident Research for Better Safety Teaching*, reviews many more.[4] The most comprehensive publication in this field is *Accident Research, Methods and Approaches*, by Haddon, Suchman, and Klein, and published in 1964 by Harper & Row.

[1] Center for Safety Education, New York University, *The Human Element in Industrial Accident Prevention* (New York: The Center, 1953).

[2] Ross A. McFarland, *Human Variables in Motor Vehicle Accidents* (Cambridge, Mass.: School of Public Health, Harvard University, 1955).

[3] National Commission on Safety Education, *Research in Safety Education: A Source Book for Research Studies* (Washington, D.C.: The Commission, National Education Association, 1961).

[4] C. Stratemyer, *Accident Research for Better Safety Teaching* (Washington, D.C.: National Commission on Safety Education, 1964).

The problem in the safety field is not only the need for research, but also the collection, publication, and utilization of research findings. The National Commission on Safety Education of the National Education Association recognizing this need, has recently developed a new publication, *Safety*,[5] in which contributions of individual studies are summarized. Digests of studies are also included in the *Transactions* of the School and College Conferences of the National Safety Council.[6]

To the average teacher research often means dull reports written in an alien language by persons lacking imagination. In an effort to be profound, researchers have tended to isolate themselves behind stilted language and highly scientific statements. Many teachers will not bother to read research of this kind, for it is too obscure and difficult to understand. As would be expected, the applications of research in practices lag a great deal behind the recommendations of the studies. For example, several researchers have shown that the psychophysical characteristics of drivers have little to do with their driving performance as measured in terms of accidents and traffic violations. Attitudes have been shown to be much more important. Yet the average teacher is prone to spend too much time on the psychophysical factors and too little on types of lessons that would tend to improve attitudes.

WHAT RESEARCH IS

Research may be thought of as the steps of reflective thinking. It involves careful or critical inquiry or examination in seeking facts or principles as well as a continued search after truth. It is concerned in education with the improvement of present practices and the determination of improved procedures with a view of ultimately increasing the sum total of knowledge in the field.

There are those who feel that real research will only be carried on by the scholars—the experts. On the other hand, Hubbard[7] contends

> . . . for those of us in education the term "research" may properly be applied to a variety of processes ranging from the preparation of a bibliography to the completion of a highly complex psychological study. All complex studies are made up of a number of processes such as reviewing previous studies, preparing bibliographies, and locating sources of information. After that comes the planning of the scope of the study, preparing outlines, selecting methods, collecting data, analyzing facts, testing results, and reporting findings.

[5] National Commission on Safety Education, *Safety* (Washington, D.C.: The Commission, National Education Association). Published five times a year.

[6] National Safety Council, *Transactions of the National Safety Congress* (Chicago: The Council, published annually).

[7] Frank W. Hubbard, "Research in the Improvement of Education" *Pi Lambda Theta Journal*, 31, Spring, 1953, pp. 131–32.

Thus, research studies in education can be carried on by high school students and their teachers as well as by graduate students and professors in colleges and universities. For example the following types of studies could be carried on by high school students:

Faulty Pedestrian Practices in Selected Intersections.
Observance of Stop Signs by Drivers in Ten Locations.
The Distribution of Accidents and Injuries in a High School.

Studies of this kind, under the direction of the teacher, would not be difficult to conduct. There are also many opportunities for research by the teacher. This is especially true when he is a candidate for an advanced degree. Teachers who are taking a minor or a major in the safety field should be required to plan research projects and carry them through to completion. Many colleges, however, permit the substitution of credit hours for a thesis or research project, which limits the amount of research.

In the National Commission on Safety Education publication *Research in Safety Education*, many of the studies reported are for the master's degree. The following are examples of typical studies: [8]

Funston, John, "An Approach to Traffic Problems Around a School." Adams State College (Colorado), 1956.
Leo, Violette P., "A Survey of the Safety Program in the Secondary Schools of the United States." Chicago Teachers College, 1955.
Lack, Chester, "Social Attitudes of Adult Traffic Violators." University of Southern California, 1955.

Although some of these projects might well have been the problems for the doctoral degree, the topics below involve a higher type of research, a more comprehensive study, usually in greater depth than that required for a master's project. The following doctoral researches are included in the Commission report mentioned above. (In only rare cases are these studies published as a whole. Sometimes they appear as abstracts or magazine articles.):

Heath, Earl D., "The Relationship Between Driving Records, Selected Personality Characteristics and Biographical Data of Traffic Offenders and Non-Offenders." New York University, 1957.
Seals, Thomas A., "An Evaluation of Selected Driver and Traffic Safety Education Courses" (doctor's thesis and abstract). Tallahassee, Florida: Florida State University, 1966.
Goldstein, Leon George, "A Factor Study of Drivers' Attitudes" (unpublished doctor's thesis). St. Louis: George Washington University, 1956.

[8] National Commission on Safety Education, *Accident Research in Safety Education: A Source Book for Research Studies, op. cit.*

EARLY DAYS OF SAFETY RESEARCH

In the early days of the safety movement there was little or no research on which schools could build their safety programs. Mention should be made of some of the first research studies for they were the forerunners of a series of studies that have had much to do with the organization of safety programs. Beginning in 1926, a series of fellowships was established at Columbia University and New York University by the National Bureau of Casualty and Surety Underwriters. Out of these first fellowships came Streitz's *Safety Education in the Elementary Schools*, Heuig's *Safety Education in the Vocational Schools*, and Stack's *Safety Education in the Secondary Schools*.[9] (Several of these studies can be found in university libraries.) These were all published and used for many years as guides for organizing school programs. They were followed by Lloyd's *Safety in Physical Education in Secondary Schools*, Sanders' *Safety and Health in Organized Camps*, and Eastwood's *Study of Safety in College Physical Education*. The last three have had considerable influence in physical education and recreation.[10] (Beginning in 1937, and extending until 1940, the Research Division of the National Education Association issued six research studies which have been combined in a volume *Safety Education Publications*. These were financed by the Highway Education Board.)

When the Center for Safety Education was organized in 1938 at New York University the donors of the original grant, the Association of Casualty and Surety Companies, suggested to the University that a number of fellowships be awarded each year. Since that time well over eighty-five fellowships have been awarded in addition to hundreds of scholarships. These awards have resulted in many doctoral theses as well as master's degree studies. In addition, many universities provide grants for doctorate candidates. The doctorate studies listed in *Research in Safety Education* cover a variety of fields and have had considerable influence in the organization of safety programs. (The Federal Government provided a new source of funds for research in the provisions of the *Highway Safety Law of 1966*.) The methods by which research findings are being utilized will be discussed later.

SELECTING A RESEARCH PROBLEM

Selecting a research problem is a highly important step. Only too often a graduate student selects a problem that is too broad, requires too much in the way of travel and other expenses, or involves too many other diffi-

[9] National Safety Council and Center for Safety Education, *Research in Safety Education* (Chicago: The Council, 1956). Out of print.
[10] *Ibid.*

culties. There are some guiding questions that may be helpful in making a selection:

1. Is it a subject in which the student is greatly interested? Has he been working in a related field?
2. Is it one which leaders in the field feel needs to be studied? Does it have priority on the basis of need?
3. Is it duplicated in any way by previous research? Obviously, the proposed study may be planned from a different point of view, or the use of a different population or geographical area.
4. Are the populations or groups to be studied available and are tools or instruments obtainable or must they be developed?
5. Is the problem within the range of capabilities of the student? The faculty advisor can give guidance on this.

Most students will spend considerable time in selecting a problem. It is important to go through the research literature to find out what studies have been completed. The publication *Research in Safety Education* [11] lists the doctoral theses up to 1956; the *Annual Transactions* of the National Safety Council School and College Conferences [12] carry abstracts of other doctorate studies completed since that time. Yost's doctoral thesis [13] involved an analysis of many master's studies, and Bookwalter's "Critique of Selected Research Studies in Safety," reported in the *1957 Transactions of School and College Safety Conference*. National Safety Council [14] would be most helpful. The reports of the National Conferences on High School Driver Education [15] also lists studies as does *Accident Research for Better Safety Teaching*.[16] A review of these three publications will be helpful.

In his critique of safety research, Bookwalter lists certain weaknesses:

1. Many of the problems started with titles or purposes that were too expansive.
2. Assumptions of randomness of sample, validity of measure, adequacy of the controls were too often overlooked.
3. Paucity of survey returns frequently injected biases into the findings which could have been far greater than criterion differences sought for.
4. Appropriate research method not used.

[11] *Ibid.*
[12] National Safety Council, *Transactions of the National Safety Congress. op. cit.*
[13] C. P. Yost, "An Analysis of Graduate Theses in School Safety in the United States from 1925 to 1950," *1957 Transactions of the School and College Safety Conference*, National Safety Council (Chicago: The Council, 1957).
[14] Karl W. Bookwalter, "Critique of Selected Research Studies in Safety," *1957 Transactions of School and College Safety Conference* (Chicago: The Council, 1957).
[15] National Conference on High School Driver Education, *Practices and Policies for Driver and Traffic Safety Education* (Washington, D.C.: National Commission on Safety Education, 1964).
[16] Stratemeyer, *op. cit.*

5. Data not statistically evaluated and tested. The statistical significances of the difference were rarely reported.
6. Results not presented in usable form. Lack of definitions of terms and explanations of techniques used.
7. Conclusions not limited to the data and not properly classified.
8. Experiment not designed, described, and executed so it could be repeated and verified.

All of these points should be kept in mind in selecting a problem, preparing an outline, and carrying on research.

Priority Problems

Several years ago the National Safety Council and the Center for Safety Education published a list of 189 research studies needed in safety education. This list was prepared by consulting safety experts, supervisors, college teachers, and others, and was published in *Research in Safety Education*. More recently, Malfetti, at that time Chairman of the Research Section of the Division of Safety of the American Association for Health, Physical Education and Recreation, working with his committee, developed a list of 20 priority problems.[17]

This Division set up the following program of action: (1) develop a list of needed research and establish priorities; (2) work with other divisions of the A.A.H.P.E.R., departments of the N.E.A., colleges and universities, national organizations, professional groups and government agencies to accomplish this research; (3) seek funds to implement it; (4) encourage research by graduate students; (5) encourage teachers to conduct research at the classroom level and to cooperate in the research activities of others; and (6) set up machinery to serve long-range aims and yet remain flexible enough to accommodate changing research needs.

The following is a list of the most important topics:

1. What safety preparation is needed by the general teacher?
2. What is the present status of teacher liability in accidents?
3. How should driver education courses be organized and taught to give adequate attention to desirable attitudes?
4. What recommendations can be made regarding techniques for influencing the safety attitude of adults?
5. What has educational research shown regarding methodology for the development and modification of attitudes, and how may this knowledge best be applied to safety education?
6. How good are present teacher education programs in safety? On the elementary level? On the secondary level?
7. What is the validity and reliability of apparatus commonly used for

---

[17] James L. Malfetti, "Research Needs in Safety Education," *Journal of Health, Physical Education, and Recreation* (January 1962).

testing psychophysical characteristics of drivers and driver education students?

8. How may the curriculum adequately provide for the development of desirable attitudes in elementary school children? Junior high school and high school students?
9. What relationships exist between driver attitudes and general personality characteristics?
10. What are opportunities for television as a medium of safety education?
11. What does the psychology of motivation have to contribute to effective teaching of safety?
12. What are the relative merits and conditions of use of the unit approach, integration, and other methods in the organization of safety education content?
13. How are emotional stability and personal adjustment related to athletic accident experience?
14. How effective are schools for traffic violators in reducing subsequent violations and accidents?
15. To what extent are responses on attitude tests reflected in actual driving practices?
16. How may valid tests of safety attitudes be developed?
17. What evidence exists pointing to emotional disturbances as direct causes of motor vehicle accidents?
18. What evidence can be gathered pointing to attitudinal defects as direct causes of motor vehicle accidents?
19. How can safety education content be correlated with the characteristics or patterns of growth and development at the various age levels?
20. What procedure should be followed in developing a course of study in safety education for a city school system?

The National Commission on Safety Education publication of the National Conferences on High School Driver Education also include lists of recommended studies. The following is a list appearing in the 1964 publication.[18]

1. Determination of extent to which current text and instructional materials incorporate existing research findings on accident occurrence, psychomotor skills, tracking, perception, and problem solving.
2. Updating of text materials to reflect current research.
3. Development and dissemination of guidelines to teachers for program evaluation.
4. Determination of the need for driver and traffic safety education for such special groups as adults, drop-outs, and students in nonpublic schools.

[18] National Commission on Safety Education, *National Conference on High School Driver Education* (Washington, D.C.: The Council, National Education Association, 1964).

5. Comparison of the relative effectiveness of summer and after-school programs with the regular school year program.
6. Reevaluation of detailed specifications for the critical knowledge, skills, and attitudes students need to acquire.
7. Identification of the critical risk problems that the younger driver is likely to encounter in the driving task, in order to incorporate instruction on facing such risks into the content of the high school course.
8. Study of the current "reading level" of textbooks and a determination of how this reading level can be raised and/or lowered to provide for all students.

TYPES OF RESEARCH

A review of several textbooks shows a variety of methods for classifying research into various types. Some include more than ten classifications. However, the following will cover the types most frequently used in safety studies:

1. Surveys of present status.

Studies of this type are the most numerous, both for master's and doctoral degrees. It would include such problems as "State Administration and Supervision of Safety Education in the United States" or "Driver Education Practices in Florida." This type of problem is especially suited for master's or Ed.D. studies.

2. Experimental decision.

The experimental type of study is often used to compare the relative values of methods of teaching, to experiment with various techniques, and compare different procedures—for example, studies such as Vaughn's *Positive Versus Negative Instruction* and Birnbach's "A Comparative Study of Accident Repeaters and Accident Free Pupils." Although these are usually on the doctoral level, there is no reason why similar studies could not be undertaken for the master's degree.

3. Adjustment.

"Adjustment" includes a wide variety of problems involving adjustment or changes in procedure. For illustration, "A Critical Study of the Effect of Newspaper Publicity" and "A Comparative Study of the Values of High School Driver Education" belong in this classification as does "The Development of a Program of Driver Selection, Training, and Education for Commercial Motor Vehicle Fleets."

4. Basic investigations.

Studies of this kind are most needed in the safety education field. It is probable that one reason why so few are completed is that they are apt to be more difficult. Subjects such as "Motives that Underlie Unsafe Behavior" and "Role of Attitudes in Accident Prevention" would be good illustrations. *The Personal Characteristics of Traffic*

Accident Repeaters and *Measuring Attitudes Toward Safety in Driving Motor Vehicles* are examples of research that have already been completed.

5. Historical-philosophical studies.

Although historical studies are quite common, philosophical ones are rare. Many master's theses belong in the historical group, and even though there may be sections devoted to philosophy in a number of studies, there are but few that could be called philosophical research. *The History of Driver Education in the United States* would be an example of the former; "The Philosophy of Safety Education in the Public Schools" an illustration of the latter.

STEPS IN PROBLEM SOLVING

Bookwalter, in an article appearing in *Research in Safety Education* [19] entitled "Steps in Problem Solving," considers briefly some of the essential steps.

Statement of the problem. The statement of the problem must be concise, descriptive, and accurate and must include only the general delimitations of the field, time, place, and size or scope of study and the kind of study. One does *not* start out with "A Study of," if it is obviously a study. One should state his problem in the nominative form not as an interrogation. For example, a good title could be "A Survey of High School Health and Physical Education Programs for Boys, in the United States, 1950–1954."

Purpose of the study. The purpose of the study must not be the same as the title of the study. The purpose should be stated in terms of the uses to which the study results are to be put.

Limitations and delimitations. The difference between limitations and delimitations should be indicated. *Limitations* affect the assurance or scope with which generalizations are made. Such limitations must be reviewed at the time of generalizations. The limitations must be admitted and indicated. Examples of limitations are: smallness of sample, soundness of measures, unreliability of opinions, human errors of operation and manipulation, and absence of desired controls.

Delimitations are prescribed boundaries of scope and size, the extent of which determine the frame of reference to which subsequent generalizations will apply. The limits are set by expediency or necessity of finances, personnel, time, and such conditions.

Basic assumptions. Underlying conditions, assumed to exist without need for proof, should be reasonably and approximately met. Likelihood that basic assumptions are met should be high. An example of a violation of an assumption is assuming a normal distribution when the distribution is actually biased or skewed. Another example is assuming that the data for a correlation are linear when actually they are curvilinear. A frequently

[19] Bookwalter, *op. cit.*

violated assumption is that subjects are randomly selected when a definite bias exists. Errors of this sort may be greater than differences experimentally obtained.

Hypothesis. An hypothesis is a preconceived conclusion—which it is the purpose of the study to test. Generalizations made must be with reference to the tenability of the preconceived hypothesis. For example, the null hypothesis states that there is no difference between the groups under consideration. Definite statistical techniques are available, under proper circumstances, for testing such an hypothesis.

PREPLANNING OR ANALYSIS OF PROBLEM

A properly selected problem is unitary. It deals with one well-defined problematical area. Its solution is usually needed for some social purpose or is a contribution to a field of learning. A well-defined problem can usually be resolved into from two to four sub-problems.

Determining the sub-problems. A sub-problem is an aspect of the main problem upon which another aspect is dependent or which depends upon another aspect for its solution. The solution of the main problem is accomplished through the resolution of its sub-problems. The solution of a sub-problem is usually of little value except as it contributes to the main problem.

A sub-problem is solved by a separate technique or through a unique medium. For example, the *exploratory* aspect of a problem usually depends upon related literature, experience, and/or some other authoritative source and its technique is a gleaning, inquiring, or observing, and recording in a logical useful manner.

Through this sub-problem, the researcher is informed of the nature and relevancy of his potential data and of appropriate means for collecting the same.

A second logical step is the *collection* of needed data through the medium suggested and formulated in the first sub-problem. The application of the interview sheet, check list, score card observation or measurement to appropriate sources or objects and the recording of obtained units or observations in comparable manageable form for subsequent organization and analysis.

A final step is usually the classification, *organization, and analysis* of data to ascertain the tendencies, relationships, and inferences from which generalizations may reliably be drawn with regard to the initial statement of the problem and its purposes.

What is needed. For each sub-problem there are two or more related objects or items of information necessary for the solution of the problem. One common error of beginning research workers in planning their problem is to make a major issue or sub-problem out of a mere item which one may need to have or know. How many such items must be brought to a conclusion will depend upon the complexity of the sub-problem and the naivete of the researcher. The more complex the problem aspect or the more naive the researcher, the greater the potential list of items. In the final sub-problem these items may be the kinds of *analysis* needed.

Where to get necessities. Every item one needs must be obtained from some source. Criteria, principles, authorities, jurors, tests, measures, controls, and such sources of data must be either logically acceptable as basic assumptions or their source must be indicated in specific texts, dissertations, or reports or through appropriate procedures. The better read and experienced and grounded the researcher the more specific these sources will be.

How to get the necessities. In this step, the researcher indicates *how* he will glean the literature, appeal to authorities, select the tests, determine the relevancy of controls and the like. Sometimes the step will be obvious and simple as in gleaning a text or dissertation. At other times, it will be more difficult as in the stratified random selection of experimental subjects.

Organization and analysis. This aspect of the outline of proposed procedures is the most vital. All other parts such as "What We Need To Know," "Where Do We Get It," etc., are usually merely intellectual traps to force one to take the proper steps preliminary and subsequent to organization and analysis. In the description of this phase, one must be functional. That is, avoid "weasel statements" such as "logically defined," "tabulate," "find the average," "find the variability," "correlate," or "determine reliability."

For example, in definition, one must show *how* he proposes to include only commonly accepted terms, to make his definition inclusive of all that is relevant, exclusive of all that is irrelevant, concise, and in good English, and to avoid overlapping or contradiction in meaning of terms or phrases.

Following these steps, Bookwalter discusses some of the essential steps in experimental or psychological studies in which the investigator must be familiar with statistical procedures. It is highly important that the proper techniques be used. Certain other researches such as the philosophical, sociological, curriculum building, and survey might require little or no statistics. For a more complete discussion of research see Haddon *et al.* in the References.

However, in addition to the steps above, practically all researches will have a "Summary and Conclusion" and some will have a section dealing with "Recommendations" of "Suggestions for Further Research."

The natures of Ph.D. and Ed.D. studies differ. In some instances the conclusions of a Ph.D. research can be stated in a single paragraph. They are narrower and more sharply defined than Ed.D.'s. The contribution of an Ed.D. document may be a course of study, an organized program, or even a book.

PUBLICATION OF FINDINGS

One of the great weaknesses in research has been the lack of facilities for the publication of findings. Most of the studies completed find their way to the college library where they have little use and gather dust. Even though the research made an important contribution to the literature, it will be seen by but few educators, and therefore have little effect on practices. One great advantage of the first studies mentioned in this chapter is that funds were made available for their publication. Each of these studies was given a wide distribution and was used in schools as a basis for organizing programs.

There are, however, several ways in which research contributions can be made available:

1. Abstracts and articles.

Many studies appear in the form of abstracts or articles in journals. Each year the School and College Conference of the National Safety Council publishes in the *Transactions of National Safety Congress* reports of research given at the Congress. In addition, some of these studies are reported in another National Safety Council publication, *Traffic Safety Research Review*.[20] Still others are included in the *Research Quarterly* and the *Annual Safety Education Review* of the American Association for Health, Physical Education, and Recreation, and other journals. The American Bar Association published Tossell's [21] study of driver improvement schools in North Carolina. Several universities issue digests or abstracts. Stratemeyer reviewed many studies in *Accident Research for Better Safety Teaching*.[22] The National Commission on Safety Education also has a policy of publishing abstracts of certain studies in the magazine *Safety*.

2. Conversion into books.

As a rule doctoral studies make dull reading. But the findings of some can be converted into books. For example, Seaton's research on safety education for teachers of health and physical education was utilized in *Safety in Sports;* Rosenfield's study on liability was published as *Liability for School Accidents;* Wagner's research on the work efficiency of physically disabled industrial workers was published as *Selective Job Placement.* Moreover, authors of safety textbooks have a general policy of quoting from the findings of relevant studies. Instructors in college courses and, to a lesser degree, high school teachers, make use of research findings.

3. Reports at conferences and conventions.

The Safety Education Division of the American Association for Health, Physical Education, and Recreation provides a useful service. At the national and district conventions an opportunity is provided to report research studies at various sectional meetings.

In recent years state associations of driver and traffic safety education in many states have held annual conferences. In addition, the American Driver and Traffic Safety Education Association, a department of the National Education Association, has an annual conven-

---

[20] National Safety Council, *Traffic Safety Research Review, op. cit.*

[21] Tossell, Richard, "Raising Driver Education Teacher Qualifications" *National Safety Council Transactions* (Chicago: The Council, 1962), V. 23, pp. 60–62.

[22] Stratemeyer, *op. cit.*

tion. These meetings give further opportunity for the presentation of research papers. In spite of the various avenues for the promotion of research that have been described, the fact remains that far too many studies are completed and never see the light of day. After they are accepted by the committee on higher degrees, only too often they are filed in the college library, or are passed on to the microfilm collection.

4. Utilization of research findings.

Research is of little value, except to the individual who has conducted it, until it is made use of in effecting changes in practices and techniques in education. No matter how significant the contribution, until its findings are utilized it will be of little value. Although this may be true in many other disciplines of education, it is especially conspicuous in the field of safety education. Though research may be lagging, the utilization of findings is the greater laggard.

As an illustration of this, consider the following: During the past decade many studies have been conducted showing the importance of attitudes in the training of younger drivers. These studies have shown that the chief reason why young people are involved in accidents is because of faulty attitudes. Recently, Sauers [23] completed a doctoral thesis in which he showed the use of group discussion techniques for driver education. An abstract of this was published, and the research reported at several conventions.

It has been established that group discussion is one of the best ways, if not the very best way, of influencing attitudes. It follows that the high school teachers of driver education should make greater use of the discussion technique. But persuading teachers to make changes in their patterns of instruction is a very slow process. Moreover, group discussion takes time; in most high schools, classroom instruction in driver education is limited to 30 periods and there is a great deal of material to be covered. It is to be expected that the adoption of group discussion methods will be a very slow process.

Another illustration of the value of research is the action of casualty insurance companies in reducing the insurance premium for school-trained drivers. Some 25 studies have been conducted in various states of the comparative accident record of school-trained, versus untrained drivers. Although some of these studies were not reliable, nearly all concluded that the safety record of the trained driver was considerably better than that of the untrained. The insurance industry followed this study by conducting their own studies of the loss-cost or claim costs of the two groups. As a result of these studies the industry adopted a policy of reducing the premium over the manual rates when a student had completed a standard course in driver education. In some areas this reduction amounts to as much as $30 a year, and with some ex-

[23] Kenneth Sauers, *Group Discussion Techniques for Driver Education* (New York: Center for Safety Education, 1961).

ceptions is good up to age 25. This is a good illustration of the dollar-and-cents value of driver education. In a given city, if the per-pupil cost of driver education is $50, the actual saving in reduced insurance premiums over a period of years will total several times this amount.

REFERENCES

American Association for the Advancement of Science, *Symposium on Basic Research* (Washington, D.C.: The Association, 1959).

Association for Supervision and Curriculum Development, *Research for Curriculum Improvement* 1957 Yearbook (Washington, D.C.: The Association, 1960).

Barad, Phillip, "What Data Processing Can Do for the School," *School and College Transactions* (Chicago: National Safety Council, Vol. 23, 1965).

Good, C. V., *An Introduction to Educational Research* (New York: Appleton-Century-Crofts, 1963).

Haddon, W. B., *et al.*, *Accident Research: Methods and Approaches* (New York: Harper & Row, 1964).

Malfetti, James L., "Research Needs in Safety Education," *Journal of Health, Physical Education, and Recreation* (Washington, D.C.: American Association for Health, Physical Education, and Recreation, January, 1962), p. 38.

Mouly, G. V., *The Science of Educational Research* (New York: American Book, 1963).

National Safety Council, *Accident Facts* (Chicago: The Council, published annually).

Stack, H. J., and J. D. Elkow, *Education for Safe Living*, 4th ed. (Englewood Cliffs, N.J.: Prentice-Hall, 1966).

Strasser, M. K., J. E. Aaron, R. C. Bohn, and J. R. Eales, *Fundamentals of Safety Education* (New York: Macmillan, 1964).

Stratemeyer, C. G., *Accident Research for Better Safety Teaching* (Washington, D.C.: National Commission on Safety Education, 1964).

Suchman, E. A., and A. L. Scherzer, *Current Research on Childhood Accidents* (New York: Association for the Aid of Crippled Children, 1960).

Tate, M. W., *Statistics in Education and Psychology* (New York: Macmillan, 1965).

Traffic Safety Inventory (Chicago, The Council, published annually).

Travers, R. W. M., *An Introduction to Educational Research* (New York: Macmillan, 1964).

Yost, Charles Peter, "An Analysis of Graduate Theses in Safety Education in the United States from 1925 to 1950," Ph.D. dissertation, University of Pittsburgh, 1956, 460 pages.

PART IV SAFETY
IN SPORTS

Teach a boy to play football safely, or to sail a boat safely, or to use a gun safely; in each case you are showing him how he can have a good adventure instead of a bad one. Instead of the bad adventure of breaking his collarbone he can have the good adventure of carrying the ball across the goal line; instead of the bad adventure of tipping his boat over and either ending his adventure by drowning or temporarily by a stupid wait for help, he can have the good adventure of sailing on to a thrilling finish; instead of ending his hunting adventure with a bullet in his leg, he can have better adventure of the chase.

ALBERT W. WHITNEY

INTRODUCTION

In athletics, physical education, and recreation, accidents and injuries are largely accepted as the inevitable risk of participation. Undoubtedly the possibility of injury in sports will always exist, since the human factor is involved, and the very nature of competition is usually dangerous. It is this attendant danger that often makes it appealing to the participants. It has been found, however, that injuries in sports can be reduced by 50 per cent or more and not deprive games of the element of danger that engenders participation. Inasmuch as athletics, physical education, and recreation are accepted programs of schools and colleges, every effort should be made by all administrators, as well as the coaches and physical educators, to meet the challenge of reducing the number of injuries.

The success of an athletic team or program of physical education and recreation rests to a great extent upon the vital factor of injury prevention. Many leaders lose their positions and worthwhile programs are often abandoned because of an unwarranted death in a sport or activity. It behooves every leader and administrator to watch carefully the accident incidence and to apply effective preventive measures. In general this calls for the determining of basic causes through a thorough accident reporting and analyzation system, by judiciously removing the hazards, and by providing the training and supervision necessary for the development of safe practices.

A Credo for Safety Education

J. Duke Elkow [1] summarized the beliefs, obligations, and aspirations of safety education for our schools and colleges.

This we believe

That education for safe living is a basic responsibility of the schools and colleges of the country.

That safety education has clearly demonstrated its value in reducing accidents to children of school age.

That safety education, rather than discouraging the adventures in physical activity and recreation, actually encourages good adventure by doing away with preventable accidents.

That there is a close relationship between health, physical education, recreation and safety.

That accident prevention programs properly carried out will reduce the injuries in athletics and physical education.

That safety education is the art of cultivating the attitudes, skills, and knowledges that make for safety. Accidents do not just happen; they are caused.

That accidents in physical education and recreation can be controlled by proper training, enforcement of regulations, adequate equipment and facilities, and effective supervision.

That increased participation in recreational activities has been remarkable, and safety education has been responsible for a significant decrease in accidents in sports activities.

That good leadership and adequate facilities and equipment may prevent at least half of the injuries in competitive athletics.

That all schools shall participate in an approved program of accident reporting, determine causes (where possible), and take corrective action for preventing recurrences.

As long as accidents are the leading causes of death among our young people, health educators and health departments should devote more time to safety instruction.

Safety education enables us to choose between experiences that are unproductive, absurd, and even stupid, and those which enrich life and make it more interesting and worthwhile.

[1] J. Duke Elkow, "Safety Education and Accident Prevention," *Annual Safety Education Review* (Washington, D.C.: American Association for Health, Physical Education, and Recreation, 1964), p. 48.

CHAPTER 15 ACCIDENTS AND INJURIES IN SPORTS

WHAT CONSTITUTES AN ACCIDENT

An accident is described by Webster's as, "An event that takes place without one's foresight or expectation especially one of an afflictive or unfortunate character."

If a person were walking in a crowd going to a football game and lightning "selected" him to kill, we would say it was an Act of God. At the other extreme, a certain number of neurotic people choose to injure or kill themselves. Relatively few people suffer injury or death from these two causes but most persons are prone to ascribe all accidents to Acts of God. The majority of the victims are, however, injured by an unplanned event immediately caused by an unsafe act or a mechanical or physical hazard, which is ordinarily spoken of as an accident caused by carelessness. In other words, most accidents are caused; they do not happen. Schulzinger[1] claims that "Universal risk is an ever-present condition of life; hazard, not safety, is the normal state of existence."

SPORTS ACCIDENTS AND INJURIES

Ordinarily, injuries (or even fatalities) in sports are not considered to be the results of accidents. This is particularly true of team and combat sports such as football, soccer, and wrestling. On the other hand, in most individual and dual sports, such as golf or tennis, when the participant is injured it is called an accident. Actually we differentiate within the same sport. If a cross-country runner pulls a muscle it is referred to as an injury, but if he steps in a hole and sprains his ankle it's an accident.

Regardless of the common use of terminology, all accidents in sports are result of an unskillful act, lack of good leadership, improper conditioning, or the use of inadequate equipment or facilities. For example, if a football player tackles another and breaks his clavicle, we do not say that he was injured accidentally. We usually ascribe his injury to hard

[1] Morris S. Schulzinger, *The Accident Syndrome* (Springfield, Ill.: Charles C. Thomas, 1956), p. 234.

luck, to the player's hard hitting, or to the opponent's size. We consider it one of the risks of the game. But is this a complete explanation? Coaches, trainers, and athletes realize that there are true causes of such injuries in sports as well as in other areas. They can readily ask such questions as was the injured player tackling properly? Was he in top condition with his shoulder muscles fully developed? Were his shoulder pads of the proper type and well fitted? Finally, they ask if he is a skilled player or an unskilled one who is often injured and considered accident prone.

MOST ACCIDENTS DO NOT RESULT IN INJURY

It should be realized that most "accidents" in sports do not result in injury. This is especially true in contact sports, where players are constantly "hitting" each other without resulting injuries. One safety engineer points out a similar situation in industry claiming that in a unit group of 330 similar accidents, 300 will produce no injury whatever, twenty-nine will result in minor injuries and only one will result in serious injury. The proportion of mishaps in sports activities could probably never be determined but it is assumed that a much higher ratio of noninjurious acts occur than in industry. However, one should also note that in assessing the risk involved in various sports we have to take into account the frequent chronic microtraumatic lesions which are the result of prolonged participation in sport, and which should weigh heavily in any final assessment of the risks involved.

This higher ratio of noninjurious acts is difficult to determine because of the nature of sports and the nature of athletes or competitors. No two games were ever played exactly the same and no two athletes were ever identical.

THE NATURE OF SPORTS

Sports competition provides the only peace-time activity in life in which one's expression of aggression is socially acceptable. All other forces in daily living impel the individual to sublimate tendencies toward physical aggression.

In all ages sports have been associated with the release of pent-up emotions—pugnacious, chivalrous, religious, sexual, patriotic, or adventurous—for both players and spectators. Play provides an opportunity for the participant to lose himself, to participate in a cause. Play has also been described as "an escape from life." The player (and often the spectator) is usually totally engrossed in the game and is stimulated to go all out, to "give it all he's got." Adolescents, especially those who have a strong distaste for restraint, welcome this opportunity to let go and to be adventurous. This spirit does not generate or even tolerate cautiousness, timidity, or faintheartedness. It calls for complete fitness, total attention, knowledge of the rules and sports strategy, expert leadership, and skillful participation.

ADVENTUROUS SPORTS

Logan,[2] in a study to develop techniques to explore the reasons that people participate in adventurous and dangerous activities such as mountain climbing, spelunking, white-water canoeing, skiing, auto racing, sky diving, and scuba diving, showed the desire for a search for something new and different, to escape from the ordinary, to be active, and to seek worthwhile, exciting activities.

In another study of the values and need of risk activities such as skiing, hunting, archery, mountain climbing, flying, and horseback riding, Rosenthal[3] found that they are necessary for our well-being, and that they persist in our evolution and aging process. Sapora[4] quotes Rosenthal, "He contends that people are deserting risk, exercise-type activities in all phases of life because they are from childhood being encouraged from all sides to do only things that are 'safe' and to avoid taking any chances of getting hurt, of failing in a task, or encountering some other similar 'traumatic' experience."

THE NATURE OF ATHLETES

Physical fitness is an adjunct to safety, and skill is a deterrent to injury. An athlete possesses both fitness and superior neuromuscular coordination. This coordination, or agility, becomes skill when it is trained to perform a movement or series of movements with dexterity and proficiency, and the higher the degree of skill possessed, the more proficient the athlete. Such skill usually assures the athlete of superior speed and often endurance, two characteristics which together with strength, enable him to perform beyond the ability of the nonathlete. It is also reasonable to assume that an athlete is ordinarily endowed with a keener sense of sight and hearing and that he maintains his body in a better state of health than does the ordinary person. In addition, he usually has a highly developed spatial perception, balance, and kinesthetic sense which enables him to "feel"

[2] Annette Logan, "A Study of Individuals Participating in Adventurous Types of Activities," unpublished research paper (Urbana: University of Illinois, 1964).

[3] Sol Roy Rosenthal, "Re-Risk Exercises," unpublished research paper (Chicago: Illinois Medical Center, N.D.).

[4] Allen V. Sapora, "Ascertaining Interests for Recreation Program Planning," *Recreation Research* (Washington, D.C.: American Association for Health, Physical Education, and Recreation and the National Recreation and Park Association, 1966), p. 101.

danger in the form of approaching "enemies" and to protect himself when hit or grasped by an opponent. It is this latter sense by which one's own muscular movements are perceived. Besides these obvious physical abilities, the outstanding athlete usually possesses certain fine qualities of character and judgment, such as courage, leadership, and level-headedness, which enable him to act quickly and correctly in a crisis.

These many characteristics are undoubtedly qualities that help one avoid accidents and injury. Athletes, then, would ordinarily be potentially better accident risks than nonathletes. Despite the fact that an athlete may have the ability to avoid many accidents that an ordinary person could not, it is possible that he experiences more nonathletic injuries than a nonathlete because of his daring and the fact that he participates more often. In discussing longevity of life among athletes, L. I. Dublin[5] of the Metropolitan Life Insurance Company said "He [the athlete] is also a more physically adventurous man who is likely at times to take chances, believing in his superior health, strength, and agility, thus exposing himself to unnecessary risks." Greenway and Hiscock, who compared the mortality rates of Yale letter winners with nonathletes, confirmed this, saying:

> This suggests that the mortality among athletes is higher than among nonathletes, not because they have been injured by their athletic interests, but primarily due to the fact that they are the type of men who, being full of physical energy, are naturally courageous and expose themselves to danger both in war and in time of peace.[6]

In other words, many former athletes tend to overestimate their abilities when they become less active and often more obese.

SAFETY THROUGH SKILLS

As noted, all sports require varying degrees of agility and skill in performing the various fundamental movements, and persons vary greatly in their innate motor capacities and mastery of skills. Poor neuromuscular coordination, displayed in awkward bodily movements, is undoubtedly the principal *physical* cause of injury among sports participants.

The principle of reciprocal innervation in muscular control here enters into the picture. When an impulse to contract is sent to a group of muscles, another to relax is sent to the antagonistic muscles so that they will not inhibit the action. This explains in part the stiffness of the beginner. The awkwardness may also be caused by one's mental state, or it may result from overdeveloped muscles resulting from too much practice in other movements. And so we often judge the caliber of an athlete by his ability to relax and by the free movement he exhibits in performing the required skills. We say that "he makes things look easy." There

[5] L. I. Dublin, "Longevity of College Athletes," *Harper's* (March 1928).
[6] J. C. Greenway and I. V. Hiscock, "Athletic Mortality Among Yale Men," *Yale Alumni Weekly* (June 11, 1926).

are at least two major implications involved here: *First,* a beginner in a sport should always receive scientific instruction. The more dangerous the sport, the more necessary the instruction. Skiing is a splendid example. Literally thousands of beginners are injured each year because they do not get adequate instruction. *Second,* a person who remains awkward at a hazardous sport and who seems unable to master it, incurring many injuries, should give it up and try one less hazardous or one to which he is better adapted. Nature usually helps out here because a person tends to participate only in those sports he enjoys because of his competency.

ACCIDENT REPEATERS AND ACCIDENT PRONENESS

Safety engineers have discovered that, as a general rule, less than one third of the employees in industry are responsible for more than two thirds of the accidents. In Connecticut it was found that 4 per cent of 30,000 drivers figured in 36 per cent of the accidents reported over a six-year period. In fact, in some states it has been estimated that only one tenth of the population experiences three fourths of the accidents. Statistics are not available regarding the prevalence of accident repeaters among participants of physical education activities, but it is reasonable to assume that a similar situation exists. Every coach and teacher is cognizant of the fact that certain members of the squad or class are always getting hurt. These members are usually considered accident prone. On the other hand, accident repeaters may not be prone but are exposed so often that they are injured more often.

What causes a person to be accident prone? This question is only partially answered by scientists in the field. Some believe that those whose motor reactions are quicker than their perceptual level are accident prone. It may be that the causes are to be found in a lack of emotional balance or improper attitude, in a lack of knowledge or skill, or in bodily defects. Although the first, lack of emotional balance or improper attitude, is usually considered the major cause of accidents and probably is a basic cause of accident proneness, it *may not* play a major role in athletics. Almost all players participate because they want to. They enjoy the game and ordinarily become completely absorbed in it. Then, too, there are comparatively few "poor sports" in athletics, and very few persons with bodily handicaps participate. This, then, leaves lack of knowledge and lack of skill as the probable major causes of accidents in sports participation. The lesser is the lack of knowledge. The important factor, then, is skill (See Pechar's study, p. 229.) Marcus [7] feels that any techniques

[7] Irwin M. Marcus, *et al., An Interdisciplinary Approach to Accident Patterns in Children,* Monographs of the Society for Research in Child Development, Vol. 25, No. 2, Serial No. 76 (Lafayette, Indiana: Child Development Publications, Purdue University, 1960), 76 pages.

that tend to control impulsive responses and encourage thoughtful behavior would tend also to lessen accident liability.

Because the obvious *physical* cause of accidents and injuries among sports participants is poor neuromuscular coordination, it is safe to say that in sports the accident repeater is usually the awkward performer. Meredith [8] says:

> Undoubtedly some of the awkward are motor morons, hereditarily and incurably awkward, possibly because of defective kinesthetic sense. But with many, the difficulty is remediable in four ways: (1) by due physical training; (2) by overcoming any sickness, malnutrition, or fatigue which plays a part in muscular weakness and incoordination; (3) by making sure that vision, if defective, is corrected by glasses; and (4) by acquiring pride in precision of motion. The latter is all that is necessary in most cases.

Of course, the above facts, with modification, apply to the performer in physical education and intramural activities as well as to athletics.

EMOTIONS AND ATTITUDES

It should not be inferred that emotional makeup or mental attitude does not play a vital and basic role in the accident-prone person's or accident repeater's record just as it does in a "normal" person's life. Pechar's study of sports accidents [9] reported that

> Of the six groups of contributing factors reported, the *mental-emotional* appeared to be the most important single group with regard to contributing most frequently to the reported accidents. . . . The most frequent contributing mental-emotional factor was reported as "disregarding instruction." Taking an "unnecessary chance" ranked second and "acting impulsively" ranked third.

Emotions and attitudes undoubtedly play a role but possibly not to the extent in sports participation that they do in industry, in the home, or on the streets. For instance, the factor of inattention, which is the bugaboo of industrial safety, or bad manners, the pitfall of motorists, are seldom found among participants of sports. Other attitude factors, such as wilful disregard of instructions, recklessness, violent temper, absentmindedness, wilful intent to injure, or nervousness and excitableness, are present in varying degrees, but sports participants must learn to control them or be penalized, and serious offenders may even be excluded from further participation. It is generally believed that athletic coaches and physical education instructors are usually successful in handling such cases. Because of his propitious position every physical

[8] F. Meredith, *Science and Health Hygiene* (Philadelphia: Blakiston, 1962).

[9] Stanley F. Pechar, "Accidents and Prevention in Secondary School Physical Education," *National Safety Congress Transaction*, School and College Safety (Chicago: The Council, 1962), p. 107.

educator should recognize his responsibility to understand and help these students overcome their tendencies to deviate from the normal. The following quotation from *The Physical Education Teacher and Safety* summarizes the role played by emotions and attitudes.

> Strong emotional states tend to set the stage for accidents. Such conditions may be brought on by fear, anger, and unusual excitability. Worry, sorrow, tensions, and anxieties limit the normal functioning of the individual. The tendency of students to have accidents has frequently been attributed to poor mental health or to more or less intangible psychological factors, such as conflict between judgment and desire, surplus energy, worry, distraction, foolhardiness, wish fulfillment, and other factors or characteristics of which the student himself may not be aware. Such students may become very depressed, boastful, disinterested, or in various ways preoccupied with their own thoughts and feelings. Frequently such conditions are accompanied by slowness of comprehension, poor concentration, loss of energy, indecision, poor muscular control, or impulsive activity. To varying degrees these characteristics are manifested by individuals whom we usually identify as neurotic, nervous, high-strung, or temperamental.[10]

A number of psychiatrists advise accident-prone persons to experience satisfying achievements in a hobby or sport.

In summary, we find that sports are adventurous and satisfy youths' normal demand for risk and daring activity, but the hazards that are not inherent in the game should be eliminated, and every effort should be made to prepare the participant for safe play. The teaching of skills is a basic control in this effort because the more skilled a person is in performing the fundamentals, the less likely he is to be injured. His physical condition, mental attitude, and emotional stability are also controlling factors. The overt reason an accident-prone person or an accident repeater has more accidents is that he acts unsafely more often than others. Similarly, the person who experiences more accidents is usually injured more often. Finally, it must be remembered that the person who is exposed to danger most often is also most likely to be exposed to accidents and injuries.

INJURIES IN SPORTS

There have been at least two critical periods in the history of football when the public demanded abolition of the sport because of its brutality and the high mortality and injury rate. With the possible exception of boxing, no other sport has raised the ire of the American public to the extent that the rules have been modified to protect players. Boxing has been virtually eliminated as a school sport for this

[10] National Safety Council, *Safety in Physical Education and Recreation* (Chicago: The Council, 1941).

reason. In fact the fear of injuries in contact sports causes many parents to forbid their sons to participate. Schools and colleges have it within their power to dispel fear by the administration of a sound safety program.

Before we begin the study of accident prevention in sports it will be necessary to review the many studies of the causes of accidents and injury that have been made in this field. Stratemeyer [11] warns that the exact meaning of accident statistics is difficult to assess. She claims, "That even the accuracy of the data presented must, to a degree, be regarded as open to question. Investigators in this area have not yet arrived at accepted methods for securing and reporting accident information. . . . Nevertheless, even when accident statistics presently available are viewed with an awareness of their shortcomings, some useful descriptive statements may be formulated."

Although it is difficult to compare the relative hazardousness of various activities or areas, the incidence of accidents in sports participation is surprisingly low when compared to others. It is probable that sports participation in properly supervised situations is less hazardous than staying at home or driving an automobile, and it certainly is less hazardous than walking or playing in the streets. Kenneth S. Clark,[12] of the American Medical Association, in his "Calculated Risk of Sports Fatalities," claims the fatality-rate ratios by man-hour exposure, football to daily living, was 1:1 and football to riding in a car 1:9.

As can be seen in Tables 15-1 and 15-2 Clark compares the hazardousness of football with a few other activities as well as with daily living. He cautions that, "These data have utility only for internal comparative

TABLE 15-1

FATALITY RATES FOR SELECTED ORGANIZED COMPETITIVE SPORTS *

SPORT	DEATHS	AVERAGE ANNUAL PARTICIPANTS	RATE †
Football, college and high school	26	666,000	3.9
Power boating	1	6,000	16.7
Auto racing, all types	30	25,000	120.0
Horse racing	1.6	1,200	133.3
Motorcycling ‡	5	2,800	178.6

* Based on totals for 1960–1964 published in the *Statistical Bulletin*, Metropolitan Life Insurance Company.

† Fatality rates are expressed as deaths per 100,000 population.

‡ Motorcycling data referred to average registration totals in sponsored events. Figures were derived by using an arbitrary assumption of five registrations annually by each participant.

(Courtesy of the Journal of the American Medical Association)

[11] Clara G. Stratemeyer, *Accident Research for Better Safety Teaching* (Washington: National Commission on Safety Education, National Education Association, 1964), p. 13.

[12] Kenneth S. Clark, "Calculated Risk of Sports Fatalities," *The Journal of the American Medical Association* (September 1966).

TABLE 15-2
FATALITY RATES PER MAN-HOUR EXPOSURE,* 1964

Step	MALES, 15–19 YEARS (HIGH SCHOOL)	MALES, 18–22 YEARS (COLLEGE)
1. Population		
Total	8,133,000	6,728,000
Football players	850,000	65,690
2. Annual fatality rate		
Daily living, all causes	130.1	162.8
Daily living, accidents	84.4	104.4
Football, all causes	0.4	0.1
Football, accidents	0.2	0.1
Motoring	55.4	74.2
3. Fatality rate during football season		
Daily living, all causes	32.5	54.3
Daily living, accidents	21.1	34.8
Football, all causes	3.6	6.1
Football, accidents	2.2	4.6
Motoring	13.9	24.7
4. Hours exposure, football season		
Daily living	1,232	1,680
Football practices and games	110	180
Motoring	77	105
5. Fatality rate per hour exposure, football season		
Daily living, all causes	0.0264	0.0323
Daily living, accidents	0.0171	0.0207
Football, all causes	0.0327	0.0339
Football, accidents	0.0200	0.0256
Motoring	0.1805	0.2352
6. Comparative fatality-rate ratios by man-hour exposure		
Daily living, all causes: football, all causes	1:1.2	1:1.1
Daily living, accidents: football, accidents	1:1.2	1:1.2
Football, accidents: motoring	1:9.0	1:9.2

* Fatality rates are expressed as deaths per 100,000 population.

(Courtesy of the Journal of the American Medical Association)

purposes (i.e., periodic fluctuation of risk within a given sport). Even then, a rate must be used to avoid overdramatization of year-to-year fluctuation with such small totals: If in 1965 the 1964 fatality tally for college football increased by but one (from four to five), a 25 per cent increase in college football deaths is an 'accurate' finding." Dr. Clark summarizes his study as follows:

In 1964, for every 25,000 varsity football players, one died from football-related causes; each football-related fatality occurred for approximately every 3 million man-hours exposure. Calibration of this risk of death from football demonstrated numerous pitfalls in judging the relative hazards in sports from fatality data. Moreover, we do not know what the football candidate otherwise might have been doing during those hours on the football field. Certainly, he would not choose football over riding in a car on the basis of the relative risk of death resulting from this exercise. Neither can the decision to begin, continue, or end participation in interscholastic or collegiate football be justified from these findings. Fatality rates do not depict the conditions under which the potential hazards outweigh the potential benefits.

What constitutes undue risk from participation in sports remains intuitive. Understanding what goes into a yardstick of risk plus a respect for the limited utility of fatality-risk figures are a sound combine for rebuttal of intemperate conclusions.

The more a sound research design is incorporated into a sports program, the more the undue-risk question can be put on an individual basis.

Various other studies have disclosed the comparative dangers of other sports in the United States and a recent study in Sweden indicates very little variance among nations.

CITYWIDE INJURIES IN SPORTS

In Oslo, Norway, according to a study made by Dr. Otto Johansen,[13] injuries in sports and open-air activities accounted for only 8 per cent of a total number of 75,481 injuries embodying occupational accidents (31 per cent); traffic accidents, 3.4 per cent; other street accidents, 11.4 per cent; brawling and assault, 2.1 per cent; accidents in homes, and other places, 44.1 per cent. See Tables 15-3.

TABLE 15-3
SPORTS INJURIES RANK FOURTH

	PER CENT
Home	44.1
Occupational	31.0
Street (other than traffic)	11.4
Sports	8.0
Traffic	3.4
Brawling and assault	2.1

The 6,053 sports injuries represented the vast majority of acute sports injuries occurring in Oslo, which has a population of approximately 430,000. Skiing was found to be the cause of the largest number of sports injuries. Table 15-4 shows the totals for each sport.

[13] Otto Johansen, *Idrett og Skader* (*Injuries and Sports*) (Oslo, Norway: The Royal Norwegian Ministry of Church and Education, State Office for Sport and Youth Work, 1955).

TABLE 15-4

DISTRIBUTION OF INJURIES ACCORDING TO SPORTS IN OSLO, NORWAY

SPORTS	TOTAL	BREAKS	FRAC-TURES	SPRAINS	HITS	CUFFS	BRAIN CONCUS-SION	OTHERS
Skiing	1783	665	55	586	276	144	31	26
Soccer	1320	314	51	372	217	309	14	43
Gymnastics	622	205	16	240	91	50	3	17
Swimming	523	50	12	40	35	375	1	10
Handball	393	112	18	171	50	35	2	5
Ice Skating	363	140	7	66	50	90	8	2
Cross-Country Skiing	279	82	2	35	51	101	8	–
Training	245	76	6	67	40	48	0	8
Ice Hockey	132	19	3	7	36	65	2	–
Wrestling	116	48	7	28	17	11	0	5
Boxing	100	41	0	14	16	26	0	3
Track	90	23	1	36	4	21	1	4
Orienteering	57	6	2	24	7	18	0	–
Tennis	30	3	3	14	1	5	0	4
Totals	6053	1784	183	1700	891	1298	70	127

Idrett og Skader—Otto Johansen.

These results are based on the total number of patients treated at a casualty clearing station and not on the total number of participants or degree of exposure and therefore may not present a complete picture. It cannot be said with certainty that skiing is the most hazardous sport in Norway because many more people may have participated in this sport than in the others.

NATIONAL SPORTS DEATH STATISTICS

According to statistics gathered in the United States by the Metropolitan Life Insurance Company among its policy holders, water sports (315 deaths during 1959) are the most dangerous. Two other aquatic activities rank next—boating, with 55, and fishing, with 46.

COLLEGE ACCIDENTS

There have been several surveys of college accidents and injuries in athletics and physical education with all producing similar findings.

At the University of Florida, Solly [14] made a study of the injuries treated at the University infirmary which disclosed the usual finding that

[14] William H. Solly, "Nature and Causes of Accidents on the University of Florida Campus," *National Safety Congress Transactions, School and College Safety* (Chicago: The Council, 1960), p. 29.

TABLE 15-5

NUMBER OF DEATHS FROM SPECIFIED SPORTS AND RECREATIONAL ACCIDENTS

According to Activity of Person. Personal Life Insurance Policyholders, Ages 10–64 Years. Metropolitan Life Insurance Company,* 1959

Type of Activity	Number of Deaths	Type of Activity	Number of Deaths
Total	315	Horseback Riding	5
Water Sports	138	Baseball, Softball	5
Swimming or playing in the water	119	Playing in sand pit or tunnel (cave-in)	5
Diving from docks, banks, etc.	12	Basketball	3
Skin and scuba diving	5	Target shooting	3
Water skiing	2	Aviation	3
Boating	55	Football	2
Fishing	46	Playing on ice–drowning	2
Boat accidents	29	Picnicking–drowning	2
Drowning (excluding boat)	11		
Other	6		
Hunting	35		
Firearm accidents	19		
Drowning	12		
Boat accidents	10		
Other than boat accidents	2		
Other	4	Other specified	11

* Exclusive of Pacific Coast States and Canada, and of military personnel.

athletic areas were the scene of almost twice as many accidents as other identifiable areas or facilities. There were 1,634 reported accidents, of which 97 per cent were not serious and 75 per cent of the victims were men.

TABLE 15-6

INCIDENCE OF ACCIDENTS IN SPECIALIZED AREAS

Specific Area	First Semester	Second Semester	Total
Play Area	214	257	471
Residence Room	82	74	156
Work Area	18	56	74
Stairway	33	31	64
Hallway	22	22	44
Classroom	16	24	40
Dining Area	6	17	23
Lavatory	2	13	15
Lounge or Recreation Room	8	9	17
Locker or Shower Room	6	4	10
Other	316	218	534

It will be noted that only ten locker or shower-room accidents were treated. This is an area that many people mistakenly believe to be the most dangerous.

In view of the fact that the University of Florida is noted for its tremendous number of motor scooters and bicycles on campus, it is quite revealing to find that more injuries were caused by the use of balls and play equipment.

TABLE 15-7

INCIDENCE OF ACCIDENTS ACCORDING TO
CAUSATIVE AGENTS

CAUSATIVE AGENT	FIRST SEMESTER	SEMESTER SECOND	TOTAL
Furniture	17	27	44
Auto	43	22	65
Motorcycle	35	35	70
Bicycle	31	17	48
Door or Gate	18	17	35
Gun or Knife	19	18	37
Other Cutting Devices	13	72	85
Other Person	183	99	282
Fire or Heat	23	20	43
Chemicals	6	16	22
Tools	6	18	24
Balls and Play Equipment	111	128	239
Other	302	262	564

As would be expected, freshmen experienced the largest number of accidents. It is easy to understand because this was the largest class and its members were confronted with a new environment for the first time. Similarly, the most dangerous time of day for the accidents was between 3 and 6 P.M., when most students are out of class and out for recreation.

TABLE 15-8

FREQUENCY OF ACCIDENTS BY TIME OF
DAY OR NIGHT

		FIRST SEMESTER	SECOND SEMESTER
A.M.	12–3	25	20
	3–6	10	5
	6–9	55	30
	9–12	130	105
P.M.	12–3	195	185
	3–6	240	240
	6–9	80	120
	9–12	75	85

TABLE 15-9

School Accidents by Type of Period and Percentage of Accidents Which Occur

TYPE OF PERIOD	COLLEGE						HIGH SCHOOL		
	WOMEN			MEN					
	PER CENT	INCIDENCE	SEVERITY INDEX	PER CENT	INCIDENCE	SEVERITY INDEX	PER CENT	INCIDENCE	SEVERITY INDEX
Class Instruction	55.4	2.2	4.1	24.1	.7	.8	49	6.4	4.1
Intramural	19.6	1.7	2.8	5.1	.2	1.5	10	.98	8.5
Intercollegiate Competition	5.8	20.9	2.7	19.7	7.4	1.8	43	94.0	6.5
Intercollegiate Practice	4.6	8.1	3.9	26.2	5.0	2.1			
Unsupervised (Free Play)	3.9		2.2	7.8		1.2	1	.88	5.5

Source: W. B. Saunders Company.

Florio [15] attempted to survey 296 colleges and universities and received returns from 131, but only thirty-five sent usable data. He found, based upon 100,000 man hours exposure, that touch football, ice skating, and personal defense were the three most hazardous sports. As would be expected, team sports and contact activities had the highest accident frequency rate and as usual the extremities were the parts of the body most often injured with the sprained ankle most prevalent. Contrary to other studies, he found 59.4 per cent of the injuries occurring in the gymnasium rather than on the outdoor fields.

Condon [16] reported 448 injuries to 920 athletes at Boston College over a five-year period that disqualified the players temporarily or permanently. He claimed that an athlete runs a fifty-fifty chance of receiving such an injury.

The danger spots on college campuses, according to a survey made by the American College Health Association and the National Safety Council, are the athletic fields and gymnasiums, the physical science laboratories, and the walking surfaces. It was found that 55 per cent of all campus injuries in eleven universities were the result of sports accidents. The experience of the University of Minnesota in succeeding years disclosed an identical rate of sports injuries. These accidents were caused by poor field conditions, crowded or confined areas, inadequate rules, poor or ineffective officiating, and improper protection equipment.

A compilation of other studies indicates a more definitive nature of the cause of injuries among college athletic, physical education, and recreation activities.

TABLE 15-10

CONTROL CAUSES OF ACCIDENTS

| | COLLEGE | | HIGH SCHOOL |
| | MEN | WOMEN | (BOTH SEXES) |
	PER CENT		PER CENT
Equipment	10	27	20
Leadership	16	29	51
Nature of Sport	74	43	29

Source: W. B. Saunders Company.

As would be expected, these figures disclose better leadership and facilities on the college level than in high school, and that college women often inherit the poorer facilities and equipment.

[15] A. E. Florio, "Accidents and Injuries in College Physical Education Programs for Men," *National Safety Congress Transactions, School and College Safety* (Chicago: The Council, 1962), p. 109.

[16] R. V. Condon, "Athletic Trauma and Incidental Disease: Principles and Analysis at Boston College, 1950–55," *New England Journal of Medicine* (August 25, 1955), pp. 312–15.

High School Accidents

In a study of accidents and injuries in the physical education programs of 96 junior and senior high schools in New York state Pechar [17] found 1,408 accidents reported over a ten-month period. Approximately 46 per cent of these occurred during September and October when the most hazardous sports, six- and eleven-man football, are played.

The eleventh-grade participants experienced the largest number of accidents (383) with the tenth and twelfth grades following with 353 and 348 respectively.

As found in practically all such surveys, 60 per cent of the accidents occurred on the athletic field and 32 per cent in the gymnasium. Two thirds of these accidents occurred during practice and games of interschool sports.

TABLE 15-11
New York Injuries in Secondary Sports (Pechar)

Gross	Severity
Six-man football	Six-man football
Eleven-man football	Eleven-man football
Ice Hockey	Ice Hockey
Lacrosse	Lacrosse
Wrestling	Soccer

Sprains were the most frequent type of injury reported, followed by fractures and wounds. The parts of the body most frequently injured were the leg and foot, followed by the arm and hand and the head.

Contributory Factors to Accidents

The personal factors (physical and mental-emotional) were contributory to the reported accidents 62 per cent of the time as compared to the administrative factors (equipment, facility, program, etc.) which accounted for 38 per cent of the total. The mental-emotional factors (inattention, haste, disregard of instructions, etc.) were contributory to the largest number of reported accidents.

"Poor skill" was the single most important contributory factor to accidents. This was followed by "disregarding instruction" and "poor surface of play area."

High School Athletic Accidents

High school athletic benefit plans provide an excellent source for the compilation of injuries in sports, particularly in athletic competition.

The state of Michigan found that it made injury payments to over

[17] Pechar, *op. cit.*

nine per cent of its insured athletes over a twenty-year period. Table 15-12 shows the distribution of payments to 60,263 students among 672,503 registered.

TABLE 15-12
INSURANCE PAYMENTS FOR SPORTS INJURIES

	PER CENT
Football	68.8
Basketball	13.2
Physical Education and Intramurals	6.2
Baseball	4.1
Track and Cross Country	3.9
Wrestling	3.0
Swimming	0.4
Other	0.4

Table 15-13, compiled from records in three midwestern states, is typical of the claims filed as a result of injuries in participation. As would be expected, football is the most hazardous, accounting for four or five times as many injuries as any other sport. Claims for physical education are surprisingly low when one considers the much larger numbers involved as compared to athletics. The table disclosed how similar the statistics are for the various states.

TABLE 15-13
ATHLETIC INJURIES IN THREE STATES

Claims Paid for Athletic Benefit Plans

	MICHIGAN (20 YEARS) PER CENT	MINNESOTA (23 YEARS) PER CENT	WISCONSIN (1 YEAR) PER CENT
Football	68.8	59.0	60.6
Basketball	13.8	21.0	18.5
Wrestling	3.0	4.2	6.4
Track	3.9	3.4	5.7
Physical Education	6.2	4.0	1.5
Swimming	0.4	0.2	
Hockey		3.1	
Other sports	7.3		

After Forsythe, Charles C., *Administration of High School Athletics*, 4th Edition (Englewood Cliffs, N.J.: Prentice-Hall, 1962).

EIGHT-YEAR STUDY OF PREP-SCHOOL INJURIES

Donald M. Clark, M.D.,[18] made an eight-year study of injuries in sports at Phillips at Andover, Massachusetts, where all 850 students participated in an extensive sports program. Table 15-14 summarizes his study.

[18] Donald M. Clark, M.D., "Some Medical Aspects of Pre-College Sports for Boys," in *Proceedings of the Sixth Annual Conference of the Medical Aspects of Sports*, A.M.A., Nov. 1964.

TABLE 15-14

EIGHT YEARS' PREP-SCHOOL SPORTS INJURIES 1956-1963

	FRAC-TURES	DISLOCA-TIONS	CONCUS-SIONS	LACERA-TIONS	ABRA-SIONS	SPRAINS	STRAINS	CONTU-SIONS	TOTAL
Football	150	9	36	55	93	234	132	353	1062
Soccer	58	–	18	37	57	131	101	294	696
Track	20	–	–	30	174	91	204	61	580
Lacrosse	33	1	1	39	46	69	68	163	420
Hockey	36	7	7	77	48	39	76	135	418
Basketball	85	–	–	35	41	87	48	77	380
Baseball	21	9	4	24	62	49	74	59	302
Wrestling	5	2	–	–	30	44	54	54	189
Skiing	17	–	1	5	30	21	25	41	140
Squash	–	–	–	24	27	19	34	28	132
Tennis	2	–	–	1	20	11	22	24	80
Cross Country	7	–	–	–	9	6	32	1	55
Crew	–	–	–	1	–	3	16	–	20
Total	434	28	67	328	637	804	886	1290	4474
Yearly Average	54	4	8	41	80	100	111	161	559

From D.M. Clark, M.D., "Some Medical Aspects of Pre-College Sports for Boys," in *Proceedings of the Sixth Annual Conference of the Medical Aspects of Sports.* A.M.A., Nov. 1964.

TABLE 15-15
Incidence of Accidents, Number of Days Lost, and Severity Index

Activity	Boys			Girls			Total		
	Inc. Acc.	Days Lost	Sev. Ind.	Inc. Acc.	Days Lost	Sev. Ind.	Inc. Acc.	Days Lost	Sev. Ind.
Basketball	169	114.00	.67	50	18.00	.36	219	132.00	.60
Football	142	162.00	1.14	0	.00	.00	142	162.00	1.14
Softball-Baseball	35	18.00	.51	20	7.50	.38	55	25.50	.46
Volleyball	23	15.00	.65	29	8.50	.29	52	23.50	.45
Stunts-Tumbling	21	21.00	1.00	22	12.00	.54	43	33.00	.77
Track	33	36.50	1.11	11	11.50	1.04	44	48.00	1.09
Team Games	29	59.50	2.05a	12	7.50	.62	41	71.50	.17
Locker-Shower Room	18	14.50	.80	12	6.50	.54	39	21.00	.54
Wrestling	29	33.50	1.16	0	.00	.00	29	33.50	1.16
Trampoline	12	7.50	.62	14	5.75	.41	26	13.25	.51
Soccer-Speedball	9	3.50	.39	14	10.00	.71	23	45.00	.20
Apparatus-Gymnastics	11	3.00	.27	7	3.50	.50	18	6.50	.36
Relays	8	6.00	.75	6	5.50	.92	14	11.50	.82
Calisthenics	6	4.50	.75	5	.50	.10	11	9.50	.86
Swimming-Diving	3	4.50	1.50	4	3.00	.75	7	7.50	1.07
Field Hockey	0	.00	.00	3	1.00	.33	3	1.00	.33
Ice Hockey	2	.00	.00	0	.00	.00	2	.00	.00
Dance	0	.00	.00	2	.50	.25	2	.50	.25
Archery	0	.00	.00	1	.00	.00	1	.00	.00
Badminton	0	.00	.00	1	3.00	3.00	1	3.00	3.00
Ice Skating	0	.00	.00	1	.00	.00	1	.00	.00
Judo	0	.00	.00	1	.00	.00	1	.00	.00

a Deleting the absence of 41 days to one student, this severity index equals .36.
Courtesy of Jean Katharyn Dissinger Research Quarterly (December 1966).

Clark makes the following observations regarding his study.

These statistics dealing with the various types of sports injuries in an independent school vary so little from year to year that perhaps it would not seem impractical to collect comparable statistics for a decade from any type of a secondary school or a group of them, and from these figures be able to predict quite accurately within certain limits what kinds of injuries would be encountered during the coming years. This, of course, could lead to selection of an improved school program for the care of sports injuries.

ACCIDENTS IN JUNIOR HIGH SCHOOL

A study by Dissinger [19] investigated the incidence, resultant injuries, and prevalent causes of accidents in 207 public junior high schools.

Data evinced that three-fifths of the 1,626 accidents occurred either in physical education or in activities related directly to this field. Activities responsible for the greatest percentage of accidents to both sexes and of accidents to boys only were basketball, football, softball, and baseball. Uppermost for girls were basketball, volleyball, and stunts and tumbling. Accidents pervading interscholastic practice, interschool games, and intramurals induced higher severity indexes than did accidents in the physical education classroom. Activities incurring the most severe student injuries were wrestling, football, and track. Diagnosed in the highest percentage of cases were the sprain, fracture, and bruise. The extremities were the parts of the body involved most frequently. Prevalent immediate causes of injury were falling, striking, or being struck by play equipment, and collision. Evidence relating to predisposing cause proved inconclusive.

Elementary School Accidents

Each year the National Safety Council [20] tabulates accident reports of a large number of schools throughout the country. It can readily be seen from Table 15-16 that the activities of athletics, physical education, and recreation account for nearly 60 per cent of school accidents; with unorganized activities, games and football accounting for most accidents. The seventh, eighth, and ninth grades seem to be the most dangerous grades (not shown on Table) for most activities.

Drowning Deaths

School and college aquatic programs have been so safe that their accident rates—especially for drowning—are extremely low. Some college

[19] Jean Katharyn Dissinger, "Accidents in Junior High School Physical Education Programs," *The Research Quarterly* (December 1966), Vol. 37, No. 4 (Washington, D.C.: American Association for Health, Physical Education, and Recreation, 1966).
[20] National Safety Council, *Accident Facts* (Chicago: The Council, 1966).

TABLE 15-16

SCHOOL JURISDICTION ACCIDENTS

(Grades 1 through 12)

ATHLETICS, PHYSICAL EDUCATION AND RECREATION		OTHER SCHOOL AREAS	
Unorganized activities	10.4	Auditoriums and Classrooms	9.3
Football	9.9	Going to and from school	8.2
Other organized games	9.6	Other grounds	5.2
Basketball	6.6	Shops	4.3
Apparatus (playground)	5.6	Stairs and stairways (inside)	3.0
Baseball and softball	5.0	Corridors	2.7
Volleyball and similar games	2.7	Steps and walks (outside)	2.2
Track and Field events	2.3	Special activities	2.0
Soccer and soccer type games	2.0	Other building	1.9
Playrooms	1.9	Toilets and washrooms	1.2
Showers and dressing rooms	1.0	Fences and walls	1.0
Swimming	1.0	Laboratories, Homemaking	.5
Lockers (room and corridor)	.8	Laboratories, Science	.5
Circle games	.7		
Hockey	.3		

Adapted from *Accident Facts,* National Safety Council, based on 57,779 school jurisdiction accidents from schools with enrollment of 3,222,000. Accidents included are those requiring a doctor's attention or causing absence from school of one-half day or more.

pools have been operated for over 30 years without a drowning. There were, however, 6,800 drownings in the U.S. last year. Only nine of them were school drownings.

The number of drownings in public and home pools have increased tremendously in the last few years because of the rapid growth in pool construction. In 1947 there were an estimated 10,800 pools of permanent construction in the U.S. In 1967 there were over 566,800, of which over 400,000 are home pools. In 1958 it was estimated that there were only 62 swimming pool drownings in the U.S., but newspaper accounts reported 226 swimming and wading pool drownings in public places in 1967. Fifty-three of these were in motel pools. They occurred primarily among youths; 46 per cent were 5 to 14 years old, 20 per cent 14 to 24, and 17 per cent under 5. Only 17 per cent were 25 or older.

Accident Facts further reported that public pools had the highest drowning rates with 38 per cent. Private club drownings totaled 6 per cent, youth or athletic organizations, 6 per cent and schools only 4 per cent.

SCUBA DIVING AND SKIN DIVING

Accident Facts also reports an upsurge of drownings in connection with skin diving and scuba diving. It records that newspaper accounts reported eighty-six underwater-diving drownings in 1965, sixty from scuba diving and twenty-six from skin diving. Ages of the victims ranged

TABLE 15-17

RESULTS OF BOATING ACCIDENTS

TYPES OF CASUALTY	FATALITIES					INJURIES					AMOUNT OF DAMAGE (Dollars)				
	1961	1962	1963	1964	1965	1961	1962	1963	1964	1965	1961	1962	1963	1964	1965
Grounding	9	12	12	15	12	63	43	84	65	49	570,700	386,100	627,700	555,400	455,200
Capsizing	404	443	463	517	549	27	32	49	41	19	126,900	125,400	158,400	173,800	134,600
Flooding	74	30	36	54	41	4	9	4	3	1	35,500	56,200	51,300	47,000	36,200
Sinking	87	112	100	89	152	13	6	2	5	3	230,500	473,500	608,000	494,400	580,400
Fire or Explosion of Fuel	21	14	15	13	18	258	198	224	237	214	1,384,500	1,035,300	1,220,300	1,325,400	1,391,300
Other Fire or Explosion	2	2	2	....	2	17	11	24	12	12	761,300	496,200	595,400	957,000	491,200
Collision with Another Vessel	30	32	32	29	38	334	286	343	394	243	712,100	892,800	758,100	935,100	824,800
Collision with Fixed Object	26	24	35	31	29	82	101	132	120	92	215,500	236,100	325,600	380,400	254,500
Striking Floating Object	23	12	29	20	24	13	6	13	22	29	151,300	194,200	329,400	245,500	364,600
Other Casualty to Vessel	25	27	43	26	58	28	15	25	21	7	182,700	147,700	122,000	54,500	107,300
Falls Overboard	256	279	251	289	340	12	10	8	7	9	1,200	2,000	400	3,000	1,700
Falls Within Boat	....	....	....	....	....	10	21	21	16	12	....	....	....	....	....
Struck by Boat or Propeller	20	12	17	19	8	125	137	126	152	160	....	100	200	200	100,700
Other Personnel Casualty	124	56	69	90	89	102	102	109	98	77	....	100	700	100	300
TOTAL	1101	1055	1104	1192	1360	1088	977	1164	1193	927	4,372,200	4,027,700	4,797,500	5,171,600	4,742,800

(Courtesy of U.S. Coast Guard)

from eleven to fifty-nine years, but more than half were between eighteen and twenty-five years. Of the 86 victims, eighty-two were males.

Many victims were reported as unusually skillful swimmers and about half were experienced divers. Among those with little diving experience, nearly half were making their first solo or deep-water dive.

Exhaustion, frequently related to panic, was mentioned as the proximate cause of the majority of cases. Entrapment or entanglement resulted in drowning of sixteen victims. Lack of equipment or defective equipment was related to twenty-three cases. Adverse conditions, including cold water and heavy surf contributed to twenty-two drownings.

In virtually all cases, disregard of recognized rules or procedures was a contributing cause.

ACCIDENTS AND INJURIES IN GYMNASTICS

Most accident and injury surveys find that gymnastics usually rank among the top three of the most hazardous sports. A recent survey of interscholastic gymastic accidents by Ralph W. Beecher [21] of the Lincoln, Nebraska, Public Schools, reveals the injuries experienced in the various events. (See Table 15-18.)

PLAYGROUND ACCIDENTS

The largest number of accidents on the playgrounds occur in connection with the use of playground apparatus. Such accidents account for 63.5 per cent of the total. Organized play and athletics account for about 23.6 per cent and the remaining 12.9 per cent occur during free play.

Accident Facts discloses that rate of accidents (accidents requiring a doctor's attention or leading to at least one-half day of absence) per 100,000 student days is .44 for apparatus, .84 for ball playing, .50 running, and .80 miscellaneous for all grades. It also ascribes 4.16 to physical education, .25 to intramural sports, and 1.39 to interscholastic sports.

CAMPING

It has been found that in a camp of seventy-five persons one accidental injury can be expected weekly, but in only one camp in twenty would an injury be so severe that the injured party would be forced to leave the same during the season.

The camp activities engaged in when injured include walking and running, 20 to 31 per cent; swimming, 12 to 14 per cent; general recreation, 6 to 11 per cent; baseball, 3 to 9 per cent; shop and craft, 4 to 7 per cent; hiking, 6 to 7 per cent; and unclassified, 28 to 34 per cent.

[21] Ralph W. Beecher, "Gymnastic Accident Survey," *Annual Safety Education Review* (Washington, D.C.: American Association for Health, Physical Education, and Recreation, 1966), p. 49.

TABLE 15-18
INTERSCHOLASTIC GYMNASTIC ACCIDENTS
—DATA FOR 1963–64 SCHOOL YEAR

ESTIMATED NUMBER OF GYMNASTS PARTICIPATING: 2,675

NEW YORK	1,225
MINNESOTA	454
WASHINGTON	278
ILLINOIS	718
	2,675

Number of Accidents Resulting in

Do you include the use of the following apparatus or events in your program		Sprains	Strains	Dislocation	Fractures	Head and Neck Injuries	Others	Paralysis	Deaths	Total Accidents
	Yes	No								
Horizontal Bar	36	2	8	2	1	11	2				24
Rings	36	2	3	9		3	1	2			18
Trampoline	37	1	9	5		5	1	3			23
Parallel Bars	37	1	4	5		3		2			14
Tumbling	36	2	27	3		7					37
Free Exercise	36	2	7	1		3		1			12
Horse	35	3	10	1	1	3					15
Long Horse	15	23	1	2		4					7
Rope Climb	8	30	1	1							2
	276	66	70	29	2	39	4	8			152

AIR FORCE ACCIDENTS

A report [22] made in 1959 disclosed that one out of five disabling injuries incurred by Air Force personnel resulted from sports participation. Of the 81 sports fatalities, 76 occurred in the aquatic sports—boating, diving, fishing, and water skiing.

INCIDENCE OF INJURY

As would be expected, the incidence of injury in the various sports varies with the nature of the activity. Those involving bodily contact would be expected to be more hazardous than the noncontact sports such as golf and tennis. On the college level, for men, football, wrestling, and lacrosse seem to be the most hazardous; with soccer, heavy apparatus, boxing, and touch football following close behind. For women, heavy apparatus, riding, and field hockey are the most dangerous, while basketball, tumbling and stunts, and speedball, follow.

Among high school students, touch football, heavy apparatus, and football seem to be the most hazardous; whereas ice hockey, lacrosse, wrestling, and soccer follow, in that order.

Giuseppi La Cava [23] of Italy, in a five-year study of Italian Olympic athletics, found the following frequency of sports injuries compared with casual factors.

TABLE 15-19

	SPORTS	
	COMBATIVE	INDIVIDUAL
Trauma caused by another participant	50.0%	7.43%
Trauma due to strain	8.1	15.25
Trauma due to fall	28.3	60.25
Trauma due to equipment or fixed object	5.5	6.65

La Cava also found that a higher ratio of sports injuries occur between the ages of 15 and 20 than between 20 and 24. He postulates that these youngsters have not yet perfected sports techniques, making them more susceptible to injury.

PARTS OF THE BODY INJURED

Injuries are most prevalent to the leg and foot among both college and high school participants. Arm and hand injuries usually rank second and head and neck injuries follow closely.

[22] "Sports Injuries Cost Air Force $1,165 each," *Scope Weekly* (February 11, 1959).

[23] G. La Cava, "A Clinical and Statistical Investigation of Traumatic Lesions Due to Sports," *The Journal of Sports Medicine and Physical Fitness*, Vol. I, No. 1 (June 1961), p. 8.

TABLE 15-20

COMPARATIVE INCIDENCE OF INJURIES IN
DIFFERENT SPORTS SUFFERED BY ITALIAN
OLYMPIC ATHLETICS

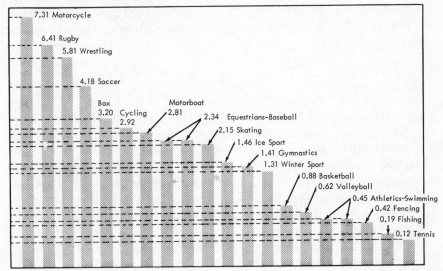

From La Cava, *op. cit.*

TABLE 15-21

FINAL OUTCOME OF SPORT INJURIES
(IN PERCENTAGE).

SPORT	TEMPORARY INVALIDITY	PERMANENT INVALIDITY	DEATH
Motorboat racing	75.00	–	25.00
Motorcycling	79.47	17.45	3.08
Equestrian sport	86.55	13.45	–
Winter sport	86.81	12.83	0.36
Fencing	87.50	12.50	–
Sporting	89.02	8.24	2.74
Ice sports	90.67	9.33	–
Light athletics	93.18	6.48	0.34
Hockey	93.23	6.77	–
Gymnastics	93.69	5.99	0.32
Swimming	94.12	5.88	–
Cycling	94.65	3.96	1.39
Football	95.41	4.56	0.03
Basketball	95.51	4.49	–
Baseball	95.83	4.17	–
Boxing	95.84	4.16	–
Rugby	95.97	3.54	0.19
Wrestling	97.61	2.28	0.11
Volleyball	98.25	1.75	–
Tennis	100.00	–	–

From La Cava, *op. cit.*

In a statewide survey in Oregon, Harr and Martin [24] found that the types of injuries occurring most often in physical education were sprains, contusions, fractures, lacerations, strains, dislocations, infections, hematomas, abrasions, concussions, eye injuries, and sacroiliac slips, in that order. More than 80 per cent of these injuries were sprains, contusions, or fractures. This finding follows the common pattern except that sprains usually rank second.

REFERENCES

Allen, Homer, and Robert Lynch, "Student Accidents at Purdue University," *Fourth Annual Safety Education Review* (Washington, D.C.: National Education Association, 1965), pp. 80–82.

Bernard, Douglas M., "A Selective Survey of Accidents Occurring in New England YMCA Physical Departments Between the years 1960 and 1962 and a Suggested Preventive Program for Use by Physical Directors," *Completed Research in Health, Physical Education, and Recreation* (1964), Vol. 6, p. 89.

Blyth, Carl S., *Annual Survey of Football Fatalities*, Committee on Football Injuries, American Football Association. National Collegiate Athletic Association, Kansas City, Missouri. Annual edition.

Boyd, Scott, *A Survey of Safety Practices in the Physical Education Program for Boys of Secondary Schools in North Carolina*, 1955. Ph.D. Dissertation, Indiana University, p. 277 (6 cards).

Drake, Charles A., "Accident Proneness: A Hypothesis," *Character and Personality* (June 1940), pp. 335–41.

Dzenowagis, Joseph G., "Injuries in Men's Physical Education and Intramural Sports," *Safety Monographs for Colleges and Universities* (Chicago: National Safety Council 1962).

——, "College Sports, Accidents, Injuries," *Safety Education* (March 1962), pp. 3–5.

Eastwood, Floyd R., "Causes of Sports Accidents," *Research Quarterly* (October 1934).

Eichenlaub, John E., "Psychological Causes of Accidents," *Today's Health* (July 1956), p. 40.

"Faulty Coordination Held Cause of Injury," *Scope Weekly* (January 7, 1959).

Hase, Gerald James, *The Nature and Frequency of Accidents in a Selected Sample of Schools in New York State*, 1956. Ph.D. Dissertation, Indiana University, 165 pages.

Metropolitan Life Insurance Company, "Fatal Injuries in Sports," *Statistical Bulletin* (April 1957), pp. 8–10.

[24] Frank B. Harr and Don B. Martin, "Student Injuries in Secondary Schools in Oregon," *Research Quarterly* (October 1953), pp. 276–83.

————, "Hazards in Competitive Athletics," *Statistical Bulletin* (June 1954), pp. 1–30.

Lloyd, Frank S., George D. Deaver, and Floyd R. Eastwood, *Safety in Athletics* (Philadelphia: W. B. Saunders, 1936). Out of print.

McGann, N. E., "Frequency of Accidents, Elementary School Children," *Recreation* (December 1957), p. 378.

Marcus, Irwin M., *et al.*, *An Interdisciplinary Approach to Accident Patterns in Children*, Monographs of Society for Research in Child Development, Vol. 25, No. 2. Serial No. 76. (Lafayette, Indiana: Child Development Publications, Purdue University, 1959), 76 pages.

Mizumachi, Shiro, and Kabuo Saito, "Sports Injuries in Japan," *Proceedings of the International Symposium of the Medicine and Physiology of Sports and Athletics at Helsinki* (Helsinki: Finnish Association of Sports Medicine, 1953).

Mohr, Dorothy R., "The Contributions of Physical Activity to Skill Learning," *Research Quarterly*, Part II (May 1960), pp. 321–50.

Pechar, Stanley F., "Accidents in the Secondary School Physical Education Programs," *Annual Safety Education Review* (Washington, D.C.: American Association for Health, Physical Education, and Recreation, 1963), p. 34.

President's Committee for Traffic Safety, *Health, Medical Care and Transportation of the Injured,* The Action Program, Basic Highway Safety Documents (Washington, D.C.: U.S. Government Printing Office, 1965).

"Preventing Trauma—A Goal at Air Academy," *Scope Weekly* (February 11, 1959).

Rhodes, Charles A., "A Study of 641 Injuries Involving Elementary School Children in the State of Iowa from 1950–1955." Unpublished master's thesis, State University of Iowa, 1957.

Rosenblatt, Morris S., *A Critical Examination of the Accident Proneness Concept* (Master's thesis, New Haven, Conn.: Yale University, 1955).

Seaton, Don Cash, *Safety in Sports* (Englewood Cliffs, N.J.: Prentice-Hall, 1948). Out of print.

Staton, Wesley M., and L. C. Butler, "Fitness and Safety," *Journal of Health, Physical Education, and Recreation* (September 1960), p. 31.

U.S. Department of Health, Education and Welfare, *The Facts of Life and Death* (Washigton, D.C.: Public Health Service, National Center for Health Statistics). Annual edition.

————, *Accidental Death and Injury Statistics* (Washington, D.C.: Division of Accident Prevention). Annual edition.

Wedlick, L. F., "Sports Injuries," *Medical Journal of Australia*, 1:159, pp. 800–801.

CHAPTER 16 PLANNING
A SPORTS SAFETY
PROGRAM

Suggested School Safety Policies [1] states that, "It is axiomatic that the strength of the school program and the attitudes of the students and staff toward accident prevention are dependent upon administrative leadership and the initiation of sound supervisory practices." Among a number of suggested policies which this helpful bulletin recommends are the following:

1. In establishing policies, participation should be invited of all persons and groups concerned: students, teachers, administrative staff members, school employees, board of education members, school patrons, representatives of community groups, and other interested community citizens.
2. There should be a continual evaluation and updating of accident-prevention policies and practices.
3. Provisions should be made for the use of advisory services from outside sources such as physicians, attorneys, insurance, health, and safety specialists to help in checking and formulating accident-prevention procedures.
4. Administration has the primary responsibility for adherence to legal provisions of school law; state and local laws, codes and ordinances; and contractual agreements with other organized bodies in the conduct of physical education, athletic, and recreational activities.
5. All curricular and extracurricular school activities in the physical education, athletic, and recreation program should be under direct supervision and control of the school.
6. Regulations regarding the use of school facilities by outside groups should include specific provisions for safety and accident prevention. Copies of these regulations should be provided to all concerned.
7. No athletic or recreation device shall be brought onto the school property without the express permission or approval of the school officials.

[1] American Association for Health, Physical Education, and Recreation, *Suggested School Safety Policies*, Accident Prevention in Physical Education Athletics and Recreation (Washington, D.C.: National Education Association, 1964).

It is also axiomatic that effective school or college programs of safety education must be guided by idealistic and realistic aims and objectives. Administrators and faculty must devise their own goals but the following paragraphs are suggestive of an ideal program.

SUGGESTED OBJECTIVES OF SAFETY EDUCATION

In selecting the objectives of safety education in physical education, it is patent that they should be consistent with those of general education. Furthermore, safety education must look to sociology, psychology, and philosophy for the desirable outcomes of education. From these, objectives that can most easily be accomplished through the type of activity represented by physical education and which are consistent with the local situation to be served can be decided. Aim, as used here, refers to the ultimate goal. It may be unobtainable but it is desirable as an objective toward which to strive.

SAFETY EDUCATION. The aim of safety education stated by the White House Conference on Child Health and Protection is consistent with the purpose of general education and acceptable for use:

> The development of such safety habits, safety attitudes and safety skills as will cause a decrease in the number of accidental deaths and injuries to children, produce safer adults for the future, and give to each individual freedom from fears and conditions which may restrict his enjoyment of life.[2]

FOR TEACHERS OF HEALTH AND PHYSICAL EDUCATION. A more specific aim for teachers of health and physical education in training would be *to develop among prospective teachers of health and physical education a knowledge of safety problems, efficient safety skills and habits of performance, and proper attitudes that will insure safer programs for their future pupils.*

It is recognized that each teacher and school should select, formulate, and activate those objectives best suited to the local situation. The selection of these objectives would be based on accepted educational procedures, including, among others, an analysis of existing materials in terms of objectives in general education and safety and material in various courses of study, and data secured by various fact-finding organizations; social responsibilities of the students; needs of the students, determined by analysis of accident records and hazards; and analysis of the interests and desires of the students. The objectives should be analyzed in terms of the aim, and should be consistent with those of general education;

[2] White House Conference on Child Health and Protection, *Safety Education in Schools* (New York: Appleton-Century-Crofts, 1932), p. 24.

they should be concise but inclusive; they should be possible and desirable of attainment; they should serve local purposes.

OBJECTIVES OF SAFETY IN PHYSICAL EDUCATION

1. To develop among participants of physical education activities a wholesome safety consciousness that will reduce the number of avoidable accidents but will not restrict unreasonably the enjoyment and benefits of the activity.
2. To teach fundamental leadership, equipment-and-skill controls, and the physical, mental, and emotional facts related to accident prevention in physical education.
3. To provide for the development of proper safety skills, habits, and attitudes in the health and physical education program.
4. To provide safe facilities and adequate and proper equipment and supplies to carry on a successful program.

STEPS IN ORGANIZING A PHYSICAL EDUCATION SAFETY PROGRAM

The organization of the safety program for physical education can be visualized as a definite procedure involving a series of steps. These steps are listed for the guidance of the safety planning committee.

1. First set up the type of organization within the school or department that will best cope with the safety problem. Regardless of the size of the school, a plan of attack is necessary. Some type of committee organization is recommended. Such an Athletic Safety Committee (it can be called by some other name) should include:
   a. Members of the health and physical education staff.
   b. Representatives of the Student Leaders' Club.
   c. Representatives of the Lettermen's Club.
      This committee should, of course, be a subcommittee of the general School Safety Council.
2. The next step is to determine where, why, how, and to whom the accidents in the Department are occurring. This requires the establishment of a thorough and efficient accident-reporting and record-keeping system.
3. The Athletic Safety Committee should then draw up a definite safety program in accordance with the results of the accident record plus the opinions of safety experts, the staff, and committee. Suggestions for this procedure follow.
4. Establish a definite system of caring for the injured in accordance with school policy. This procedure should include such vital issues as

who shall render first aid, who shall notify the parents, and how the injured shall be transported. All persons concerned must be made completely familiar with the correct procedure. Sufficient first-aid supplies must be available at all times and at strategic locations. Some schools find student first-aid clubs very helpful in caring for the injured.

5. If the health-instruction curriculum is to include various other phases of safety, the nature and placement of this material must be determined by the instructors concerned, in conjunction with the principal, curriculum committee, and the School Safety Council.

6. Provide for some form of athletic accident insurance. (If your state does not support such a plan, it may be that your league or community can evolve some workable type of medical reimbursement.)

7. Provide sufficient and appropriate safety education materials.
   a. Recommended textbooks and reference materials.
   b. Current safety pamphlets such as those furnished by the federal and state governments, motor clubs, the National Safety Council, and the various centers for safety education.
   c. Visual aids such as posters, motion pictures, film strips, and charts. (See the lists provided by the National Education Association, the National Safety Council, and the various centers for safety education.)

8. Determine methods of evaluating the program.
   a. Reduction of accidents.
   b. Development of attitudes.

SAFETY COORDINATOR. Because so many physical educators are selected to serve as safety coordinators or chairmen in their respective schools, it may be judicious to outline their duties.

1. The interpretation of the philosophy and objectives of the school safety program to teachers, principals, pupils, building custodians, and parents.

2. Collection of data on student accidents through an accident-reporting system, and the careful study of such data to determine local problems and points of emphasis. More general accident data should also be collected through the local police, fire department, and other sources.

3. Interpretation of accident data through published materials, such as monthly accident reports going to the individual schools, and faculty meetings.

4. Preparation or provision of teaching aids to give children the information they must have if they are to avoid accidents. Obviously the content of the material will be determined by a study of the student accident data. The manner in which the material is presented will vary with the system. A special course in safety education may be desirable, safety materials may be integrated in selected courses, and current materials may be provided through the school library.

5. Encouragement of faculty-supervised cocurricular safety activities to insure children opportunities to "learn by doing." These activities may be safety councils, safe drivers' schools, motor traffic clubs, school safety patrols, and others.
6. Periodic surveys of buildings and grounds to keep them in as good condition as possible, thereby aiding in giving pupils maximum protection while they are on school property.
7. The development of definite cooperation for child safety between home, community, and school.
8. Cooperation of police in securing adequate traffic signs, signals, and traffic direction near schools.
9. Supervision of the school safety patrols and other school safety organizations.[3]

RESPONSIBILITIES OF DEPARTMENT MEMBERS. No administrative plan, regardless of how carefully it is planned, can succeed without the delegation of responsibility to those who are a part of the department. It is difficult to outline the responsibilities and duties of all people in the department of physical education because of variance of administrative setups and programs, but the following suggestions are made in the hope that each school will be able to make proper adaptations. In general, the responsibilities of all individuals in the department may be grouped as follows.

1. Providing and maintaining a safe environment in which the health and physical education program is conducted.
2. Organizing and conducting safety services for the students.
3. Influencing safe behavior of the students through example and safety instruction.

The responsibilities will naturally overlap, but in general, each teacher or coach will be responsible for his or her own class or team activity. The difference between the responsibilities of the supervisor and teacher is one of degree rather than kind. In many elementary and rural schools and in smaller high schools one person serves in both capacities, which eliminates some of the problems of allocation of responsibility.

All instructors, coaches, and administrators should be thoroughly familiar with the legal liability aspects of their profession.

LEGAL LIABILITY IN PHYSICAL EDUCATION AND ATHLETICS

In most states the probability of liability law suits is rare. Protection, however, for the physical education instructor, athletic coach, and the

[3] National Safety Council, *Safety Teaching in the Modern School* (Chicago: The Council), pp. 4–5. Out of print.

school or college is to be found in an understanding of the principles of liability. (See Chapter 4.) Steinhilber [4] lists seventeen reminders of appropriate action for the teacher or coach to act as a reasonably prudent and careful person.

A reasonably prudent and careful physical educator (or teacher, coach, supervisor)

1. Knows the health status of his students and/or players if he has them engage in highly competitive and/or rough activities.

2. Requires medical approval for participation following serious illness or injury.

> The Supreme Court of Washington held for the plaintiff—a high school football player—on the grounds that the coach who induced the boy to play even though he was injured should have required medical approval before permitting him to return to play following an injury.

3. Inspects all class and personal equipment at regular intervals.

4. Does not expose students to possible injury by using defective equipment.

> Plaintiff who had received an injury to his nose in a previous football game had notified the coach before the game that his helmet had been broken; the strap was defective, and the face mask removed. He had asked for a new helmet with a face mask. In spite of his notice and request, the plaintiff was *directed* to go into the game wearing the defective helmet. Subsequently he was knocked unconscious and his nose broken. Recovery granted.

5. Conducts an activity in a safe area.

> A player who broke his leg in a championship softball game was awarded damages in an action against two playground supervisors. The player was hurt while chasing a foul fly along the third base line. He tripped over a spectator who was sitting on a bench close to the field. Evidence showed that the supervisors had moved the spectators back on several occasions, but they again allowed the base line to be crowded.
>
> The court pointed out that ropes and standards were not used to keep the crowd back; that the supervisors were negligent in allowing spectators to congregate close to the base line; and that they were also negligent in permitting the bench to be obscured from the view of the players.

6. Foresees possible injury if activity is improperly conducted.

> In *Brooks v. Board of Education, City of New York* (189 N.E. 2d 497 N.Y. 1963) the Court of Appeals affirmed the decision of the lower courts in holding that a teacher was negligent in the supervision of a class in which random pairs of pupils were to compete in kicking a ball when their numbers were called.

[4] Augustus Steinhilber, "A Reasonably Prudent and Careful Physical Educator," *Annual Safety Education Review* (Washington, D.C.: American Association for Health, Physical Education, and Recreation, 1966).

7. Analyzes his teaching and coaching methods for the safety of the students and players.

8. Assigns only qualified personnel to conduct or supervise an activity.

9. Keeps the activity within the ability of a student.

In *Keesee* v. *Board of Education,* 235 N.Y.S. 2d 207 (N.Y. Sup. Ct. 1963) an action against a physical education teacher, the court held that the teacher was negligent in permitting eight inexperienced girls to compete for a ball in a game of line soccer. The court also held that the pupil sustaining the injury was not guilty of contributory negligence as the participation was involuntary.

10. Performs the proper act in the event of injury.
    a. Renders first aid.
    b. Summons medical attention.
    c. Removes injured to medical attention.

Welch v. *Dunsmuir Joint Union High School District* (326 P. 2d 633 Cal. 1958) also concerns injury. During a preseason high school football scrimmage, the plaintiff—the quarterback on one of the teams—attempted a "quarterback sneak."

After being tackled, the plaintiff continued to lie on his back. The coach of the high school, suspecting that the plaintiff might have suffered an injury to the neck, had him take hold of his hands to determine if he were able to grip. Plaintiff was able to do so at that time.

The plaintiff was carried from the field by eight players. There was testimony to the effect that no one directed the moving. There was also conflicting testimony as to whether or not a doctor who was admittedly present examined the plaintiff before he was moved to the sidelines. The undisputed (and only) medical testimony was that the plaintiff is a permanent quadriplegic caused by damage to the spinal cord. It was the medical witness's opinion that the injury *was caused by the removal of the player from the field without the use of a stretcher* and that this failure to use a stretcher was improper medical practice. Medical opinion also held that the player's ability to grip things with his hands while on the field was proof that the damage had not been done by the tackle but had occurred afterward.

Of particular interest were (a) the claim by the defendant that the doctor was an agent of the district, and (b) the defendant's effort to obtain an instruction to the effect that his responsibility ended when the physician's began. The court refused to grant this instruction because it proceeded on the theory that when "the negligent acts or omissions of two or more persons, whether committed independently or in the course of jointly related conduct, contribute concurrently to the injury of another each of such persons is liable."

The court felt that from the evidence in the case, the jury could reasonably infer that both the doctor and the coach were negligent in the removal of the plaintiff from the field to the sidelines—"the coach in failing to wait for the doctor and allowing plaintiff to be moved and the doctor in failing to act promptly after plaintiff's injury."

Judgment—$206,804 plus interest and *costs*.

11. Does not diagnose or treat injuries.

12. Instructs adequately prior to permitting performance.

13. Keeps an accurate record of all accidents and action(s) taken.

14. Uses school buses or public utility motor vehicles to transport members of athletic teams to and from contests; does not use privately owned motor vehicles.

> In general, the courts have held that if privately owned autos are used for this purpose, the athletes are *not guests,* and recovery for injuries sustained while in the car may be granted for mere negligence—not gross negligence. Owners of the cars are usually held liable.

15. In cooperation with administration, makes arrangements for adequate care of injured pupils in emergency situations.

   a. Physicians at all football games and *readily available* for practice sessions.

   b. Ambulance service, preferably at field.

16. If he serves as an athletic trainer, performs only in areas in which he is directed by medical personnel.

17. Fulfills his duty to supervise within the scope of his employment, especially in situations in which the risk of harm is exceptionally high and in those situations in which it is reasonable to foresee that injury might occur if supervision is not provided.

> In *Stanley Miller, et al.* v. *Board of Education of the Borough of Chatham* (N.Y. Sup. Ct. L. Div. No. L-7241-62 1964), a student received $1,215,240 from the school board and gymnasium teacher for injuries resulting from use of a spring board in the gym. The teacher was found negligent because at the time of the accident he had left the gym to escort another student, who had suffered a rope burn, to the nurse. (It has been reported that by process of remittitur the damages were reduced to $300,000. Contributory negligence was not admissible.)

(See Chapter 4 for a more complete explanation of a school's legal position in relation to accidents and injuries.)

References

Creason, Frank, "Build Your Safety Program with Your School," *Safety Education* (April 1956), p. 4.

Danford, Howard G., *The Organization and Administration of School Safety Education Program.* Unpublished Final Document, New York University, 1943.

Dzenowagis, Joseph G., "College Sports, Accidents, Injuries," *Safety Education* (March 1962), pp. 3–5.

Englehardt, Melvin E., *The Administration of Safety Education in Selected School Systems.* Dissertation, Columbia University, 1961.

Florio, A. E., and G. T. Stafford, *Safety Education* (New York: McGraw-Hill, 1962).

Forsythe, C. E., *The Administration of High School Athletics,* 4th Edition (Englewood Cliffs, N.J.: Prentice-Hall, 1962).

Harris, W. H., "Suggested Criteria for Evaluating Health and Safety Teaching Materials," *Journal of Health, Physical Education, and Recreation* (February 1964), pp. 25–27.

Hein, Fred V., "Health Aspects of Accident Prevention," *Second Annual Safety Education Review* (Washington, D.C.: National Education Association, 1963), pp. 81–87.

Henry, F. J., and C. C. Hawkins, *Constructing the Teacher-Education Curriculum in Safety* (New York: Center for Safety Education, New York University, 1941).

Kralovec, Dalibor W., *The Safety Education Program of Philadelphia Public Schools—Historical Background, Description, and Evaluation.* Dissertation, Temple University, 1961.

Larson, Leonard W., "Medicine Is Concerned with Johnny, Too," *First Annual Safety Education Review* (Washington, D.C.: National Education Association, 1962), pp. 4–9.

Malfetti, J. L., "The Family Ties Between Health Education and Safety Education," *Journal of Health, Physical Education, and Recreation* (September 1961), pp. 35–37.

Mallory, Ann, "A Team Approach to Safety and Physical Fitness," *Safety Education* (May 1962), pp. 10–12.

Miles, James B., "The School Principal and Accident Prevention," *Safety Education* (February 1957), p. 6.

National Commission on Safety Education, *Checklist on Safety and Safety Education in Your School* (Washington, D.C.: National Education Association, 1953).

————, *Our Schools Plan Safe Living* (Washington, D.C.: National Education Association, 1956).

————, *Safety in Physical Education for the Classroom Teacher* (Washington, D.C.: National Education Association, 1951).

National Safety Council, "A Job Analysis for Safety Education Supervisors," *Safety Education* (February 1959).

Pechar, Stanley F., "A Study of the Nature, Frequency and Related Person and Administrative Factors of Physical Education Accidents Among Boys in Junior and Senior High Schools of New York State." Unpublished Ed.D. Dissertation, New York University, 1961.

Pittsburgh Public Schools, "Pittsburgh Writes Guide for Physical Education Teachers," *Safety Education* (September 1962), p. 27.

Rappaport, Mary B., "An Apple a Day," *Safety Education* (February 1960), pp. 4–7.

Roundtree, William, *The Formulation of a Guide Book in Safety Education for Teachers of Health and Physical Education in the Public Schools of the District of Columbia*, Washington, D.C.: Ph.D. in Physical Education 1960, 190 pages.

Schneider, Nathaniel O., *Teacher Preparation for Safety Education*, Center for Safety Education. New York University, Ed.D. dissertation, 1940.

Seaton, Don Cash, *Preparation of a Course in Safety Education for Teachers of Health and Physical Education*, Ed.D. dissertation, New York University, 1947.

Stack, H. J., and J. Duke Elkow, *Education for Safe Living*, 4th ed. (Englewood Cliffs, N.J.: Prentice-Hall, 1966).

Suggested School Safety Policies, Accident Prevention in Physical Education, Athletics, and Recreation (Washington, D.C.: American Association for Health, Physical Education, and Recreation, 1964), 28 pages.

CHAPTER 17 SPORTS FACILITY AND EQUIPMENT CONTROLS

Introduction

Administrators and physical educators have faced many perplexing problems in attempting to provide and maintain adequate and safe facilities and equipment to carry on the ever-changing and expanding program of physical education and athletics. Many of the present gymnasiums were constructed at a time when formal gymnastics or basketball dominated the physical-education program and do not lend themselves to accommodating the varied activities of the present-day program. Similarly, the locations of most schools were not selected with a view to sufficient outdoor play space, and all too many are limited in this respect. Add to this the fact that many schools are forced to accommodate double and sometimes triple the number of pupils for which they were constructed and it can readily be seen that the physical educator often meets a complexity of facility safety problems.

When the physical educator is called upon to make suggestions or submit requirements for the construction of new facilities, it is recommended that he confer with his state Department of Education, the United States Office of Education, university officials, and other authorities, to make certain that the plan suggested will be functional and will meet future needs. For items of safety in construction and suitable sizes of playfields and gymnasiums the reader is referred to *Planning Areas and Facilities for Health, Physical Education, and Recreation*.[1] In the following discussion, *facilities* refers to permanent play areas and dressing rooms, and *equipment* to the expendable gear used by the participants.

INADEQUATE FACILITIES AND ACCIDENTS. The role played by inadequate or faulty equipment and facilities in accident causation tends to be overemphasized by teachers and coaches. When they were polled on the question, it was found that they attributed ap-

[1] *Planning Areas and Facilities for Health, Physical Education, and Recreation* (Chicago: The Athletic Institute, and American Association for Health, Physical Education, and Recreation, Washington, 1965).

proximately 70 per cent of all accidents to such causes. Actually, Lloyd and Eastwood's study [2] showed that in high schools only 20 per cent of accidents were due to inadequate equipment; in colleges for women, 27 per cent; and in colleges for men, 10 per cent. Pertinent figures are not available for elementary schools or playgrounds, but it is reasonable to assume that the percentage would be higher because more apparatus is used, and especially higher out of doors where apparatus is subject to deterioration because of the vagaries of the weather. Although the actual percentage of accidents resulting from inadequate or faulty equipment tends to be lower than that caused by leadership or nature-of-the-game accidents, they are accidents that can be almost completely eliminated. *There is no excuse for accidents occurring because of negligence in the care and maintenance of facilities or equipment.*

PRINCIPLES OF PROCEDURE IN ELIMINATING HAZARDS

There are certain specific principles in the elimination of hazards which, if followed, should result in a safer environment and program in physical education, athletics, and recreation. They are:

1. Recognition and understanding of the hazards of all activities and facilities.
2. Removal of all unnecessary hazards of facilities, equipment, and programing.
3. Compensation through education and protective equipment for those hazards that cannot be removed.
4. Creation of no new hazards.[3]

Such knowledge and comprehension cannot be gained from a study of textbooks and safety rules, nor is it necessarily a by-product of participation in athletics; rather, it requires a goodly share of each, plus administrative experience. Furthermore, each school presents certain hazards, especially facility hazards, that are peculiar to that particular school. The most efficient and accurate means of determining facility and equipment hazards is through an analysis of well-kept accident reports and by thorough inspections.

GENERAL CONTROLS

The following safety controls were determined by a questionnaire survey of experts in the field of physical education and from regulations advocated by various official agencies.

[2] Frank S. Lloyd, George G. Deaver, and Floyd R. Eastwood, *Safety in Athletics* (Philadelphia: W. B. Saunders, 1936). Out of print.

[3] H. J. Stack and J. Duke Elkow, *Education for Safe Living*, 4th ed. (Englewood Cliffs, N.J.: Prentice-Hall, 1966), p. 115.

INSPECTION AND CORRECTION. All apparatus and facilities should be inspected and tested thoroughly before the opening of a sports season or semester, and should be observed carefully by each instructor at the time of use. It is probably best to make the inspection of facilities at the end of each semester so that repairs and replacements can be made before school reopens. Likewise, an inspection and inventory of equipment should be made at the close of each sports season so that equipment may be cleaned and repaired and orders placed for the following season. In large schools the semi-annual inspection requires considerable time and effort. The use of a checklist [4] as outlined in Table 17-1, may be found useful in the survey. Similarly, a repair request blank, filled out by the teacher who discovers a faulty facility or a piece of apparatus, will not only facilitate the correction, but many exonerate the teacher and department in the event of a lawsuit. (Sample form on page 358.) When possible, the defective apparatus or facility should be put away, roped off, or in some way kept away from students. Custodians and students, particularly the safety leaders, should be encouraged to help with such surveys and be on the alert to report hazardous conditions. On page 255 are suggestions made by the National Safety Council for use in the survey of apparatus, with recommendations for general care of apparatus.

TABLE 17-1

SAFETY CHECKLIST

Health and Physical Education Department

SEMIANNUAL INSPECTION _____   MADE BY: _____
                          (Date)

(See preceding instructions)   CUSTODIAN: _____

GENERAL SAFE PRACTICES

No.	Item	Yes	No
1.	Are facilities checked by the custodian-engineer and the director or equipment and facility manager for safety at least twice each year?		_____
2.	Do instructors check equipment and facilities before each usage?		_____
3.	Is there an established system of writing to the proper authority to report needed repairs to facilities?		_____
4.	Is apparatus put away, locked, roped off, or covered with mats when not in use under supervisor?		_____
5.	Are any activities conducted for which adequate protective equipment cannot be furnished?		_____

[4] Don Cash Seaton, *Safety in Sports* (Englewood Cliffs, N.J.: Prentice-Hall, 1948). Out of print.

No.	Item	Yes	No

6. Are intramural and physical education class participants furnished the same adequate protective equipment as the varsity?

7. Is there an established method of accident reporting and follow-up?

8. Is there an established policy of rendering first aid and treating injuries received in physical education classes, intramurals, and athletics?

9. Is there an established policy of notifying parents regarding transportation and hospitalization of injured pupils?

10. Are the students taking physical education and participating in intramurals covered in the athletic benefit plan?

11. Are pupils assigned to activities or permitted to play on teams on the basis of health examinations, tests, and ability?

12. Are any classes or activities overcrowded for the facilities available?

13. Are passage facilities safe and is there a safe system of pedestrian traffic within the athletic plant?

14. Are doors locked at any time in violation of fire ordinances?

15. Is the number of spectators that is safe for each area determined and the limit strictly adhered to?

16. Are there adequate fire extinguishers in every area, and are all staff members trained in the methods of correct operation?

17. Are students trained in the proper fire-drill procedures for all areas and activities of the department?

INSPECTION OF APPARATUS. The National Safety Council proposes the following inspection procedures:

1. Apparatus in which wood is employed, such as slides, swings, teeters, and giant strides, should be inspected for worn or split portions or slivers.

2. All apparatus should be examined for broken parts, rough corners, projecting corners or clamps, and loose joints, bolts, and fastenings.

3. Chains, ropes, fastenings, and clamps should be examined regularly for signs of deterioration or looseness.

4. All minor repairs and adjustments should be made immediately.

5. All unsafe apparatus should be removed or roped off so that it cannot be used while it is in a dangerous condition.

6. All needed repairs or parts should be reported to the principal at once.

7. All movable parts and connections should be frequently inspected and well lubricated. It is good practice to replace yearly the parts of apparatus subjected to the most strenuous wear.

8. All exposed surfaces should be treated regularly with a preservative coating. Metal surfaces may be painted and wood surfaces treated with linseed oil and varnish.

Before the safety checklist is used, it is recommended that the users acquaint themselves with the various safety controls enumerated in this chapter.

BLEACHER ERECTION AND MAINTENANCE. Bleachers and grandstands are probably the most neglected and the most potentially dangerous facilities of the school athletic plant. It is usually assumed that permanent stands will remain safe forever and that manufacturers will sell only trustworthy, demountable bleachers. Yet each year bleacher collapse is responsible for dozens of deaths and injuries. Administrators are urged to give serious consideration to the erection and maintenance of bleachers.

Demountable bleachers should be erected only by reliable workmen who will follow the directions of the manufacturer and realize the implications of careless workmanship. It is not advisable to give students this responsibility. A solid foundation must be provided for the A-frames. Seat stringers and A-frames which can be dislocated should be wired into place. They must never be erected on soft or wet ground which will allow dislocation. One manufacturer stated, "We urge the careful inspection of our bleachers prior to and during their use. Small boys can remove sustaining members which immediately affects the strength of the entire bleacher." Because *permanent outdoor grandstands* are more likely to deteriorate, special care must be taken to test and repair them before the opening of each season. This responsibility is best delegated to a competent engineer. Only his official approval will protect the administrator in case of failure. All permanent structures should be inspected regularly for such relatively minor items as protruding nails, splinters, and broken boards.

Manufacturers of demountable bleachers and builders of permanent grandstands should be engaged to inspect the stands for safety periodically. Not only are these engineers best qualified to pass upon the safety of the stands, but also they should take pride in their product's being well maintained and in its security.

HEAVY APPARATUS. Much of the so-called heavy apparatus of the gymnasium and playground has stood the test of time as to value and safety, but accident records reveal that certain pieces cause more accidents than others. According to the National Safety Council it is possible to gain the same value through other, safer apparatus and equipment, and the dangerous kind should therefore be eliminated.

In addition to periodic inspection and intelligent leadership, the *proper placing* of apparatus will do much to eliminate the danger of collision. Indoors the instructor must arrange the movable apparatus so that sufficient space is available for all exercises, and performers are not likely to be struck by equipment or participants of other sports. All permanent outdoor apparatus should be located in a fenced-off space or around the edges of the playground where it is less likely to interfere with the sports areas.

SAFE PLACE FOR STORAGE. All equipment and movable apparatus should have a safe place for storage and should be kept there at all times when it is not in use under supervision. Although it is not possible for all schools to follow this procedure because of inadequate storage space, the practice is a desirable one from the standpoint of safety. Often apparatus can be set away from the practice area in a safe location. Although much of the playground apparatus cannot be so put away, it is customary to permit its use only under supervision. On the college level such provisions for safety are probably less necessary, for the students are more mature and usually less likely to experiment with dangerous stunts. Some coaches feel, too, that unless the apparatus is available, students will not have an opportunity to develop an interest in recreation during leisure moments.

PLAYING SURFACES. Except for such sports as cross-country running, golf, horseback riding, and aquatics, all playing surfaces should be level, smooth, dry, free from harmful extraneous materials, and of proper texture for the sport or activity. It is understandable, of course that the playing field cannot always be dry, but from the standpoint of safety this is desirable. The proper texture of the field depends on local weather and ground conditions, as well as on the use to which the field is put. In football, soccer, speedball, and other games in which falling to the ground is common, grass provides the most suitable surface. Crowded play areas demand an all-weather surface which is both practical and safe, and to date no one formula has proved successful under all conditions. However, the new synthetic surfaces such as Tartan and Astroturf may eventually solve this problem. A good play surface should have resilience, good drainage, freedom from dust, durability, nonabrasiveness, cleanliness, firmness, smoothness, general utility, good appearance, and be procurable at a reasonable cost.

No matter what type of surface exists, constant care must be taken to keep the play areas free from extraneous materials that may cause injury, such as rocks, cinders, glass, and tin cans. Also it is necessary to keep the surface free from holes and bumps, because uneven surfaces cause many ankle and knee injuries as well as a large variety of other falling injuries. Dust is a hazard to health and safety and must be controlled. It can best be allayed by the use of calcium chloride or one of the commercial compounds developed for this purpose.

INDOOR SURFACES. Indoor surfaces seldom present the problem of unevenness, but are more likely to cause injuries because they are slippery. The most satisfactory finish for wooden floors has been the so-called bakelite treatment. This finish provides a very attractive and cohesive surface which insures safe footing when good rubber-soled shoes are

used. Many schools using this finish have found it advisable to provide
a canvas cover, not only for use when the gymnasium is converted into an
auditorium but for dancing as well. As mentioned above the new synthetic
surfaces that are being developed may prove far more safe and satisfactory for indoor surfaces.

REPAIR REQUEST

To the Maintenance Department: The following facilities or equipment
are in need of repair:

Faulty Equipment _____

_____

Place _____

Suggestions _____

_____

Signed: _____ Room_____ Date_____

REPORT ON REPAIR REQUEST

To _____ The following disposition has been
made of your repair request:

_____

_____

_____

Signed _____ Date_____
(Maintenance Department)

FIGURE 17-1. Suggested Repair Request Form and Report. The use of such
a form fornishes a record for reporting repair needs and may protect the instructor
in case of a misunderstanding or even a law suit.

The use of the old-fashioned powdered wax for dancing should be
discouraged, because it leaves the floor too slippery for the safe conduct
of classes or games. If it is used, it is essential that the floor be thoroughly
scrubbed afterward with a caustic soap and hot water to restore the required friction. It is recommended that boric acid powder be used for a
dance surface; this powder is quickly dissolved in water and has antiseptic properties.

According to the National Safety Council, water waxes (emulsions), if properly applied, will permit a floor to be used safely for physical education activities. When a dancing surface is required, a thin film of wax can be applied and buffed to a high gloss. If floors are not specially filled and sealed, they should be thoroughly cleaned as often as necessary and mopped at least once a week.

All playing surfaces should be free from surrounding or overhanging obstructions likely to cause injury. This requirement is impossible to fulfill where supporting pillars, stairs, or other permanent construction hazards exist. Rather than abandoning activity in that area, the activity in the area can be restricted or the hazard may be padded or otherwise lessened. On the other hand, there, are certain facilities, such as drinking fountains, radiators, and permanent apparatus, that can and should be relocated if they present unusually hazardous conditions. Eight to ten feet in customarily considered a safe height above which projections are permissible. See Table 17-2. Empty bleachers in the gymnasium are often dangerous, especially when cross-court play is in progress. The safest bleachers from this standpoint are the folding type, which can be removed from the playing court when they are not in use. The type of bleacher that folds flat against or into the wall is probably safer than those types that leave an uneven front. If they are of the permanent or knockdown type that is not removable, it may be necessary to place mat covers over them at dangerous locations. Insufficient space between the side lines of the play area and the wall, bleachers, or fences is a common hazard. When such distance cannot possibly be widened, steps should be taken to pad them, or otherwise lessen, the danger.

SUITABLE OUTDOOR PLAY AREAS. Outdoor facilities have often been provided solely for interschool competition in the various sports. It has been a too common practice for high schools to build a football field enclosed by a running track and stadium and then put up a "keep out" sign for all other activities. Almost any remaining undeveloped space has been considered good enough for the other sports, with the exception of tennis. The mass of the student body has been compelled to play on inadequate space and hazardous surfaces. Many facility-caused accidents occur because of overcrowding and because of playing a number of sports at the same time in a restricted area. This is particularly true of the so-called free play periods and other loosely organized and unsupervised groups of activities.

Outdoor play areas should be sufficiently large and well cared for, and when it is necessary to use a common area, the space should be properly allocated according to the various activities for the age and sex of the players. In planning such allocation, the prescribed areas required for various sports should be considered. (See Table 17-2.)

MARKING PLAY AREAS. Most sports require that their play areas be defined by lines. Such lines often mark danger zones and should

TABLE 17-2
NEEDED SPACE FOR SAFE PLAY (Measurements in feet; Bleacher space not included)

Sports	Dimensions of Playing Area	Sq. Feet Playing Area	Outside Safety Zone End (Minimum) To Wall or Fence	Outside Safety Zone End (Minimum) Between Courts or Bleachers	Outside Safety Zone Sides (Minimum) To Wall or Fence	Outside Safety Zone Sides (Minimum) Between Courts or Bleachers	Total Area Needed (Minimum) Dimensions Plus Safety Zones	Total Area Needed (Minimum) Square Feet
Archery (outdoor)	500 to 300 x 450	22,500	10	150	10	50	50 x 450	22,500
Badminton (double)	20 x 44	880	8	6	8	5	32 x 56	1,792
Basketball	42 x 72 (minimum)	3,024	8	6	6	6	54 x 84	4,536
Baseball (hard)	90 x 90 (diamond)	8,100	60*	550**	30	30	300 x 300	90,000
Baseball (soft)	60 x 60 (diamond)	3,600	30*	350**	30	30	250 x 250	62,500
Boxing (ring)	20 x 20	400	8	4	8	4	28 x 28	784
Fencing (strip)	5'10" to 6'6" x 40	233	4	6	6	8	18 x 48	874
Field Hockey	150 to 180 x 270 to 300	40,500	20	10	10	10	160 x 280	44,800
Football and Touchball	160 x 360	57,600	20	10	15	10	180 x 380	68,400
Golf Driving Net	9 x 18 x 9 high	162	8	4	4	4	17 x 30	510
Handball (one wall)	20 x 30 x 34 to 45	680	8	6	4	6	32 x 46	1,472
Handball (four wall)	20 x 40 x 20	800	8		8		20 x 40	800
Ice Hockey	60 to 110 x 165 to 250	9,900					60 x 165	9,900
Lacrosse	210 to 260 x 450 to 500	94,500	15	10	15	10	230 x 470	108,100
Soccer (men)	150 to 300 x 300 to 390	45,000	15	10	15	10	170 x 320	54,400
Soccer (women)	120 to 180 x 240 to 300	28,800	10	6	10	6	143 x 252	33,264
Speedball (men)	160 x 240 to 360	38,400	15	10	15	10	180 x 260	46,800
Speedball (women)	180 to 200 x 300 to 340	54,000	10	6	10	6	192 x 312	59,904
Swimming Pool	40 x 75	3,000	15		8		56 x 105	5,880
Tennis (double)	36 x 78	2,808	21		16		60 x 120	7,200
Track (outdoor)	24 x 440 yds.	31,680	10	6	10	6	260 x 610	158,600
Volleyball	30 x 60	1,800	8	6	12	8	46 x 72	3,312
Wrestling (ring)	24 x 24	576	10	10	10	10	34 x 34	1,156

* To backstop. ** Between home plates of facing diamonds. Safety In Sports, Prentice-Hall, Inc., 1948.

not be allowed to become indistinct or to be omitted entirely. There is a tendency to omit such lines in track and field events where their use is most helpful in defining the danger zones of such events as the discus, javelin, and running broad jump. Lines are also helpful around apparatus areas and for use in segregating groups, thus preventing playground accidents. Slacked lime of whiting, applied wet, water paint, or white sand should be used to mark outdoor play areas. *Unslaked lime should never be used* because of the danger of burns. White tape lines are often used in court games, but care must be taken to keep them well pinned down or they become a tripping hazard. It is customary to use different colors to distinguish the various play areas in the gymnasium and to indicate danger zones of apparatus and swinging doors.

Temporary areas for special squad events in physical education classes should be carefully designated to avoid the dangers of collision. The permanent areas, such as jumping pits, outdoor running track, and indoor horizontal bars and ladders, are definitely established and provide segregation to a certain extent, but many activities do not possess such designated areas. When a class is divided into squads participating in games of low organization, relays, and hand wrestling, as well as basketball, apparatus, and soccer, care must be taken to define clearly the areas of activity, or injury may result from collisions. It may be advisable to indicate these various areas on a blackboard located where the classes form.

S A F E I N D O O R A R E A S .   Indoor play space is usually at a premium. Since the physical educator can do little to expand the space available, it becomes necessary for him to restrict the number of persons who may use the facility at one time and to adjust the activity program in accordance with the number permitted. In most schools it has been customary for the student to schedule all other classes and then "fill in" gym at a vacant hour. This has often resulted in overcrowded classes at certain hours and classes too small at others. It is therefore recommended that administrators arrange to schedule physical education classes first, so that an equal distribution of class and teacher loads can be made.

Doors swinging into play areas should be reversed or slowed down by means of doorstops, or lines should be painted on the floor to show danger areas, or leaders posted where it is necessary to protect the players. Such doors can be extremely dangerous, because students coming to the gymnasium are usually in a hurry and feel active and rush through the doors with little thought of the consequences. Another precaution that can be used on doors is the painting of signs such as "Open Slowly" or "Caution." Doors that swing in both directions should be eliminated, and where possible, no doors at all should be used. All gymnasium doors should have recessed handles.

P O O L A N D S E R V I C E R O O M S .   *Locker, shower, and drying room floors and pool decks should be of nonslip material.* If they are not, corrugated rubber mats or wooden platforms can be used. The matter of slippery floors in these areas has perplexed architects and safety engineers for many years. There is no satisfactory method of correcting the slipperiness of the usual floors constructed of tile, terra cotta, and terrazzo. The use of rubber mats and wooden platforms has not proved satisfactory from the hygienic standpoint, and some instructors feel that their use does not reduce the number of accidents. The use of nonslip marine paint on certain floors may be desirable. One of the best solutions to the accident problem is to prohibit running and roughhousing on the part of users of the locker rooms. Keeping the locker room floors dry by not allowing bathers to enter the room until they are dried off in the drying room is another important administrative control. Floor panel-heating used in these areas in modern buildings practically eliminates the hazard of wet floors.

To prevent scalding, showers should be equipped with mixing valves. The temperature of the water should be thermostatically controlled and should never be permitted to exceed 100°F. If such safety devices are not available, an effort should be made to keep the temperature from exceeding 100°, and users should be constantly instructed in the method of safe usage. Liquid or powdered soap is safer than bar soap for use in shower rooms because bar soap is often left on the floor and becomes a slip hazard. It is also recommended that the dispensers be of metal and that the soap be of good quality.

If footbaths are used they should have nonskid bottoms, because the antiseptic used usually adds to the slipperiness of the container.

The bottom and sides of the swimming pools should be cleaned as often as necessary to keep them from becoming slippery. The use of a modern vacuum cleaner usually suffices. Also the pool decks must be mopped or squeegeed often to prevent them from becoming dirty and slippery. *The instructor should inspect the diving board* before class or team usage for possible weakness and hazardous surface. The principal danger from a broken board is to those who happen to be underneath it at the time of breakage. It is advisable not to allow swimmers to go beneath the board while it is in use.

Gym and locker room doors should not be locked in violation of fire laws as a means of controlling attendance and theft. It is a common practice in departments of physical education to employ this very dangerous method of policing the various rooms. It is recommended that a check be made with the fire marshal, and if the practice is judged by him to be dangerous, it should be discontinued.

PROPER LIGHTING. All play areas, shower and locker rooms, and corridors should be properly lighted. This is a safety factor that is very often neglected in passageways, on stairs, and in dressing rooms, particularly when they are located in the basement. If an unusual number of accidents occur in those areas, it is advisable to check the illumination. (See Table 17-3.) Usually there is not much that can be done about improving the natural lighting of an existing gymnasium. Some type of shade should be provided, however, to keep the sun out of the players' eyes, because temporary blinding may be responsible for an accident. Many new gymnasiums have been built without windows for this reason.

With the rapid growth of night football and baseball, the lighting of outdoor areas has become of paramount interest. From thirty to sixty footcandles are recommended for such play, and unless this minimum can be provided, a school would be wise, from a standpoint of safety, not to attempt staging night contests. However, Forsythe, in a survey of night contests in Ohio, Pennsylvania, Kansas, and Michigan, reported that the schools "were virtually unanimous in indicating that there was no difference in the number or severity of athletic injuries received in night football as compared with the daytime game." [5] In this connection it must be considered that both teams and spectators are required to go to and from the game at a time when the traffic-accident rate is highest.

TABLE 17-3
LEVELS OF ILLUMINATION CURRENTLY
RECOMMENDED FOR SPECIFIC SPORTS AREAS

AREA	FOOTCANDLES ON TASKS
Gymnasiums	
Exhibitions, matches	30
General exercising and recreation	20
Dances	5
Lockers and shower rooms	20
Badminton	
Tournament	30
Club	20
Recreational	10
Basketball	
College and professional	50
College intramural and high school, with spectators	30
College intramural and high school, without spectators	20
Volleyball	
Tournament	20
Recreational	10
Swimming pools	
General and overhead	50
Underwater	#

#100 Lamp lumens per square foot of pool surface.
(Courtesy of Planning Areas and Facilities for Health, Physical Education, and Recreation by Participants in National Facilities Conference.)

[5] Charles E. Forsythe, *Administration of High School Athletics*, 4th ed. (Englewood Cliffs, N.J.: Prentice-Hall, 1962).

ADEQUATE PERSONAL EQUIPMENT. Adequate protective equipment should be furnished to, and worn by, all contestants in those sports or activities that require it. In the preceding section it was recommended that a school should not sponsor an activity for which adequate facilities or equipment cannot be provided. The practice of requiring players to furnish part of their own equipment, such as shoes and shoulder pads in football, is to be condemned from the safety standpoint, because often poor equipment is purchased and allowed to deteriorate. Football, hockey, lacrosse, and boxing are sports that require especially adequate gear. It will be noted that these sports rank high on the hazard list because they are contact sports. The rules may specify the equipment necessary for game participation in these sports, but there is no such requirement with regard to the practice field. Also, there are very few or no rules requiring that equipment be of the most effective style or that it be properly fitted. Since statistics indicate that the largest number of accidents occur during free play and practice periods, it behooves the coach or instructor to insist that players be supplied with adequate protective equipment and to see that they *wear* it. Usually coaches and trainers are better qualified than the players to select the proper style of protective equipment, as well as to place it properly.

The best quality, most efficient, and most protective equipment should be purchased. Coaches learn from experience the brands and styles of equipment that are most satisfactory. Many, especially college coaches and equipment men, are also adept at devising special types of equipment for the protection of their athletes. It is recommended that all coaches study this important phase of safety and bend every effort to see that the best protection possible is made available to all athletes in all sports. The secretary of one state High School Athletic Association points out, however, that the most expensive equipment is not necessarily the safest.

ATHLETIC SUPPORTERS AS A SAFETY FACTOR. Opinion varies regarding the safety factor involved in the use of the common elastic supporter. Many coaches feel that its use prohibits the testes from floating to the side, as nature designed, when one is hit in the groin, thus making the use of a supporter a hazard rather than a protection. Others contend that such support prevents the testes from being pinched between the legs and otherwise protects them from harm. The author believes that each individual must experiment and decide this issue for himself, but recommends the elimination of elastic supports whenever possible. The use of the aluminum or plastic cup is a definite safety factor when it is properly fitted and used. Its use in all contact sports is recommended.

WRAPPING OF ANKLES AS A SAFETY FACTOR. Taping of normal ankles to prevent injury in athletics is a moot question among coaches. One school of thought holds that reliance upon this support tends to weaken the ankle, whereas others believe that such support only at the time of play could not possibly have this effect. Many coaches require such wrapping for both practice sessions and games, which practice Coach Adolph Rupp of Kentucky says has a definite tendency to weaken the ankles. All are agreed, of course, that weak or injured ankles should be wrapped for play. Many trainers believe that ankle wrapping, especially rigid taping, is responsible for a large number of knee injuries, because the ankle is rendered unable to absorb some of the necessary twist. There is sufficient evidence supporting this theory to limit the amount of wrapping.

EYE PROTECTION. *If a participant must wear spectacles for team play, guards or nonshatter glass should be worn.* This rule applies to any activity in which there is danger of the person being struck by another player or by a piece of equipment. The spectacle frames should be made of plastic and should be form-fitting. In contact sports, such as soccer and lacrosse, the guard can be worn successfully as a part of the helmet, whereas in other sports it must be self-supporting and is less satisfactory.

Another development, the nonbreakable contact lens, offers the ametropic athlete a convenient and safe type of correction that may become universally adopted in sports participation. These lenses have proved satisfactory for use in noncontact sports and in baseball and basketball. Their use in football is doubtful but eventually they may prove most convenient and safest for such contact sports. The prohibitive cost and short periods that contact lenses can be worn with comfort have retarded their use. Their loss on the floor or field has become a recurring problem.

SAFE TRAINING SUPPLIES. School and college training and first-aid departments should retain and dispense only the simplest medical supplies necessary to render first aid. Poisons, of course, should be properly labeled and made inaccessible for general use. It is not a wise practice to transfer medicines, especially poisons, to bottles not intended for their storage.

Flammable materials should never be stored or used within the athletic plant. There have been several explosions with serious results from using flammable materials in training rooms for the removal of adhesive tape. Ether is another highly explosive chemical that must be handled with care. Those responsible for the purchasing of training and first-aid supplies should make certain that they are nonexplosive.

ROLE OF SERVICE PERSONNEL IN SAFETY

Physical educators are prone to underestimate and to capitalize upon the influence that service personnel exerts in the safe conduct of the program. To this staff falls the responsibility for maintaining the physical plant, and whether or not they provide maximum safety depends upon the attitude and diligence of the workers. The director of physical education and athletics (and staff) should consider the custodial staff as an integral part of the department and make every effort to dignify their work. When the service-staff members feel that they are accepted and relied upon, and when they are made conscious of the important safety role they play, better maintenance results.

CUSTODIANS AND ENGINEERS. To enumerate the safety aspects of the custodian's and engineer's work would require the listing of all their jobs. Almost all such work has some safety significance; these men are not dealing with safety in the abstract. It can be readily recognized that many of the items previously discussed in this chapter are controlled almost entirely by the service staff. They are particularly warned not to sacrifice safety for beauty in the maintenance of the plant. The following safety contributions can be made by custodians and engineers:

1. The custodian, with the director of physical education or designated persons, should make the semi-annual safety inspection of facilities.
2. The custodian should check the grounds and indoor facilities daily for defects or extraneous materials that may cause accidents and injury.
3. The custodian should declare in writing to the proper authority when a facility or piece of equipment is unsafe for use. He should first render the item unusable until made safe again.
4. The engineer should inspect the bleachers for safety before each usage, and if he is in doubt, prohibit their use.
5. A custodian should be present during all athletic contests to provide maximum safe use of facilities for both spectators and players.
6. The custodian and engineer must be aware of the special hazards of the swimming pool and shower rooms, and of the water heating and purification plant.
7. Engineers and custodians must rigidly enforce all fire laws and fire-protection measures.
8. Engineers and custodians should be qualified to render first aid when necessary.

REFERENCES

Bischoff, David C., "Design for Participation," *Journal of Health, Physical Education, and Recreation* (March 1966), pp. 28–31.
Fabian, Dietrick, *Modern Swimming Pools of the World* (Florence, Alabama: National Pool Equipment Company, 1958).
"Focus on Facilities," *Journal of Health, Physical Education, and Recreation* (April 1962), p. 37.

Gabrielson, Alexander M., and Caswell M. Miles, *Sports and Recreation Facilities* (Englewood Cliffs, N.J.: Prentice-Hall, 1958), 370 pages.

Illuminating Engineering Society, *Current Recommended Practice* for Sports Lighting. (Current issue.)

Johnson, Burt, and S. A. Abercrombie, "A Safe Environment for Learning," *National Education Association Journal*, Vol. 49, No. 7 (October 1960), p. 24.

National Commission on Safety Education, *Checklist of Safety and Safety Education in Your School* (Washington, D.C.: National Education Association, 1963).

National Industrial Recreation Association, *Standard Sports Areas* (Chicago: The Association, 20 N. Wacker Drive, 60606, 1963).

Ryser, Otto E., "Safety—The Administrators' and Teachers' Responsibility," *Athletic Journal*, Vol. XLI, No. 3 (November 1960), p. 32.

Scott, Harry A., *From Program to Facilities in Physical Education* (New York: Harper & Row, 1958).

Seaton, Don Cash, *Safety in Sports* (Englewood Cliffs, N.J.: Prentice-Hall, 1948). Out of print.

Silverwood, George P., "Safety in the School Environment," *Journal of Health, Physical Education, and Recreation* (March 1960), p. 30.

Stack, Herbert J., "Supervisors Set Up Schedule," *Safety Education* (January 1960), pp. 11–13.

Wilcox, Harry, "Safer Athletic Fields: *Athletic Journal* (June 1965), p. 34.

CHAPTER 18 SAFETY IN PHYSICAL EDUCATION AND RECREATION

INTRODUCTION

A number of studies have shown that over 50 per cent of all school and college injuries occur in the field of sports participation—athletics, physical education, and recreation. The National Safety Council reports that 67 per cent of all school jurisdiction accidents involve boys and 59 per cent girls in these areas.

Practically all physical education and active recreational activities are potentially dangerous. Some, such as tennis and folk dancing, are relatively safe while others, such as football and hockey, are considered most hazardous. It is this very element of danger and adventure that makes certain sports more appealing to certain people than to others. Many young men and women have lost their lives or have been maimed for life as a result of participation in the so-called recreational activities as well as in the combat sports.

Undoubtedly the possibility of injury in sports will always exist, since the human factor is involved, and leaders would not have it otherwise because man seems to need this risk of participation, total engrossment, and all-out effort that is demanded.

Since it is virtually impossible to teach all of the safety skills of all sports and activities, it is incumbent upon our schools and colleges to attempt to teach the proper attitudes and controlled emotions that help prepare students to avoid accidents and injuries in all situations.

Because physical education is required and recreation encouraged in most all schools and colleges it is the duty of every administrator to organize and administer these programs as safely as possible. It has been estimated that accidents and resultant injuries in sports can be reduced by 50 per cent through proper administration, leadership, and facility and equipment controls.

ADMINISTRATIVE AND PROGRAM CONTROLS

The administration of school or college physical education may be defined as that part of the program which is concerned with the organization, management, regulation and control of personnel, program, and materials so that they will function smoothly, efficiently, and effectively as an integrated whole in achieving the desired goals.

The principal task of administration in physical education, then, is to integrate the objectives of the program, the activities of the pupils and instructors, and the facilities and equipment used. The success of the program would be judged by the effectiveness in reaching these objectives. One of the stumbling blocks in attaining these objectives may well be an ineffective safety program and an excessively high accident incidence. Pechar [1] lists the most important contributing factors to accidents in the following rank order:

Physical
   (1) Poor skill; (2) Fatigue; (3) Poor condition.
Mental-Emotional
   (1) Disregarding of instructions; (2) Impulsive actions.
Equipment
   (1) Inadequate or faulty protective equipment; (2) Inadequate or faulty personal equipment; (3) Inadequate or faulty activity equipment.
Facility
   (1) Poor playing surface; (2) Limited space; (3) Obstructions in play space
Leadership
   (1) Inadequate amount of instructions; (2) Poor officiating; (3) Inadequate amount of supervision.
Program
   (1) Too many participants in activity; (2) Level of performance demanded by activity too high; (3) Ratio of activity to leader too high.

As can readily be seen, most of these factors are the responsibility of an efficient administration, and effective supervision as well as capable leadership.

An analysis of existing studies in this field and the findings of the author's own study indicate a number of desirable and effective adminis-

[1] Stanley F. Pechar, "Accidents in Secondary School Physical Education Programs," *Second Annual Safety Education Review* (Washington, D.C.: National Education Association, 1963), pp. 34–37.

trative and program controls for departments of health and physical education.

LEADERSHIP CONTROLS

Leadership is probably the most important of the safety controls. With good leadership even poor administration and inadequate facilities can be overcome, and a fine record for the safe conduct of sports can be established. The qualities and training necessary among coaches and instructors to insure a high type of leadership is discussed later, but it might be well to point out here that teachers and coaches must be or become *safety-conscious*. Such a vital factor should not be a hit-or-miss policy of department conduct. To determine leadership success or failure, the attitude and methods used by every instructor and coach should be studied and the accident statistics analyzed from season to season.

LEADERSHIP QUALITIES

Qualifications for intelligent leadership have been outlined by a national conference of physicians and educators as follows:

To provide leadership . . . such persons will need a thorough knowledge of:

1. The principles of child growth and development.
2. The health needs of boys and girls.
3. Desirable health practices—particularly those related to athletics.
4. The principles of first aid and accident prevention.
5. The physiology of exercise.
6. The games they teach and their rules and strategy.

A noted pediatrician John Reichert [2] says, "In addition, good leaders understand the needs, desires and limitations of growing children. They have a sound knowledge of child (and parent) psychology, and they can at least partially match participants."

Fortunately, most graduates of schools of physical education have had training in all of these aspects for leadership and should therefore be qualified leaders. Unfortunately, many school systems permit the employment of coaches and often teachers of physical education who are *not* qualified and should not be utilized to assist with school or college programs.

SOURCES OF LEADERSHIP CONTROLS. There are three main sources of leadership controls: the instructor or coach, the official,

[2] John Lester Reichert, "A Pediatrician's View of Competitive Sports Before the Teens," *Today's Health* (October 1957).

and the player. All are important, but vary in influence. It has been contended that 31 per cent of all accidents and 30 per cent of the days lost are caused by improper leadership controls, and that of these accidents 44 per cent can be blamed on inadequate officiating, 40 per cent due to improper supervision during the activity, and the remaining 13 per cent to inadequate conditioning of students. Breaking these statistics down further, 13 per cent of high school accidents were caused by poor conditioning; among college women approximately 56 per cent were caused by poor leadership, including lack of training, old injuries, fatigue, and overtraining; and among college men approximately 46 per cent were blamed on lack of training, fatigue, and old injuries. It is evident that those responsible for the safety controls are not giving sufficient attention to the conditioning of the body or training in the skills required for the activity.

QUALIFIED INSTRUCTORS

Only qualified instructors should be employed to teach physical education. Because more than 50 per cent of all school accidents occur in this field of school activity, this admonition is self-evident. However, universities and colleges vary considerably in their preparation of teachers of physical education and state requirements for certification also vary. Likewise, most teacher-education institutions teach safety in the sports skills but relatively few require sufficient training in this field to produce good teachers or administrators of safety education. It is therefore recommended that the administrator select prospective teachers of physical education whose credentials show sufficient training in safety education. If the prospective teacher also possesses great empathy for students' welfare, and thoroughly understands the general and specific safety procedures in the activities he teaches, then the administration will not be plagued by excessive accidents and injuries.

Nyman [3] Principal of La Fayette School in Salt Lake City, has compiled a pertinent list of qualifications that he looks and hopes for in selecting teachers of physical education:

1. Intelligent enough to talk about sex problems objectively.
2. Tactful enough to referee disputes fairly.
3. Altruistic enough to want to do some social service.
4. Trained enough in psychology to counsel young people.
5. Professional enough to serve his fellow workers in their improvement.
6. Kind enough to win young folks to his leadership.
7. Big enough to distinguish trifles from giants.
8. Doctor enough to heal the heartbreaks and soul injuries common to a big school.

[3] Emil Nyman, as quoted by Charles A. Bucher, *Administration of School Health and Physical Education Programs* (St. Louis: C. V. Mosby, 1963), p. 78.

9. Cultured enough to be a model in taste and language.

10. Creative enough to be able to put art into physical education activities and to appreciate originality in others.

No. 11. Vision enough to tolerate the antics of young folk and to make the most of them.

12. Big enough to overflow into the lives of other teachers in the school to keep them balanced and encouraged.

13. Funny enough to be the clown of the organization if no one else turns up.

14. Wholesome enough to set the mental health climate of the school.

15. Religious enough to be secure, clean, optimistic, and courageous.

16. Skillful enough to provide practices in wholesome, constructive group living.

17. Moral enough to be a part in the development of conscience.

18. Adaptable enough to make a physical education health program in spite of weather, interference, and lack of equipment.

19. Young enough to catch new ideas.

IN-SERVICE TRAINING. There are many courses in safety education available in colleges throughout the country, by extension or summer courses, where teachers may take such courses as Safety Education, Safety in Sports, First Aid, Driver Education, and many others. Nine hours of safety education is the minimum recommendation for certification to teach.

USE OF WOMEN INSTRUCTORS. The practice of using men instructors to teach girls physical education classes is questionable from a safety standpoint. Most female organizations and leaders believe that the use of male instructors, especially in team sports, is not wise. They feel that the hard-driving, win-at-any-cost methods used by men in their sports is not appropriate to the conduct of female activities.

USE OF ATHLETIC COACHES. Unless athletic coaches are graduates in physical education or have had at least nine years of teaching experience, they are not good safety risks to employ as instructors of physical education. On the other hand, many coaches become fine instructors of driver education after they have taken sufficient courses in this field.

THE INSTRUCTOR'S CONCERN. The instructor of physical education is vitally concerned with the safe conduct of his classes and intramural sports. Often, of course, the athletic coach and the instructor of physical education is the same person, serving in both capacities. Fundamentally, the obligations and approaches to the problems are the same for both. The physical education instructor, however, is more often forced to conduct sports and other activities for which adequate protective equipment and sufficient space are not provided. The participants are less skilled and less fit than those reporting for athletics. His problem, therefore, is often more difficult even though there is not the pressure to produce winning school teams.

METHOD IN ACCIDENT PREVENTION

The method of instruction and organization is basic in the control of accidents and injury in physical education. The efficient coach or instructor who has good organization and uses good teaching techniques will have better control of his squads and classes, and fewer accidents and injuries will result. When participants are kept busy learning the proper skills and playing according to the rules of the game they are less likely to experience accidents and injury through forbidden stunts and horseplay. Staley [4] commented upon this point.

> A class that is conducted efficiently is so busy performing necessary and worth-while activities that there is little or no opportunity for "cutting capers." Disorder arises when interest and action begin to lag, or when confusion exists. The instructor who assumes a negative approach is defeating his own end. He is so concerned about disorder, so on the alert for it, so ready to squash it, that he is prone to neglect the very thing which is the best check against it—efficient management and direction. He would do much better if he centered his attention on teaching and learning procedures, and then handled disorder when it arose.

It is assumed that all teachers are aware of the principles of learning and that they will apply those techniques that are apropos to physical education. In applying the principles of learning to the teaching of skills the teacher must also be aware of and trained in the safety devices and procedures for all sports and activities that he is called upon to teach.

STUDENT SAFETY LEADERS. The use of student leaders in the physical education program is a common and desirable practice. Properly selected and trained, these leaders can serve an extremely important role in the safety education program. Research indicates that their use is valuable in accident prevention at all levels, especially in the high school, where they are also responsible for a decrease in the severity of the injuries. The degree to which students can help in the reduction of accidents is in part affected by the training in safety they have received and the degree to which they are allowed to take an active part in the teaching situation, preferably with small squads. It is therefore recommended that the department have a plan for selecting and training student leaders to assist in conducting the activity program. It is common practice on the secondary level to form a leaders club, the members of which can be selected by the students, the faculty, or the club members themselves.

[4] Seward C. Staley, *Sports Education* (New York: A. S. Barnes, 1939), p. 240. Out of print.

Many instructors feel that it is more democratic and effective to give every member of the class an opportunity to serve in the capacity of leader. It can be readily seen, however, that the former method would ordinarily provide safer leadership, because the fewer numbers would be easier to train more thoroughly.

The National Safety Council suggests two criteria for the selection and use of these leaders:

1. The experience should be an educative one which the particular pupil needs.
2. The pupil should be capable of assuming the responsibilities of a safety leader.

Some safety responsibilities of student leaders are the following:

1. To assist in the daily inspection of play areas, apparatus, and equipment.
2. To instruct new students in all activities, especially in the use of apparatus and facilities.
3. To supervise activities and assist in their safe performance.
4. To assist in the setting up and proper use and storage of equipment and supplies.
5. To conduct groups safely from school to playground and back, particularly where it is necessary to cross traffic lanes.
6. To help develop an attitude of safety on the part of fellow students.
7. To learn the rules of the various sports and to officiate well.
8. To learn first aid and how to report accidents.[5]

Safety patrols may be used on crowded playgrounds. This is a practical adaptation, particularly where traffic is a hazard. The advantages of using the patrols are that they are already organized and the students have a distinguishing badge or Sam Browne belt that adds authority to their office of supervision. Unless pupils are trained to assist in the conduct of various activities, they are of little value in this respect. Class or team equipment should be delivered by managers or class leaders to the playing field and distributed for use *only* upon permission of the instructor. When such equipment as balls and bats are distributed in the gymnasium, the players in their exhilaration or anxiety to get to the field, are likely to race and throw bats or balls promiscuously. Broken windows and other property damage may result as well as occasional injury caused by collisions or falls.

HEALTH EXAMINATIONS. Among the controls set up for the department of health and physical education, the health examination is one of the most important single administrative precautions for the pre-

[5] National Safety Council, *Safety in Physical Education and Recreation* (Chicago: The Council, 1941). Out of print.

vention of injury.) It has been found that the accident incidence for schools having such examination was 11.6 per 1,000 exposures, as compared with 17.4 for schools *not* having such examinations, a 39 per cent lower incidence. Outstanding teachers of health and physical education, when polled by the investigator, unanimously agreed that such an examination was a primary safety control and should be required periodically of all participants in the physical education program and of all members of interschool teams before participation in *each* sport. The trend is away from superficial examinations made annually, to less frequent but more thorough examinations supplemented by an intelligent program of detection and referral at all times. Most experts agree that the frequency of periodic examinations should vary with the age of the participants. The younger the participant the more frequent the examination.

The examination should be recorded on the cumulative record, which is kept on file in the department where it can be used constantly for guidance of the student's program. This blank should contain a space for the recording of the injury-accidents experienced by the student. Such a record may prove helpful in studying the underlying causes among accident repeaters and in determining means of correction. It is important that the examining doctor or doctors be familiar with the physical requirements of each sport to enable them to eliminate those students who have conditions that might prove dangerous in a specific activity.

The health examinations should include items that affect a person's safety, such as colorblindness, range of peripheral vision, and reaction time. Although such items are usually a part of the testing program in the school's driver-education course, too few schools have such a course, or else have one that all too often reaches only a small segment of the school population. It is therefore desirable that such psychophysical tests be included in the regular health examinations, which ordinarily reach all of the pupils. In those schools and colleges in which the Department of Health and Physical Education conducts an extensive testing program, it might be desirable to include certain psychophysical tests there.

Because of the importance of *vision* in the role of safety, it is recommended that an effort be made to provide tests of the range of *peripheral vision, colorblindness, depth perception,* and possibly *double vision* and *dark adaptation,* in addition to the customary *visual acuity* test. Floyd R. Eastwood, one of the country's outstanding leaders in safety in athletics said, "Tests of depth perception and peripheral vision should be given in the medical examination, and *practice on split vision should be instituted.*" The services of an ophthalmologist would be required to make such tests on a scientific basis, but since the school's role is assumed to be one of screening only, the more common driver-testing devices, under direction of a nurse or other competent person, are adequate to provide such examinations. These devices can be purchased or borrowed from safety organizations or constructed in the school shop.

Although reaction time has probably received undue and disproportionate emphasis in the testing of drivers, it nevertheless is an important factor in safe living and is especially vital in physical education. Such a test can usually be incorporated in the health examination or testing program. Keller [6] reported that athletes responded faster than nonathletes, also that baseball, basketball, football, and track athletes comprised a group significantly faster in reaction time than the group including gymnasts, swimmers, and wrestlers, but that no significant difference was found between the sports within these groups. Harry R. McPhee,[7] team physician at Princeton University, commented on the slow reactor, "Because of his subnormal reactions, he is injury fodder of a malicious type. His awkwardness will result in injury not only to himself but to other players. A wise coach will encourage him to take a physical education course in coordinating exercises before going out for football."

Hearing is almost universally included in the health examination, but its relation to safety is seldom pointed out to the unfortunate ones. This brings us to the next point, that not only should the examination or tests include such items, but that *students should be made aware of such deficiencies in relation to safe living, and informed of proper methods of compensation or correction.* The real value of the health examination lies in effective education at the moment of examination and during the follow-up. It is at these times that the relationship between deficiencies and the student's safety should be brought home. If the coaches and instructors of physical education are also aware of these deficiencies, a safer and more profitable program can be planned for the individual.

Since health, or physical fitness, is not a static factor, it must be recognized that an examination does not preclude the possibility of a player's competing when he is not fit. In order to insure safety by this method, an examination would be required before each participation, which would be administratively impossible. For this reason, each individual's participation following the health examination must rest upon the expert scrutiny of the coach or instructor, supplemented by consultation with the individual. The latter usually takes place only when the participant reports some injury or ailment or the instructor suspects there is something wrong. In fact, through constant association, there are many signs which indicate to the teacher or coach unnatural conditions of which the student himself may not be aware, and which

[6] Louis B. Keller, "The Relation of Quickness of Bodily Movement to Success in Athletics," *Research Quarterly* (May 1936), pp. 146–155.

[7] McPhee, Harry R., "Prevent Football Injuries," *Scholastic Coach,* 1948, p. 47.

may be missed by the physician who seldom observes the student at play. Manner of response to a command and lack of "life" are common warnings of illness. The observant instructor becomes adept at spotting such ailments and in distinguishing between the real thing and "gold-bricking." In the last respect, experience indicates that the instructor should err on the side of leniency when judging a student's fitness for participation in the required physical education program. To let an occasional malingerer slip by is far less harmful than to harm irreparably a truly ill or injured student who is not capable of adroitly pleading his case.

PHYSICIAN'S PERMISSION FOR READMITTANCE. Students absent from school for three or more days because of illness or injury should present a *physician's written approval for readmittance* to physical education classes, intramurals, and interschool athletics. This precaution has been accepted in principle almost universally, but the physical education departments have found its administration so difficult that few schools follow the procedure. The administration is relatively simple for those schools supporting a school nurse or physician, but a practical method must be worked out for those not having one. The use of a form similar to the one in Figure 18-1 is recommended. The use of such a permit guides the physical educator in planning a scientific

---

PERMIT TO RESUME PARTICIPATION IN
ACTIVITY PROGRAM

Township High School   Date_____

_____has been out of school for _____ days
         (name)

because of _____

_____
                          her

In my opinion it will be safe for him to resume the activity program as follows:

1. Physical education classes _____
                                          (date)

2. Intramural or interschool athletics _____
                                          (date)

Remarks: _____

              (Signed)_____
                              Physician

FIGURE 18-1. Physician's Permit to Resume Participation

and safe reconditioning period for the returning student and protects the department from possible criticism should something go wrong.

HOMOGENEOUS GROUPING. *Homogeneous grouping of students in physical education and athletics is helpful in reducing the number and severity of accidents.* The extent of such grouping from the safety standpoint is debatable, but most leaders feel that it is desirable to divide the sexes above the third grade for the majority of activities, and to segregate each grade for participation. Lloyd and Eastwood found that grouping by age is a superior safety technique to grouping by combinations of height, weight, and judgment of the teacher. Such classification, however, would be administratively impossible in many schools. Some schools find it advisable in physical education to divide these groups still further, through the use of physical tests or other selective methods, into various classifications of adeptness. This method of classification is commonly used in the teaching of swimming, gymnastics and tumbling, wrestling and boxing, and similar sports because of the danger in superior performers competing with the less effective. Coaches almost universally find it necessary and advisable to segregate their squads according to ability, not only as a means of improving team play, but as a safety measure.

COMPETENT FIRST AID. A physician, trainer, nurse, or competent first-aider should be available for all class and intramural activities. If the instructor is a qualified first-aider, as has been recommended, his presence should suffice. In fact, it is customary in most schools where a nurse or physician is not employed for the department of physical education to act in all school first-aid cases. However, a doctor should always be available and it is recommended that the names and telephone numbers of approved physicians be on file for emergencies.) (In case the injured person does not express a desire to call his family physician, this is useful.) It has been found that the availability of a medical doctor for class instruction results in an average reduction of severity of the injuries of two thirds—approximately 36 per cent—and for intramurals of approximately 40 per cent.)

CORECREATIONAL ACTIVITY. So far as is known no studies have been made of the accident incidence in corecreational activities. It would seem logical to assume, however, that the tendency would be toward an increased rate because of the inherent urge of the males to demonstrate their prowess and the girls to feign weakness. The desire to show off is definitely an accident producer. The late Howard Danford, a leader in the field, commented, "On the other hand, we have found the boys holding back in order not to injure the girls." The University of Kentucky's service program has been completely coeducational for many years and accident reports show no increase over the rates reported for segregated classes. Instructors in charge of corecreational activities should be aware of various safety controls needed and the possibility of an increased accident rate.

PHYSICAL TESTS. Maturity, strength, speed, endurance, and agility are factors not usually measured by the health examination, but they should be considered when students are being classified for safer participation. Therefore, physical tests that measure these qualities are also helpful in planning the students' program, and can be considered a safety factor. Such classification as that mentioned in the two categories above makes instruction easier, provides continuity in the program, and assures adequate progression of skills, all of which make for safety.

SIZE OF PHYSICAL EDUCATION CLASSES. No other problem has plagued the administration and the physical education departments more than the one of overcrowded classes. Physical educators have been demanding smaller classes for years, but there still remain too many overcrowded physical education classes throughout the country. That overcrowding causes accidents is a fact accepted by most authorities who have studied the problem. Every effort should be made to gauge the size of classes according to the limitations of the facilities and equipment and the availability of teaching and supervisory personnel. Although educational authorities advocate that the size of physical education classes not exceed that of academic classes, many instructors are required to teach classes far in excess of the normal load. When an instructor is required to handle a class with more than approximately thirty-five students, it becomes very difficult to conduct the class so as to avoid excessive accidents among the participants. Under these conditions many instructors devote most of their time to safety supervision rather than to instruction. Physical educators are urged to refuse to endanger the students by scheduling overcrowded classes.

School administrators are urged to schedule physical education classes first on the student's program so that he will be homogeneously assigned to classes of proper size. Often, when the scheduling of physical education is relegated to last, unequal distribution results because there is usually but one gymnasium, swimming pool, or play field available so that students cannot be shifted to other classes within the department.

ADEQUATE PROTECTION. *Schools should not sponsor or conduct those sports or activities* in physical education, intramurals, or interschool athletics for which *adequate protective equipment and safe facilities cannot be provided.* Many small schools are guilty of promoting activities that require expensive equipment that they are unable to afford. Also, large schools often conduct activities in areas that are entirely inadequate from the standpoint of space and safety. When he is contemplating the conduct of an activity where either the facilities or equipment are not adequate or safe, the school administrator must always weigh the possibilities of injuries in the light of the benefits to be derived. Likewise, when unusual numbers of accidents are occurring, the administrator should *first* investigate the adequacy of facilities and protective equipment.

Closely allied with this problem is that of climatic conditions. School administrators should conduct a seasonal program of sports that is suited to the climatic conditions of the particular community. Daily activities of the physical education and sports program must be adjusted to adverse weather conditions such as snow, ice, rain, fog, heat, and cold. Alternate activities or spaces should be available for such occasions.

⌐ SAFETY INSTRUCTION. *Safety instruction in health and physical education should be an integral part of the program.)* This instruction would range from the formal teaching program of the health class to the informal warnings of the coach to his players as they scuffle in the showers, and would include direct and correlated teaching, the use of visual aids, and the posting of rules and regulations and posters.

Every well-ordered department will establish certain safety rules and regulations for the proper use of the facilities. Observance will depend upon the effectiveness of the educational program, enforcement, and accident experience.

At an early meeting of each class the teacher should instruct the members concerning the rules and regulations for health and safety, the reasons for their existence, and the methods of compliance. Many schools find it helpful to place this information on the same mimeographed sheet with the course objectives and grading plan that is given each student at the beginning of the class.

The health class instruction, now a part of every modern school's program, should include pertinent materials on safer participation in sports, similar to the contents of this text.

Various hazards of the facilities often warrant warning signs, such as for instance •

1. Never enter pool alone.
2. Keep locker doors closed.
3. Don't jump from steps.
4. Dry off in this room only.
5. Walk—don't run.
6. Use this equipment only when instructor is present.
7. Keep right.
8. Open door slowly.
9. Remove football shoes outdoors.

⌐ INFORMED PLAYERS. To help avoid injury to others as well as to themselves, participants should know the safety implications and should observe the rules of the game. Playing according to the rules and spirit of the rules reduces injuries, and those players who know the rules are more likely to observe them. It is therefore recommended that coaches and instructors make special efforts to familiarize all participants with the rules before participation. Progressive instructors frequently give written tests on the rules of the game being learned.⟩

No Furthermore, *participants in all physical education activities should be instructed on the facts of accident causes, incidence, parts injured, and severity.* Each sport and activity has certain inherent and attendant hazards about which participants should be informed. Players should also be cognizant of the safety role played by one's attitude and knowledge in such participation. It is the responsibility of the instructor and coach to teach these knowledges and attitudes as well as skills for safety. The imparting of such information need not take the form of rote classroom work, but might rather be interwoven with the activity instructional period. Such admonitions as "Don't forget, Bill Jones had his ankle broken doing that last year," or "Most of the injuries we've had on the parallel bars have been caused by spotters putting their arms over, instead of under, the bars" are very effective and are often employed by teachers of physical education. Such instruction need not be predominantly negative in nature, because most instructors feel that "scaring" is not good methodology. It is generally understood that unless there is ample justification for it, negative instruction in safety education should not be used. School spirit and group approbation are of immeasurable value as incentives in teaching safety education.

FIRE DRILLS. *Fire drills must be thoroughly planned, organized, and carefully practiced in all areas of the physical education plant.* Correct exits for each area including emergency obstructions and the proper clothing procedure for each activity must be worked out and practiced in accordance with general school fire-drill plans. If the weather is favorable, students can carry on the drills in gym clothes, but in inclement weather they should be permitted to secure coats.⟩ If the drill occurs while students are showering, dressing, or in the pool, they should be instructed to secure sufficient clothing and participate. The instructor must be sure to carry his roll book and take the roll to make certain that all students have left the building.

SUITABLE ACTIVITIES. *In planning the physical education program, activities should be selected that are safe for the given sex, age level, and pupil abilities.* It is understood, of course, that because of their inherent qualities, very few sports activities are entirely safe, but there are certain recognized limitations. For instance, touch football is considered unsafe for girls, cross-country too strenuous for elementary school children, and horse polo too hazardous for unskilled riders. One proven method to reduce the accident incidence is to have a large variety of activities, provided they can be properly supervised.

The writer wishes to make it clear that he would not eliminate hazardous games. As it is so ably expressed by the late Howard Danford,

"If we select only activities which are safe, we will devitalize the program. Much of the value of some activities lies in the hazards. Our job is not to eliminate all these hazards, but to help youth overcome them." In discussing the trends in high school athletics, Forsythe says, "It is very probable that, in the near future, an accounting will be taken to determine whether high schools are sponsoring athletic activities which do not properly belong in the high school category of sports."

ADAPTED ACTIVITIES. Activities that involve a variety of different interests, skills, social situations, and emotional outlets should be provided, and students assigned to these various activities according to capabilities and to need. Many students have organic defects or physical impairments that prevent them from taking part in all phases of the regular program. In these cases the examining physician should prescribe suitable activities and the department of physical education provide needed supervision and instruction within the regular class activity or in special classes. Present educational policy does not call for complete segregation of handicapped children, which poses the added problem of protecting, as well as developing, these youngsters.

SUPERVISION AT ALL TIMES. All activities, including free-play periods of the physical education program, should be adequately supervised by the teaching staff at all times. From the standpoint of safety, this control is a necessary one. According to Lloyd, Deaver, and Eastwood, inadequate supervision during the activity accounts for 40 per cent of the improper leadership controls which cause 31 per cent of the total accidents. Many school systems make it mandatory that a teacher be present at all times for every activity of the program. "Teaching" supervision makes for greater safety than "sitting" supervision. Although records do not show conclusively that the incidence of accidents is higher during free play, they do disclose that the severity index is much higher. Experience indicates the desirability of supervision at this time. (See Chapters 4 and 16 for liability in case of inadequate supervision.)

Clubs sponsored by the department, such as those for skiing, camping, archery, rifle, riding, and others, must be supervised by a knowledgeable member of the department or faculty because of their potential dangers. Special rules of safe conduct must be established and observed. If they are supervised by a faculty member who has not had physical education training, the procedures should be worked out with the physical education department.

Classes in physical education are usually limited to the length of the regular school periods, and ordinarily are considered too short. Those schools that find the double gym period better suited to instructional needs must avoid undue fatigue on the part of the students, for it might result in a higher accident incidence. There seems to be no particular class period during the day when the accident incidence is higher than normal.

Sufficient time for showering, dressing, and getting to the next class must be allowed. When students are forced to rush to and from showers, dress hurriedly, and rush to the next class, it increases the possibility of accidents. Although most school physical education periods are too short for the usual class activities, it is not wise economy to rob the students of needed minutes for dressing. Table 18-1, which indicates the time allotment advocated by the State University of New York, the New York State Education Department, is recommended as a basis for scheduling:

TABLE 18-1
GENERAL TIME ALLOTMENT FOR INSTRUCTIONAL PERIODS

CLASS AS A WHOLE		CLASS IN SQUADS OR IN SPECIAL FORMATION	CLASS AS A WHOLE
10 to 12 per cent of the period	4 to 6 per cent of the period	60 to 75 per cent of the period	12 to 20 per cent of the period
Dressing for class	Assembly, preliminaries, warming-up, and body building activities	Instruction, practice, and evaluation of activities adapted to the needs of each group; rotation of squads	Reassembly, showers, dismissal

No No No

LARGE-GROUP SAFETY

In handling large groups, the coach or instructor must be wide awake and assume comprehensive control if accidents are to be avoided. He must not become intensely absorbed in one or two individuals while the remainder of the group runs wild; nor can he afford to loaf on the job. The handling of large numbers, especially in combat sports, is a difficult task that must be undertaken with a knowledge of the proper methods of accident prevent as well as the best procedures of organization and instruction. It is not within the province of this text to discuss the various methods of instruction, and the reader is referred to the many good texts on this subject.

PROGRESSIVE SKILLS. *The fundamental skills of all activities should be progressively taught and thoroughly learned.* Just as the success of a team or individual depends on the acquisition of skills, so does the safety of each individual depend to a great extent on such mastery. Performance in good form is usually a safety factor. Athletic coaches, therefore, are ordinarily very thorough and meticulous in the teaching of fundamental skills. On the other hand, the athletic coach and some instructors of physical education do not always take the time and energy necessary to teach thoroughly in their classes or in intramurals. This is often the situation when classes are so large that individual instruction is impossible.

Activities and teaching procedures should be organized so that the student will pass through a progression of logical skills. Particular care should be given in those skill areas where the greatest incidence or severity of accidents occur, such as sliding in baseball and blocking and tackling in football. Progression of players from physical education classes and intramural sports to varsity squads seems to be a desirable factor. In speaking of this point, a famous football coach once said that football coaches probably don't think of it as safety, but every sound coaching instruction has a double purpose: (1) To point out the most effective execution of the maneuver, and (2) to protect the players involved to prevent them from being injured and thus keep them in the game. *The use of lead-up games in teaching sports is a factor for safety.* This is true because the teaching of lead-up games is actually an advanced step in bringing together the learned fundamental skills that make the transition to the actual playing of the game less complicated and hazardous. Such lead-up games as "keep-away" in basketball, tag tackling in football, and "pepper" in baseball are interesting combinations of desirable fundamentals that help condition the players as well as teach progressive skills.

PROGRESSIVE CONDITIONING. Simultaneous with the proper development of fundamental skills should come progressive conditioning. As previously noted, Pechar [8] reported that the most important factors in high-school accidents were lack of skill, fatigue, and poor conditioning of the student or athlete. *Progressive conditioning of all participants is necessary for safe participation in all sports and activities.* Almost the same admonitions are applicable here that were listed above, however, the extenuating circumstances are far more numerous. Not only the player's training schedule while he is at school, but also his health habits throughout the rest of the day are involved. The condition in which each individual reports for the team or class and the time required to get into condition are important considerations to the coach or teacher.

The normal body possesses remarkable qualities for withstanding the

[8] Pechar, *op. cit.*

rigors of a physical education or varsity sports program, and its ability to recover, especially in the young and well-conditioned person, is even more astonishing. It is essential, however, that the teacher or coach work out an intelligent progressive conditioning schedule for each individual to insure keeping all participants in perfect condition. Each sport, of course, requires a type of conditioning different from other sports. The player who is in perfect condition for football is not necessarily able to step onto the basketball court and last out a full game. Nor is the basketball player necessarily in condition for track events or wrestling. There is only a partial carry-over from one sport to another and different neuromuscular skills must be established for each one, and the cardiovascular system adjusted to the different types of endurance and power required. The coach or instructor who succeeds in bringing all participants to maximum condition in the shortest length of time with the fewest injuries and illnesses is the one most likely to be rewarded with success.

ACCIDENTS CAUSED BY EXCITEMENT OR FEAR

During gym shows and exhibitions, students are likely to be overstimulated and unaware of new hazards, and therefore special precautions must be made for their safety. The situations that arise during such shows are too numerous and problematical to be discussed here. However, it would seem wise to explain to the participants that they will probably be overadrenalized, which tends to stimulate a person to go beyond his usual endurance and to attempt more difficult feats than can be safely accomplished. It should also be pointed out that the noise, glamour, and confusion that accompany the usual exhibition create an artificial atmosphere, which, when combined with the average student's stage fright, may hamper his ability, particularly until he has become accustomed to the strange circumstances.

IN CLASS. *Likewise, the teacher should be quick to restrain the overstimulated student when his actions might lead to injury.* It is not unusual for participants in the physical education program, especially children in the lower grades, to become highly emotional and hence dangerous to others as well as to themselves. Such conduct is less rare but not unknown on the higher levels, even in college, where players may "lose their heads." The teacher or coach must be able to recognize these persons quickly and to restrain or withdraw them from the activity or contest. Then, to try to correct the tendency would be a worthy goal.

THE TEACHER SHOULD NOT COERCE. The obese, the weak, or the uncoordinated pupil should not be chided or coerced into attempting skills or stunts beyond his ability. In those schools where these handicapped persons are members of the regular classes, the instructor must be cognizant of the fact that each person has a physiological limit and not prod him too far. This does not mean, necessarily, that such pupils should not be encouraged to extend themselves and to go beyond what they usually feel possible. It means rather that the instructor must use good judgment in handling them. Controlling the attitude and conduct of other pupils toward these unfortunate ones may also be necessary.

COURSE IN HORSEBACK RIDING
Physical Education

The University of Kentucky is offering a course in horseback riding, designated as "Physical Education_____," for the purpose of giving students healthful outdoor exercise and training in this art and recreation under the supervision of competent instructors. The University will supply reasonably gentle horses suitable for use by inexperienced riders or will contract with owners of riding horses for such horses and proper equipment. The course would not be offered if it were believed to be dangerous, but since horseback riding involves risks not found in the usual classroom courses, it is the policy of the University not to allow students to enroll or participate unless they assume these risks, nor to enroll students under the age of twenty-one years unless their parents give their consent and agree to release the University and those connected with the course from any liability by signing the attached agreement.

ASSUMPTION OF RISK
RELEASE OF LIABILITY

In consideration of allowing me to enroll in the course offered by the University of Kentucky, designated as "Physical Education–, (Horseback Riding)," I assume all risks inherent in or which may attach to the course and hereby agree to release the University of Kentucky and those connected with the course from all liability for injuries which I sustain as a result of my participation therein. I am _____ years old.

_____
(Signature of Student)

FIGURE 18-2.

There are also activities that are too difficult and hazardous for certain pupils. Participation in the very hazardous activities should not necessarily be required of all students. This is particularly true in heavy-apparatus and combat activities. The high incidence of severe accidents found in high school, where it is often required that all students participate in every activity, and the comparatively small incidence of accidents in colleges, where students usually follow their own interests, in small groups, is evidence for this principle.

Horseback riding is such a dangerous activity that a special permit or release should be required. (See sample, Fig. 18-2.)

HIKING TRIPS AND OUTINGS. If hiking trips and outings are sponsored as an activity of the physical education program, the laws governing liability apply. It is recommended, however, that parental consent in writing be obtained before allowing a student to participate in such activities. The value of obtaining written permission is that it shows that the parents had a knowledge of the activity and were willing that their child should participate. The permission does not, however, excuse actionable negligence on the part of the teacher.

Those with valid doctor's excuses should not be allowed to participate. The key words in this admonition are *valid* and *allowed*. A valid excuse is one given by a doctor for a real cause, not because a student wants to avoid physical education. The instructor should follow the physician's recommendation and not allow the student to participate.

FALLING RELAXED. Physical educators have found that it is unwise to teach students to fall completely relaxed or completely taut. Tumblers are the most adept at falling and they soon learn to retain a sufficient amount of muscular tone to protect the bones and joints from unnecessary strain. Many football coaches spend a great deal of time teaching their players to fall safely, and this practice is recommended in all sports where there is the hazard of falling. Hartley Price,[9] a gymnastic coach at Florida State University, calls attention to the importance of proper falling.

> From the safety point of view, *the breakfall is the most important single skill in athletics.* But it is one of the most neglected areas of directed learnings. The viewpoint seems to have been taken that the art of falling will take care of itself. Falling is a part of all types of sports and therefore should be regarded as a necessary fundamental which should be included in the training of every individual.

SPECIAL SAFETY PROBLEMS FOR GIRLS

The physical education program for girls presents a few special safety problems. Among these are the advisability of interschool competition,

[9] Hartley Price, "Tumbling and Stumbling Safely," *Journal of Health, Physical Education, and Recreation,* 1942, p. 533.

the advisability of exercise during menstruation, and the rather minor problem of hazardous accessories and fingernails.

EXERCISE DURING MENSTRUATION. *During menstruation, adolescent girls should not be compelled to participate in strenuous activities or swimming.* The key words *adolescent* and *compelled* should be noted in this sentence. There have been many exhaustive studies and volumes of learned discussion with regard to the pros and cons of exercising during menstruation, but the above principle is promulgated on the basis of pure safety. An instructor or department can "play safe" by adopting the above policy. Steinhaus [10] comments on this issue, "The best authorities recognize great differences in women's ability at this time. They usually recommend that a girl carry on her regular program throughout this period, in so far as she feels herself capable of doing, avoiding both excessive exertion and cold baths." (See Chapter 19.)

In contact sports and gymnastics girls should not be allowed to wear hazardous pins, jewelry, or long fingernails. Although such items may be considered minor details, they have been responsible for accidents that can be quite painful. Many departments forbid the wearing of these accessories during physical activities, and provide a jewel box in which girls deposit their jewelry during the class.

RECREATION

It is neither possible nor necessary in a text of this nature to include the administrative and supervisory functions of all forms of public recreation. Most of the material of this chapter and the following one, Safety in Athletics and Intramurals, applies to the field of school recreation and should be considered in that relationship.

The following hints to the directors of recreation are included because they are discerning and can apply to all areas of school and college administration. The material on playgrounds is included because most schools provide some type of playground recreation and the unsupervised aspect of school play often is the most hazardous.

How to Be an Adroit Executive

George S. Hjelte,[11] General Manager of Los Angeles Department of Recreation and Parks, and a respected leader in the field of recreation, compiled the following do's and don'ts for recreation leaders.

[10] Arthur H. Steinhaus, *Toward an Understanding of Health and Physical Education* (Dubuque: William C. Brown, 1963), p. 146.

[11] George S. Hjelte, "How to Be an Adroit Executive," *American Recreation Journal* (February 1961).

1. Know the community.
2. Have a plan with immediate and long range objectives for the development of the recreation service.
3. Be not covetous of the whole field of recreation.
4. Be loyal to his colleagues.
5. Be patient.
6. Preserve his professional identity.
7. In association and communications with elected officers and with board members, accord all equal attention and avoid intimate associations with any.
8. Try to understand the apprehensions of the elected officers who are held strictly accountable by their constituents for their acts, often when they are not legally responsible.
9. Receive job applicants bearing recommendations from politicians for employment with courtesy and consideration, yet without surrender of principle.
10. Leave the credit for commendable actions to those accountable to the electorate.
11. Remain in the shadows, publicity-wise.
12. Keep elected representatives informed of programs, events, and actions which take place or affect their constituents, especially if they represent a ward or district.
13. When complaints from citizens are answered by letter, send a copy of the letter to the elected official in whose district the complainant resides.
14. Avoid public mention of financial costs when possible.
15. Keep an open door to all employees and to the public. Try not to get a reputation for "being hard to see."
16. Avoid the peremptory NO which is the immediate answer that precludes discussion.
17. Preserve an open mind.
18. Display an interest in the constructive hobbies and activities of everyone, for they constitute the recreation culture of the whole community.

SAFETY IN PLAYGROUND ACTIVITIES

A high percentage of playground accidents occur in the use of apparatus. With the exception of apparatus, sports constitute the principal activity of the playground and are the second largest source of accidents. The safety controls for the various aspects are discussed in other chapters and need not be repeated here.

Apparatus activities may cause as many as 65.5 per cent of all playground accidents. (See Chapter 15 where accident statistics are covered in detail. The arrangement of play areas, care of equipment, and surfacing of grounds were treated in Chapter 17 and other leadership controls discussed in Chapter 19.) Parents have been led to believe that the playground has been built to provide a safe place for their youngsters to play. The administration, especially the director, should realize that this trust exists and bend every effort to be worthy of it.

SPECIFIC ADMINISTRATIVE CONTROLS

Regulations governing participants should be established for the use of all apparatus in accordance with their age, sex, and abilities. Usually such designations and restrictions are determined for all playgrounds in a system. If they are not, the playground director should determine which pieces of equipment should be used by various groups. For instance, older children should not be allowed to use the swings, teeters, and so on, and the very young children or the unskilled should not be permitted to use the parallel or high bars.

Safety lines, walks, or fences should be provided to separate all dangerous apparatus or play areas. The well-arranged playground has various separated areas for different groups. If natural barriers or fences are not provided, it may be possible to rope off or paint lines to designate the areas. Playground leaders, who may be members of school safety patrols, should be selected and trained to protect younger or less experienced performers on all apparatus. *Apparatus should not be used except under supervision.* Rings, ropes, and poles should be tied when they are not in use or when no supervision is possible. Children should not be allowed to use wet or icy apparatus. Children should be instructed to report unsafe apparatus, unsafe conditions, and injuries to the instructor. This instruction might well be included among the various posted rules and regulations. It is a necessary precaution because the playground director may miss some weakness in his daily inspection or may not be present when some apparatus gives way.

Children should not be allowed to run or play with sharp, dangerous objects in their mouths or hands. Children often play with lollypops in their mouths, and it is a very dangerous practice unless the sticks are of the harmless paper type. Similarly, craft tools must not be taken to the play areas nor should children be allowed to use knives, sling shots, BB guns, or other dangerous items on the playgrounds. Children should be taught how to use the apparatus correctly and safely. No supervised playground would be worthy of the name if a constant program of safety education were not carried on. It need not be the negative "don't do this" type, but it should be the positive "do it this way" type. Children should be taught to observe the rules of the game as well as the playground safety rules. If apparatus is to be used safely, it must be used properly, and the only method of insuring proper usage is through instruction and careful supervision. The *landing areas around apparatus should be soft;* when feasible, mats should be provided, otherwise there should be sand, shavings, sawdust, or other suitable material. Since most apparatus injuries are the result of falls, this provision is an important one.

References

American Association for Health, Physical Education, and Recreation, *Suggested School Safety Policies, Accident Prevention in Physical Education, Athletics, and Recreation* (Washington, D.C.: National Education Association, 1964).

"Are Your Playgrounds Safe?" *American Recreation Annual,* 1962 Edition, p. 14.

Bonahoom, J. E., "Safety Program Recommendations," *Recreation* (April 1957), p. 149.

Edgren, H. D., "Spotlighting Dangers for Physical Education," *Safety Education* (February 1958), p. 16.

Elkow, J. D., "Safety Education and Accident Prevention," *Third Annual Safety Education Review* (Washington, D.C.: National Education Association, 1964), pp. 43–49.

———, "Accident Problems in Physical Education and Athletics," *Second Annual Safety Education Review* (Washington, D.C.: National Education Association, 1963), pp. 94–97.

Fait, H. F., "Interscholastic Athletics in Junior High and Elementary Schools," *First Annual Safety Education Review* (Washington, D.C.: National Education Association, 1962).

Florio, A. E., and G. T. Stafford, *Safety Education* (New York: McGraw-Hill, 1962).

Fox, M. G., "Implications for Physical Education of the Conference on Accident Prevention," *Third Annual Safety Education Review* (Washington, D.C.: National Education Association, 1964), pp. 50–52.

Frederick, M. M., "Play Safe in Technicolor," *Journal of Health, Physical Education, and Recreation,* 27:10 (April 1956).

Glaser, P. A., "School Playground Council in Action," *Journal of Health, Physical Education, and Recreation,* 32:27–28 (September 1961).

Halsey, M. N., *Accident Prevention* (New York: McGraw-Hill, 1961).

Hjelte, G. S., and J. S. Shivers, *Public Administration of Park and Recreational Services* (New York: Macmillan, 1963).

Howard, G. W., and E. Masonbrink, *Administration of Physical Education* (New York: Harper & Row, 1963).

Loft, Bernard I., "A Positive Approach to Safety," *Journal of Health, Physical Education, and Recreation* (May–June, 1961), pp. 34–35.

Memmel, R., "Developing Safety Consciousness in Physical Education," *Third Annual Safety Education Review* (Washington, D.C.: National Education Association, 1964), pp. 33–37.

Michale, S., "The Teachers' Responsibility for Safety," *First Annual Safety Education Review* (Washington, D.C.: National Education Association, 1962), pp. 37–43.

Miller, N. R., "Install Playground Devices Properly for Safety and Economy," *American School Board Journal*, 133:72 (September 1956).

Nagle, F. J., "The Identification of the School Health and Safety Concerns of the Secondary School Physical Educator," *Research Quarterly* (December 1960), p. 53.

Safety Education, "Safety is Everybody's Business," *National Education Association Journal*, Vol. 49, No. 7 (October 1960), pp. 18–19.

Seaton, D. C., I. A. Clayton, H. C. Leibee, and L. Messersmith, *Physical Education Handbook*, 5th ed. (Englewood Cliffs, N.J.: Prentice-Hall, 1968).

Shaw, F., "How Teachers Get Hurt," *Safety Education*, No. 42 (March 1963), pp. 3–5.

Thacker, E. H., "Five Keys to Safety on the Playground," *Journal of Health, Physical Education, and Recreation*, 30:24–25 (April 1959).

Vernier, E., "Concern for Safety Awareness," *Third Annual Safety Education Review* (Washington, D.C.: National Education Association, 1964), pp. 30–32.

Williams, E., "A Physical Educator Looks at Safety," *Third Annual Safety Education Review* (Washington, D.C.: National Education Association, 1964), pp. 38–42.

Yost, Charles Peter, "Total Fitness and Prevention of Accidents," *Journal of Health, Physical Education, and Recreation* (Washington, D.C.: American Association for Health, Physical Education and Recreation, March 1967), p. 32.

CHAPTER 19 SAFETY IN ATHLETICS AND INTRAMURALS

INTRODUCTION

The administration of the school or college program of interscholastic or intercollegiate sports competition is often one of the administrator's major problems. Any serious accident in connection with a school's sports program, especially one resulting in death, may bring about the curtailment of the athletic program or the removal of an administrative officer.

It is therefore necessary that all administrative officers, from the president or principal down to the coach and his team managers, bend every effort to foresee and forestall accidents and injuries. It has been found that coaches with nine years or more of experience have fewer injuries among their players than coaches with less experience.

Suggested School Safety Policies,[1] mentioned in an earlier chapter, also prescribes responsibilities for the control of athletics and intramural sports. They caution the administrator to observe the following policies:

1. All school personnel should conform with recognized authoritative rules and regulations governing safe practices and procedures, particularly in the conduct of sports and athletic activities.
2. All schools should be affiliated with accredited federations and organizations, which set standards and establish rules governing competition and activities in physical education, athletics, and recreation.
3. All physical education, athletic, and recreation activities should be instructed and supervised by professionally trained personnel employed by the board of education or control.
4. School activities conducted at nonschool facilities should be under the direct supervision of school personnel; appropriate measures should be taken to assure the safety of students.
5. Adequate health histories and medical examinations should be required

[1] American Association for Health, Physical Education, and Recreation. *Suggested School Safety Policies, Accident Prevention in Physical Education, Athletics and Recreation.* Washington, D.C. 1201 Sixteenth St., N.W. 20036, 1964.

for all athletes immediately before participating in interscholastic sports and as needed during each year of participation.

6. All officials with primary responsibilities for the conduct of interscholastic sports should be certified or accredited.

7. The unique aspects of activities in physical education, athletics, and recreation should be considered in the development and conduct of all emergency drills.

8. There should be a detailed plan for handling spectators and crowds at all athletic contests and other public events.

ADMINISTRATIVE CONTROLS

There are a large number of administrative controls affecting the safe conduct of school and college athletics and intramural programs. In general, these controls can be divided into two major groups; those exercised from within the school or college organization and those imposed from without.

The *external administrative controls* include: (1) governing bodies such as the Amateur Athletic Union, the National Collegiate Athletic Association, the National Association of Intercollegiate Athletics, the Commission on Intercollegiate Athletics for Women of the Division for Girls and Women's Sports of the American Association for Health, Physical Education, and Recreation, and the State and National Federation of State High School Athletic Associations; (2) the national rules governing sports contests and the officials; (3) league and conference regulations; and, (4) state laws or regulations of the state high school athletic association or the chief state school officer.

The *internal administrative controls* include the school and college policies established by the school board of education or the college or university board of trustees, and those policies promulgated by the school superintendent, principal, or the president and his administrative assistants in the colleges and universities. These controls range from setting standards of safety in transporting teams to the wearing of ankle wraps to prevent injuries. Let us first examine the external administrative controls.

NATIONAL ORGANIZATIONS

The National Collegiate Athletic Association, the major governing body among colleges since 1905, the National Federation of State High School Athletic Associations, established in 1920, and the Division of Girls and Women's Sports of the American Association for Health, Physical Education, and Recreation are the three national organizations exerting the most influence upon interschool competition and the establishment of sports rules in this country. The health and safety of players has been a primary objective of these organizations since their inception.

✳ *The National Federation of State High School Athletic Associations* has always regarded safety in competition as one of its primary objectives. To provide safer and more equitable competition among schools, the organization has established and published rules for such sports as football, basketball, and track. Its many accomplishments to adjust athletic competition to the high school age athlete, include the reduction of the standard size of the football and basketball; introducing the 39-inch hurdle, the high-school discus, and the shorter low-hurdle race, and, most important of all, instituting a safer football game through the adoption of many precautionary rules such as the one requiring players to wear a football helmet at all times during play.

The National Collegiate Athletic Association was an outgrowth of the desire to curtail the injuries and deaths occurring in football during the early 1900's. K. L. Wilson, for many years associated with the N.C.A.A., made the following statement regarding the birth of the organization.

> It is significant that the very origin of the National Collegiate Athletic Association is identified with a concern for safety in sports. In 1905 intercollegiate football was being condemned for its brutal and admittedly dangerous aspects and a conference was called of college and university heads who, in advance of the meeting, were strongly disposed to abolish the sport as a collegiate activity. The result of that meeting was a decision to reform rather than outlaw the game, and from this came the Football Rules Committee of the N.C.A.A., whose initial concern from its inauguration may be said to be standards and rules that assure the safety of participants. Its enactments against the flying wedge, as an early instance, and other types of play which were thought to provoke injuries are examples of that primary interest.
>
> Its concern for proper equipment is another example. . . . Through the years the Football Rules Committee has encouraged and legislated in favor of equipment providing maximum protection for players. One result of that sponsorship has caused great current concern in the committee— that so much protective equipment has been provided it can actually be of danger to an opponent. Now a sort of negative legislation, limiting the type and extent of protective equipment, is being sponsored. Rules in all other sports, as written by N.C.A.A. Committees, follow the same pattern of primary concern for the safety of participants. Boxing is an outstanding example, from its restrictions on men with undue experience, to its protection for an injured fighter, as is wrestling, which bars a great variety of holds considered likely to invite injuries.

The Division of Girls' and Women's Athletics, a division of the American Association for Health, Physical Education, and Recreation, is a comparative newcomer to the family of sports associations. It supplanted the National Committee on Women's Athletics in 1947 and since that time has become the sole authority in the conduct of female school athletic activities and has issued rule books for practically every competitive sport. Their rules and articles in the rule books reflect a concern for safety more ardently than do the men's organizations. This organization has co-sponsored with the National Association of Physical Education for College Women, a Commission on intercollegiate sports for women for the regulation of competition.

The Division of Safety Education, another division of the American Association for Health, Physical Education, and Recreation, was established in 1957 for the express purpose of coordinating all safety activities of the AAHPER and to publish materials for use in health, physical education, and recreation activities.

Two other organizations vitally concerned with safety in these fields are the *National Commission on Safety Education,* which is also a division of the National Education Association and the *National Safety Council.* None of these organizations publish sports participation rules but they all exert considerable influence through their publications and leadership.

SPORTS RULES FOR SAFETY

Possibly the greatest single force for safety in athletics has been the establishment of national rules by which sports are played. Such rules are usually formulated by committees of the national organizations for the various sports. These organizations, such as those listed in the last section, are primarily interested in improving the game. In the contact sports, their main concern is to make the sport safer.

A large number of other national associations interested in certain sports such as the United States Lawn Tennis Association, the Amateur Fencer's League of America, the U.S. Ski Association of America, the Judo Black Belt Federation, the Babe Ruth and Little Leagues, the United States Soccer Football Association, the American Bowling Congress, and many others, prepare their own rules and regulations that are often followed in school and college competition. The professional football, basketball, and baseball leagues have established their own rules, many of which have proved so successful that the school and college rule makers have adopted them. In fact most baseball teams compete under the national professional rules.

In general, however, high schools compete under the rules established by the National Federation of High School Athletic Associations; colleges compete under rules of the National Collegiate Athletic Association, and women compete under the rules of the Division for Girls and Women's Sports of the American Association for Health, Physical Education, and Recreation. *For safety's sake it is recommended that all schools and colleges play under the rules designed especially for their respective groups.*

When necessary, local ground rules should be established to provide protection against special hazards. Often a traditional tree or some structural hazard makes it necessary to adopt special ground rules in various sports. This practice is quite customary in baseball and leaders should not hesitate to do the same in other sports when safety is involved.

⋆ LEAGUE REGULATIONS. Most schools have also found it advisable to form leagues with schools of similar classification to provide equitable competition and friendly association. Such leagues as the Western Intercollegiate Conference of colleges and the various State High School Athletic Associations have established their own rules governing eligibility, length of seasons, and various other regulations, including many that are definite safety factors

OFFICIALS AND SAFETY

An official is directly responsible for the safety of the players through the interpretation and enforcement of the rules of the game. The degree to which the rules of safety are enforced depends entirely on the judgment and skill of the persons acting as officials. The caliber of officials, especially in high school athletics, has greatly improved during the last few years. This improvement has been brought about largely by the establishment by state high school athletic associations of a plan for the qualification, registration, training, certification, and classification of officials.

College officials are similarly controlled by the various conference authorities. Usually, however, the college system is better in that it goes one step further and *assigns* the official for the various games. The method of assignment varies, but in general it has provided better officiating. It should be noted that an increasing number of high school leagues use this same method for the assignment of officials.

Competent officials in sufficient numbers should be provided for all sports competition in which there is an element of danger. Although players should be instructed to play according to the spirit of the game as well as the rules, it is the obligation of an official to maintain this atmosphere and to enforce the rules most rigidly, especially where danger is involved. In high schools, officiating indicates the least degree of efficiency from the point of view of safety. It is recommended that only "certified" or "approved" officials, who realize that their duty extends beyond the mere calling of fouls for the safe conduct of the game, be employed for interschool contests. Officials should be held responsible and accountable for excessive accidents if it seems clear that other causal factors are normal.

Probably the poorest officiating takes place in the intramural and extra-mural contests. The department of physical education should make every effort to provide well-trained officials for these contests. One of the best solutions lies in the careful selection and thorough training of student leaders.

The Division for Girls and Women's Sports of the American Association for Health, Physical Education, and Recreation has been conducting an intelligent and energetic plan for the upgrading of officials within their ranks. Their program to select and train student leaders is particularly commendable.

SELECTION, TRAINING, AND ASSIGNMENT

It has been estimated that approximately 45 per cent of sports accidents where inadequate leadership has been a factor (which accounts for about 30 per cent of all sports accidents) are the result of poor officiating. If the safety of players depends to such a large extent upon officials, it follows that great care must be taken in their selection, training, and assignment.[2]

In securing officials for games or contests, especially contact sports, the men selected should not only be highly skilled in the technical aspects of officiating but must recognize their responsibilities for the prevention of accidents and discharge these responsibilities efficiently. The too common practice of permitting opposing coaches to agree upon officials whom they think less likely to penalize their respective teams often results in incompetency. Poor officiating usually results in a greater than normal number of injuries. *It is therefore recommended that officials for all contests be selected, trained, and assigned by competent nonpartisan authorities.*

OFFICIAL CONTROL. From the start of the game or contest, the safety of the players is almost entirely in the hands of the official or officials. Upon their interpretation of the spirit of the rules, as well as the rules themselves, and their strict enforcement depends not only the outcome of the game but also the number of injuries, and possibly fatalities, that will occur. The more experienced officials are very careful to enforce penalties for even the slightest infraction of a rule when violating it may result in injury. The rules of almost every sport require officials to inspect equipment and to interpret questionable sections in such a way as to provide maximum safety. Such arbitrary authority should always be invoked whenever it is necessary to protect a player from possible injury.

Women or girls only should officiate girls' team sports. It is generally felt among women instructors that male officials lack the necessary under-

[2] Most athletic benefit plans will not pay an injured player if the officials in charge of the contest do not qualify according to the requirements of registration.

standing of the psychology of girls' competition to be safe officials. It should be noted that this principle is applied only to *team* sports, because many women instructors feel that male officials are satisfactory or more desirable for such individual or dual sports as tennis, golf, and badminton.

The safeguarding of players should be a primary objective of all officials and officials' associations. An official's attitude plays an important role in the safeguarding of players. If he assumes a hardboiled I-don't-care attitude, players will naturally react unfavorably and the play will become rougher. This type of official, popular a number of years ago, seldom lasts long in the game today. On the other hand, the official who is vitally concerned with the welfare of the players, and at the same time performs in a businesslike manner, will usually promote fewer injuries during play.

Efforts should be made to discuss the various safety precautions pertaining to each sport during meetings of officials' associations. Rules interpretation meetings, where both coaches and officials are present, afford excellent opportunities for an exchange of opinion on safety through officiating. Allen,[3] in an article on the official's responsibility in preventing accidents, said, "In many instances, it has been the far-reaching vision of athletic officials which has been responsible for improvements in the rules, equipment, and facilities of a game. The officials, not being directly connected with a school or college, have been able to recognize hazardous situations which have gone unnoticed by those in close proximity to the scene."

FITNESS OF OFFICIALS. It is strongly recommended that *every official have a thorough physical and medical examination prior to working in each sport.* Officials' organizations are urged to require such an examination. Pennsylvania has been a leader in this field. The examination would serve a twofold purpose: (1) It would give the official an appraisal of his health status, and (2) it would inform the association of his physical ability to perform his duties. Requiring an examination prior to participation in each sport might appear unnecessary, but when one considers that many officials are quite old (athletically speaking), and that a strenuous season such as football or basketball, in addition to occasional illnesses, may take too much out of a man, it will be adjudged the sensible thing to do. A regular officials' examination blank should be used which informs the examining physician of the strenuousness of the sport, the approximate number of games to be worked, the distances to be traveled, and the capacity in which the examinee will serve. Figure 19-1 is a suggested form.

Officials should keep fit by engaging in some form of regular and suit-

[3] Homer Allen, "Responsibility of Athletic Officials for Accident Prevention," *Journal of Health, Physical Education, and Recreation* (February 1947), p. 61.

PENNSYLVANIA INTERSCHOLASTIC ATHLETIC ASSOCIATION
Report of Official's Physical Examination

(Note to official: The continuance of your registration as a P.I.A.A. Official depends upon the receipt of this blank (filled in and signed by your physician, or the reverse side signed by yourself) on or before dates specified. This is a Board of Control requirement.)

Consideration for the physical welfare of officials, due to deaths which have occurred on playing fields and in dressing rooms in the past, has prompted the Board of Control of the P. I. A. A. to formulate requirements that all football and basketball officials, before entering upon an active season, shall subject themselves to a rigid physical examination. The examination may be conducted by the official's personal physician or other physician of his own selection.

There are many reasons why this examination is desirable. The official owes it to himself as a precautionary measure; to his reputation as an official; to his family; to the schools which employ him; to the boys whose games he administers; and to the public in general.

FOOTBALL OFFICIALS are required to return the physical examination blank, properly filled and signed by a physician, BETWEEN THE DATES OF AUGUST 15 AND SEPTEMBER 1 TO THE P.I.A.A., 1613 N. FRONT ST., HARRISBURG, PA. 17102

BASKETBALL OFFICIALS are required to return the physical examination blank, properly filled in and signed by a physician, BETWEEN THE DATES OF NOVEMBER 15 AND DECEMBER 15 TO P.I.A.A., 1613 N. FRONT ST., HARRISBURG, PA. 17102

In case an individual officiates in more than one of the above named sports, it will not be necessary for such an individual to undergo two physical examinations. It is necessary for him to submit his physical examination blank before officiating in any one year in the first of his sports in which he is registered. For example: the physical examination before the football season will be sufficient for both football and basketball seasons.

NAME OF EXAMINEE .... DATE OF BIRTH ....

ADDRESS ....

RECENT ILLNESS ....

Eyes R .... L ....   Are eye glasses recommended for
                                                work as an athletic official? ....

Ears R .... L ....

CARDIOVASCULAR SYSTEM: Blood Pressure S .... D ....

PULSE: Sitting .... After Exercise, Immediately .... Two minutes ....

        Is heart action clear and response to exercise normal? .... Is there any murmur or enlargement? .... Is pulse full, compressible and strong? ....

        Is pulse regular? .... What is the rate? .... Is there any atheroma of the arteries? ....

CHEST: Normal .... Inspiration .... Expiration ....

ABDOMEN: Masses? .... Hernia? .... Measurement at umbilicus ....

FIGURE: (Good) (Fair) (Poor)   FRAME (Heavy) (Medium) (Light) Height ....

WEIGHT: .... Is this over or underweight for general make up? ....

HEMORRHOIDS .... HERNIA? .... VARICOSITIES? ....

URINALYSIS

        Specific Gravity——
        Albumin: Presence .... Absence .... Sugar: Presence .... Absence ....
        Microscopic examination if there is any history of diseases that produce kidney damage.

....

Does examinee meet all physical requirements for employment as an official in strenuous athletic contests? ....

If not, in what way is he deficient and to what extent? ....

....

Remarks and corrective measures: ....

....

....

                                                                        D. O.
Place .... M. D.
                                              Signature
Date ....
                                              Address

TO THE EXAMINING PHYSICIAN: Other information may be submitted in a separate letter. Such additional information will be treated as confidential.

(OVER)

FIGURE 19-1.   Report form for Official's Physical Examination (Pennsylvania). (Courtesy Pennsylvania Interscholastic Athletic Association.)

able exercise, especially between seasons and before the opening of a season. Officials' organizations should encourage a physical fitness program among its members. Too many officials lead a sedentary life between seasons and work strenuously to get into shape a few days before the opening of the season. Calisthenics, particularly when taken under the supervision of a competent instructor, are especially recommended for officials. Such games as volleyball and golf are advocated for older men. Badminton, squash, and handball are excellent conditioners for younger men. An out-standing official of the Big Ten and Big Eight Conferences says,

> An official owes it to the game to keep in physical shape the year around, and it is imperative that every man working football start special preparations in the summer for the next football campaign. In this way, the official can keep on top of the play and help prevent many injuries. Golf early in the summer, followed by handball later, are excellent conditioners for the veteran football official and I always play regularly every day from July on until the first game.

John W. Bunn, the herald of sports officiating, claims that leg strength and endurance should receive the most attention and prescribes preseason practice.

Officials should be well schooled in first-aid procedures. It often becomes necessary for an official to render first aid and to have sufficient knowledge to keep others, especially players, from injuring the victim further through improper treatment. It is recommended that officials' organizations spend some time in first-aid training of their members. It should not be a course in bandaging, but one that will teach officials how to recognize various injuries and how to prevent further harm to injured athletes before they receive medical attention.

Officials should not overeat, especially before working a game or contest. Many officials have been former athletes who are prone to under-exercise and overeat following their active competitive careers. These men are cautioned against this tendency and urged to look upon officiating as the strenuous activity that it is. The mental and emotional disturbances prior to, during, and often following a game make it especially necessary for the official to eat moderately and wisely during this time. He should eat at least three hours before the contest and wait at least one hour following his work before eating again. Each official has usually worked out a diet he considers agreeable for such periods but he is warned to avoid excessive fats and carbohydrates, especially greasy foods.

PREGAME CHECK-UP. Probably the first pregame precaution that should be taken by an official is to make certain that he is properly dressed for the occasion. He must wear sufficient clothing to keep warm and sufficient protective equipment to protect himself from injury. Vanity concerning his attire should not deter him from these sensible precautions. With the usual protective gear necessary for sports such as baseball and hockey, officials should have their ankles wrapped snugly for most activities and should be careful to wear only perfectly fitted shoes.

It would be wise for officials of basketball, football, and such sports to *warm up thoroughly before beginning their duties.* Light calisthenics in the dressing room and jogging to the field would help many an official avoid a painful sprain or strain.

Before beginning any game or contest the official should report to the field or floor in sufficient time *to make a thorough safety check* of playing facilities and equipment. The rules of many sports require officials to report at a specified time, but do not always obligate them to make an inspection for the safe conduct of the contest. Such an inspection should include the condition of the playing surface, the proximity of the spectators, and the hazards of trees and walls, and the equipment of the players. When hazards exist—such as players' benches being too close to the field of play or insufficient padding about the wrestling mat—the official should correct the conditions before beginning play. There may be other hazards such as shortened corners of a football field or a fence on a baseball field that require the establishment of special ground rules or play compensation. When weather conditions, unruly spectators, or other unusual happenings make it hazardous to begin or continue a contest, the official should have the good judgment and moral courage to call off the play.

When it is necessary an official should remove from a game or contest any player who is dangerously belligerent, obviously fatigued, or painfully injured. Luckily, this action is seldom necessary, because the coach or captain usually recognizes these cases and removes them; however, in case of oversight, officials should realize their obligation. This action need not be done in an officious manner, but carried out through a diplomatic suggestion to the captain or coach. In wrestling and boxing the official must accept this responsibility and realize that the life of a contestant may rest on his judgment.

ATHLETIC INSURANCE PLANS

The factor that has probably been the most effective in reducing injuries in high school athletics—second only to the formation of the state associations and the National Federation—is the development of insurance plans for the players. These plans are often referred to as athletic benefit plans, accident benefit plans, or athletic protective funds.

There are at least five types of such insurance plans according to the Joint Committee report of the AAHPER and the AMA: [4]

1. Commercial insurance policies written on an individual basis.
2. Student medical benefit plans written on a group basis by commercial insurers.
3. State high school athletic association benefit plans.
4. Medical benefit plans operated by specific city schools systems.
5. Self-insurance.

[4] American Association for Health, Physical Education, and Recreation, Joint Committee, *Administrative Problems in Health Education, Physical Education and Recreation* (Washington, D.C.: The Association, 1953), p. 105. *School Health Services*, 1964.

The Joint Committee recommends the following steps in selecting and establishing an insurance program:

1. The insurance problems and needs.
2. A survey should be made to ascertain the need for insurance before it is purchased.
3. After the need has been established, specifications should be constructed indicating the kind and amount of insurance needed.
4. The specifications should be presented to several insurers to obtain estimates of coverage and costs.
5. The plans presented to the school by the several insurers should be studied and the one best suited to that particular situation should be selected.
6. Parents should be given full information about the insurance.
7. Workable and harmonious relations should be established with the insurer selected.
8. Continuous evaluation of the insurance program should be carried out.
9. Records should be carefully kept of costs, accidents, claims payments, and other pertinent data.

School administrators should insist upon the following conditions and requirements when purchasing accident insurance:

1. The coverage should include all school activities and provide up to $500 for each injury to each pupil.
2. The medical services should include:
   a. cost of professional services of physician or surgeon
   b. cost of hospital care and service
   c. cost of trained nurse
   d. cost of ambulance, surgical appliances, dressings, x-rays, and other possible needs
   e. cost of repair and care of natural teeth
3. The policy should be tailored to fit the needs of the school.
4. The coverage should be maximum for minimum cost.
5. All pupils, as well as all teachers, should be included.
6. A deductible clause should be avoided unless it reduces the premium substantially and the policy still fulfills its purpose.
7. Blanket rather than schedule-type coverage should be selected.
8. Claims payment must be simple, certain, and fast.[5]

SAFETY VALUES OF ACCIDENT BENEFIT PLANS. Probably the most important benefit of these plans next to relieving parents of the financial burden for athletic accidents, is that the system invariably makes the school officials safety conscious. An accurate accident-reporting record must be kept, which makes self-diagnosis and evaluation more common. Schools with unusually high accident rates are investigated and if the poor record persists, they are sometimes denied renewal of con-

[5] *Ibid.*

tract. State tabulation of results makes it possible to judge schools in relation to one another and for the state to compare its program with that of other states. Another important benefit is the provision for better care in the case of severe injuries. Victims will be cared for even though the parent or school is unable to bear the expense for treatment. Also, the physician has been given more responsibility for the decision as to whether or not an injured player should return to the competitive sport, because insurance companies will not make a second payment to a school for an injury that has already been compensated for unless there has been a reexamination of the injured student by a physician who will certify that the player is fit to return to the sport.

Individual playing equipment and facilities have improved, rules have been modified for the better, the importance of warm-up periods has been emphasized, and the many other precautions advocated have made athletics safer for participants in those states supporting such plans.

HARMFULNESS OF ATHLETIC COMPETITION

The question of a sport's being physically harmful brings up two questions for general considerations. (1) Is it too strenuous or hazardous for a player of given age and ability? (2) Is the player physically fit to participate at a given time? Arthur H. Steinhaus [6] answers the first question as follows:

> Barring accidents, which of course occur occasionally in events involving great exertion and bodily contacts, there are very few sports whose proper pursuit, even to extremes, brings harms to the body. *What are these few exceptions?* Some surgeons have reported that the cartilage covering bones in the knee and elbow joints of soccer players and boxers, respectively, may become pulped or shredded in consequence of the continual pounding they receive in such sports, even in the absence of accidental injuries. Since cartilage has no blood supply, such deterioration is not repaired. Boxing is further condemned on more serious charges. In most sports head injuries are purely accidental and everyone is sorry. Only in boxing are such injuries planned and gloried over. Jolting or concussion of the brain by any severe head blow may rupture tiny blood vessels. Even in the absence of a knockout or temporary unconsciousness, pinpoint hemorrhages follow the breaking of the little blood vessels and cause the destruction of a small amount of surrounding brain tissue. This brain tissue is never replaced. Such injury oft repeated adds up until it shows in emotional disorders, in the slurred speech, slowed responses, and shambling gait of the "punch drunk." Too many boxers act a bit on "the punchy side." Of course, head injuries from football and other games may have the same

[6] Arthur H. Steinhaus, *How to Keep Fit and Like It* (Chicago: Dartwell Corporation, 1957), pp. 54, 58.

after effects. Only in boxing, however, do men proceed systematically and deliberately to inflict such injuries. This is a valid charge against boxing. Arguments extolling the virtues of boxing as a builder of courage, speed, etc., often uttered in the slurred speech of an ex-boxer, appear weak and hollow in the face of these condemnatory facts. As a means of self-defense it has proved far inferior to wrestling and "rough and tumble" (jiu jitsu).

The second question, that of being physically fit for participation or competition, is more difficult to answer. In general, however, a person can be considered fit for participation *when declared so by a competent physician,* and fit for competition when adjudged so by a coach or trainer. It can be readily seen that neither decision is foolproof. The danger usually arises when a person participates without either the consent of a physician or the advice of a coach. A person is especially foolish to participate in any sport without the approval of a physician, especially if the would-be participant is past school age.

How Exercise Affects the Heart. Some people believe that participation in athletics, especially distance running and rowing, causes an "athletic heart," which will bring about an early death. Nothing could be farther from the truth. As a matter of fact a "loafer's heart" more aptly describes most cardiacs. Let us again consider what Steinhaus says on the subject.[7]

> The heart of a well-trained distance runner at rest beats fifty to sixty times a minute. That of an average non-athlete must contract seventy to ninety times. But the athlete's heart is not lazy. With fifty beats it puts out more blood in a minute than does the non-athlete's with eighty, because it can pump more blood with each beat (almost three ounces instead of only two). Under the influence of exercise it speeds up correspondingly less.
>
> Why is a slow beat an advantage? Only when the heart is resting between beats can blood flow through its walls to supply it with oxygen and food. The slower the heart, the longer the rests, and these add up. The heart beating sixty times per minute gets eighteen days more of rest in a year than does the eighty-beat heart.
>
> Strenuous exercise that is continued over a long period of time is particularly good for training the heart. Trained hearts are larger, stronger, slower, and steadier. Exercises that emphasize strength, such as weight lifting and short sprints, develop powerful body muscles but do not tax the heart muscles enough. Wise athletes in these sports, therefore, balance their exercise program with some distance running, basketball, water polo, or other sports that develop heart and lungs and therefore endurance. Many sports are good heart developers.
>
> There is an old-fashioned notion that exercise injures the heart. For this belief there is no scientific foundation. The term "athlete's heart" as

[7] *Ibid.*

applied to a heart supposedly injured by athletics has disappeared from scientific and medical writings. But this is true: A heart already injured by disease or other factors will suffer extra abuse under exercise. When the motor of a car is in good shape, fast driving will not hurt it; but should the pistons slap and bearings rattle, even slow driving is dangerous.

It is very important to have your heart, lungs, and other organs examined by a physician before engaging in any strenuous work. If the physician finds some defect, he will advise accordingly. The normal heart in a young person cannot be hurt by exercise. The middle-aged heart is different. It has lost resilience with age and very possibly may be already somewhat damaged. Therefore, the middle-aged person should not play like a twenty-year-old. Often persons with slightly affected hearts profit by moderate exercise if carefully supervised.

Smoking stands convicted not only of unnecessarily speeding up the heart but, what is more serious, of often having produced real and lasting damage by the time a smoker reaches his forties or early fifties.

INTERSCHOLASTIC COMPETITION FOR GRADE SCHOOL BOYS

Interschool competition for boys below the ninth grade has long been a controversial issue. The controversy revolves around two concerns—the health and safety aspects and the social and psychological implications.

As a matter of fact, early teen-agers are competing in sports, especially in track, gymnastics, and swimming. Clubs have sprung up all over America and thousands of even prepubescent youngsters are undergoing intensive training and extensive competition. Since parents and coaches have been convinced by scientists that a healthy heart cannot be damaged by excessive exercise, the mystic veil of the "athletic heart" has disappeared. That youths are competing at an earlier age has been dramatically brought home to the American people by their accomplishments in the Olympic Games.

Thompkins and Roe,[8] in a survey made for the National Association of Secondary School Principals, found that 85.2 per cent of the 2,296 junior high school schools they surveyed supported interscholastic athletics. Many educators, however, hold certain reservations about the sociological and psychological effects of athletic competition and its attendant effects.

A report of the Joint Committee on Athletic Competition[9] for children of elementary and junior high school age takes the following stand:

[8] Thompkins and Roe, *Interscholastic Athletics in Junior High Schools, A Survey* (Washington, D.C.: National Association of Secondary School Principals, 1958).

[9] American Association for Health, Physical Education, and Recreation, *Desirable Athletic Competition for Children*, Report of the Joint Committee on Athletic Competition for Children of Elementary and Junior High School Age (Washington, D.C.: The Association, 1952), p. 4.

Interschool competition of a varsity pattern and similarly organized competition under auspices of other community agencies are *definitely disapproved* for children below the ninth grade.

Participation in any program involving high-pressure elements of the kind mentioned below would be considered a violation of this principle. Boxing (all levels) and tackle football (below the ninth grade) are considered undesirable under any conditions. [Condensed.]

1. Leagues, championships, tournaments, and little bowl games.
2. Overemphasis by publicity—especially individuals and "all star" selections.
3. Games and contests at night (other than the usual school or recreation hours).
4. Travel beyond the immediate neighborhood or community.
5. Encouragement of partisan spectators.
6. Grooming players for high school, proselyting.
7. Commercial promotions.
8. Permitting the few players a disproportionate share of the facilities and attention of the staff members to the neglect of the many other school children.

The Committee on School Health of the American Academy of Pediatrics made the following recommendations, among others, for the guidance of the interschool programs of athletics.

Competitive programs organized on school, neighborhood and community levels will meet the needs of children twelve years of age and under. State, regional and national tournaments; bowl, charity and exhibition games are not recommended for this age group. Commercial exploitation in any form is unequivocally condemned.

All competitive athletic programs should be organized with the cooperation of interested medical groups who will ensure adequate medical care before and during such programs. This should include thorough physical examinations at specified intervals, teaching of health observation to teachers and coaches, as well as attention to factors such as: (a) injury; (b) response to fatigue; (c) individual emotional needs; and (d) the risks of undue emotional strains.

Charles A. Bucher [10] makes two other observations that school authorities should be aware of in inaugurating or conducing an athletic program.

The interscholastic athletics program, if offered, should be provided only after the prerequisites of each physical education class, adapted, and intramural and extramural programs have been developed, and only as special controls in regard to such items as health, facilities, game adaptations, classification of players, leadership, and officials have been provided.

Competitive athletics, if properly conducted, have the potential for

[10] Charles A. Bucher, *Administration of School Health and Physical Education Programs* (St. Louis; C. V. Mosby, 1967), p. 617.

satisfying such basic psychological needs as recognition, belonging, self-respect, and feeling of achievement, as well as providing a wholesome outlet for the physical activity drive. However, if conducted in the light of adult interests, community pressures and other questionable influences, they can prove psychologically harmful.

JUNIOR HIGH SCHOOL ATHLETIC PROGRAMS

Most criticism of an interschool or other highly organized competitive programs of athletics in junior high schools has been based on assumptions rather than facts. Fait,[11] examined the scienctific support available in ten areas of alleged danger. His findings in several of these areas follow.

IS PARTICIPATION PHYSICALLY HARMFUL TO THE PUBESCENT BOY?

One of the greatest concerns has been that the heart will be overtaxed by the strenuous exertion of competitive play. The preponderance of evidence indicates that, if the heart is sound and not predisposed to cardiac enlargement, possible danger to it from strenuous exercise is very remote.

Another concern is that the increased elimination of fatigue products resulting from the strenuous activity of competition will cause kidney damage. There are no scientific findings which would indicate that the normal kidney can be damaged as the result of strenuous physical activity.

Pubescence is also generally thought of as a period of awkwardness, supposedly due to the rapid increase in skeletal growth. This gives rise to the opinion that accidents will occur more frequently among pubescent boys engaged in competitive play. Surveys of accidental injuries in athletics show that a lesser percentage of accidents occur among pubescent athletes than among the post-pubescent group. But they also demonstrate that a higher proportion of accidents occur during supervised school competition than in sand lot and free play time.

The conclusions based upon scientific findings are: Accidents can and will occur during competitive play; there is insufficient evidence to indicate how growth is affected; other concerns about physiological damage are unsupported by evidence if the boy is normal and healthy.

DOES COMPETITION ENGENDER MENTAL AND EMOTIONAL STRESSES WHICH ARE HARMFUL TO THE IMMATURE PARTICIPANT?

Concern is frequently expressed that harm may be done to the emotional development of an immature participant under the pressure of competitive athletics. Physiological and phychological evidence indicates that strenuous physical activity prevents bodily disturbances engendered by strong emo-

[11] Hollis F. Fait, "Interscholastic Athletics in Junior High and Elementary Schools," *Annual Safety Review*, 1962, pp. 18-24 (Washington, D.C.: The American Association for Health, Physical Education, and Recreation).

tions. It would appear, then, that for the normal well-adjusted boy the emotions aroused by the game would have sufficient release in the activity of the game. However, there may be intermittent periods when emotions do cause some discomfort to a participant which may result in lessened efficiency for that period.

What Other Problems May Arise from the Establishment of an Interscholastic Athletic Program at the Junior High Level?

1. Because of the cost of supplying uniforms, equipment, and so on, the school may be forced into the position of having the interscholastic program become chiefly a money-making venture.
2. The interscholastic sports program may displace the intramural and physical education programs. It may cause the girls' physical education program to be placed in a secondary position.
3. Part-time coaches may neglect other phases of their work to concentrate on coaching.
4. The program may place more importance on winning than upon the welfare of the boys who are participating.

Should Your School Sponsor Interscholastic Competition in Sports in the Junior High School, it is necessary to consider four questions.

1. Is the program greatly desired by the school and the community?
2. Are sufficient funds available to support the program so that it can be the best possible type of educational experience without jeopardizing other phases of instruction?
3. Can the necessary controls be exercised to keep the program in its proper educational perspective?
4. Can the proper safety precautions, training procedures and playing situations be maintained to keep the accident rate to a minimum?

Athletic Competition for Females

For many years there has been an unsubstantiated belief, especially in America, that strenuous exercise, particularly that experienced in athletics, is detrimental to the health of females. This generally accepted concept has been based on such vague assumptions that athletic women become mannish and have difficulty bearing children, that activities that require jumping may cause damage to healthy pelvic organs, and that girls should participate only in expressive, artistic, and rhythmical forms of exercise.

These assumptions have gradually been disproved by the research of physiologists and the general observation of experts. Studies, by Jokl,[12] indicate that female athletes find that child bearing is easier, of shorter delivery duration, and that fertility ratios are no different than for non-athletic females. Many women have been found to improve their physical efficiency during early pregnancy and following childbirth by exercise. The normal menstrual period is not disturbed by exercise—even competitive forms and often a girl's best athletic performance is recorded during a menstrual period.

These facts have led to a liberalization of the restrictions on athletic competition for females.

As observed previously, both boys and girls are competing in athletics earlier in life than in previous decades. In fact, girls have been more successful at earlier ages than the boys, because girls mature earlier.

Astrand, et al.[13] made a study of 30 of the best Swedish girl swimmers, ages 12 to 16. Among them they held two world records, three European records, and four Swedish championships. They found that the mean age at which the girls learned to swim was 5.8 years. Their training distances per week ranged from 5,000 to 68,000 meters and the time they spent in the water varied from 3 to 28 hours per week, with the champions taking the most strenuous workouts.

DGWS STAND ON ATHLETIC COMPETITION FOR WOMEN. Following is a statement concerning competition approved by the Division for Girls and Women's Sports [14] of the American Association for Health, Physical Education, and Recreation in 1958.

> The Division for Girls and Women's Sports of the American Association for Health, Physical Education, and Recreation believes the competitve element in sports activities can be used constructively for achievement of desirable educational and recreational objectives. Competition in and of itself does not automatically result in desirable outcomes, but competitive experiences may be wholesome and beneficial if they occur under favorable conditions and result in desirable conduct and attitudes.
>
> The adoption of the best practices for the attainment of desirable outcomes is the responsibility of all associated competitive events. Sponsoring agencies, players, coaches, officials, and spectators must share responsibility for valid practices in competitive sports if essential values are to be realized.
>
> DGWS believes participation in sports competition is the privilege of all girls and women. Sports needs, interests, and abilities are best met through sports programs which offer a wide variety of activities and pro-

[12] Ernst Jokl, "The Athletic Status of Women," *The British Journal of Physical Medicine* (November 1957).

[13] Astrand *et al.*, as quoted by Jokl, Seaton, *et al.* "Sports Medicine," *The Biology of Human Variation* (New York: Annals of the New York Academy of Sciences, 1966), p. 912.

[14] American Association for Health, Physical Education and Recreation, *Desirable Practices In Sports for Girls and Women* (Washington, D.C.: The Association, 1958). Standards, 1961.

vide for varying degrees of skill. Limiting participation in competitive sports to the few highly skilled deprives others of the many different kinds of desirable experiences which are inherent in well-conducted sports programs. Development of all participants toward higher competencies and advanced skills is a major objective in all sports programs.

Where the needs of highly skilled girls and women are recognized and served, broad physical education intramural and informal extramural programs take precedence over an interscholastic program. The latter may be an outgrowth of such programs but is not a substitute.

QUALIFIED COACHES

The National Federation of State High School Athletic Associations has the following rule: "A school shall not permit coaching by anyone who is not a certified teacher regularly employed by the Board of Education and *whose entire salary is paid by that body; or who has fewer than three regular periods of classes, gymnasium or study-hall duty per day.*" Forsythe [15] says, "Frankly, if a school cannot provide a man or woman who is properly trained to teach the sport desired, that sport should not be an activity of its athletic program." It is quite common in some states to violate this rule by selecting athletic coaches from the faculty who do not hold physical education certificates. Such practice may lead to an increased accident incidence.

Instructors and coaches should be aware of the school policies relating to safety and well-informed regarding the safe practices of the activities they are selected to teach. Before selecting a coach to "fill in" for some sport until a qualified person can be secured, the administrator should consider the hazards involved. Not only should they be qualified, but, according to Lloyd, Deaver, and Eastwood: [16]

> Teachers must be made safety conscious and trained to recognize hazards, know how to prevent them where possible, and what to do when an injury occurs. They must recognize the signs of overtraining as well as lack of training, and know when a student is physically fit to reenter a game. They must know the expectancies of injuries for various sports, and prevent unnecessary injuries. Full-time teachers of physical education give more satisfactory safety results than part-time teachers.

HEALTH EXAMINATIONS

Practically all state high school athletic associations and college-university athletic associations require competing athletes to undergo health

[15] Charles E. Forsythe, *Administration of High School Athletics* (Englewood Cliffs, N.J.: Prentice-Hall, 1962), p. 289.
[16] Frank S. Lloyd, George G. Deaver, and Floyd R. Eastwood, *Safety in Athletics* (Philadelphia: W. B. Saunders, 1936). Out of print.

examinations before they are permitted to report for competition. An equally important safety factor, that of requiring a physician's permit for the injured athlete to return to the game or practice, has become common practice. This sensible procedure not only protects the athlete's health but relieves the coach and trainer of the perilous risk of making a mistake. For further information see Chapter 18.

FIRST AID AND TREATMENT OF ATHLETIC INJURIES

Rosenfield reports that a number of court decisions clearly indicate that school officials have a duty to render first aid, but no treatment beyond that. A lay teacher should attempt to give only emergency treatment, and should not continue to dress a wound over a period of time. Courts have refused to permit school boards to pay for continued nonemergency treatment on the ground that their legitimate scope of action ended with the rendering of first aid. The question of liability for the *treatment of athletic injuries* by the coach or trainer, a common practice in most schools and colleges, is not so clearly defined. A California attorney general ruled that the district could not provide hospital or medical care to athletes beyond first aid. Rosenfield points out that the scope of the treatment must necessarily vary with the person who is rendering it. This, plus the moral obligation, would indicate that those persons rendering continued treatment to athletes should be well qualified to act. See Chapters 4 and 16.

WEIGHT CHECK AS HEALTH SAFEGUARD. Coaches keep close tab on the weight fluctuations among their players so that they may help them attain fitness and to be forewarned of any organic disorder or disease as well as of overwork. Some coaches require daily checks before and after practice; others believe a weekly check is sufficient. All agree that it is a desirable safeguard. Many instructors of physical education encourage class members to keep similar records of their weights.

WARM-UP. *Participants should be thoroughly warmed-up before performing strenuously or competing.* The physiological necessity of the warm-up is well known and accepted in athletics and physical education. Each coach and instructor has pet theories about the proper method of warming-up for the various sports or activities.

Stevens and Phelps [17] make the following observations:

> The warming-up process can never be the same for all individuals, nor can it be the same in all climates or types of weather or sports. Sweating is important in the elimination of waste products, and sweating varies markedly with change of temperature.
>
> Warming up is thought of by some athletes as simple limbering up of the joints, and these men run a few steps, lifting the knees high, turn a few

[17] Marvin A. Stevens and W. M. Phelps, *Control of Football Injuries* (New York: A. S. Barnes, 1933), p. 37. Out of print.

somersaults and present themselves as ready to begin. This is not recommended. A carefully worked out system of warming up should be developed by each athlete to fit what he has found by experience to be his particular needs. In general, this should be a gradually increasing set of activities which should increase the heart rate, not too much at a time, until he feels himself at a peak. If carried too long, he will be likely to begin tiring and thus waste valuable energy. At the peak of the warming up, a man should feel a slight beginning of sweating, provided he is warmly clothed, and should feel a definite increase in his muscular efficiency.

As these physicians point out, the requirement of warming up varies with sports, and even for events or positions within sports. A distance runner in track will usually require a lengthy and vigorous leg and body warm-up so that he will acquire his "second wind" before the race, whereas a shot-putter may require a less vigorous leg warm-up and a more vigorous arm warm-up. In fact, there are very few sports or activities that do not require a good warm-up if injury is to be avoided and if maximum efficiency is to be gained.

PREGAME WARM-UP. The character of the pregame warm-up depends on those factors mentioned above, plus that elusive quality of being "keyed up." When a team has been keyed to the extreme, its members cannot be subjected to the same long and thorough group of exercises followed in practice or they will become exhausted before game time. The sagacious coach will weigh all of these factors in planning his pregame warm-up periods. In relation to safety, there are two principles of warming up for both practice and pregame that are often neglected and therefore are mentioned here: (1) Sufficient stretching exercises should be employed; and, (2) the initial warm-up period does not guarantee a proper physiological tone indefinitely. The first precaution is particularly necessary in avoiding pulled muscles or tendons. The second is mentioned because too many coaches and instructors forget how long a player sits on the bench, and send him into the game after he has lost the benefits of the original warm-up period. The cooling-off period is also important, especially in such sports as track and field, wrestling, and basketball. Cooling off is best accomplished by mild exercise, such as walking, until recovery is made.

EQUALLY MATCHED TEAMS AND CONTESTANTS. It is obvious that matching teams or contestants of unequal strength, size, age, or ability is to court unwarranted danger. Since at least 50 per cent of the causes of sports accidents are due to the nature of the game and hence are probably unavoidable, the important role played by fair competition is to be emphasized. This is particularly true in contact sports. The practice of small schools, with comparatively weak teams, of scheduling larger ones because of financial returns is to be frowned upon. Also the matching of opponents in such individual sports as boxing or wrestling who are entirely out of each other's weight class is not to be condoned. If by chance such uneven matching occurs, a good official or a conscientious coach will stop the matches before the weaker fellow gets hurt.

It is therefore recommended that, *in contact sports, contestants and teams be as equally matched as possible.* This matching is recommended for contact sports only because the chief concern here is safety. Although it may not be desirable to match tennis players or swimmers of extremely different abilities, very little harm could result from the safety viewpoint. This principle of fair competition should, of course, apply to all competition whether it is in athletics, intramurals, or in physical education classes.

FEAR AND INJURY IN ATHLETICS

An inexperienced athlete usually experiences a sinking feeling of fear during his first game, as well as before large crowds and important contests, but he soon learns to adapt himself to the situation. Most athletes say, "I was scared to death until the whistle blew, and then I forgot all about the crowd." However, a *player's fear of injury may make him more liable to injury.* Although there is not, and possibly there never will be, any scientific proof of this, most coaches believe it to be true. To offset it, it is necessary that the player's confidence be built by improving skill and "losing" himself in the game. Skill is improved through constant and intelligent practice, and the wise coach leads the timid player progressively through a series of "fear situations" until he learns to conquer his fear of such daring stunts as doing a backward dive, a giant swing, or tackling a hard-driving fullback.

Players, particularly in combat sports, are often overstimulated by pep talks before games and between halves of contests. Such "adrenalization" often boomerangs by exciting the players beyond their ability to think clearly and act intelligently and may result in an unwarranted number of injuries.

"BUTTERFLIES" AID ATHLETES

Morehouse [18] tells us that most great athletes experience "butterflies" before an important game. He studied "pregame tensions" in his laboratory and concluded that the player who has them is the man the coach can count on for a brilliant effort. Morehouse says, "The effect of adrenaline secretion is to accelerate heart action, causing the blood pressure to soar driving the blood through the muscles, this triggers off the glycogenalytic system, increasing blood sugar."

These superior athletes are seldom injured during their moments of glory but may succumb later during a period of let-down. The wise coach knows when to make substitutions for his star players.

[18] Lawrence Morehouse (UCLA).

Virginia High School League

Box 3697 University Station, Charlottesville, Virginia 22903

Athletic Participation — Parental Consent — Physician's Certificate Form

(Separate form required for each school year. File in Office of Principal)

PART I—ATHLETIC PARTICIPATION

(To be filled in and signed by the candidate)

Name: _____School Year: _____

Home address: _____Home address of Parents: _____

Date of birth: _____Place of birth: _____

This is my _____semester in _____ High School, and my _____ semester since entering the ninth grade of

any high or prep school. I attended _____school last semester. I passed in_____subjects last semester,

and am carrying _____ subjects this semester. I have read the condensed individual eligibility rules of the Virginia High School League as they appear below and believe I am eligible to represent my present high school in athletics. If accepted as a squad member, I agree to make every effort to keep up my school work, and to abide by the rules and regulations of the school authorities and of the Virginia High School League.

Date: _____Signed: _____

(Student)

ATTENTION, ATHLETE!

TO BE ELIGIBLE TO REPRESENT YOUR SCHOOL IN ANY INTERSCHOOL CONTEST YOU:

——must be a bona fide and regular enrolled student in good standing, carrying not less than four classes.
——must have been promoted to the ninth grade (students in the eighth grade for the first time are eligible for the junior varsity).
——must be enrolled not later than the tenth day of the current semester.
——must have passed at least four subjects the previous semester.
——must not have reached your nineteenth birthday on or before the March first which precedes the current semester.
——must have been in residence at your present school or its "feeder" junior high school the last full semester.
    —unless you are transferring from a public or private school with a corresponding move on the part of your parents into the area serviced by your present school.
    —unless you are entering the ninth grade for the first time.
    —unless your former school was discontinued or consolidated and you were required to transfer to your present school.
    —unless you are a foreign exchange student, under the guidance of State Department of Welfare and Institutions, or are required to change residence by court order.
    —unless you are transferring for the first time from one public school to another within the same school division to obtain a desegregated education.
——must not have graduated from or completed the requirements for graduation from high school.
——must not have attended classes at an institution of higher learning except as a student making normal progress toward high school graduation or participated in any college athletics.
——must not, after entering the ninth grade for the first time, have been enrolled or been eligible for enrollment in high school more than eight consecutive semesters, nor have represented a high school in a varsity sport more than four years.
——must be an amateur as defined by the NCAA: ". . .one who engages in sports for the physical, mental or social benefits he derives therefrom, and to whom the sport is nothing more than an avocation."
——must have submitted this form to your principal prior to becoming a member of any school athletic squad, completely filled in and properly signed, attesting that you have been examined and found to be physically fit for athletic competition and that your parents have approved your participation.
——must not have been asked or unreasonably encouraged by any individual or group of individuals to transfer to your present school for athletic purposes.
——must not have received in recognition of your ability as a high school athlete any award not presented or approved by your school or League.
——must not have been a member of an organized team or participated in an organized meet or tournament in a sport during the school year after having represented your school in the same sport.
——must not have participated in an all-star contest between squads of individual contestants elected from more than one high school.
Eligibility to participate in interscholastic athletics is a privilege earned by meeting not only the above listed minimum standards but also any other standards set by your League, district, or school. If you have some question regarding your eligibility or are in doubt as to the effect any activity might have on your eligibility check with your principal or athletic director who is aware of the various interpretations and exceptions provided under League guides. Meeting the intent and spirit of League standards will prevent your team, school, or community from being penalized.

PART II—PARENTAL CONSENT

(To be filled in and signed by the parent or guardian)

In accordance with the rules of the Virginia High School League, I give my consent and approval to the participation of the student named above for the sports NOT MARKED OUT BELOW:

BASEBALL	FOOTBALL	SOFTBALL	TRACK
BASKETBALL	GOLF	SPEEDBALL	VOLLEYBALL
CROSS COUNTRY	GYMNASTICS	SWIMMING	WRESTLING
FIELD HOCKEY	SOCCER	TENNIS	OTHERS——

I will not hold the school authorities responsible in case of accident or injury as a result of this participation. *Please check appropriate space:* He (She) has student accident insurance available through the school ( ) has football insurance coverage available through the school ( ) is insured to our satisfaction ( )

Date: _____Signed: _____

(Parent or Guardian)

(over)

FIGURE 19-2. The State of Virginia combines the three forms of permission for athletic competition. (Courtesy Virginia High School League.)

PARENT'S CONSENT FOR PARTICIPATION

All students below college level should present their parents' *written consent* for participation in each sport of the interschool program. Although such consent has no legal significance, this procedure has become common practice because it is a method of informing the parents of the student's activity. It can be considered a safety measure, because a parent may be aware of certain weaknesses or family responsibilities because of which the son or daughter should not participate. Among the coaches and teachers polled by the writer, 60 per cent felt that permits were desirable, and the remainder felt that they were unnecessary. If intramural contests are conducted after school, it seems reasonable that these permits would be just as important as a safety factor as they would be for interschool competition.

USE OF TRAVEL FORMS FOR PARTICIPATION. Although the use of travel forms provides extremely limited legal protection, there are certain psychological and public relations advantages connected with their use. They assure parental knowledge of and permission for the proposed trip. Both of these forms may discourage the filing of suits by parents who, unless they consult an attorney, are likely to think that they have waived all rights in court.

SAFE TRANSPORTATION OF TEAM MEMBERS

With the ever-increasing rise of traffic accidents [19] the problem of transporting athletic teams safely has become extremely difficult. A school

---

TRAVEL FORM
PARENTS' NOTIFICATION OF CONTEST

Your son has been selected to represent his High School in _____

on _____ in competition with _____ High School.

He will need _____.
He should be neat in appearance.

He must be at the gymnasium not later than _____.

He will leave at _____ by _____ and return at approximately _____.

Should he not return by this time, information may be obtained by calling _____. Every care will be taken for his safety.

If for any reason your son will be unable to compete on this date please note the reasons and return the card by him.

Signed _____
Coach

FIGURE 19-3.

[19] School-age persons (15–24 yrs.) experience the highest motor vehicle death rate of all age groups. (See Chapter 2.)

should *never* allow team members to be transported in a private automobile with a fellow student driving, and it is questionable whether they should be so transported even with an adult driving. It is even more questionable regarding the coach driving. This precaution should be applied to transportation to and from practice fields as well as to other communities. Some school officials even require an adult to accompany each car of student *spectators* when traveling to games away from home. Schools forced to allow transportation in private cars should be certain of the following points:

1. The driver should be a careful, accident-free, licensed adult operator.
2. The automobile should be an all-steel-body sedan and has been currently inspected and approved.
3. Only the number of passengers prescribed by law should be allowed in each vehicle.
4. Insurance policies should adequately cover the players under all circumstances.
5. Parents should be informed of method of transportation and their consent should be obtained.

It is recommended that contests be cancelled when unusually inclement weather makes driving hazardous. This precaution is particularly applicable when private cars are used and the roads are unsafe because of ice, snow, fog, or rain. Such action may also save the lives of spectators who may brave the dangers to see their team in action.

Team players should be transported only in insured school buses or public carriers (including airplane travel) if utmost safety is desired. Comparison between the relative safety of this type of travel and the private automobile leaves little doubt about this choice. Even in this type of transportation, however, it must be pointed out that the capabilities and attitude of the driver are paramount. While they are traveling, the coach should enforce among his men the common rules and regulations governing safe conduct in the given mode of transportation. These rules and regulations are too numerous to mention here, but every coach should be on the lookout for unsafe acts on the part of his players which might lead to injury or death. Such trips provide numerous opportunities for effective safety education, because the players are keenly interested in new and novel situations.

SAFETY FOR SPECTATORS. *Adequate safety controls should be provided for spectators,* such as safe bleachers, police and fire protection, ushers and guards, fencing of areas, control of concession hazards, and traffic regulations. (See Chapter 17.)

Fire prevention rules and regulations must be strictly enforced during the use of indoor spectator areas. Some school gymnasiums are potential fire traps when they are filled with spectators. The administration should make certain that all exits are unlocked and available for use. In extremely hazardous situations it might be wise for the administration to consider the advisability of conducting fire drills occasionally. Such drills could be most easily conducted during intermission.

In larger schools police protection should be provided to curb the small percentage of persons who sometimes attend games to create trouble. Traffic officers should also be utilized, when necessary, to direct traffic to and from the games. The school's safety patrols and safety leaders can be used to assist in directing pedestrian traffic and in otherwise assisting with the handling of spectators. Ushers and guards are usually necessary to restrain the spectators from getting too close to, or even wandering onto, the field of play. Proper fencing or roping off of areas is also useful in keeping the spectators and players safe.

Concession wares, particularly empty bottles, present an added hazard if they are not properly regulated. Paper cups for beverages are much safer.

LIMITING THE NUMBER OF CONTESTS. The question of how many contests should be permitted among the various sports has been the object of much discussion and investigation. Again, from the standpoint of safety, there can be little doubt that certain reasonable limitations should be made in interschool competition, because as has been noted the incidence of accidents is much higher at this time than during practice. On the college level the problem is not ordinarily an issue, because the number of contests usually is limited by league or college officials to the time available. It is felt that the college players are sufficiently developed mentally to make their own judgments and sufficiently developed physically to be well beyond the dangers of immaturity.

The high school situation, however, presents a very troublesome question. In most states the limits for interscholastic contests in football and basketball are set by the state high school athletic associations, but athletic leagues and local school administrators often decide that a lesser number be played. With no state limitation and where the decision is left to local school administrators, the pressure from overzealous fans often forces the number of contests to be increased beyond all reason. For example, a few years ago, one school in a midwestern state played thirty-four basketball games during a single season. Various national organizations have gone on record regarding the maximum number of contests that should be scheduled for various sports during a season. A compilation of these and various state standards are summarized as follows.

Similar standards have not been promulgated for the junior high schools or elementary schools, because it has been rather generally felt that interschool competition should not be encouraged below the high school level. If such competition does exist, it is recommended that re-

TABLE 19-1

RECOMMENDED NUMBER OF GAMES (EXCLUDING TOURNAMENTS) FOR HIGH SCHOOL COMPETITION

Baseball	16	Soccer	14
Basketball *	18	Swimming	12
Cross Country	8	Tennis	14
Football	9	Track (indoor and out)	17
Golf	16	Lacrosse	9
Ice Hockey	14	Wrestling	12

* In some states, schools that do not sponsor football permit more basketball games.

strictions be adopted according to the immaturity of the students and the dangers of the sports.

INTRAMURAL CONTESTS. In general, it is deemed necessary to limit the number of intramural contests only by the condition of the contestants, the time and facilities available, and the strenuousness of the sport. This viewpoint is valid in light of the low accident incidence of intramurals as found by various studies.

LIMITING PRACTICE PERIODS. Closely allied with the limitation of the number of contests scheduled is the question of controlling practice periods. As would be expected, a greater percentage of injuries occur on the college level in practice than during intercollegiate competition because so much more time is spent in practice. It is surprising to learn that the severity index of injuries received at this time is higher than for those received during contests. Such a record, however, should probably be ascribed to the intensity of the practice rather than to the length of the periods, because most college practice periods are governed by league or association rules. By starting football early in August and finishing the last week in October, as many school do, many of the late season injuries caused by bad weather are avoided.

Here again the high school situation is the one that calls for special controls. According to the American Association for Health, Physical Education, and Recreation, there are two definite reasons for limiting practice—to safeguard the time and health of the student, and to make for fair and friendly competition among teams playing in the same league or the same section of the country. It further suggests that practice be limited in three ways—to the date practice begins, to the number of hours spent per day, and to the number of practices per week. Most state and college associations also limit the out-of-season practice periods.

PRESEASON PRACTICE. The length of time required to condition the members of a team for the competitive season varies somewhat with the sport. Coaches in general feel that it takes approximately three weeks to condition a team, and this period of time has served as a guide for most preseason practice periods. The Wisconsin Interscholastic Ath-

letic Association requires three weeks of practice before the opening of
the football schedule and it sets dates before which the remaining sports
cannot be started. Alabama requires at least two weeks of practice for all
sports before the opening game. Other states range between these two,
and some set no limitations. Most state associations now set the date for
opening, closing, and the first game played for football and basketball.

LENGTH OF DAILY PRACTICE. The length of the daily prac-
tice session depends upon a variety of factors; and very few, if any, state
high school athletic associations have seen fit to govern this phase of
athletics. A small number of intercollegiate associations have found it
necessary to limit the practice sessions of football in particular. The Western Conference, for example, has limited football practice to two hours.

Because of the important role played by fatigue in causing accidents
and injury, the writer interrogated leaders in the field on this point. They
agreed generally that as a safety measure against fatigue, practice sessions
in high school sports should be limited for each individual to an hour and
a half. It should be noted that this limitation is for each individual, and
not for the total length of the practice period. The American Association
for Health, Physical Education, and Recreation Committee on Interscholastic Athletic Standards for boys recommends that football and basketball *practice periods* be limited to this length of time.

NUMBER OF PRACTICE PERIODS PER WEEK. The number
of practice periods per week is usually left entirely to the judgment of the
coach, but is limited by the facilities available in some schools. Preschool
football practices are almost universally conducted twice daily, and the
tendency in all sports is to practice harder and longer than formerly
thought necessary.

A physician should be present at all combat sport interschool contests.
It will be noted that this principle is applied specifically to *combat* sport
interschool contests. It is usually possible to have a physician present and
certainly it is a most desirable practice. If it is not possible, one should at
least be within calling distance. The sports for which such service is desirable are usually considered to be football, boxing, lacrosse, horse polo, ice
hockey, and possibly wrestling, field hockey, basketball, and gymnastic
matches. A physician, trainer, nurse, or competent first-aider should be
present for combat sports practice. Usually the trainer or coach is a competent first-aider, which fulfills this requirement. Some coaches do not
feel themselves sufficiently qualified, and therefore like to have a more competent person present, or at least available.

AGE AND WEIGHT LIMITATIONS. It is neither fair nor safe
for mature, twenty-year-old youths to compete against immature fourteen-
year-olds. Nor is it safe for 200-pound college players to compete in contact sports against lightweights. For these reasons most high school conferences have limited the age of eligibility to nineteen, and both colleges

and high schools have fostered lightweight or junior varsity teams for interschool competition. Likewise, some authorities feel that it may not be safe for young and immature students to compete in strenuous interschool competition. For this reason a few states have set minimum age limits for competition in certain sports. For example, in New York a boy must be fourteen years old before he may compete in football, cross country, or ice hockey, and in Michigan he must be at least fifteen years of age before he can compete in cross country or any track event of 440 yards or more. (See page 304.)

GOOD SPORTSMANSHIP AS SAFETY FACTOR. Good sportsmanship by the players and by the coach or instructor is an important safety measure for the prevention of injury. The losing player who resorts to tripping, the sorehead who clips an opponent, and the coach who leaves a player in the game who has forced an opponent into the bleachers are all examples of poor sports who cause injuries. Although the officials can, and usually do, control such conduct, it is far better that these situations never arise. In other words, good sportsmanship practiced by the instructors and students in class and by the coaches and players on the practice field will usually insure good sportsmanship on the field of conquest.

STALENESS AND FATIGUE IN RELATION TO SAFETY. The coach and instructor should realize that staleness and fatigue often lead to injury. They should be able to recognize the signs and not utilize tired players or fail to remove them from the game at the proper time. Many accidental injuries in physical education and athletics are caused by fatigue and overtraining. It is important that every coach and physical education leader be adept not only in preventing staleness and fatigue but also in recognizing and "curing" them. There are many fine studies on the nature, causes, symptoms, and methods of prevention of fatigue, especially those of the Harvard Fatigue Laboratory. The relationship between the length of practice periods to fatigue has been discussed. Industry has been particularly interested in this phase of accident prevention, and Heinrich [20] has this to say: "The workman with a fatigued mental, nervous, or muscular system is a bad risk for himself and his employer. Remove, or at least minimize, the sources of fatigue and you can radically reduce illness and accidents."

Adolescents especially should be watched for overfatigue and nervous strain. The period of adolescence is characterized by rapid growth and many changes of the organs and structure of the body. Even though adolescents often seem to have unbounded energy, moderation in contact sports should be considered for the protection of growing boys and girls.

Varsity squads should be kept as large as feasible so that sufficient

[20] H. W. Heinrich, *Industrial Accident Prevention* (New York: McGraw-Hill, 1959), p. 13.

substitutes will be available for games. It has been proven again and again and is common knowledge that small squads in combat team sports tend to have a larger accident incidence. There are various reasons for this fact but the element of fatigue and staleness is probably the most important. Small-squad players are often required to enter or reenter a game when they have minor injuries or are fatigued, neither of which is desirable. New York State prohibits football to schools that cannot muster a squad larger than 20 players. This whole problem is closely associated with the administrative principle discussed earlier of scheduling schools of equal strength for fair competition.

Injured Players

The handling of injured participants in physical education classes has been discussed previously, but the question of injured players in athletics is not so simple and requires more elaboration. (See Fig. 19-4.) Because of the pressure to win by the student body and townspeople and the usual desire of a player to play regardless of an injury, the coach often is tempted to play a man when his better judgment would dictate otherwise. It must be remembered too, that opinions vary about the seriousness of an injury. The player usually belittles it, the trainer may be optimistic, and even doctors may have conflicting points of view. A physician who is not a sports fan may prescribe the usual two or three weeks rest for a sprained or strained ankle, whereas a team physician may prescribe only a few days rest and supervised exercises. *The best policy is to employ a team physician and to abide by his decision.* Thus the decision about using an injured player is made by an authority who assumes responsibility for the action.

The type and severity of the injury as a basis for determining the

PRELIMINARY INJURY REPORT CARD—FORM D
ATHLETIC ACCIDENT BENEFIT PLAN OF M.H.S.A.A.

(Leave blank)
No.________
Completion
Date________

..................Michigan..................19......

Secretary-Treasurer, Athletic Accident Benefit Plan of the M.H.S.A.A.
Dear Sir: Pursuant to requirements outlined in the Athletic Accident Benefit Plan of the M.H.S.A.A.
I hereby advise you that.................................. a student in the
..................High School, WAS INJURED ON.................., 19......, while:

(Check and fill in appropriate one.)

- ☐ Participating in an interscholastic contest in (sport)..................
- ☐ Participating in a practice session in (sport)..................
- ☐ Participating in an intramural contest (sport)..................
- ☐ Participating in a physical education class (activity)..................
- ☐ Traveling from..................to.................. as a member of our high school squad in (sport).................. to play a regularly scheduled interscholastic contest.

The best available information shows that his injury is a..................
and he is being attended by..................
Kindly forward required Forms for benefit request. (Indicate Name of Physician or Dentist)

Yours truly,..................
(Superintendent)—(Principal) (Cross out one)

(NOTE: THIS CARD MUST BE MAILED WITHIN TWENTY (20) DAYS AFTER INJURY OCCURS.)
Form D—(67—10M)

FIGURE 19-4. Preliminary injury report form (Michigan). (Courtesy Michigan High School Athletic Association.)

advisability of a player's participating must also be considered in respect to the sport or activity. For instance, a gymnast with an injured ankle might be able to perfom creditably upon most apparatus; a right-handed tennis player with a sprained left wrist would probably not be handicapped severely, nor would his injury necessarily be aggravated.

After Illness

Possibly more important than readmittance to competition after an injury is that of returning following illness. This decision, of course, must be made by the attending physician. Jokl [21] warns:

> It is an important but insufficiently known fact that following infectious diseases, among them the common cold and flu, the organism may be more sensitive than otherwise to the strain of athletics. Sufficient time for recuperation should therefore be allowed.

Prevention of Heat Stroke

Death from heat stroke has accounted for approximately 16 per cent of deaths in high school athletics during recent years. Early fall football practice accounts for practically all of these fatalities. The Medical Corps of the United States Marine Station at Paris Island cut its casualties tenfold by curtailing training activities under the following formula (simplified).

1. Temperature 80°–90°, humidity below 70 per cent observe carefully athletes particularly susceptible to effects of heat.
2. Temperature 80°–90°, humidity over 70 per cent, or temperature 90°–100°, humidity under 70 per cent: allow 10 minutes of rest per hour; change T-shirt when soaked; observe all athletes carefully for signs of heat exhaustion.
3. Temperature 90°–100°, humidity over 70 per cent, or temperature over 100°, regardless of humidity: cancel practice or perform shortened routine in T-shirts and shorts.

INTRAMURAL SPORTS

The organization, administration, and supervision of intramural sports differs very little from that of the physical education and athletic programs except in the degree of application. The athletic program usually has the most careful supervision, even to the presence of a physician, and

[21] Ernst Jokl, "Effect of Sports on the Cardiovascular System," *Encyclopedia of the Cardiovascular System*, Chapter 25 (New York: McGraw-Hill, 1960).

the physical education program is usually under the guidance of well-prepared personnel; but all too often the intramural contests take place under little or no supervision, with poor equipment and untrained officials. Practically all of the safety precautions enumerated in the foregoing chapters apply to the administration and supervision of intramural sports but need to be more carefully observed. The administrative set-up ranges all the way from the small high school with one faculty advisor to the large university with innumerable administrators and supervisors. The principles governing the safe conduct of contests, however, are the same for all. They are:

1. Rendering and maintaining a safe environment and providing safe equipment for the various intramural contests.
2. Organizing and conducting only those activities that can be made reasonably safe.
3. Furnishing the best possible supervision and officiating.

The supervisor's responsibilities are the same as those enumerated for physical education in Chapter 18. There are, however, at least three administrative precautions that bear repeating.

1. The keeping of accident records is extremely important for intramural activities because of the "looseness" with which they must often be controlled. One supervisor may be responsible for several games that are in progress at once and in different areas so that it becomes most difficult to give proper care to the injured and to keep accurate records.
2. Because of the usual shortage of faculty supervisors it becomes necessary to use student leaders. A special effort must be made to train these leaders in the safety measures that are necessary for every activity promoted.
3. It is usually necessary to use student officials, and their selection and training become a major responsibility. Poor officiating often leads to ill feeling and rough play that may result in an increase in injuries. On the college level physical education majors are usually used as a part of their training for the profession, and they provide a good nucleus of trained officials.

REFERENCES

American Association for Health, Physical Education, and Recreation, *Standards for Junior High School Athletics* (Washington, D.C.: The Association, 1963).
Bowerman, W. J., "More Safety for Vaulters," *Athletic Journal*, Vol. XLIV, No. 9 (May 1964), p. 72.

Brashear, R. H., "Basic Areas of Prevention of Athletic Injuries," *The Journal of the American Medical Association* (November 21, 1960), pp. 140–41.

Brown, Billy Joe, "A Tub of Water and No Blisters," *Coach and Athlete,* Vol. XXVI, No. 4 (November 1963), p. 36.

Clarke, K. S., "Safety Implications for Athletics," *Third Annual Safety Education Review* (Washington, D.C.: National Education Association, 1964), pp. 33–38.

DeCarlo, T. J., "Safeguards in Gymnastics," *Scholastic Coach,* Vol. 31, No. 5 (January 1962), pp. 70–75.

Gilbertson, W. E., "Ski for Fun," *Safety Education* (January 1961) pp. 20–23.

Grambeau, R. J., "Safety Measures in Athletics," *The Physical Educator,* Vol. 21, No. 4 (December 1964), p. 168.

———, "Developing Safety in Intramural Sports," 59th Annual Proceedings, *The College Physical Education Association.* 1956, pp. 148–51.

Green, D. A., "Safety in Sports," *Safety Education* (February 1957), pp. 19–22.

Hanley, D., "Play Football Safely," *Scholastic Coach,* Vol. 32, No. 1 (September 1962), p. 24.

Harris, R., *Safety and Rebound Tumbling* (Cedar Rapids, Iowa: Nissen Trampoline Company, 1961).

Hauck, E., "Struck by Bat," *Safety Education* (April 1960), pp. 20–23.

Hein, F. V., "Tackle Football in Junior High School," *First Annual Safety Education Review* (Washington, D.C.: National Education Association, 1962), 37, pp. 25–27.

Houston, R. J., "A Safe, Portable Squat Rack," *Scholastic Coach,* Vol. 33, No. 5 (January 1964), p. 60.

Keller, Louis B., "The Relation of Quickness of Bodily Movement to Success in Athletics," *Research Quarterly* (May, 1936) pp. 146–55.

Klein, K. K., "Preventive Conditioning and Reduction of Knee Injuries," *Athletic Journal,* Vol. XL, No. 7 (March 1960), p. 28.

La Place, J., "Let's Keep Baseball Safe," *Athletic Journal* (January 1959), p. 10.

Little, B. J., "Softball Safety," *Journal of Health, Physical Education, and Recreation* (May 1965), pp. 46–47.

McPhee, H. R., "Prevent Football Injuries," *Scholastic Coach* (September 1948).

Mickelsem, M., "Ski Safety," *Journal of Health, Physical Education, and Recreation* (February 1964), pp. 65–66.

Murphy, Robert R., "You Can Prevent Heat Stroke," *Scholastic Coach,* Vol. 33, No. 9 (May 1964), p. 100.

The National Federation of State High School Athletic Associations, Chicago: *Current Handbook.*

National Safety Council, Safety Education Data Sheet, No. 94, "Safety in Archery," *Safety Education*, The Council (May 1960), pp. 9–13.

Norwick, M. M., "A Physician Looks at Athletics," *Journal of the American Medical Association* (June 1956).

O'Donoghue, D. H., "General Principles of Treatment of Injuries to Athletes," *Journal of the American Medical Association* (November 21, 1959), pp. 132–35.

———, "A Doctor Talks about Injuries to Athletes," *Journal of Health, Physical Education, and Recreation* (November 1960), pp. 22–25.

Reichert, J. L., "A Pediatrician's View of Competitive Sports Before the Teens," *Today's Health* (October 1957).

Ryan, A. J., *Medical Care of the Athlete* (New York: McGraw-Hill, 1962).

Smith, B. A., "An Investigation of the Effectiveness of Two Conditioning Programs in Reducing the Number of Injuries in Women's Intercollegiate Basketball," *Completed Research in Health, Physical Education, and Recreation*, Vol. 7, 1965, p. 80.

The Society of State Directors of Health, Physical Education, and Recreation, *A Statement of Basic Beliefs*. The Society, 1964.

Steinhaus, A. H., *Toward an Understanding of Health, Physical Education, and Recreation* (Dubuque, Iowa: William C. Brown, 1963).

Templin, P. H., "An Analysis of Health and Safety Practices for Football Players in Selected High Schools in the State of Washington, 1960–61," *Completed Research in Health, Physical Education, and Recreation*, Vol. 4, 1962, p. 77.

Thorndike, A., *Athletic Injuries* (Philadelphia: Lea & Febiger, 1962).

Tucker, W. E., and J. R. Armstrong, *Injury in Sport* (Springfield, Ill.: Charles C. Thomas, 1964).

Young, D., "Safety in Your Indoor Batting Cage," *Athletic Journal*, Vol. XLIV, No. 6 (February 1964), p. 36.

Yost, Charles Peter, "Better Leadership, the Key to Safety in Athletics," *Safety* (Washington, D.C.: National Commission on Safety Education, National Education Association. The Association, January–February 1967), p. 8.

CHAPTER 20 SAFETY IN CAMPING AND AQUATICS

POPULARITY OF CAMPING

All types of camping, organized and unorganized, have had a tremendous growth in popularity during the last ten years. It is estimated that one out of every six schoolchildren will attend a summer camp each year, totaling 5.5 million campers, which will cost their parents more than a quarter of a billion dollars. The National Park Service alone accommodates approximately 90,000 campers.

There are between 11,000 and 16,000 organized camps serving school-age children. These camps employ about 15,000 full-time persons and approximately 175,000 part-time personnel. Many of these camps are owned and operated by public school systems. California, Florida, Illinois, Indiana, Michigan, Missouri, New York, North Carolina, Ohio, Texas, and Washington have established a variety of school camps with gratifying results. Michigan has been the scene of the greatest development with more than seventy-five school districts sponsoring this type of outdoor education.

Most campers—50 million—are city folk who are often ill-prepared to cope with the hazards of outdoor life. Many are totally inexperienced and inadequately equipped to experience the benefits of outdoor life without exposing themselves to a large number of unnecessary hazards. Most camping accidents are the result of these unqualified persons attempting camp adventures beyond their ability and knowledge. Inexperienced campers should either join an organized camping group or be accompanied by someone qualified to cope with the type of country and activities to be engaged in. For this reason, and others, those persons responsible for the school-sponsored camp must be more conscious of the safety factors than others.

PEACE OF MIND THROUGH SAFETY

Parents naturally want the peace of mind that results from the knowledge that their children are in the safe and secure hands of trustworthy camp counselors. Every school and camp administrator must keep this in mind when organizing and administering a camping experience. This is equally true for the day camp as for the long-term resident camp.

ORGANIZED CAMPING

More and more educators are realizing the benefits to be derived by young people from camping. As noted before, many schools now sponsor summer camps, and there is evidence that this movement will continue to grow.

The following trends affect the camp safety problem: (1) The age of admittance for campers is becoming younger, some camps admitting children under six years. (2) The term of camp has decreased. (3) Camping has become "big business," with some persons operating camps for profit who are not fit to conduct such an enterprise. (4) Some camps have increased so in size that they have become small villages, with the accompanying problems of safe-guarding many persons. (5) There has been a rapid growth of camps for specialized groups such as the handicapped or those interested in fitness or certain sports. (6) Camping has become a factor of public health and safety in which the state has gradually assumed control.

Although there is no accurate method of comparing the accident incidence of camping with home or summer vacation records, it would be expected that youngsters coming into an entirely strange environment would be prone to experience an unusual number of accidents unless a thorough educational and preventive program were conducted.

CAMPING ACCIDENTS

Kibrick et al.[1] made an accident-injury study of 1,192 campers and staff in three summer camps which revealed a remarkably low accident rate for campers (12.4 injuries per 100 campers per month) and a much higher rate for the staff. Only 12.3 per cent of all injuries were disabling, that is, severe enough to keep the injured camper from participating in the camp program for at least one day.

They found that 42 per cent of the accidents were the result of object impact, falls caused 23 per cent, cuts 22 per cent, and others 13 per cent. The parts injured followed the usual pattern with 82.1 per cent occurring

[1] Ann Kibrick, et al., "Report on Accidental Injuries in Summer Camps," *Camping Magazine* (April 1963), pp. 28–31.

to the extremities, 13.3 per cent to the head, and 4.6 per cent to the body. It was surprising to find that the more experienced campers at a scout camp tended to have more accidents than the inexperienced. This camp also had more disabling accidents—22.8 per cent—as compared to a private camp which had 6.7 percent, and a guidance camp which had only 0.7 per cent.

ACCIDENT PREVENTION

It was estimated by Kibrick *et al.* that 80.7 per cent of the campers' accident injuries were preventable and that 51.5 per cent of staff's could have been prevented.

Saunders,[2] who made the first and probably the most comprehensive study of safety in camping, estimated that 25 per cent of the accidents could have been prevented if the sites had been well selected and the camps well equipped and cared for; that 26 per cent probably could have been eliminated by disposing of poison ivy and insects; and that by proper education and supervision in the use of axes and knives, in horseback riding, and in wearing proper footwear, another 14 per cent might have been prevented. Of the remaining 35 per cent of accidents in the camps studied, only 11 per cent seem, for practical purposes, not to have been preventable. The other 24 per cent could have been prevented only by the exercise of greater care and intelligence on the part of the injured individuals, though over half of that number might have been prevented by adequate supervision.

ATTITUDE TOWARD SAFETY

F. C. Mills, late Director of Health and Safety of the Boy Scouts of America, expressed most lucidly the attitude which the authors hope will be conveyed by this material. He said:

> It is possible to surround camping and aquatic activities with negative rules that take all the fun out of being a camper or swimmer. The philosophy of our organization is safety through skill. Over-protection, paradoxically, can cause many accidents. We believe in teaching skills which will make it possible for boys to learn to meet life's situations. I know of camps where children are robbed of their self reliance by the over-protective policies of the management.

Example is one of the greatest forces in the teaching of camp safety. Every camp leader is urged to set a good example by acting safely under all circumstances. He should also provide an inconspicuous and unob-

[2] J. Edward Saunders, *Safety and Health in Organized Camps* (New York: National Conservation Bureau, 1931; also, a doctoral dissertation, Columbia University, 1930).

trusive type of safety supervision which is motivated by a genuine interest in the welfare and safety of the boys and girls.

SPECIFIC ADMINISTRATIVE CONTROLS

A meeting of the counselor staff should be held before or at the opening of the camp to discuss and lay plans for safety and sanitation and for a complete inspection and correction of possible hazards. Herbert J. Stack [3] in addressing such a meeting said, "I do not need to call to your attention the fact that a serious accident, such as a broken leg or collarbone, may rob a camper of many weeks of happiness and adventure. A fatality—and fatal accidents are exceedingly rare—may ruin your camp." He continued by outlining the methods of attacking the problem:

> As I have repeatedly stressed, as counselors directing camp activities you have a major responsibility to reduce accidents to a minimum. You can do this in four primary ways: first, by planning activities that are reasonably safe; second, by removing hazards wherever possible; third, by proper supervision of the activity; and fourth, by teaching campers and counselors safe practices in these activities. These are parallel, in a way, to the three E's in Safety: Education, Engineering, and Enforcement.

CAMP PREPARATION

The hazards of a camp that should be removed, repaired, or compensated for include such items as glass, tin, nails, wire, unsafe flooring, steps, and ladders, uneven and rocky paths, poisonous plants, and so on. There can be little doubt concerning the advisability of removing dangerous debris and repairing flooring, steps, and such, but the desirability or possibility of making all paths foolproof is questionable. An effort should be made to eliminate a certain amount of uneven or slippery surfaces and hazardous inclines, but complete security is often impossible. A Boy Scout official cited a case where a girl sprained her arm falling on a rock in a girls' camp. The camp director the following year, at great expense, had as many of the stones removed as possible before the opening of camp, only to have three campers experience broken bones from the same source because the removal of the stones made it possible for the campers to run faster.

Sufficient bulletin boards with safety rules and regulations should be provided at strategic locations about the camp area. One of the principal faults in using the bulletin board or poster technique is that it often becomes the *only* teaching device. A propitious joke will often make a

[3] Herbert J. Stack, "Setting the Stage for Safety," *Camping Magazine* (March 1939).

point better than a serious article. The director of each camping activity should be responsible for the safe conduct of that activity, and the cabin counselor should be responsible for his cabin. The designation of persons responsible for certain areas of the camp or phases of the program is a wise and necessary administrative task.

The *health examination* and parents' statements should inform the administrative staff of each individual's handicaps and idiosyncracies, such as epilepsy and sleepwalking, which might endanger the camper's existence. These individual traits are often difficult to ascertain, but it would be well worth the effort expended if the counselors could be forewarned and instructed in the best methods of handling them. Campers should be given special health examinations before embarking on prolonged canoeing, hiking, and camping trips. It is assumed, of course, that all campers will have been thoroughly examined before coming, or upon entrance to the camp, and as often thereafter as may be deemed necessary, further examination will be made by the camp physician. To take a camper who is not capable of withstanding the hardship on a trip is not only an injustice to him but to his companions as well. Many camps also give an examination before sending the campers home.

If it is necessary for the staff to use gasoline or other inflammable materials, the materials should be safely stored and not used by the campers. Flammable materials should be stored in a fireproof, vented storage place, and the key should be kept in the possession of one person only who should be responsible for all issuances and for the uses to which the materials are put. Camp buses should be driven only by qualified, adult drivers, and campers should not use, or be driven in, camp cars unless public liability insurance is carried. State laws vary. Each camp must work out its own method of controlling this issue, which in many localities is a serious problem. Campers should not be allowed to possess firearms or to use them except under expert supervision. The possession or use of firecrackers or other explosives should be prohibited. This rule should be thoroughly understood by all before coming to camp, then careful precautions taken to make certain that none of the campers possess weapons. The archery butts and rifle ranges should be located at the edge of the camp in the safest possible area.

SPECIFIC LEADERSHIP AND SKILL CONTROLS

Campers should be instructed to drink and eat only the water and food approved by the camp staff. Although this precaution is primarily one of hygiene or sanitation, it is listed here because of its significance. The campers should be so well instructed with regard to this item that violation of the rule would be an accident! Campers should be taught to recognize and avoid dangerous animals, insects, poisonous plants, and snakes. They should also be instructed in proper first-aid treatment. These two areas of instruction are normally an accepted part of every camp program, and when they are presented in a positive, constructive manner, they should do much to reduce hazards. As Saunders points out, 25 per cent of camp accidents could be eliminated thereby. (See Chapter 4 for school first-aid procedures.) Campers should be instructed in the safe use of axes, knives, and other common camp tools. Those taking arts and crafts should receive special instruction in the safe use of such tools, machinery, and materials. The need for such instruction is so obvious that it is difficult to conceive of any responsible camp that would fail to provide it. A famous camp leader [4] has said, "Practice of these skills does not have to be either boring or monotonous. Campers readily understand how essential it is for each one to be able to take his part." Campers should be instructed and trained in the safe methods of building and controlling camp fires used for cooking and heating. Arthur H. Desgrey of the City College of New York, says: "A large percentage of camp accidents may also be traced to a lack of knowledge and information, and to the absence of safety skills necessary for camping." For this reason the last three items have been listed.

When it is necessary to travel on a highway, campers should be instructed to walk on the extreme left, and to wear something white and carry a flashlight if they are walking at night.

HIKING SAFELY

Miss Joy, a nationally known camp leader, summarizes overnight camping in this manner:

> Safety anywhere, in this day and age, is a matter of training, good sense, and good judgment. Safety on trips is assured only by mastery of camping-out and enabling skills, and by knowledge of the hazards inherent in the environment. It may be rapids in the river, poison ivy or snakes on land, squalls on the lake, slippery rocks on the mountain, or a horse which shies too suddenly on the trial. The main thing is to be cognizant of the hazards that may be met with in each situation, and then be prepared to meet them. In addition we should not take chances or become overfatigued. We should keep all equipment in good repair, keep the group together, and keep the morale high. We must know the country we are going through, be prepared for all emergencies, and keep steady when one occurs.[5]

[4] Barbara Ellen Joy. "Overnight Trips—Yes and No!," *Journal of Health and Physical Education* (April 1938).
  [5] *Ibid.*

Hikes should be thoroughly planned, with one counselor in charge and others of the staff assisting as the size of the party may require. In ascending rocky hills, the group should zigzag, and all hikers should complete the zig before changing course so that loosened rocks do not roll on those below. If there is to be swimming, at least one of the counselors should be a water sports specialist. The number of counselors necessary will vary with the age of the group being conducted, but in general the proportion ranges from six to twelve hikers per counselor. For overnight hikes, the camp site should be selected for its safe location, nearness to drinking water, shelter, and accessibility to a telephone. Accessibility to a telephone may not always be possible, but anyone who has experienced the necessity of taking care of a seriously injured or ill camper under such circumstances will appreciate the importance of this precaution.

Sufficient first-aid equipment should be on hand, including gauze, iodine or other antiseptic, bandaid, adhesive tape, bandage, tourniquet, aromatic spirits of ammonia, scissors, scalpel, safety pins, ointment for poison ivy and burns, and snakebite remedy if necessary. Other remedies may be deemed necessary for particular sections of the country, but these form the basic items for most kits. Halazone tablets to purify water might also be considered an essential of the first-aid kit.

On an overnight trip the hiker's equipment should include strong, well-broken-in shoes, knife or ax, blankets, flashlight, compass, canteen, and sufficient clothing for climatic conditions. The counselors will carry the necessary maps and matches. For daytime hikes blankets and flashlights may be omitted. The party should travel with one counselor in the lead and another bringing up the rear. *Roll calls* should be made at necessary intervals. If an injury occurs on a hike the counselor must keep the group together. By using the buddy system, which is recommended, roll calls will not be necessary so often. A hiker should stay with the party and protect the fellow behind by holding branches and warning of holes and other dangers; he should not be allowed to show off by doing dangerous stunts. Few activities promote the feeling of comradeship more than hiking does, and these acts of sportsmanship are spontaneous with most persons. There should be a prearranged *plan of operation* for group and individual conduct in case someone becomes lost. There are several different methods of procedure, but probably the best is to require the lost person or group to "sit tight" and await rescue. During this time the person or persons should conserve energy and food, seek or build shelter, and light two signal smoke fires.[6] The use of other types of signals could also be prearranged. Another plan would be to instruct lost hikers to seek to return to camp, provided some convenient stream, lake, or other landmark exists to make such a return comparatively certain. Or, if the destina-

[6] Two columns of smoke are recognized all over the world as a distress signal.

of the hike is some mountain peak or large lake, it might be advisable to arrange for the parties to meet there.

It might be desirable to combine these ideas and say something like this: "If you become detached from the party, seek to reach the destination by the use of your maps and compass until nightfall. If you are not successful, prepare to 'hole up' and await rescue, observing all of the woodcraft and rescue precautions you have learned." *Instruction in methods of survival should be a part of every camper's training.* There are many sources of information on survival available to camp leaders.

FIRE PREVENTION

The threat of fire hangs heavily over the camp director's head, because most buildings are highly flammable, and the fire-fighting equipment is of necessity limited. Everyone should know his job when a fire breaks out. Rigid rules governing the use of matches and smoking must be enforced. The kitchen should be carefully planned to control the fire in that area. Camp fires must be built in accordance with accepted safe practices and only under supervision. *Fire drills should be thoroughly organized and periodically practiced.* In those areas where there is danger of forest fires, plans for reporting and defending the camp against them must be established and practiced.

SAFETY IN AQUATICS

As pointed out in an earlier chapter, 6,800 persons were drowned in the United States last year. Gabrielsen [7] found that recreational swimming claimed most victims, 26.3 per cent, fishing accounted for the next highest percentage, 18.5, and boating claimed 16.3 per cent. He also indicated that there were no indoor pool drownings in the year studied.

It is not possible in the limited space of this text to explore all of the administrative and supervisory details needed to conduct a variety of aquatic programs. The ever-present threat of drowning and the vast numbers of people—estimated at 60 to 70 million—engaged in swimming, boating, skiing, skin and scuba diving, and fishing on a given weekend, however, calls for some school treatment of the subject.

Gabrielsen [8] claims that the public schools of our country are responsible for the fact that so many people cannot swim. He says, "It is

[7] B. W. Gabrielsen, *Facts on Drowning Accidents* (Athens, Georgia: University of Georgia Press, 1956).

[8] M. Alexander Gabrielsen, Betty Spears, and B. W. Gabrielsen, *Aquatics Handbook* (Englewood Cliffs, N.J.: Prentice-Hall, 1960), Chapter 2.

unfortunate that facilities are not being provided to allow a compulsory swimming program in the physical education programs of our schools. Huge edifices are being built to seat thousands for a basketball game, but there is not enough concern for the safety of children to provide facilities to 'drown proof' them by teaching them to swim. The first thing to be dropped in a building program when money is to be saved is the swimming pool."

It is almost unbelievable to find that there are 2,673 swimming pools in the elementary schools of Japan and 889 in the lower secondary schools. This means that 78.5 per cent of the elementary schools and 89.2 per cent of the lower secondary schools have 25-meter swimming pools. Approximately 70 deaths from drowning were recorded in these pools of Japanese schools during the school year 1960–1961.

The following material is presented primarily for the guidance of school and college administrators and is therefore limited in its scope. Also, a number of specific administrative and leadership controls have been included because relatively few safety education texts cover these vital factors.

Indoor Swimming

No other area of sports activities has been so thoroughly governed for safety as swimming. The American Red Cross, the Boy Scouts, the Y.M.C.A., and others have for many years conducted extensive water-safety education and training programs that have borne fruit. As successful as these programs have been in controlling the number of water accidents among the general population (the National Safety Council's *Accident Facts* points out that the death rate by drowning in 1902 was 10.2, whereas by 1959 it had been reduced to approximately 3.6), the school program has been even more spectacular in controlling the school pools. Lloyd *et al.*[9] found that the school accident incidence of swimming was only .6 per 1,000 exposures, which is probably as safe as sitting in the classroom.

Drowning as a Major Cause of All Fatalities. A salient point that must be kept in mind, however, is that drowning ranks second among all causes of accidental death among boys and girls between the ages of fifteen and twenty-four, also second among the five to fourteen age group, and third among the group up to four years old. This record of drownings almost entirely outside of school premises indicates the need for an even more thorough job of water-safety instruction in our schools. It must also be remembered that only actual drownings are reported and that hundreds of *near* drownings are never recorded.

[9] Frank S. Lloyd, George G. Deaver, and Floyd R. Eastwood, *Safety in Athletics* (Philadelphia: W. B. Saunders, 1936). Out of print.

There are a number of pool accidents as described in *Safety in Athletics*. Some schools believe it is desirable to seek parental permission for the participation of the students in the aquatic program and require the submission of a form similar to that displayed in Figure 20–1.

DENVER PUBLIC SCHOOLS
Department of Health Service - Health Education
PARENT PERMIT FOR PUPIL TO PARTICIPATE IN REGULAR SWIMMING CLASS

I hereby give permission and request that_____
be permitted to participate in a swimming class at school.

To my knowledge, my child does not have diabetes, epilepsy, chronic sinus or ear infection, or any other physical condition that would make it unsafe for him to swim.

_____   _____
(Date)   (Signature of Parent)

Furthermore, if my child presently needs medical clearance for swimming (a doctor's examination is required every three years) I prefer:

To have my own physician send to the school at once a recent health report. I will urge him to use the special blank furnished by school health services to private physicians_____ ☐

To have the school physician perform the swimming appraisal_____ ☐

STOCK NO. 10783
FORM 853   DSP   4-63-100 PADS   A-252-52814

FIGURE 20-1.

SPECIFIC ADMINISTRATIVE CONTROLS

Keep the pool locked. No one should be allowed to enter the pool unless he is supervised by an instructor or officially designated lifeguard. This rule is rigidly enforced in most schools and its safety importance can scarcely be overestimated. Lanoue [10] said:

> The swimming pool is an alluring aquatic medium which presents continuous elements of danger. By means of the teaching and learning of swimming and diving skills, and the mastery of aquatic breathing, human beings have developed remarkable adaptability to the water, thus greatly reducing the danger element. Nevertheless the risk of water accidents, even among skilled swimmers, is such that the most careful instruction and constant vigilance are necessary on the part of the instructors and lifeguards whenever the pool is in use.

An instructor should be the first one in the swimming pool room and the last one to leave. There should also be the established rule that no one is to enter the water until the instructor is present. All means of entrance to the pool should be locked when they are not in use. When the pool is in use, the doors should *never* be locked. If it is necessary to prevent sightseers, signs or guards should be posted. Also, special care must be taken to prevent anyone from diving or falling into the pool when it has been emptied. Swimming classes should not be scheduled for

[10] Fred Lanoue, *Drownproofing* (Englwood Cliffs, N.J.: Prentice-Hall, 1960).

the first hour following a meal. This provision is not necessarily recommended as a deterrent to stomach cramps, which has been discussed, but because of the fact that during this hour students are likely to be less alert, a condition that may lead to accidents. Experience has taught most instructors that this hour is the least desirable teaching period. Most authorities believe that exercise may not be harmful at this time if there is little emotional upset.

Flutterboards, floats, balls, and so on should *not* be used in the pool unless permitted by the instructor for special instruction or recreation. The indiscriminate use of these devices usually leads to unreasonable activities and carelessness that makes the pool a dangerous place. Some instructors find it more profitable to instruct without the use of artificial aids of any type.

The buddy system should be used in beginners classes, in all large classes, and in classes below the high school level. In small pools with clear water and adequate guards, the buddy system may not be necessary, but it is an accepted safety precaution. The system is also a good teaching device. The safe size for class instruction will of necessity be governed by the size of the pool, clearness of the water, ability of the instructor, and level of instruction. Luehring recommends that the class be limited to twenty-five, especially for beginners. "If larger classes are required, a correspondingly larger part of the teachers time is taken up by lifeguard duties, thus limiting teaching efficiency." Most universities limit the size of classes to twenty-five, and the public schools usually set a maximum limit of thirty-five pupils per instructor. The pool load for sanitation should be determined by the Gage formula.

The instructor should be dressed so that he may enter the water in an emergency. It has been accepted professionally that the instructor should be dressed appropriately for all activities, and in swimming it is a *must* from the safety standpoint. Occasionally a drowning person is unable to catch hold of or be rescued by the lifesaving devices offered, and when it becomes necessary for the instructor to go in after the one in trouble, he should be appropriately dressed. *Sufficient lifesaving equipment must be provided for the pool.* The following items are minimum recommendations.

One resuscitator.

Two fifteen-foot aluminum poles.

Two flutterboards approximately 1 foot by 3 feet by 2 inches capable of supporting not less than 200 pounds.

Two throwing ring buoys, 18 inches in diameter, with 60 feet of quarter-inch nylon line attached or torpedo buoys (especially in large pools).

One first-aid kit containing aromatic spirits of ammonia, tincture of iodine, sterile gauze, absorbent cotton, surgeon's plaster, and bandages of various sizes.

Two woolen blankets.
One stretcher.

All swimming instructors should be qualified Red Cross Water Safety In-structors. Qualification by the Y.M.C.A., Y.W.C.A., the Girl Scouts, the Boy Scouts, or other equally reliable organizations should also be accept-able. However, the American Red Cross service has been so widespread that most schools follow its leadership.

An area for nonswimmers should be roped off. Large pools with large classes need this provision especially, but it is of sufficient importance to use under all conditions. Much of the trouble comes when beginners panick after paddling unknowingly into water too deep for standing. In large classes of mixed abilities it is advisable to require nonswimmers to be identified in some manner, such as the wearing of red swim caps. Classes for instruction should not be this large, nor should there be groups of varying abilities, but if these conditions do exist, such added precau-tions are necessary.

The Joint Committee on Bathing Places of the Conference of State Sanitary Engineers and the American Public Health Association specifies, "At artificial pools all bathers of both sexes should be required to wear rubber bathing caps," because the hair oils and bobby pins are detrimental to filtration systems. If the pool is so organized that the different groups can be kept segregated, identification marks may not be necessary.

SPECIFIC LEADERSHIP AND SKILL CONTROLS

Instruction in the safe use of the pool should be given at the first class meeting, and the users repeatedly instructed in proper conduct there-after. Often the first meeting is devoted to instruction in sanitation and the safety rules are neglected. It is recommended that the safety rules be incorporated as a part of this instruction, and that printed instructions be distributed to the students. It is also recommended that the rules be posted on the bulletin board or printed on large signs so that there will be no reason for a student's ignorance of them. Beginners should be in-formed concerning superstitions associated with drowning that have no basis in actual fact. (These beliefs reduce the swimmer's efficiency and produce a fear complex.) Some of these common superstitions are that a drowning man goes down twice before the third and final time; that the lungs fill up with water when drowned; that cramps will usually drown one. To instill confidence, the debunking of such misconceptions should be a part of the instruction regarding the water's ability to support a person.

Bathers should be informed of hazards of, and instructed in the safe use of, beaches, rivers, lakes, and the ocean. This instruction can be integrated throughout the course, but the most logical time is in the lessons given before summer vacation. A number of organizations have printed water-safety lesson outlines for use in junior high school and elementary school which might prove valuable in presenting such lessons. Bathers should be instructed in the accepted best practices and trained in the proper techniques of lifesaving. All pool users should learn the accepted principles of rescue, and the various levels should be taught the procedure capable of being executed by each particular group. Just a few techniques are really necessary. It is not necessary, of course, to require all students to take a complete lifesaving course, but it is highly desirable to make such courses as the Junior and Senior Life Saving Courses of the Red Cross available. Capable and reliable student lifeguards should be qualified as Red Cross Lifesavers and used in the pool as desired. Luehring and others recommend at least one lifeguard per seventy-five persons or fraction thereof using the pool at a given time for general recreation. With more than the recommended twenty-five pupils per instructor, additional lifeguards should be provided for class work as necessary. Many instructors require one lifeguard always to remain on the side or end of the pool opposite the instructor.

Nonswimmers should not be allowed to go beyond their depth, even with artificial support. Occasionally a nonswimmer will be so bold as to jump off into deep water without assistance, but usually the trouble comes from those who have mastered a few strokes and want to try out their newly found skill. The use of artificial support is particularly risky during recreation periods. When a prankish swimmer dumps a nonswimmer off an inner tube, he may find himself in unsuspected trouble, and the nonswimmer may be so frightened that he will never again be at home in the water. Inner tubes should not be used, but when they are used the valves should be taped down so that they cannot poke one's eyes.

Persons who have chronic ear infections, damaged ear drums, or have had mastoid operations should use *special precautions to prevent water from reaching the middle ear.* The percentage of persons who are adversely affected by water is small. Some, however, if so designated by a physician, should not enter the water, and others may have to restrict their activity to surface swimming and avoid diving. Some may have to wear ear or nose plugs for safety's sake. Only those types of plugs that are approved by the physician should be used.

Running about the pool should be prohibited because of the danger of falling on the slippery surface. It seems almost impossible to develop a material suitable for surfacing the runways about the pool that will be nonslippery, and therefore most such decks are very slippery. It becomes necessary, then, to curb running and unnecessary playing about the pool. Ducking, pushing, and climbing over others in the water should not be

permitted. It seems rather heartless and not very understanding sometimes to curb youngsters who are having a good time in the pool, but the
resourceful instructor will provide activities that fulfill the needs of the
swimmers and will otherwise conduct the pool so that the problem will
seldom arise.

The diving board should be used *only with special permission of the
instructor.* By this is not meant special permission for each individual, but
for the group. There is little danger if necessary precautions are followed,
such as preventing cross-pool diving within range of the board; that not
more than one person be allowed on the diving board at one time, and
that he should not be allowed to bounce out of control; and that divers
should not be allowed to attempt dangerous dives beyond their abilities.
Divers should leave the water as soon as possible after the completion of
their dives. A line of floats should be available to string across the diving
area when it is necessary to segregate the divers. Intermediates or mixed-
ability classes should not be required to jump into deep water until the
instructor ascertains their respective abilities. (Nonswimmers often do
as they are told!) Often a student gets signed up in the wrong class or
overestimates his ability, and when he is required to jump or dive into
water over his head, he will become panic stricken and have to be
rescued. It is suggested that qualifying tests be required for all class-
work.

CRAMPS. Research tends to dispel the theory that stomach cramps
are caused by swimming too soon after eating. A study by Mason,
Franseen, Rork, and Horne [11] throws considerable light on the subject of
cramps. They conclude:

> 1. Drownings occuring as the result of cramps are very improbable.
> 2. Cramps do not occur often enough to be alarming; only 6 per cent of
> the subjects in this experiment reported them, and 92 per cent of the
> cramps reported were either in the foot or leg. 3. One is apt to call any
> pain noticed while swimming, whether it be in the side or stomach, viscera
> or abdominal wall, an abdominal cramp. The only two cases of abdominal
> cramps and the only two cases of side cramps reported in this study were
> definitely survivors. In fact, they suffered no apparent pain; they were not
> assisted in any way from the pool; they were perfectly capable of stopping
> at the end of the hour and filling out the questionnaire. 4. There seems to
> be no physiological process on which to base the assumption that eating
> before a swim is conducive to the occurrence of cramps. 5. The factor which
> seems most predisposing to cramps occurring in a pool situation is fatigue
> of untrained muscles either before or during the swimming period.

The American Red Cross and other authoritative sources have not as
yet seen fit to discard their customary precautions, so bathers should be

[11] Mason, *et al.*, *Official Aquatics Guide, 1943* (Washington, D.C.: National
Section on Women's Athletics of the American Association for Health, Physical
Education, and Recreation, 1943).

instructed not to enter the water for at least one hour after eating, and for at least an hour and a half after a heavy meal.

Water polo and other games require specific precautions with which every instructor should be familiar and should teach along with the game. Water polo has been considered one of our most dangerous games. Although no statistics are available to substantiate this belief, almost any player will vouch for the game's ruggedness. Space will not permit the discussion of its hazards or the hazards of the many other games played in swimming pools. It should suffice to say that the instructor should be aware of the attendant hazards when introducing and teaching the game. Water polo should be played only by varsity teams under trained coaches.

CORRECT LIFESAVING METHODS

In cases of emergency the instructor should use the lifesaving apparatus; if he is not successful, he should then enter the water to assist. This follows the regular Red Cross lifesaving procedure. The instructor should not enter the water to assist the pupil in preference to using the lifesaving apparatus, unless such apparatus is unavailable. Also, the instructor *should never allow students other than qualified lifeguards* to enter the water to assist. The Red Cross, however, says swimming assistance can be directed a few feet away or a human chain may be used. In cases of suspected drowning, *artificial respiration* must be begun at once and continued until the victim is revived or a physician orders it stopped. The mouth-to-mouth method of artificial respiration is generally accepted as the best, and *every person* should know how to apply it properly. It may be advisable for advanced students to discuss and practice the Sylvester, Nielson, and other proven methods of resuscitation. For other precautions and methods of application to be observed, the reader is referred to *Life Saving and Water Safety*, the American Red Cross Manual.

ADDITIONAL SUGGESTIONS. The depth markers should be kept legible. Only regulation diving boards should be used. They should not be installed in pools that do not have sufficient depth, width, and ceiling height.

SPECIFIC ADMINISTRATIVE CONTROLS FOR OUTDOOR SWIMMING

Docks, flats, ladders, diving platforms, and boards should be inspected daily for weak spots, splinters, and nails, and should be kept in repair. Regardless of how often it is made, much depends upon the thoroughness of the inspection and certainty of the correction of defects. *Roped-off areas and/or cribs should be provided at proper depths for each classification of swimmers.* Although some camps may not be able to afford cribs, all should be able to provide the ropes and floats necessary to control the nonswimmers' area. The ideal arrangement provides crib areas for beginners three-and-one-half feet in depth; for intermediates, seven-feet deep; and for advanced swimmers and divers, at least twelve-feet deep. At the beginning of the season, hazardous rocks, stumps, logs, glass, wire, cans, and so on, should be removed from the shore, from the bottom of the swimming area, and from the sink holes, and various depth should be charted. The hazards of the swimming-area bottom can be determined by the use of group surface diving and sounding. Water boxes and face glasses are helpful for this method of survey. Similar inspections may be needed if unusual weather is experienced. *Safety equipment* that should be provided should include dory skiffs, bamboo poles, grappling irons, water scope, life rings, signal bell, buddy board and tags, combination reel line and surf buoy for swimming rescues. The number and variety of these items that may be needed will be determined by the facilities and number of swimmers. These various devices must be carefully maintained and strategically located if they are to be of most value.

On hikes, swimming places should be approved by the aquatic director and plans for safeguarding the swimmers determined. This provision would include such precautions as checking the water for sanitary conditions, depth, current, and temperature; the condition of the bottom and of the beach; and the presence of poisonous plants.

A check board, for checking swimmers in and out of the dock area, should be provided. This system is particularly valuable for use during recreation periods. Unless it is efficiently managed, however, such a system loses its value. Because of its importance great care must be taken to operate it efficiently. No one should be allowed to enter the water unless *supervised* by a counselor or lifeguard. This provision is almost universal in aquatics and may necessitate constant supervision of the waterfront.

It is advisable to require swimmers on the various levels—beginners, intermediates, and advanced—to wear different colored swim caps. This is common practice in girls' programs, because they usually prefer to wear caps, but most boys object to wearing them. Some administrators require only the nonswimmers to wear them or to utilize some other mark of distinction. *Each lifeboat should have a crew of two,* one to man the oars and the other to rescue swimmers who get into trouble. The conditions and number of swimmers that make a boat patrol necessary vary, but the minimum number of swimmers is usually considered to be about fifteen. Bathers should be required to wear shoes to and from the beach. Many camp accidents occur on the paths, and going barefoot would certainly add to the casualties.

SPECIAL LEADERSHIP AND SKILL CONTROLS

A lifeguard crew, consisting of Red Cross lifesavers among counselors and older campers, should be organized, trained, and on duty when necessary. With older or more advanced groups it is, of course, not necessary to provide this ratio, but it is easily recognized that if any error in the number of lifeguards allocated is to be made, it should be on the side of too many rather than too few. They should be assigned and properly placed so that they can supervise a definite area and observe every swimmer at all times. Direct waterfront safety instruction and training, including water accident prevention, self-rescue, and lifesaving should be given all campers. Most camps maintain a regular system of instruction, including awards for attaining the various levels of efficiency. Such agencies as the Red Cross and the Boy Scouts are usually available to assist in these programs. The aquatic instruction program should begin with testing to determine the abilities of all campers, then they should be assigned to the classes for which they qualify. It is not necessary to list the various tests available because most aquatic directors are familiar with them.

The buddy system should be in force at all times, and whistle checks made about every ten minutes. Conditions may require more or less frequent checks, which should be determined by the director. The last check should come immediately following the "all out" signal, when the swimmers should immediately leave the water and file by the check board for a final checkout.

Long-distance swims should be taken *only by permission,* and each swimmer should be accompanied by one boat and a competent oarsman. It would be safer still to have two qualified persons in the boat to accompany the swimmer. By conducting a sufficient number of such swims, the swimmers' desire for testing their strength will be satisfied, and they will not be tempted to try them on their own. No roughhousing, pushing others overboard, ducking of weaker swimmers, and so on, should be tolerated. This provision naturally can be carried too far so that free swim periods are robbed of much of their fun, but as a general rule it must govern the conduct of all beaches. Good swimmers should not be permitted to play jokes on poor swimmers. Taking dares and challenging others to perform foolish stunts is another method of inviting trouble. The poorest and most dangerous joke anyone can play when swimming is to call for help unnecessarily. *Swimmers should be cautioned never to dive into strange water.* Divers should always be certain of the depth and conditions at the bottom before diving. A good rule is to dive only in regularly designated diving areas. *The diver should wait until the preceding diver returns before diving, and he should be careful to avoid other swimmers.* In addition, divers should test the board or take-off, await their turn, and not try to show off.

Beginners should not be allowed to go beyond their depth, even with artificial support. Many administrators prohibit the use of such supports, but if they are permitted, this rule should not be violated. Following are six very dangerous swimming practices even for experts:

1. Swimming too far out and in dangerous currents.
2. Swimming to rescue others when boats, buoys, and other aids are available.
3. Diving into water without knowing whether it is deep enough or whether there are other possible dangers.
4. Staying in the water too long.
5. Swimming after dark.
6. Swimming under docks, piers, or rafts.

SAFETY IN SKIN AND SCUBA DIVING

Gabrielson et al.[12] outlines the following safety rules and instructor hints for safety in skin and scuba diving.

Safety Rules for Skin Divers

1. Know the movements of the water—tides, currents, and surf.
2. Know the type of bottom—mud, shell, rock, sand, or coral.
3. Know the depth of the water.
4. Know the storm characteristics of the area.
5. Always stay with a group or at least one other person. Know where the other person is at all times. Have a system of hand signals in order to be understood if audibility is poor.
6. Before starting out, inspect all rubber fittings and safety equipment. A moment of time may well save a life.
7. Excessive shivering is a signal to stop diving. Cold water induces rapid fatigue, and the diver may become exhausted when he is far from the beach.
8. Be thoroughly familiar with the latest methods of artificial respiration.
9. Sound is magnified under water; hence, a diver should always be aware of speeding power boats in the fishing area. Always look up before surfacing.

Safety Hints to the Scuba Instructor

1. Be sure that a safe facility is available before starting a course. Do not attempt to teach in open-water areas.
2. The first concern of the course should be safety.
3. Do not leave out the theory, and design a course around the use of Scuba alone.

[12] M. Alexander Gabrielsen, et al., op. cit.

4. Every member of the class should be treated as a novice no matter what the student's diving background has been.
5. Use audio-visual aids whenever possible.
6. Doctors and science teachers should be invited to lecture when the class is studying the sciences related to diving.
7. Scuba-diving education should be divided into a basic and advanced course. Do not attempt to introduce advanced skills into the basic course.
8. Minimum-age requirements are important. The authors suggest that the minimum age be set at the eleventh and twelfth grades of the secondary school, or seventeen and eighteen years of age.
9. The instructor should know the subject matter thoroughly.
10. Some students in the class who have had some diving experience may be able to describe some situations they have experienced.
11. The instructor should include information about the underwater environment, covering the wind, waves, currents, surf, and marine life.
12. Artificial respiration should also be covered. Try also to teach its application while the divers are on the surface, returning to shore or boat.
13. Make sure the students use the buddy system throughout the course.

Boating and Canoeing

Every boy in camp should learn to row, whether he can swim or not. Swimming can be learned by most boys back home. Rowing, which can be very important, is hard to learn because little instruction is given except in camps. It is assumed that all boat counselors will make certain that their craft, including the oars and paddles are in first-class condition. All rowboats should be equipped with rowlocks that permit the oars to be feathered. The pin type of rowlock is condemned.

Boating and canoeing should be permitted only at scheduled times, when a lifeguard crew is on duty, and in accordance with qualifying tests. Some authorities do not agree that boys should learn to row even if they cannot swim, but believe that no one should be permitted in camp boats unless they are able to take care of themselves in the water. Goddard Dubois, Director of Camp Caribou, recommends a tag-checking system for boating the same as for swimming, and the hoisting of a flag to designate the times boating and swimming are permitted. Only qualified swimmers should be permitted free boating periods, within special limits and time regulations. No camper should be permitted to go out alone, either in a boat or canoe, until he has demonstrated his ability to take care of himself and his craft in an emergency. Regardless of craft, weather and water-surface conditions are important safety factors. One should not leave the shore if a storm is threatening.

Canoes should be provided with thwarts so that the canoeist will be required to sit or kneel on the bottom while paddling. This places the center of gravity lower in the canoe and makes it less likely to tip over. *Life preservers should be aboard all boats and canoes,* especially those used by novice boatsmen and camp visitors. This precaution is particularly applicable to those camps in which nonswimmers are permitted to use boats and visitors are allowed to use such craft or accompany camp members. Inexperienced canoeists and boaters should change seats only when the boat is docked. Also, a canoeist should not stand up or lean out to retrieve something. The temptation to lean out to retrieve a dropped oar is great but it may lead to a tipover.

Canoe trips should be limited to campers who have passed qualifying tests. A senior Red Cross lifesaver for approximately every ten canoeists should be along on the trip, with a senior counselor in the first canoe and an assistant in the last. By qualifying tests is meant tests of endurance and knowledge as well as of skill. There are many dangers on a trip of this sort and all of them cannot be pointed out, but a common mistake is to hitch all canoes together and then tow them with a motor launch. If a severe storm were to arise, this alignment could be quite dangerous. Campers should not be allowed to wear heavy boots or rubber boots in canoes or boats. The amount of boats and equipment would be governed by the number on the trip and its length. A tin can or other vessel to be used for bailing may be useful. Canoe and boat capacities should be determined by the director of aquatics, and the limitations should be strictly enforced. The rowboats should have their capacity painted on them. This may be determined by the following formula: Multiply the length by the breadth by the depth by .6 and divide by 7.

Beginners should work in calm water, close to the shore. It is customary to designate definite areas for the use of beginners and accomplished canoeists.

Visitors should be allowed in craft only upon approval of aquatic director. It should never be taken for granted that passengers can swim or handle the craft. This precaution was suggested by a camp director who experienced a very serious mishap because two visitors, who claimed to be competent swimmers, were allowed to go canoeing with one of the campers. Campers should be instructed to remain with the canoe or boat if it upsets. Ignorance of this basic boating safety factor has probably cost more lives than any other. Every such craft is buoyant enough to support the occupants when it is turned right side up, and the occupants should never try to make shore without help unless the craft is being borne by wind or current into a dangerous situation and the boaters are positive of their ability to reach safety. Weak swimmers can be placed in the craft, and the strong ones can tow them ashore by grasping the gunwales.

Those canoeists who cannot right an overturned canoe should not be permitted to use one alone or in rough weather. Some writers warn against holding the hands across the bottom of an overturned craft, because it is a position that is very tiresome and cannot be held for long; they also think that all canoes and most boats can be turned right side up.

With the exception of lifeboats, no boats or canoes should be allowed near the swimming area. The boating counselor should not only designate the various boating areas, but should use a water patrol to supervise, issue summonses, and so on. Likewise fishing areas must be reserved so that casting will not be a hazard to either boaters or swimmers.

ADDITIONAL SUGGESTIONS

Lloyd and Eastwood [13] say:

> It is highly desirable that more emphasis be placed on the proper handling of canoes and rowboats, rather than having swimming tests as the only prerequisite. To date little attention has been paid to adequate instruction in the handling of boats and canoes, and too much emphasis placed on jumping out of the canoe and swimming for fifteen minutes, and rules of a similar nature.

There should be separate docks for boating, so that they do not interfere with the swimming areas. The usual safety precautions governing construction hazards and the proper use of docks should be observed. Students should practice using plastic and aluminum until they can do so safely. Steel boats are not recommended.

FISHING

More people engage in fishing than any other sport. There are over 40 million fishermen in the United States, only about 30 million of whom are licensed. It is estimated that these people spend at least two and one-half billion dollars a year on the sport, which also places it at the top of the list for the amount of money spent on a sport in America. There are no studies available showing the number of persons injured each year in angling activities. Even statistics as to the number drowned while fishing are not available. It may be assumed, however, that the accident incidence is rather high because of the great number of outdoor hazards to which anglers are subjected. Among these hazards are the bites and stings of animals and insects, poisoning by plants and reptiles, cuts and lacerations from fishing and camping gear, falls from high places or rough terrain, overexertion, burns from the sun, camp fires, and gasoline engines, the dangers accompanying the use of alcohol, and, last but not least, the many water and weather hazards.

[13] Lloyd, Deaver, and Eastwood, *op. cit.*

The fish hook is a very dangerous implement and many people have suffered from being caught on one. Because of the hook's unsanitary condition it is considered a very infectious thing.

DANGEROUS FISH. There are several fish that are dangerous, among them the sting ray, electric eel, Portuguese man-of-war, the bullhead or mud-cat, and such predatory fish as the barracuda and shark. Although most of these fish are never fished for, they present a potential danger to those in or near the water. A saltwater fisherman should be wary of any odd-looking fish he catches with which he is not familiar.

FISHING INSTRUCTION. Despite the fact that more persons engage in fishing for recreation than in any other sport, schools in general do not include instruction in the methods of angling or impart a knowledge of the hazards. A small number do include bait- and fly-casting in the physical education programs. It is recommended that all schools at least teach the hazards attendant on this sport and the safe methods of its conduct.

SKILL CONTROLS

Measures applying to camping safety are also helpful and necessary to fishermen. Probably the first and most important of these precautions is that *the fisherman should never go out on the water in any small craft unless he can take care of himself in the water.* For those who cannot swim this would require the ability to stay afloat and maneuver in the water with a life preserver. Under no condition should two nonswimmers go out together, or with a third who can swim, in a small boat. It is usually unwise for any person, regardless of skill in the water, to set out on a lone fishing expedition in a boat. This precaution, of course, would not apply to fishing on small ponds or streams but to more treacherous areas. It is usually safer to have another person available in case of trouble.

The beginner should master the fundamental skills of bait- or fly-casting before fishing in this manner. Not only is the beginner dangerous to others but to himself. This is especially true when the novice attempts casting from a boat. When he is fishing from a boat, the angler should observe general safety precautions of handling a boat. Wearing boots in a boat is particularly dangerous and only the foolhardy will do it. A nonswimmer should wear a life preserver when fishing from small craft.

FIRST AID TO THE FISHERMAN. The common but dangerous and painful injury of being caught on a fish hook usually presents a very serious first-aid problem. Although the victim might be many miles from medical aid, it is advisable in most instances to allow only a physician to remove the hook. When such professional assistance is not possible, the hook may have to be removed by cutting off the barb or eye and then pushing it on through the flesh. If possible, the remaining end should be sterilized before being pushed through. Needless to say, this is a dangerous process which calls for the thorough cleansing of the wound following removal of the hook. The wise fisherman will carry the necessary first-aid equipment on all trips where supplies are not immediately available. In addition to the usual gauze, tape, and antiseptics, a good pair of strong, sharp-nosed pliers should be carried to remove fish hooks as well as for use in many other ways.

References

Andrews, H. L., and A. L. Russell, *Basic Boating* (Englewood Cliffs, N.J.: Prentice-Hall, 1964).

Brown, R. L., "Near Facts on Near Drowning," *Journal of Health, Physical Education, and Recreation* (September 1963), pp. 38–39.

Councilman, J., and B. Drinkwater, *Beginning Skin and Scuba Diving* (Belmont, California: Wadsworth, 1965).

Cross, W. D., "Accidental Drownings in Iowa," *Fourth Annual Safety Review* (Washington, D.C.: National Education Association, 1965), pp. 38–39.

Duffner, G. J., "Medical Problems Involved in Underwater Compression and Decompression," *Clinical Symposia* (July–August 1958), pp. 100–14.

Grazer, J. A., *Water Safety Instructional Material Based on an Analysis of Drowning and Present Practices in Water Safety Instruction in Lane County, Oregon*. M.S. in Physical Education, University of Oregon, 1960, p. 82.

Haugen, A. O., "Bow and Arrow Hunting," *Safety Education* (October 1960), pp. 44–45.

Helms, W. G., "Safety Aspects of Family Camping," *Third Annual Safety Education Review* (Washington, D.C.: National Education Association, 1964), pp. 75–77.

Korb, E. M., "Trends in Camp Aquatics," *Journal of Health, Physical Education, and Recreation,* 27:8–10, May 1965.

Mobil Oil Company, *Safety Afloat* (Mobil Touring Service, 150 E. 42nd Street, New York, N.Y., 1963).

Morris, W. E., "Tips for the Wagon Boss," *Safety Education* (April 1961), p. 5.

Mulroney, M. G., "Relationship of the Growth of American Red Cross Water Safety Educational Programs to Population and Drowning in Selected Chapters in the State of Washington from 1957–1961," *Completed Research in Health, Physical Education, and Recreation,* Vol. 7, 1961, p. 109.

Safety Education Data Sheet, No. 43, "Hiking and Climbing," *Safety Education* (May 1961), pp. 24–28.

Safety Education Data Sheet, No. 44, "Hook and Line Fishing," *Safety Education* (April 1961), pp. 11–13.

Sand, G. X., "Skin and Scuba Diving" (New York: Hawthorne Books, 1964).

Shaffer, J. H., *Stinging Threats to Campers, Camping Magazine* (January 1964), pp. 24–25.

Silvia, C. E. *Lifesaving and Water Safety Today* (New York: Associated Press, 1965).

Smith, J. W., "Outdoor Living," *Safety Education,* Vol. 39, No. 9 (May 1960).

Stein, C. W., "Assure Campers Fun, Follow Rules for Safe Waterskiing," *Camping Magazine* (April 1960), p. 32.

Stiles, G. E., "Prevent Accidents at Camp," *Camping Magazine* (April 1961), p. 14.

Watson, W. H., "Scuba School at Florida State University," *Safety Education* (May 1961), pp. 2–23.

PART V THE FUTURE OF SAFETY EDUCATION

He that will not apply new remedies must expect new evils, for time is the greatest innovator, and if time of course alters things to the worst and wisdom and council shall not alter them to better, what shall be the end?

FRANCIS BACON

CHAPTER 21 FUTURE DEVELOPMENT OF SAFETY EDUCATION

In what directions will safety education move in the future? Will it have a stronger position in schools and colleges? Where will growth take place? What needs are there for greater emphasis? Is safety education getting results in a reduction of accidents? These are some of the questions that will be discussed briefly in this chapter. As has been seen in previous chapters, safety is becoming more and more important. This is particularly true in the traffic field where the annual death toll has mounted to over 50,000—more than one half of the total fatalities from all types of accidents.

In order to predict some of the direction in which safety education will move, we will consider some of the trends, needs, and values. One would expect that any movement that had marked success in the saving of lives of schoolchildren would have the strong support of all schools. The death rate for children between the ages of 5 and 15 has decreased steadily. If the accident rate had continued the same as it was in 1920, in the ensuing years 50,000 more children would have been killed. Safety education has produced real dividends in saving lives. However, it should be pointed out that this reduction has not been brought about by the work of the schools alone. Many agencies have been at work in the safety field, for example, the Boy Scouts, the Girl Scouts, the Red Cross, police and fire departments, the playground associations, and youth agencies. In fact, there are dozens of community agencies that have helped in this life-saving movement.

TRAFFIC SAFETY EDUCATION

There are well-defined guideposts for traffic safety education. Alarmed by the increasing toll of automobile accidents, the federal government moved strongly into the field when the 1966 Congress passed legislation aimed to assist in strengthening the national and local safety programs. Among other features, the legislation will provide financial aid to many of the state and local municipal activities similar to the Action Program of the President's Committee for Traffic Safety. Up to 1966, the federal government had done but little in support of the traffic safety movement. For example, the major financial support for the several National Conferences on Street and Highway Safety and the President's Conferences on Traffic Safety have come from private safety organizations, industries, and state and municipal government, rather than from federal agencies. These conferences could not have been held without this support.

Funds from the new legislation should provide a strong stimulus to state and community activities. The following are some examples of progress. Only two thirds of the states now have state financial support for driver education but it is probable that laws will be enacted in other states. At present we are training only 51 per cent of the eligible students. Eventually we will be able to train *all* of them. Moreover, there are indications that within a short time *all* applicants for a driver's license will have to complete a course in driver education. This will mean more courses for both young people and adults. It will also mean the improvement of standards of high school courses and those of professional driving schools. It is expected that more use will be made of both simulators and ranges for driver education. The use of these devices enables schools to train many more students than the "behind-the-wheel" plan. It is surprising to find that one state, Florida, has 72 ranges, yet many others have none. It is also expected that the work of the colleges that are training teachers will be upgraded and certification requirements will be increased. It is possible that in addition to providing funds to states and municipalities, on a matching basis, grants will be made to other agencies that have been active in the field.

There are a number of other activities that have an indirect relationship to education, such as the work of the police, the traffic courts, state highway patrols, traffic engineers and motor vehicle departments. All of these activities will be upgraded, partly through the use of training programs.

Far more attention will be paid to vehicle safety, to uniform laws and regulations, and to standard signs, signals, and marking. It is also expected that research grants will be made available to find out more about the characteristics of accident repeaters, the causes of accidents, and methods of improving the behavior of drivers. Colleges and universities will receive many of these grants. If a state fails to introduce a comprehensive program, the allocation of federal funds to that state for highway use can be reduced.

All of these activities should also have a beneficial effect on the work of the elementary schools, including classroom instruction, bicycle safety, schoolboy patrols, and other activities. We have lost ground in recent years in the death rate for children of school age. More attention will be paid to pedestrian safety. On the other hand, it is entirely possible that it will be far more difficult to reduce the death rate because of the tremendous increase in the number of cars on our streets and highways. Recently, the number of drivers in the country passed 100 million. Many of the children killed will be riding in cars operated by these drivers.

It is also expected that far more will be done in the further training of adult drivers with refresher courses and advanced driving techniques. Motor vehicle departments will do much more than they are at present in driver-improvement schools—often in cooperation with the schools and colleges. New York, for example, now has 650 courses for adult drivers offered by the high schools. Illinois has 700, and several other states 100, but the great majority of states are doing almost nothing to reach the adult driver except in commercial driving schools.

It is expected that there will be a great improvement in the work of commercial driving schools. State supervision will be required and these schools will not only provide practice driving but will also include classroom instruction. There is every reason to believe that federal and state legislation will help increase the quantity and improve the quality of all commercial driving schools. There is plenty of work for both public and parochial schools, and commercial schools; both types need improvement and regulation.

HIGHWAY SAFETY PROMOTION

Public Law 89-564 of the Congress under Highway Safety Programs states specifically that it shall provide for comprehensive driver training programs, including

1. The initiation of a State program for driver education in the school systems or for a significant expansion and improvement of such a program already in existence.
2. The training of qualified school instructors and their certification.
3. Appropriate regulation of other driving schools, including licensage of the schools and certification of their instructors.
4. Adult driver training programs, and programs for the retraining of selected drivers.
5. Adequate research, development, and procurement of practice driving facilities, simulators, and other similar teaching aids for both school and other driving training use.

Although the amount of money available to each state is limited, the greatest value of the law will come in the setting up of standards. Today, the range in driver education programs varies from practically zero in some states to 100 per cent in others. The limited funds available have some "seeding" effect on state programs.

RECREATION AND PHYSICAL EDUCATION

It is expected that the present interest in safety in recreation and physical education will continue and undoubtedly expand. There has been a tremendous increase in recreational activities, with millions of children and adults participating in water sports, camping, hunting, fishing, mountain climbing, snow and water skiing, and dozens of other activities. Although there has been an increase in nonfatal accidents, fatalities have remained about the same. Drowning is a good illustration. Even the use of the water for swimming and other water activities has increased greatly in the last decade, the number of fatalities has remained about the same, and the death *rate* has decreased 20 per cent. This trend will undoubtedly continue since there are so many agencies active in teaching water safety. In addition, more courses will be offered in power-boat safety by the Coast Guard Auxiliary and the United States Power Squadrons. These courses will tend to reduce boating accidents, including those that result in drowning. Almost overnight, scuba diving and skin diving have become very popular and this popularity will continue to grow. Careful instruction will be required to keep accidents down. The same is true of water skiing. Youth organizations such as the Boy Scouts and the Y.M.C.A., together with the Red Cross, will undoubtedly expand their training programs. More safeguards will also be required in the use of home swimming pools.

What about accident prevention in physical education and athletics? It is expected that more attention will be given to safety in schools and colleges. Physical educators and coaches have had improved training in which greater emphasis has been given to safety. Since coaches know that accidents can undermine the strength of their teams, they will emphasize safe practices. It is also expected that more colleges will adopt accident reporting systems. This will undoubtedly develop as more institutions introduce campus safety programs.

There are many other activities that have had remarkable growth in the last decade. Fishing and hunting are two examples. State legislation and private organizations such as the American Rifle Association, the National Safety Council, and "Hunter Safety" courses have helped to keep serious accidents down. There will always be accidents in these activities, and in all areas of recreation. Safety programs will help reduce these accidents.

HOME

Interest in home accident prevention has developed rapidly in recent years. It is expected that this will continue. There has been a steady decrease in fatalities, but few facts are available regarding trends of non-fatal accidents. This reduction has, in part, been brought about by education, but modern construction, equipment, and maintenance have also contributed to safer living; for example, falls on stairs tend to be common among elderly persons and young children. One-story or ranch-type house do not have stairs. In addition, houses built of brick, stone, or stucco are more fire resistant than frame buildings. The gradual elimination of tenement housing in cities will also help increase safety.

The "do-it-yourself" movement has resulted in an increase in non-fatal accidents among home owners. If this movement grows, then there will be more injuries to unskillful handymen.

INDUSTRY

There have been important gains in safety in industry. The death rate for industrial accidents has been falling steadily. This reduction will continue but at a slower rate. Improved training of workers, the safeguarding of machinery, the implementing of safety standards and regulations, and supervision will continue to reduce accidents in factories. The key problem of the future will be to organize programs to prevent off-the-job accidents which in some industries are now five times as numerous as those in the plant.

The future of the safety movement in industry is secure. It has demonstrated that it can reduce accidents. With the federal, state, and municipal governments moving strongly into the accident prevention field, accidents will be further reduced. But it is going to require the combined efforts of all of our population to effect this reduction.

TRANSPORTATION

There has been a steady improvement in the safety of all forms of transportation with the exception of passenger cars. It is expected that school and commercial bus accident rates will continue to decrease. It is probable that there will be little change in the accident rate for passengers on railroads.

There has been a remarkable improvement in the accident record in air transport in the last decade. Jet aircraft have had a very good record based on the number of persons killed per 100 million passenger miles. No phase of airline operation gets greater concentration than safety. Not only are there federal regulations, but the airlines, also, have their own rigid safety standards.

It is also probable that there will be an increase in the safety of private passenger planes. Improved construction and maintenance of aircraft, traffic control, and better regulations and training will be needed to effect this increase.

NATIONAL FUNDS FOR EDUCATION

Public Law 89-10 is providing billions of dollars over a three-year period to be used to stimulate elementary and secondary education. Local officials in thousands of school districts are assigning members of their staff to develop plans for securing funds. Those responsible for leadership in safety education are included. Here is an opportunity to take the initiative, to outline proposals, to claim for safety education a fair share of the funds for which many specialists in the local schools will be competing. According to Maul [1] of the National Commission on Safety Education, "This is the opportunity which holds the most stimulating challenge to workers in safety education."

Funds available from the Federal Government should be most helpful in extending the work of safety education in schools and colleges.

RESEARCH

There never was a time when the possibilities for research appear so good. Funds are required for research and there are several sources for grants. The first is from PL 89-10 which would cover various phases of safety. The second is from funds provided in the Federal Highway Safety Act of 1966 in which 10 million dollars has been set aside for research in 1967, increased to 20 million the following year, and 25 million the third year. This can be used primarily for traffic safety studies and related areas. In addition, funds are also available from the Department of Health, Education, and Welfare. These three are the principal sources, but funds will also be available from many other agencies.

There is a great need for research in all fields of safety. Some years ago supervisors listed over 200 studies that should be made covering all phases of safety, but few of them have been completed. More recently a committee under Malfetti prepared a list of priority problems for the *Journal of Health, Physical Education, and Recreation*. Others have been suggested in the several publications of the National Conferences on High School Driver Education and the annual publications of the School and College Conference of the National Safety Council. These not only included research that could be carried on for the Ph.D. degree, but also

[1] Ray C. Maul, "Let's Get Help from PL 89-10," *Safety*, Vol. 2, No. 1. (Washington, D.C.: National Commission on Safety Education, 1966).

those for the master's and bachelor's degrees as well as nondegree studies by individuals and private organizations.

There is no limit to the studies that can be conducted. There is little research available on the best methods of teaching safety. There is very little in relation to the behavioral sciences—psychology, sociology, physiology, and others. There is a dearth of materials in the field of driver education and driver behavior and almost nothing on methods for measuring the attitudes of drivers. In fact, the whole field of testing and evaluation has been neglected; there are but few reliable tests for measurement. Very little is known about the influence of enforcement on the behavior of drivers or the effects of knowledge, skills, and attitudes on behavior or how children learn safety. It is probable that the greatest need is for standardized tests that will measure various aspects of safety. This is especially true for the elementary schools.

Since more colleges are establishing complete safety programs leading to a master's or higher degree and requiring research studies, the future should show much more research. Moreover, there will be more studies carried on in other departments of universities, such as psychology, engineering, sociology, visual aids, and tests and measurements. It is a curious fact that since Vaughn conducted his research on Positive and Negative Instruction at Chicago University nearly forty years ago, there has been little done to amplify his study. The same is true of the *Siebrecht Attitude Scale* published nearly twenty-five years ago.

THE EDUCATIONAL TREND

Education is fermenting. The methods, contents, and structure of schools and colleges are being challenged and new programs are being instituted almost daily. The future of safety education depends to a large extent upon its adaptation to the trends. If school and college programs of safety education are to keep up with the trends, Hahn [2] points out that in addition to accident prevention functions, they must make significant contributions toward achieving the goals of all education.

He relates:

> We must look beyond the surface forms of safety education toward educational depth perceptions, for in these lie the ultimate dimensions . . . safety educators might well direct the searchlight of analysis and inquiry toward further understanding of the total educational process, for here alone can they find the pinpoint answers to questions related to safety . . . the goals of education:
>
> The achievement of genuine understanding

[2] D. Willard Hahn, "Putting Understanding in Our Safety Education Program," *National Safety Congress Transactions* (Chicago: The Council, 1963).

The development of insight
The increase in social perception
The improvement of emotional control

Significant advances must be made in our knowledge of human be-havior, personality development, and the arts of persuasion if safety edu-cation is to keep pace in the twenty-first century.

REFERENCES

Blake, Roland P., *Industrial Safety* (Englewood Cliffs, N.J.: Prentice-Hall, 1963).

Center for Safety Education, New York University, *Family Recreation and Safety* (New York: The Center, 1960).

Cutter, Walter A., "Uniform Programming and Improved Traffic Safety," *Traffic Quarterly* (April, 1963). (Saugatuck, Conn.: Eno Foundation for Highway Traffic Control.)

National Commission on Safety Education, *Policies and Practices for Driver and Traffic Safety Education* (Washington, D.C.: The Commission, 1964).

————, *History of Driver Education in the United States* (Washington, D.C.: The Commission, 1966).

National Safety Council, *Safety in the 60's* (Chicago: The Council, 1960).

Insurance Institute for Highway Safety, *Annual Driver Education Achievement Program* (Washington, D.C.: The Institute, 1966).

President's Committee for Traffic Safety, *The Action Program* (Washington, D.C.: The Committee, 1962).

Stack, Herbert J., and J. Duke Elkow, *Education for Safe Living* (Englewood Cliffs, N.J.: Prentice-Hall, 1966).

Strasser, Marland, *et al.*, *Fundamentals of Safety Education* (New York: Macmillan, 1964).

The 89th Congress, Public Law 89-564, *Highway Safety* (Washington, D.C.: U.S. Government Printing Office, 1966).

APPENDIX
SOURCES OF
AUDIO-VISUAL
AIDS

The first place to look for audio-visual aids is in various government departments in the state where you live. Although they may not have extensive depositories, the following departments often have films available: Education, Health, Conservation, State Police, or Highway Patrol. In addition, many universities have depositories of audio-visual aids. It is best to secure films locally when they are available.

The following are among the best-known sources of audio-visual aids.

AAA Foundation for Traffic Safety, 1712 G. Street, N.W., Washington, D.C.

Aetna Casualty and Surety Company, Hartford, Connecticut

American Association of Motor Vehicle Administrators, 912 Barr Bldg., Washington, D.C.

American National Red Cross, Washington, D.C.

Association Films Inc., 347 Madison Avenue, New York, New York

Coronet Films, Coronet Building, Chicago, Illinois

Encyclopaedia Britannica Films, 1125 Central Avenue, Wilmette, Illinois

Ford Motor Company, 3000 Schaefer Road, Dearborn, Michigan

General Motors Corporation, General Motors Building, Detroit, Michigan

Liberty Mutual Insurance Company, Boston, Massachusetts

Metropolitan Life Insurance Company, One Madison Avenue, New York, N.Y.

Modern Talking Picture Service, Inc., 45 Rockefeller Plaza, New York, N.Y.

National Association of Automotive Mutual Insurance Companies, 20 North Wacker Drive, Chicago, Illinois

National Board of Fire Underwriters, 85 John Street, New York, N.Y.

National Commission on Safety Education, National Education Association, 1201 Sixteenth Street, N.W., Washington, D.C.

National Film Board of Canada, 1270 Avenue of the Americas, New York, N.Y.

National Safety Council, 425 North Michigan Avenue, Chicago, Illinois

Nationwide Insurance Company, Columbus, Ohio

Travelers Insurance Company, Hartford, Connecticut

U.S. Public Health Service, Washington, D.C.

U.S. Department of Labor, Washington, D.C.

U.S. Public Health Service, Washington, D.C.

Walt Disney Productions, 16 mm. Department, 2400 Alameda Avenue W.,
Burbank, California

Young America Films, Inc., 18 East 41st Street, New York, N.Y.

Zurich American Insurance Companies, 135 LaSalle Street, Chicago,
Illinois

INDEX